P9-EKD-752

NARUTO VOL. 63
SHONEN JUMP Manga Edition

STORY AND ART BY MASASHI KISHIMOTO

Translation/Mari Morimoto
Touch-up Art & Lettering/John Hunt
Design/Sam Elzway
Editor/Alexis Kirsch

NARUTO © 1999 by Masashi Kishimoto. All rights reserved. First
published in Japan in 1999 by SHUEISHA Inc., Tokyo. English translation
rights arranged by SHUEISHA Inc.

The stories, characters and incidents
mentioned in this publication are entirely fictional.

Printed in the U.S.A.

Published by VIZ Media, LLC
P.O. Box 77010
San Francisco, CA 94107

10 9 8 7 6 5 4 3 2 1
First printing, November 2013

www.viz.com

PARENTAL ADVISORY
NARUTO is rated T for Teen and is recommended
for ages 13 and up. This volume contains realistic
and fantasy violence.
ratings.viz.com

THE WORLD'S
MOST POPULAR MANGA
www.shonenjump.com

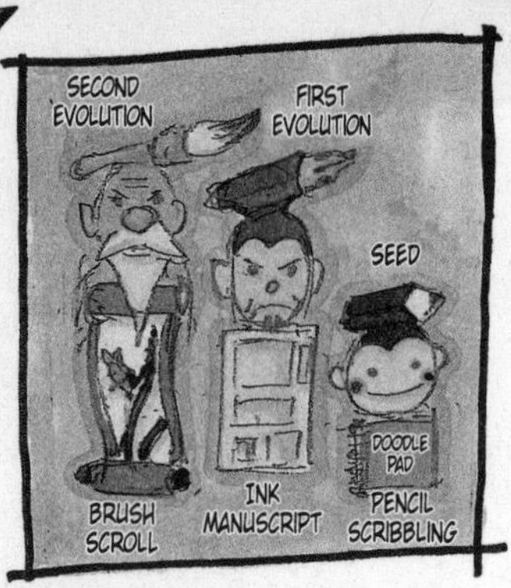
SECOND EVOLUTION
FIRST EVOLUTION
SEED
DOODLE PAD
BRUSH SCROLL
INK MANUSCRIPT
PENCIL SCRIBBLING

岸本斉史

It's really hitting me these days, that I've aged...
No matter how much I sleep, I'm still tired and my eyes are blurry.
Yet I can't sleep for very long.
I recall writing here before that I was starting to become an old man, but I've already completed my first evolution and am now in the middle of my second evolution from old man to geezer! Pokémon evolve and get stronger, but humans just get weaker!
But I'm gonna keep drawing manga!

—Masashi Kishimoto, 2012

Author/artist Masashi Kishimoto was born in 1974 in rural Okayama Prefecture, Japan. After spending time in art college, he won the Hop Step Award for new manga artists with his manga **Karakuri** (Mechanism). Kishimoto decided to base his next story on traditional Japanese culture. His first version of **Naruto**, drawn in 1997, was a one-shot story about fox spirits; his final version, which debuted in **Weekly Shonen Jump** in 1999, quickly became the most popular ninja manga in Japan.

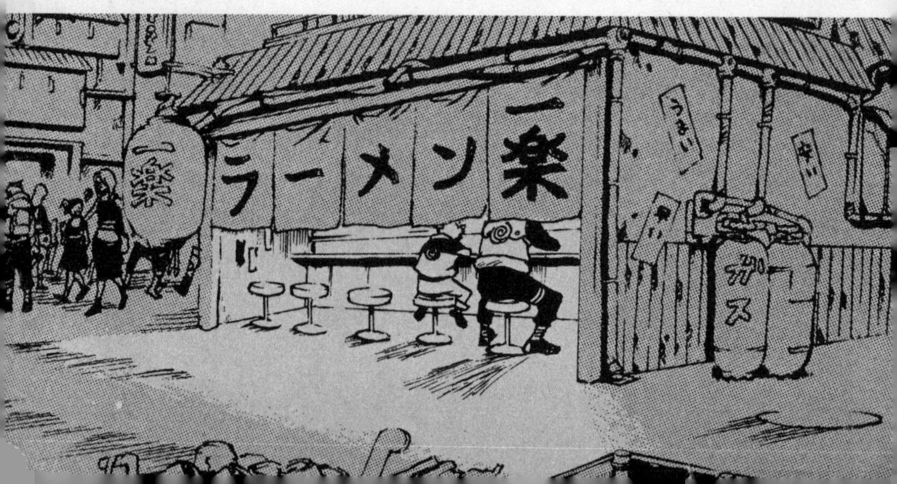
ラーメン一楽
一楽

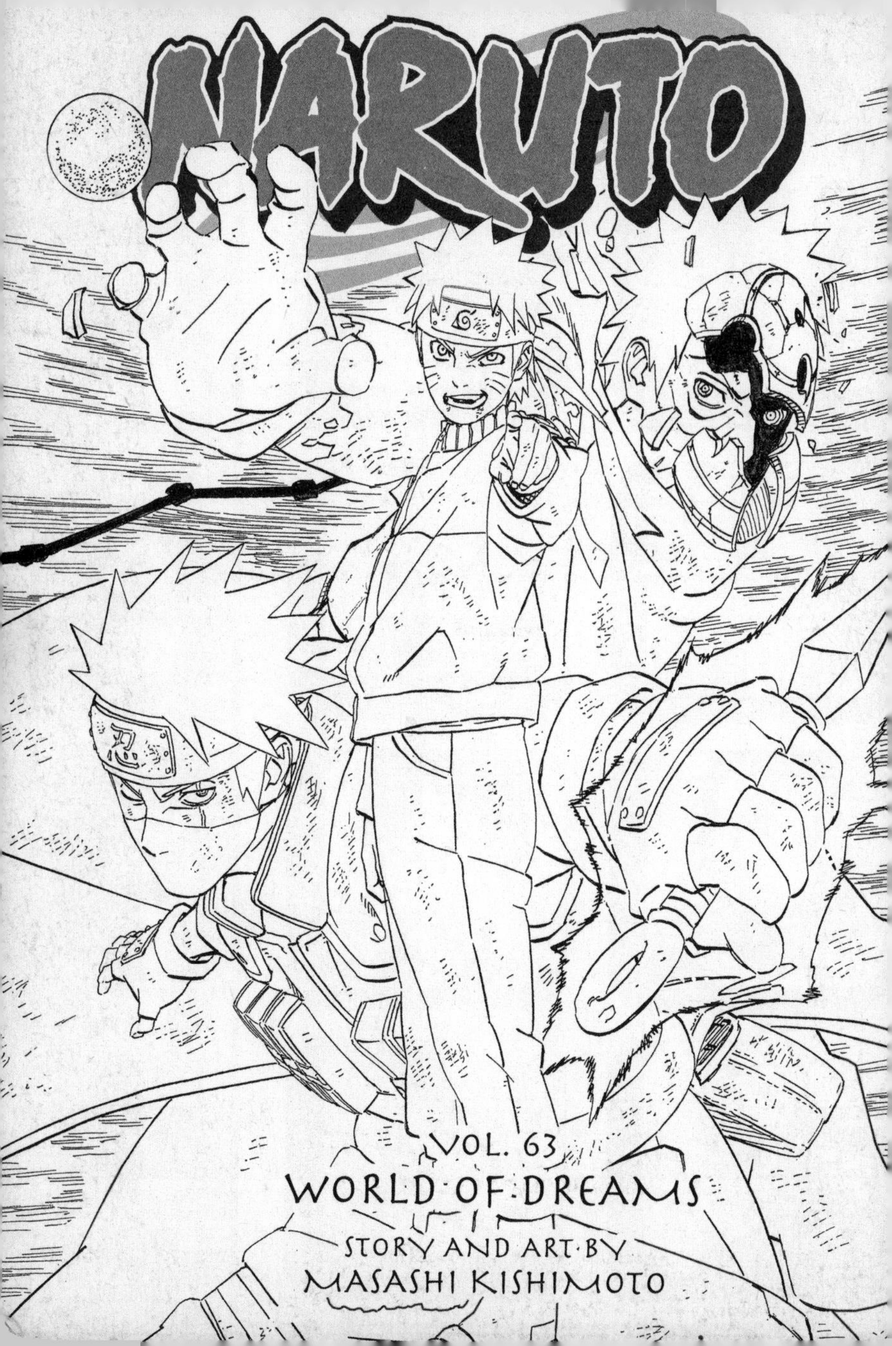

NARUTO

VOL. 63

WORLD OF DREAMS

STORY AND ART BY
MASASHI KISHIMOTO

CHARACTERS

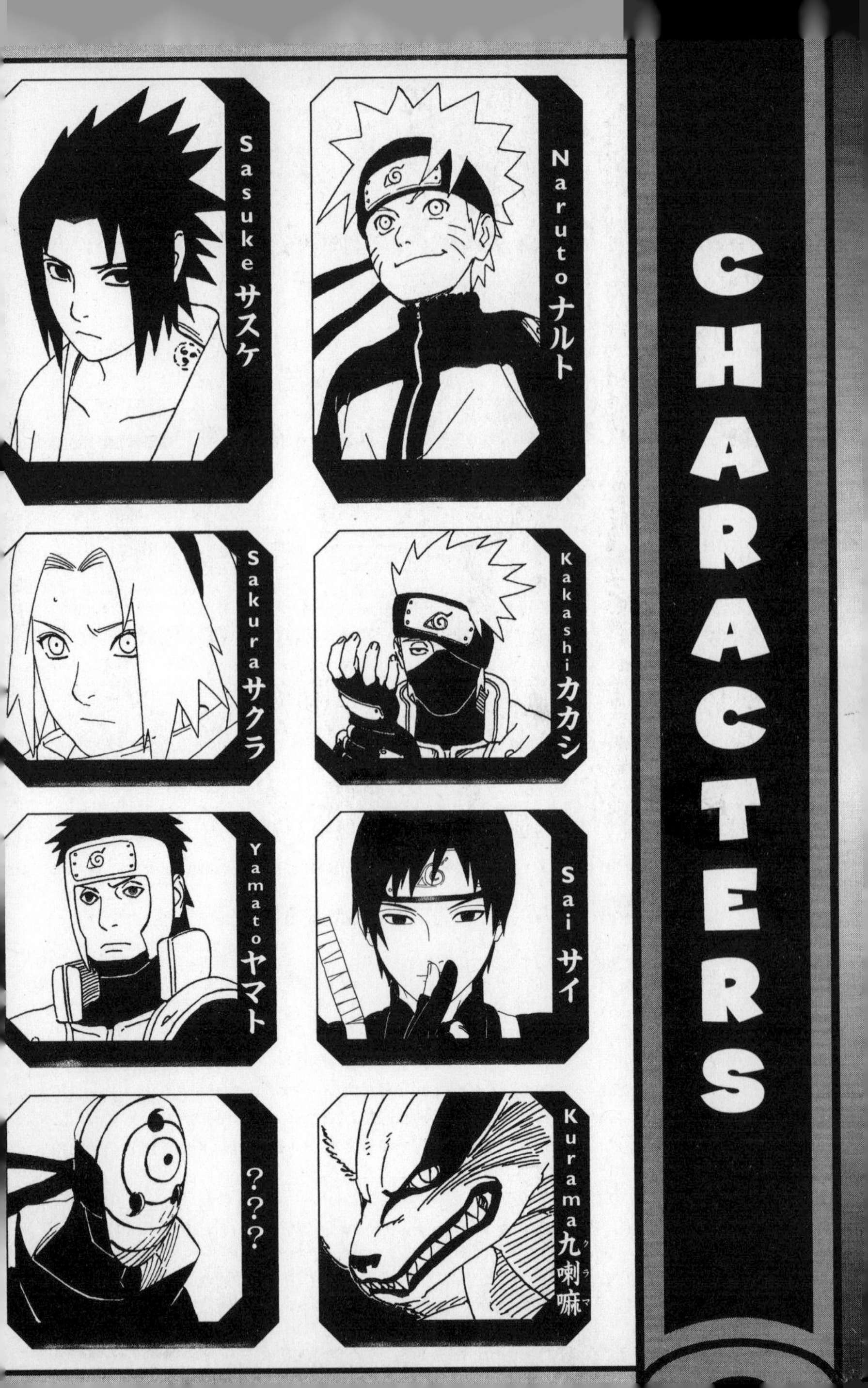
Naruto ナルト
Sasuke サスケ
Kakashi カカシ
Sakura サクラ
Sai サイ
Yamato ヤマト
Kurama 九喇嘛
???

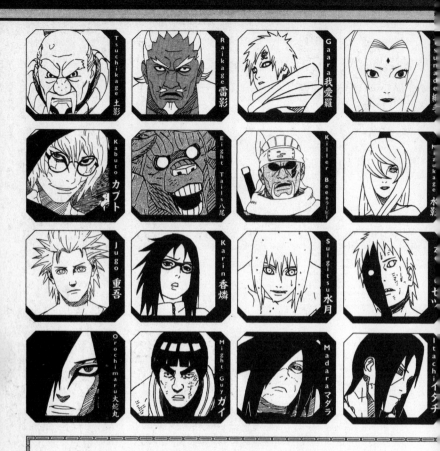

Tsuchikage 土影
Raikage 雷影
Gaara 我愛羅
Tsunade 綱手

Kabuto カブト
Eight Tails 八尾
Killer Bee キラービー
Mizukage 水影

Jugo 重吾
Karin 香燐
Suigitsu 水月
Zetsu 絶

Orochimaru 大蛇丸
Might Guy ガイ
Madara マダラ
Itachi イタチ

THE STORY SO FAR...

Naruto, the biggest troublemaker at the Ninja Academy in the Village of Konohagakure, finally becomes a ninja along with his classmates Sasuke and Sakura. They grow and mature through countless trials and battles. However, Sasuke, unable to give up his quest for vengeance, leaves Konohagakure to seek Orochimaru and his power...

Two years pass. Naruto grows up and engages in fierce battles against the Tailed Beast-targeting Akatsuki. Elsewhere, after winning the heroic battle against Itachi and learning his older brother's true intentions, Sasuke allies with Akatsuki and sets out to destroy Konoha.

The Fourth Great Ninja War against the Akatsuki begins. The Five Shadows seem powerless against the revived Madara's power. Meanwhile, Sasuke and Itachi confront Kabuto, who is dragging the battlefield into a vortex of chaos. Having surmounted their past differences, will the brothers' united front finally succeed in stopping Kabuto?!

NARUTO

VOL. 63
WORLD OF DREAMS

CONTENTS

NUMBER 598: DEMOLITION!!   7

NUMBER 599: UCHIHA OBITO   25

NUMBER 600: WHY NOT SOONER?   43

NUMBER 601: OBITO AND MADARA   61

NUMBER 602: ALIVE   79

NUMBER 603: REHAB   97

NUMBER 604: REUNION, AND THEN...   115

NUMBER 605: HELL   137

NUMBER 606: WORLD OF DREAMS   155

NUMBER 607: IT DOESN'T MATTER TO ME   173

Number 598: Demolition!!

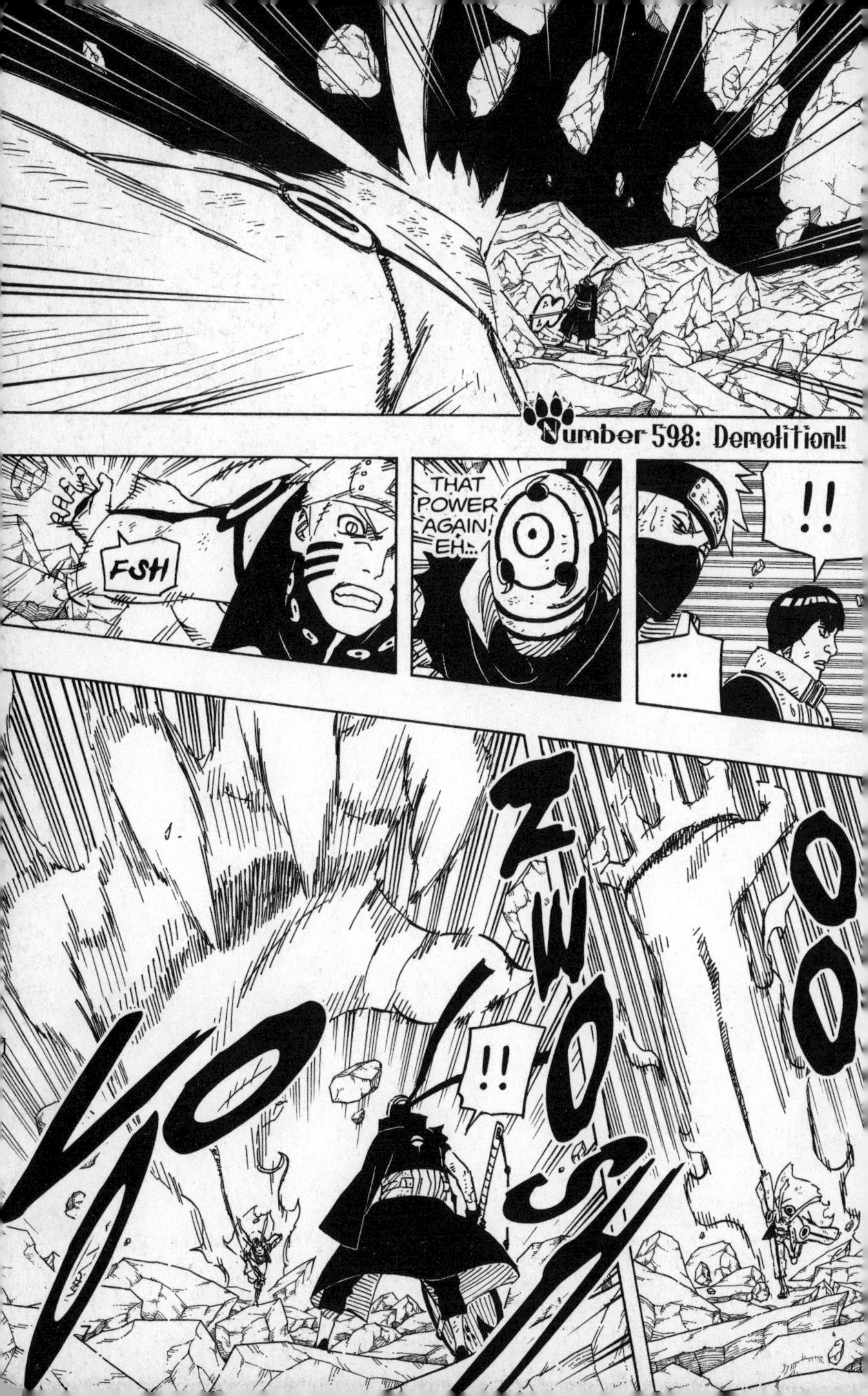
!!
...
THAT POWER AGAIN, EH...
FSH
!!
ZWOOSH

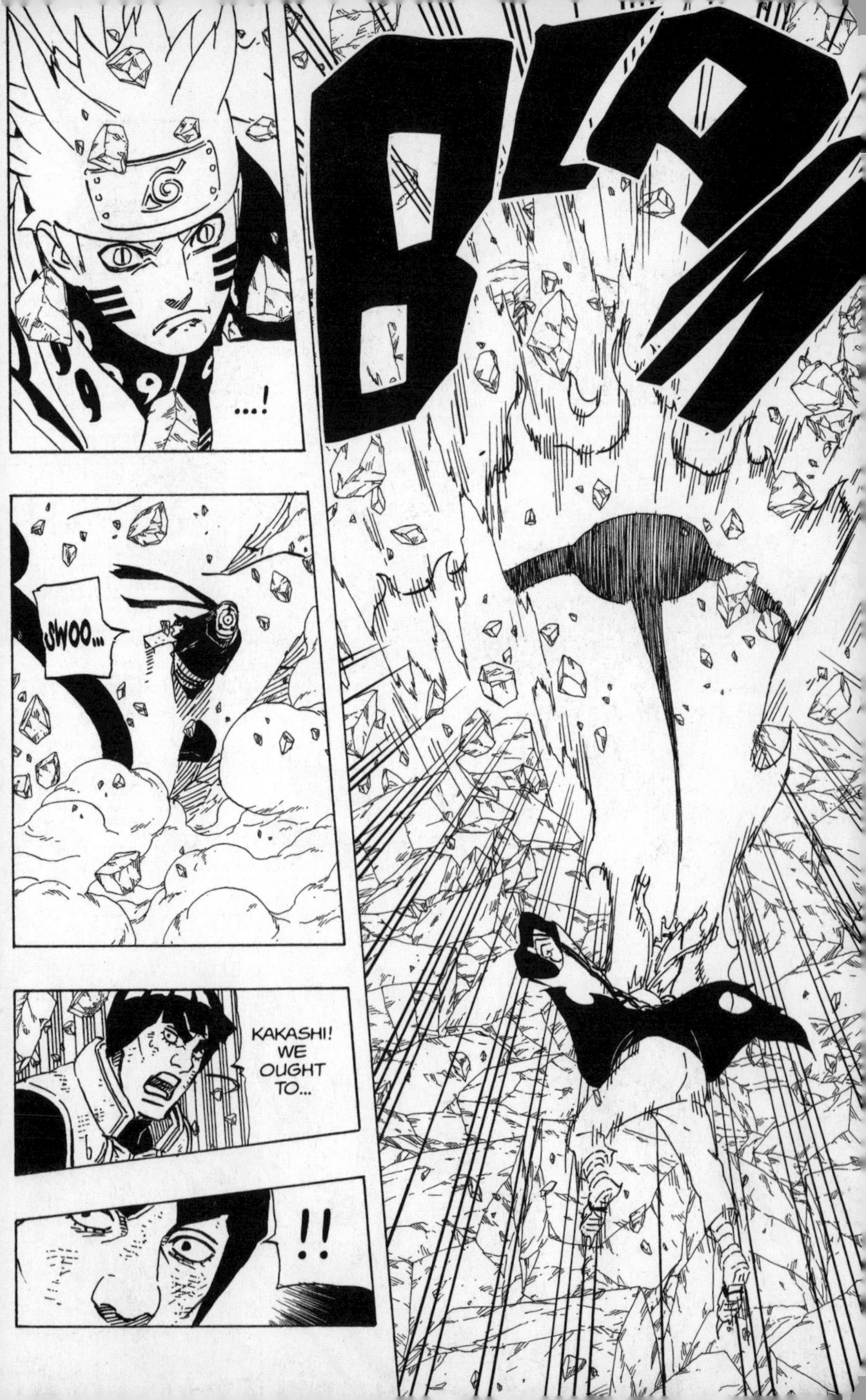
BLAM
...!
SWOO...
KAKASHI! WE OUGHT TO...
!!

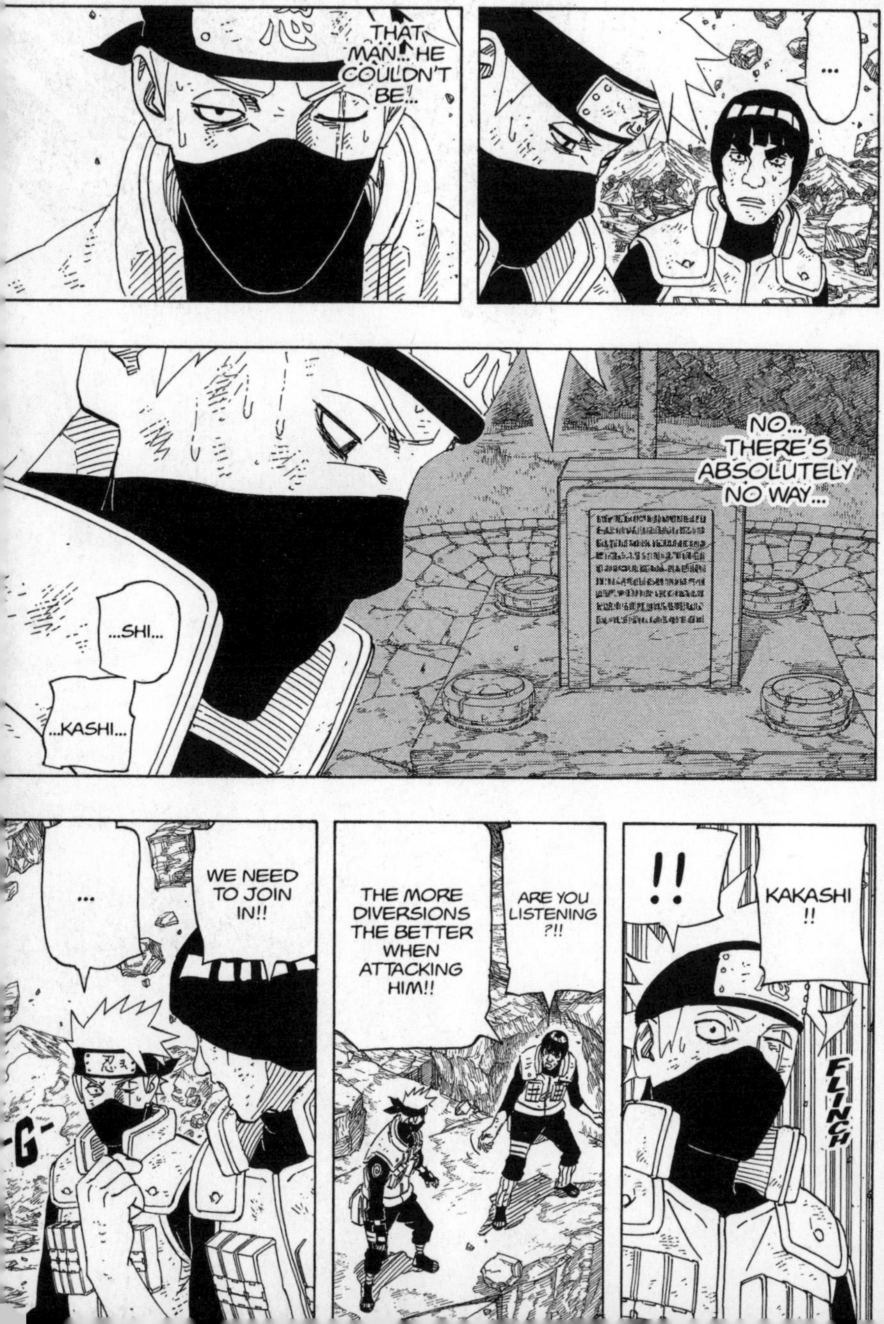
...
THAT MAN... HE COULDN'T BE...
NO... THERE'S ABSOLUTELY NO WAY...
...SHI...
...KASHI...
KAKASHI!!
!!
FLINCH
ARE YOU LISTENING?!!
THE MORE DIVERSIONS THE BETTER WHEN ATTACKING HIM!!
WE NEED TO JOIN IN!!
...
-G-

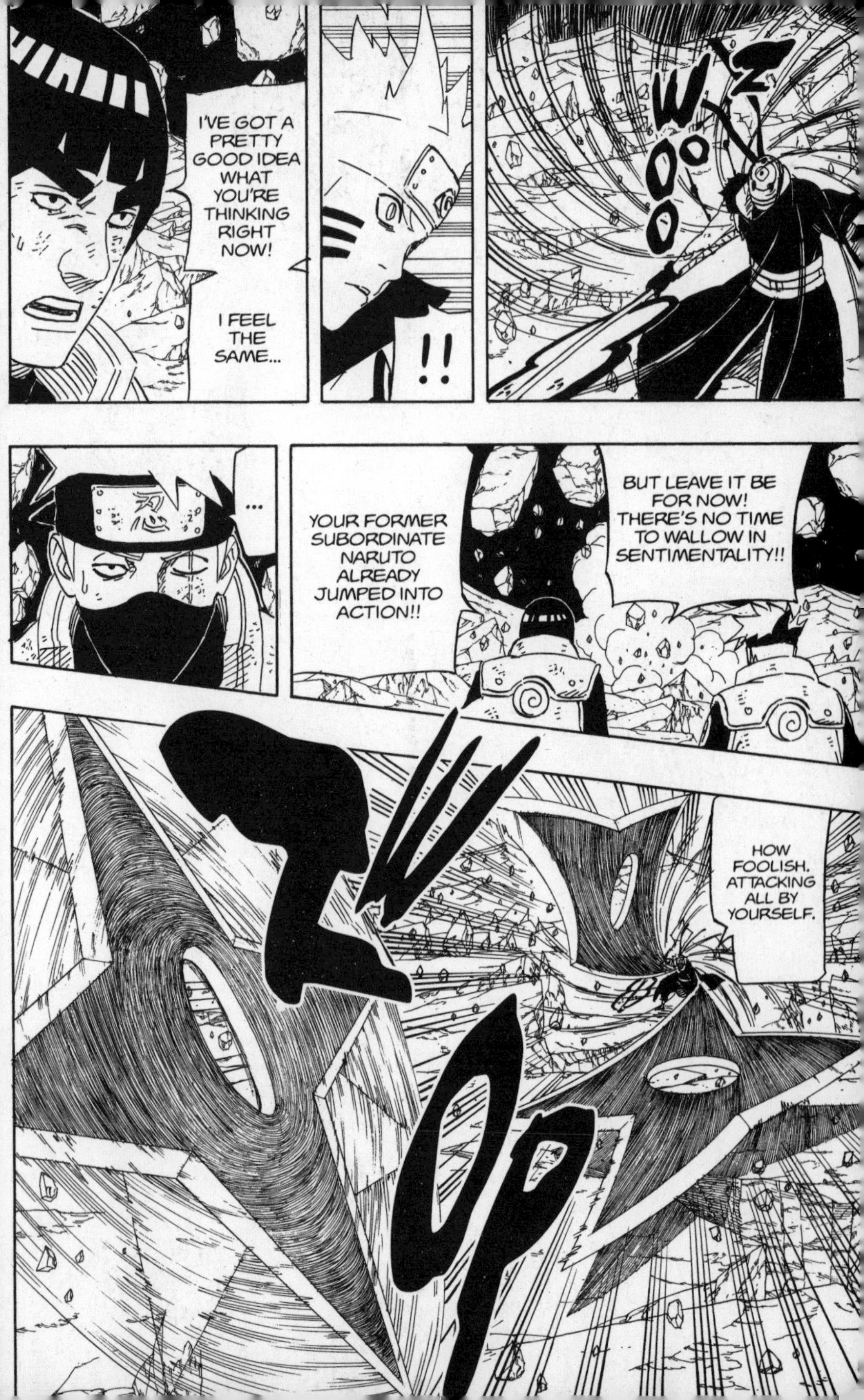
!!
I'VE GOT A PRETTY GOOD IDEA WHAT YOU'RE THINKING RIGHT NOW!
I FEEL THE SAME...
BUT LEAVE IT BE FOR NOW! THERE'S NO TIME TO WALLOW IN SENTIMENTALITY!!
YOUR FORMER SUBORDINATE NARUTO ALREADY JUMPED INTO ACTION!!
...
HOW FOOLISH. ATTACKING ALL BY YOURSELF.

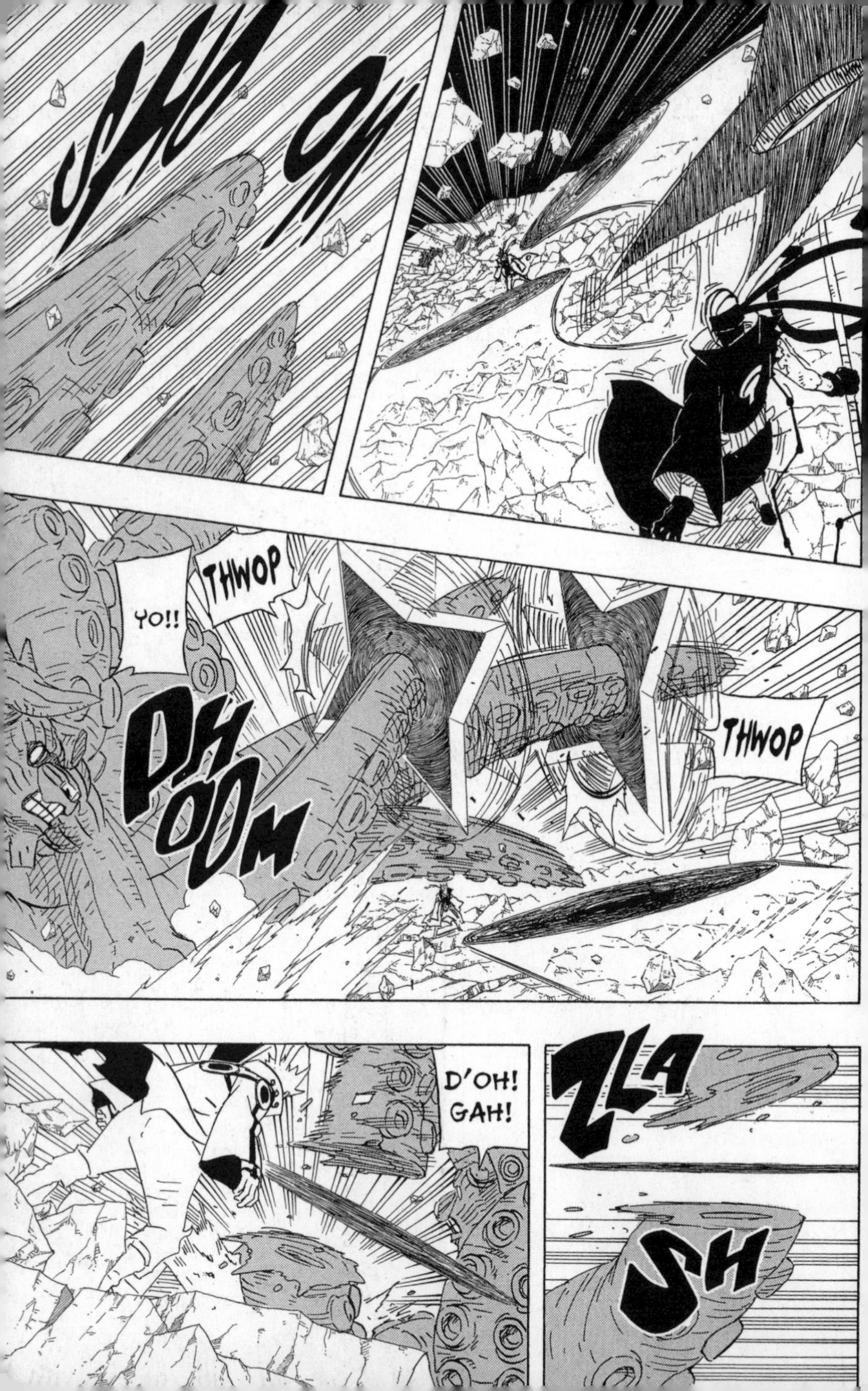
THWOP
THWOP
YO!!
ZLA
SH
D'OH! GAH!

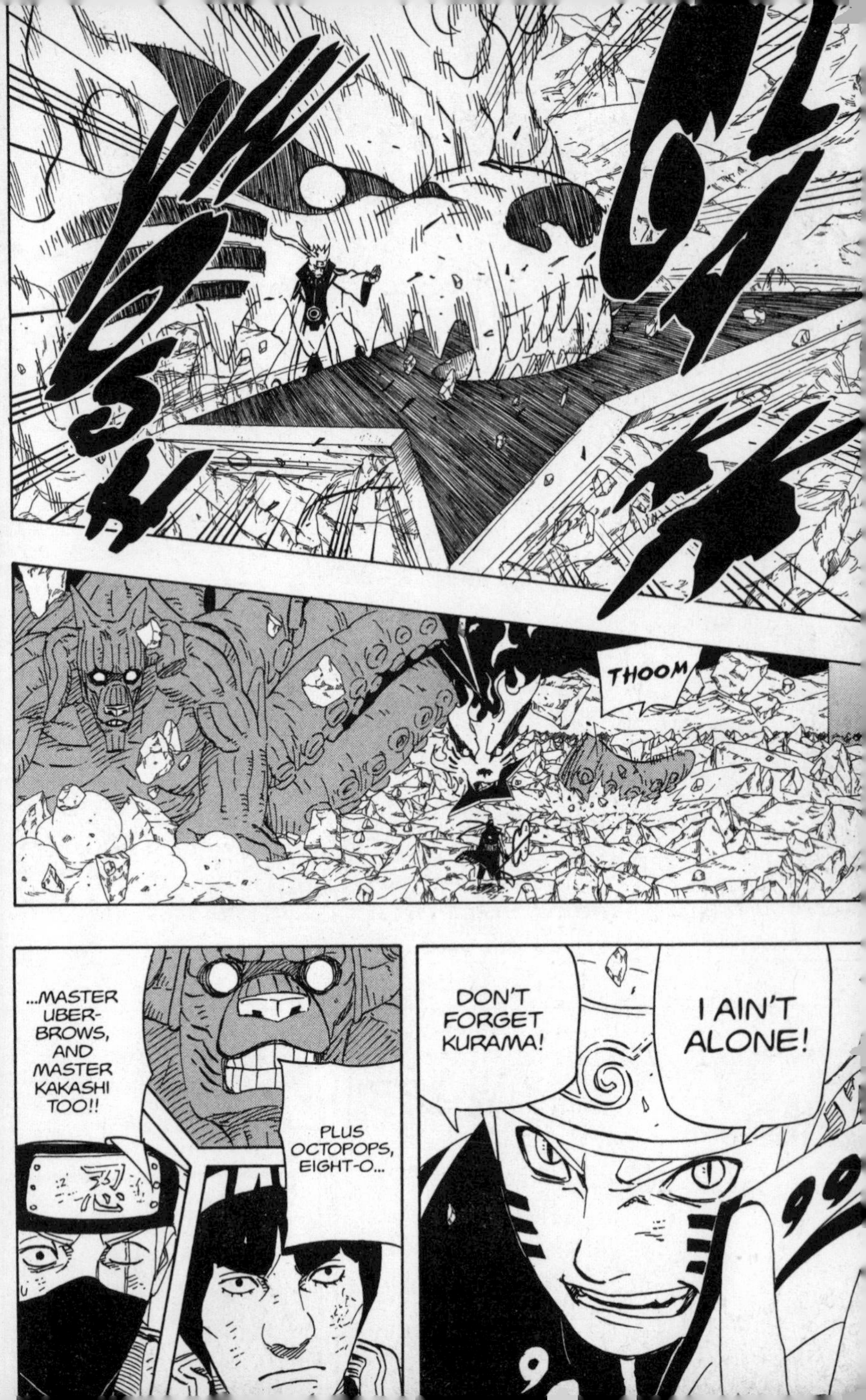
THOOM
I AIN'T ALONE!
DON'T FORGET KURAMA!
PLUS OCTOPOPS, EIGHT-O...
...MASTER UBER-BROWS, AND MASTER KAKASHI TOO!!

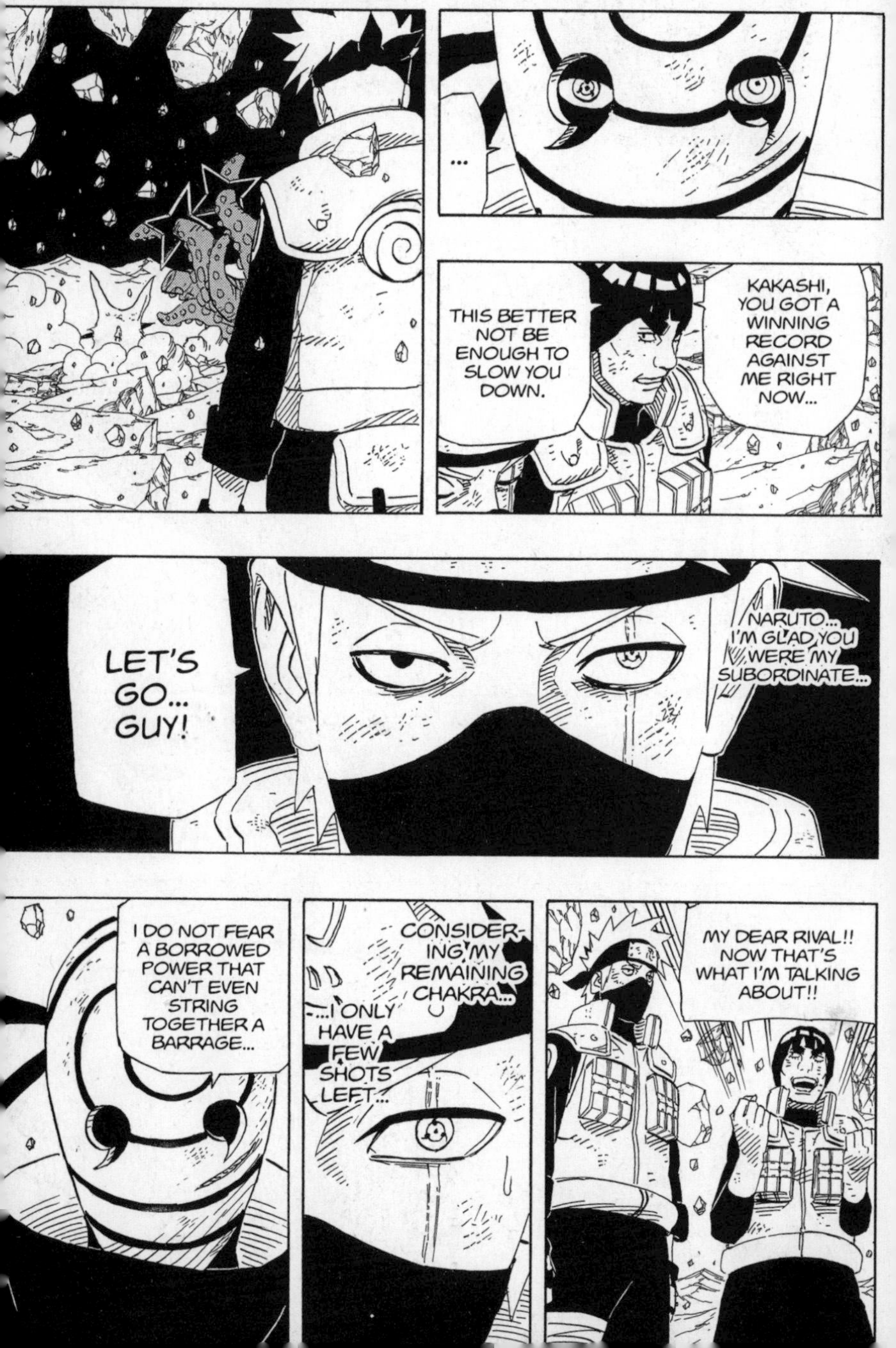
...
KAKASHI, YOU GOT A WINNING RECORD AGAINST ME RIGHT NOW...
THIS BETTER NOT BE ENOUGH TO SLOW YOU DOWN.
NARUTO... I'M GLAD YOU WERE MY SUBORDINATE...
LET'S GO... GUY!
MY DEAR RIVAL!! NOW THAT'S WHAT I'M TALKING ABOUT!!
CONSIDER-ING MY REMAINING CHAKRA...
...I ONLY HAVE A FEW SHOTS LEFT...
I DO NOT FEAR A BORROWED POWER THAT CAN'T EVEN STRING TOGETHER A BARRAGE...

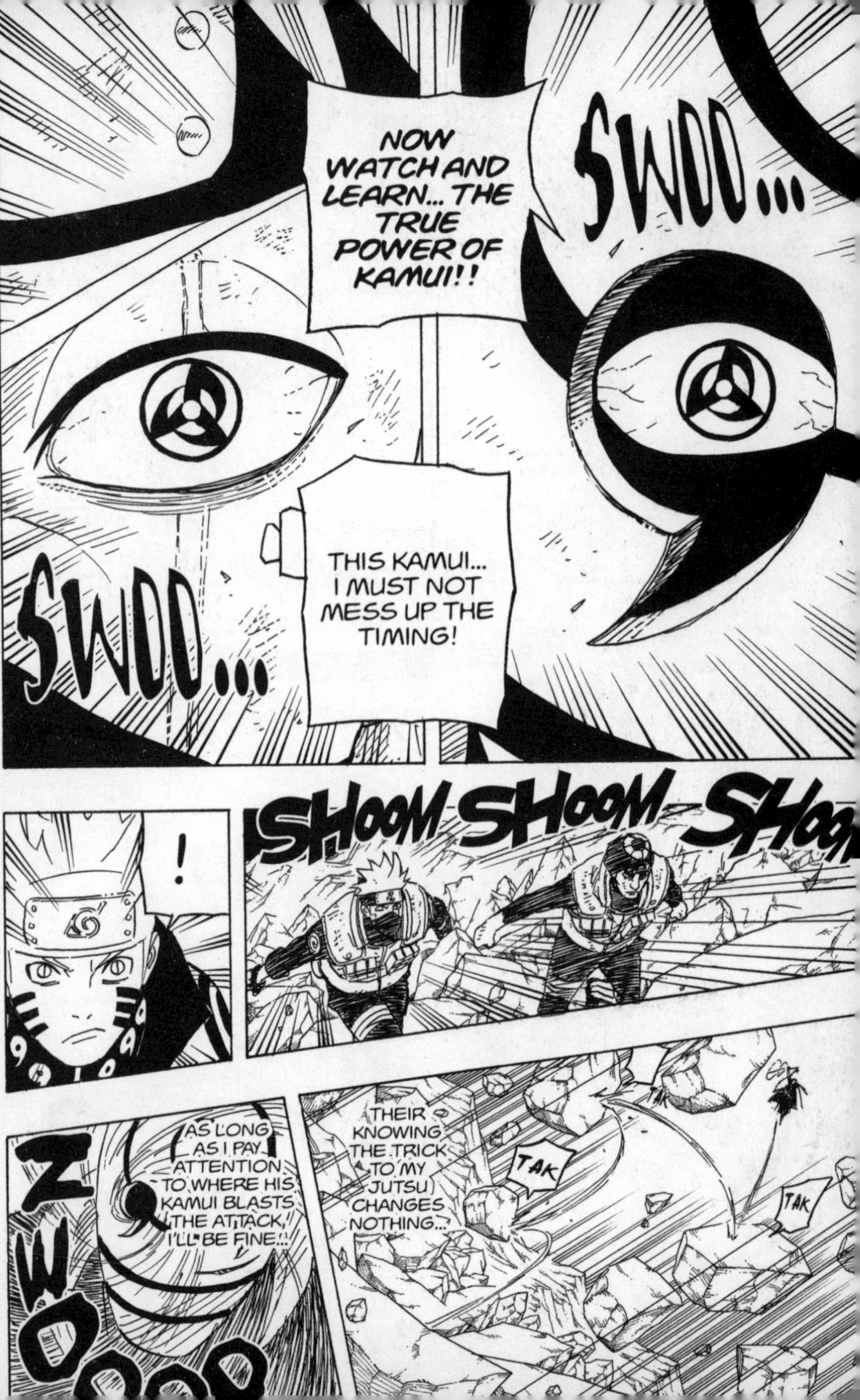
SWOO...
NOW WATCH AND LEARN... THE TRUE POWER OF KAMUI!!
THIS KAMUI... I MUST NOT MESS UP THE TIMING!
SWOO...
SHOOM SHOOM SHOOM
!
TAK
TAK
THEIR KNOWING THE TRICK TO MY JUTSU CHANGES NOTHING...
AS LONG AS I PAY ATTENTION TO WHERE HIS KAMUI BLASTS THE ATTACK, I'LL BE FINE...!

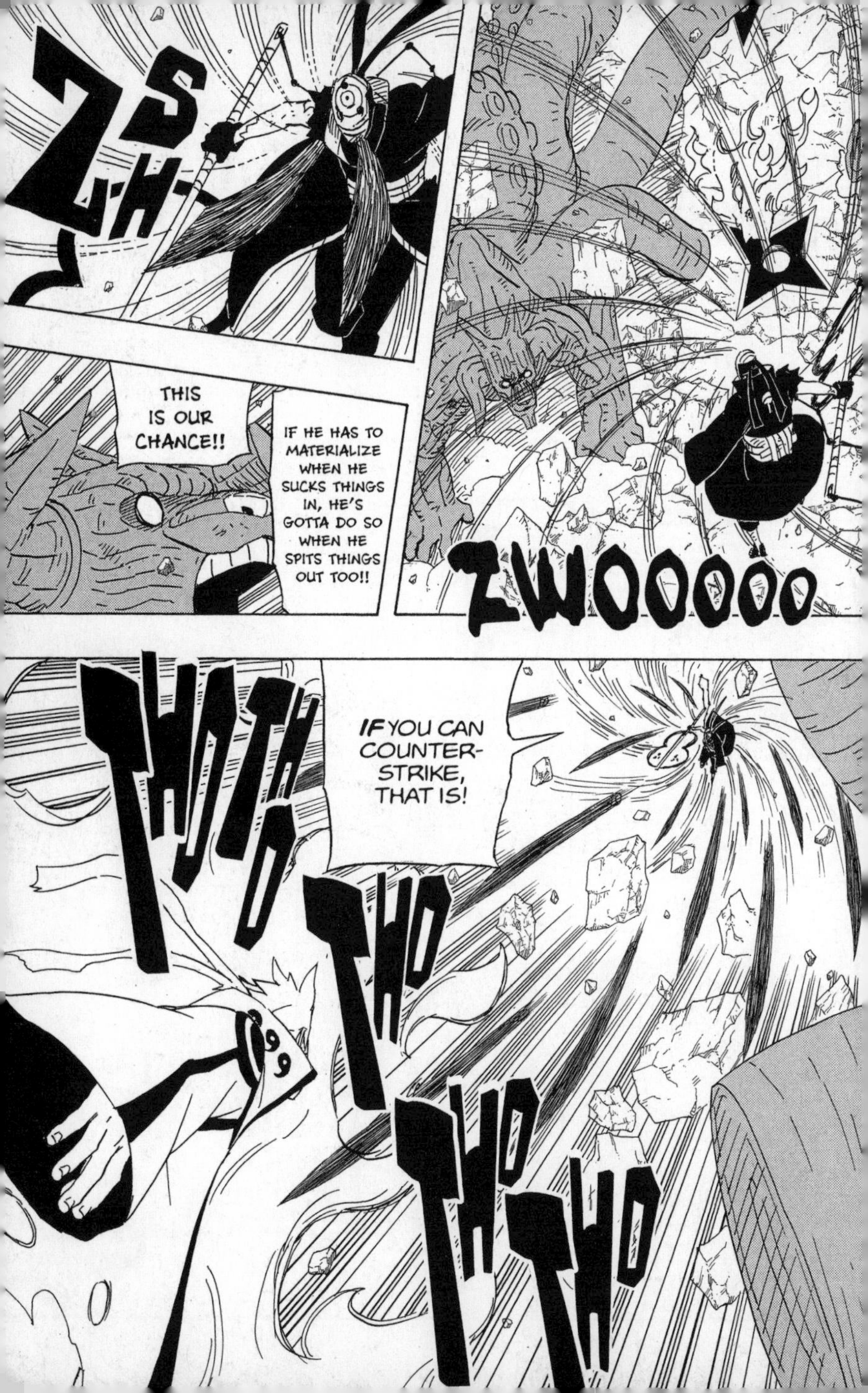
ZWOOOOO
THIS IS OUR CHANCE!!
IF HE HAS TO MATERIALIZE WHEN HE SUCKS THINGS IN, HE'S GOTTA DO SO WHEN HE SPITS THINGS OUT TOO!!
IF YOU CAN COUNTER-STRIKE, THAT IS!

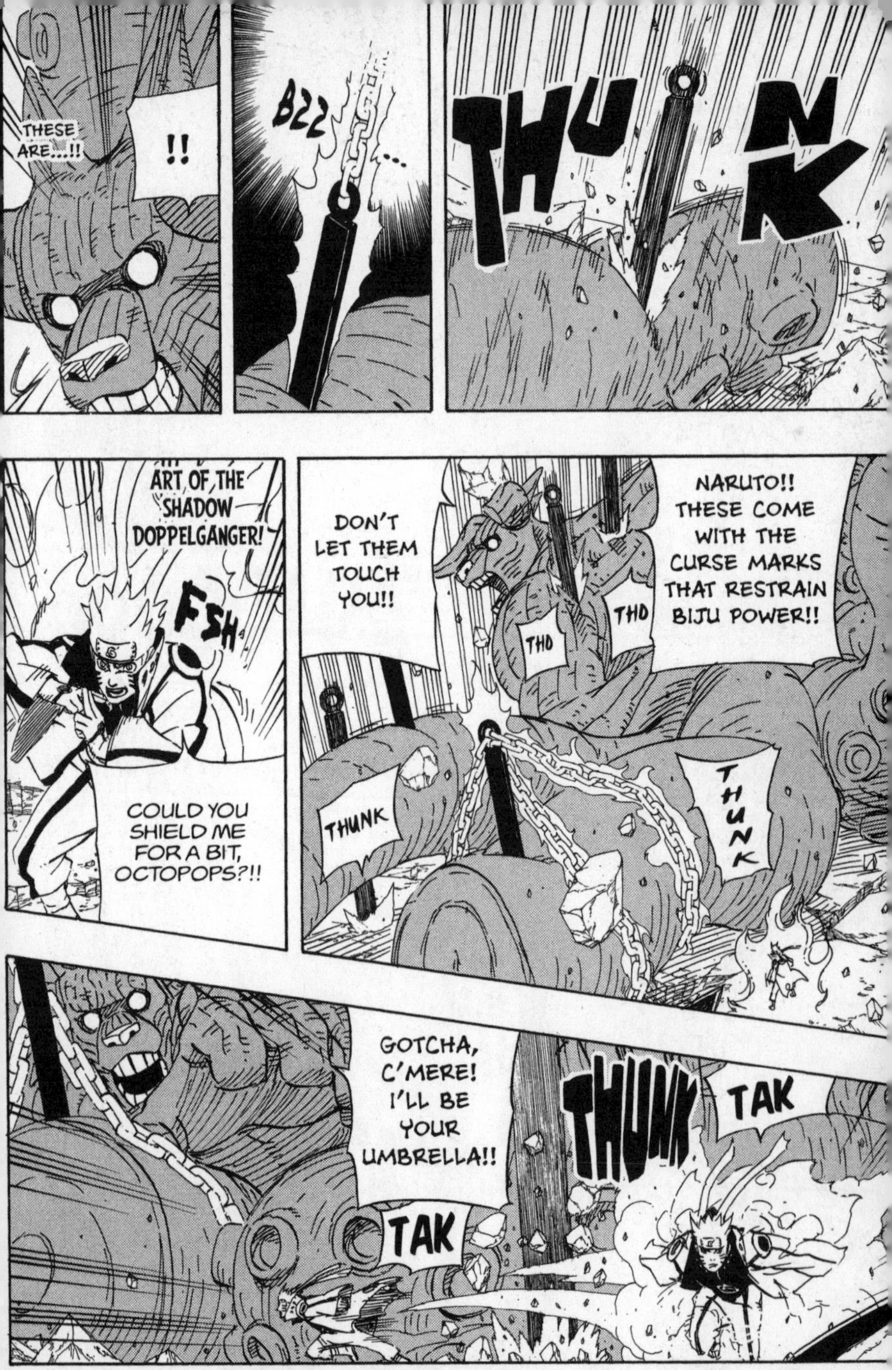
THUNK
BZZ
...
!!
THESE ARE...!!
NARUTO!! THESE COME WITH THE CURSE MARKS THAT RESTRAIN BIJU POWER!!
DON'T LET THEM TOUCH YOU!!
THD
THD
THUNK
THUNK
ART OF THE SHADOW DOPPELGANGER!
FSH
COULD YOU SHIELD ME FOR A BIT, OCTOPOPS?!!
TAK
THUNK
GOTCHA, C'MERE! I'LL BE YOUR UMBRELLA!!
TAK

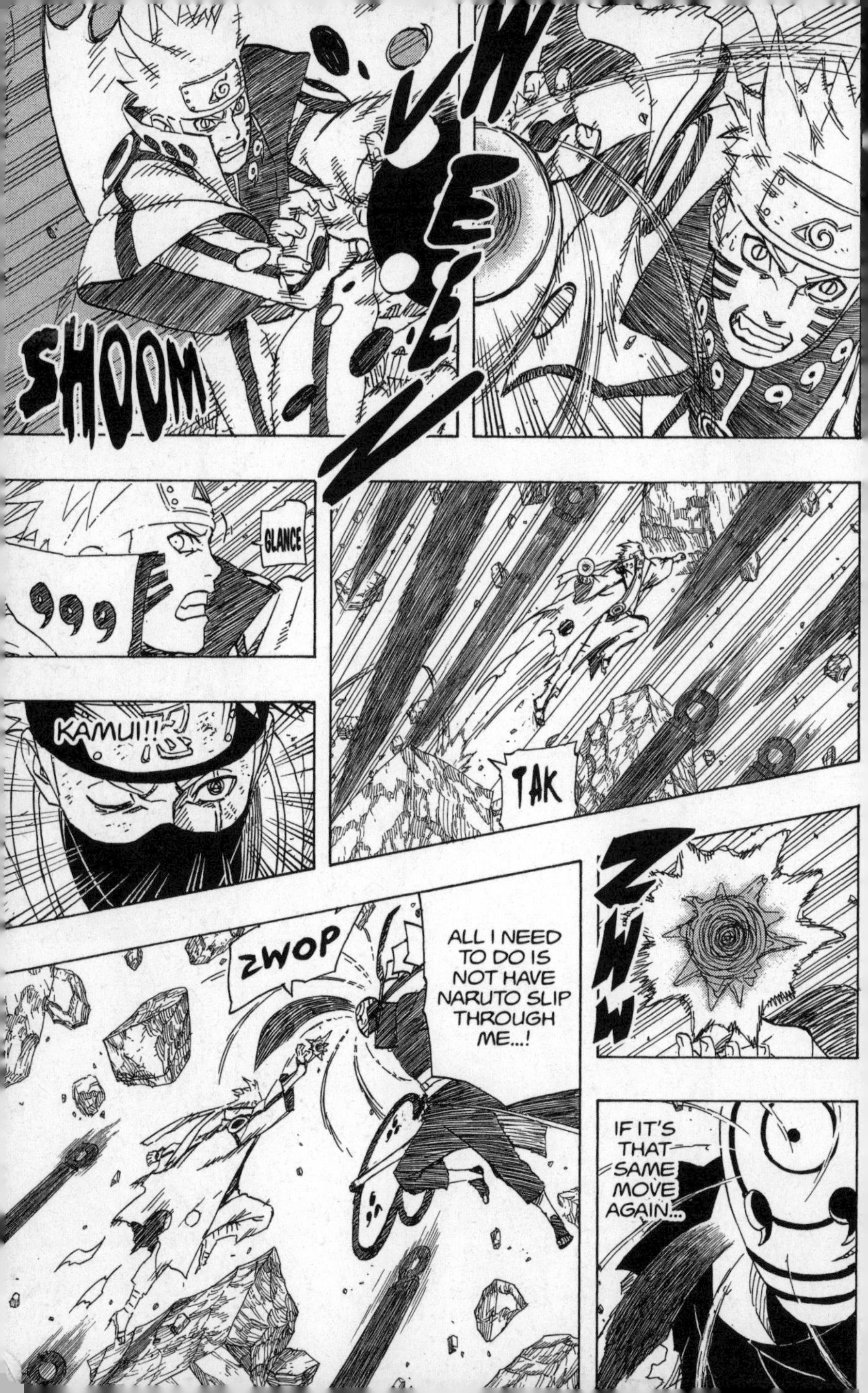
VWEEEN
SHOOM
TAK
GLANCE
KAMUI!!!
ZWWW
IF IT'S THAT SAME MOVE AGAIN...
ZWOP
ALL I NEED TO DO IS NOT HAVE NARUTO SLIP THROUGH ME...!

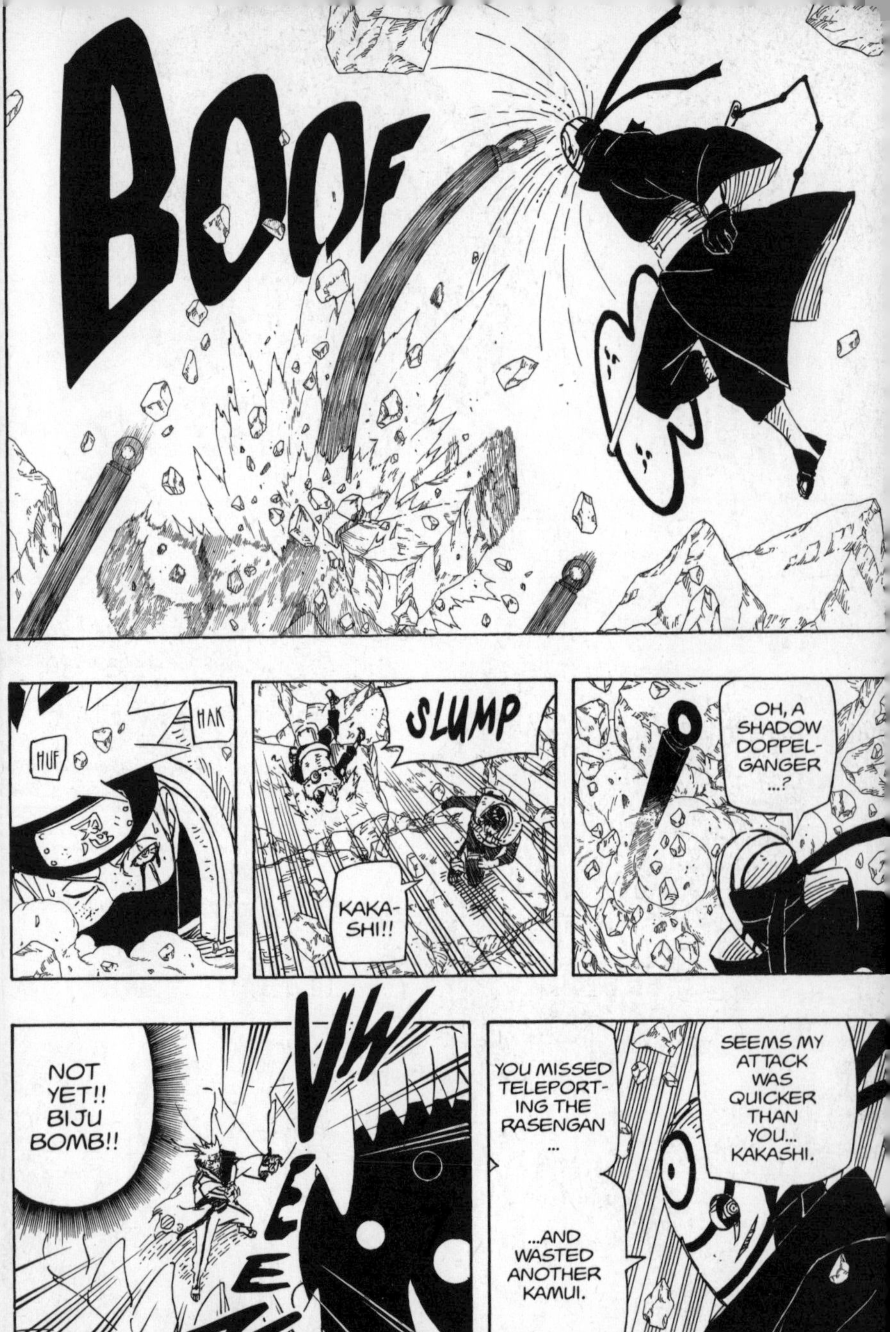
BOOF
OH, A SHADOW DOPPEL-GANGER ...?
SLUMP
KAKA-SHI!!
HAK
HUF
SEEMS MY ATTACK WAS QUICKER THAN YOU... KAKASHI.
YOU MISSED TELEPORT-ING THE RASENGAN ...
...AND WASTED ANOTHER KAMUI.
VWEEN
NOT YET!! BIJU BOMB!!

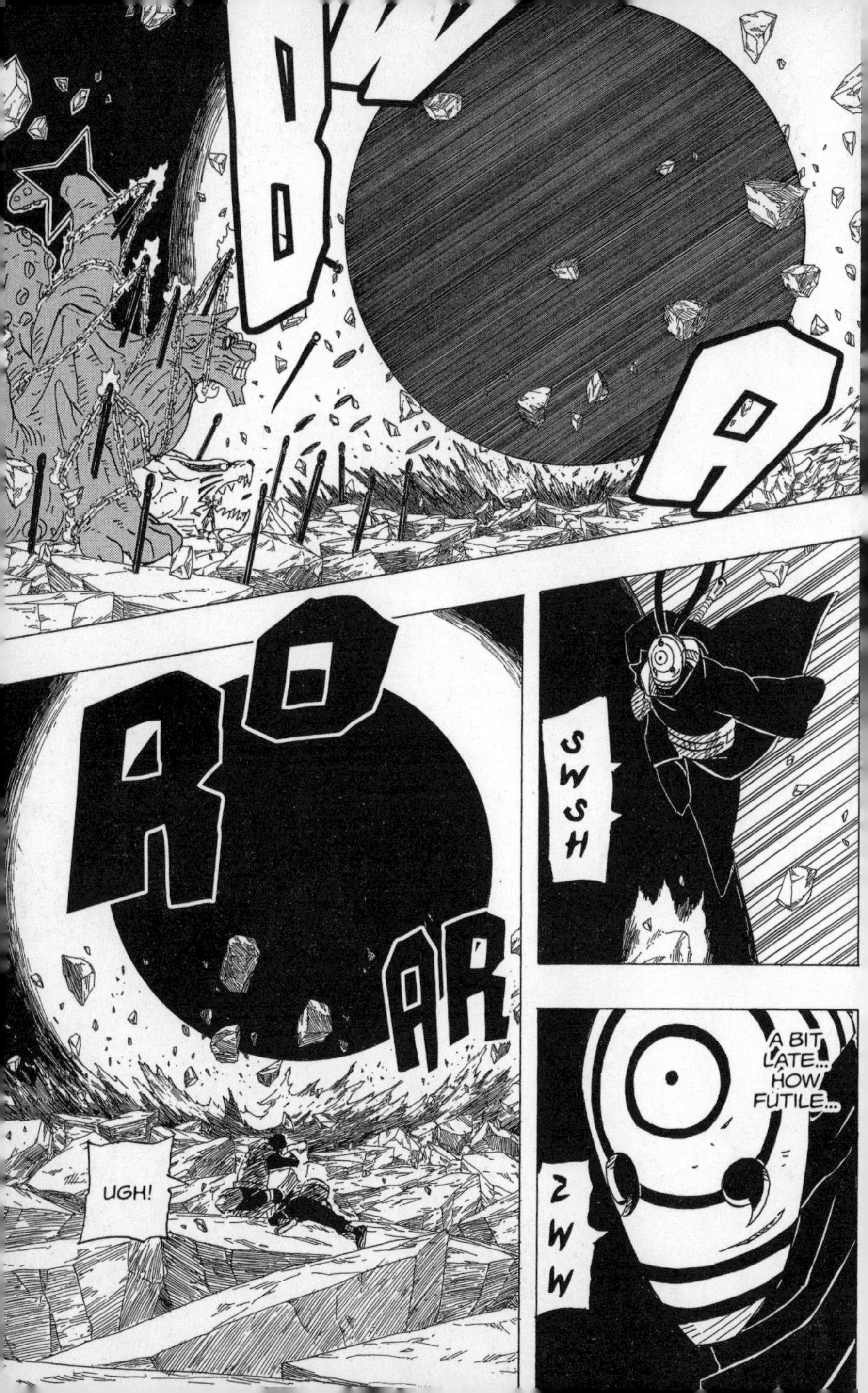
SWSH
A BIT LATE... HOW FUTILE...
ZWW
ROAR
UGH!

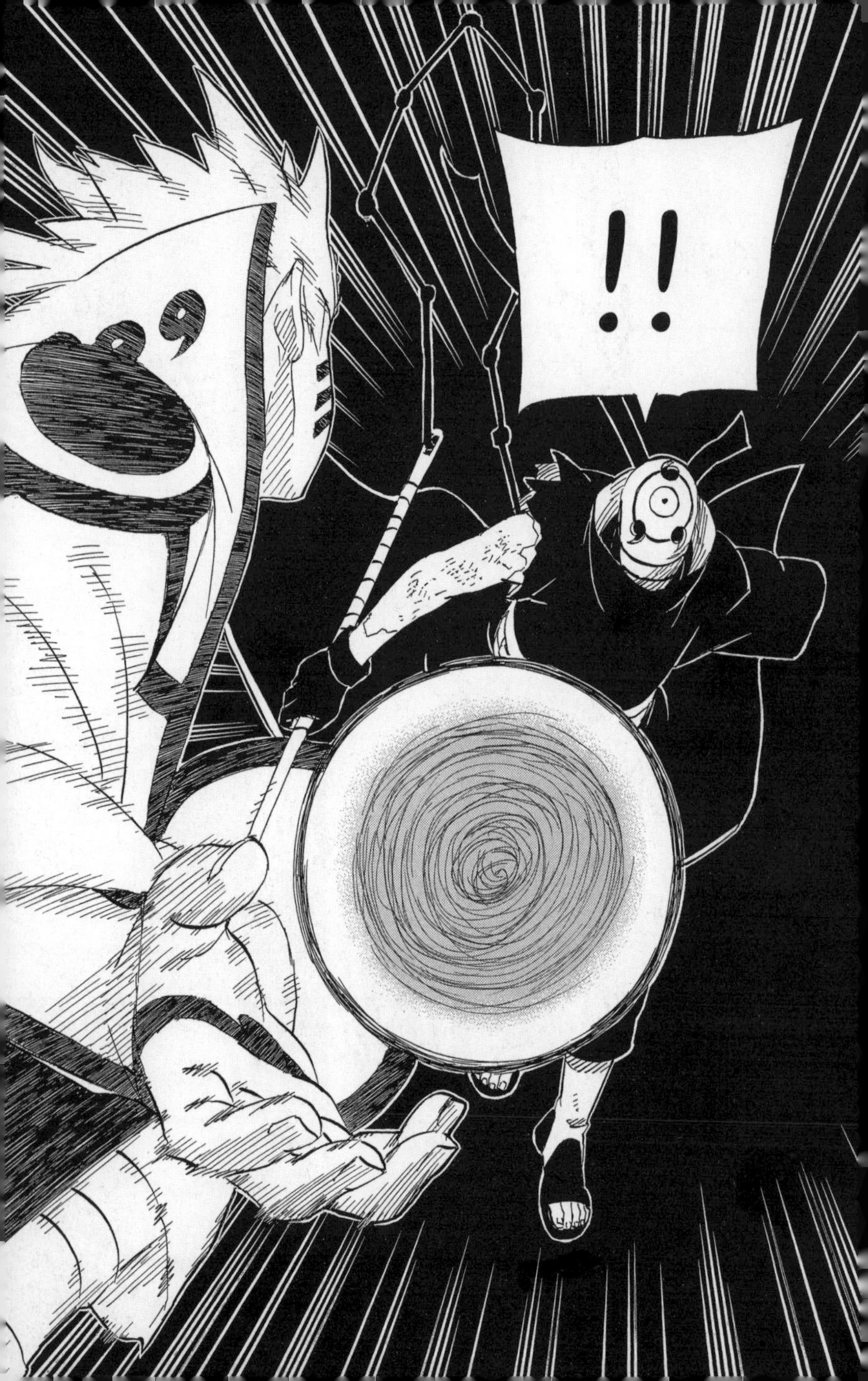
!!

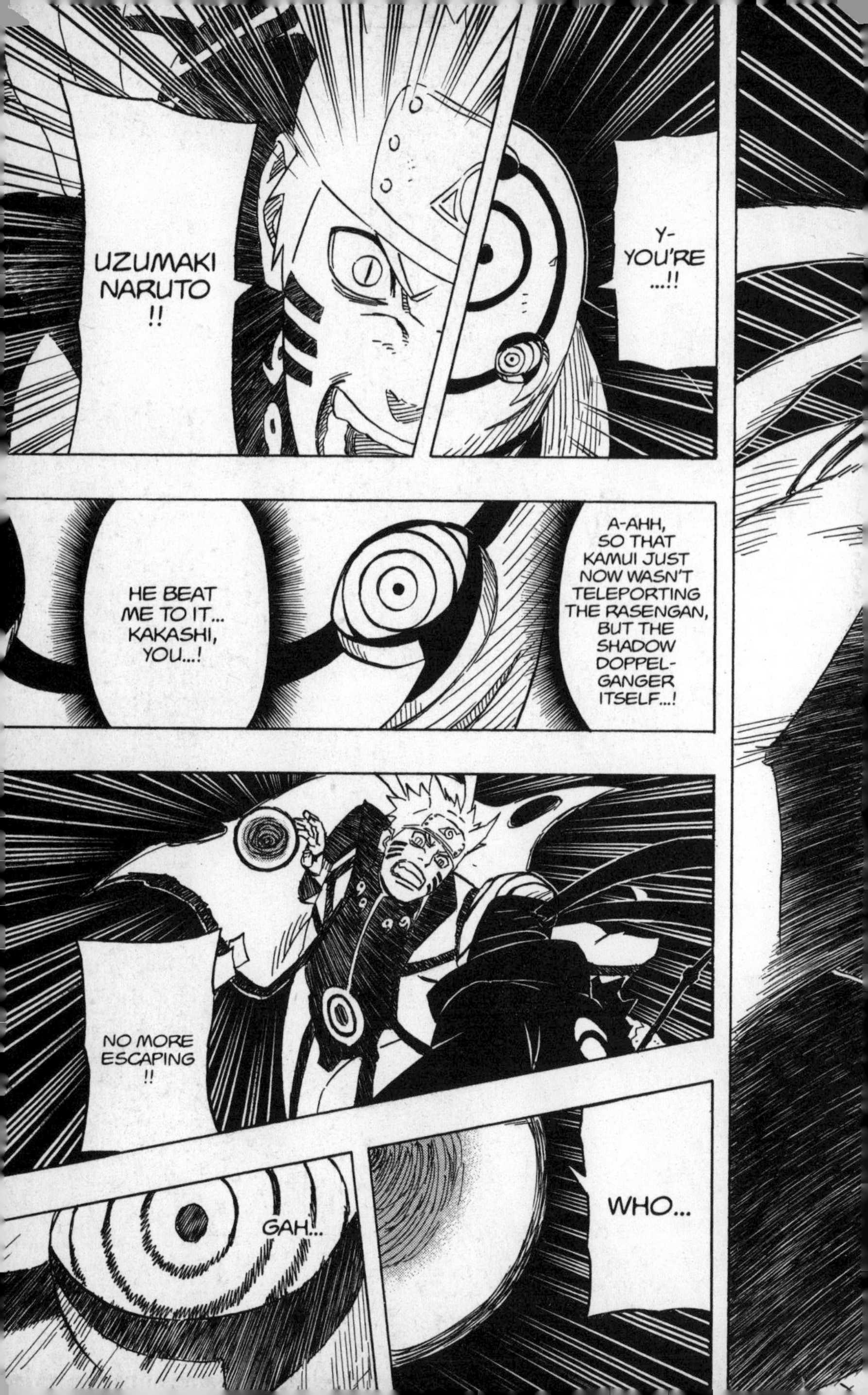

Y- YOU'RE ...!!
UZUMAKI NARUTO !!
A-AHH, SO THAT KAMUI JUST NOW WASN'T TELEPORTING THE RASENGAN, BUT THE SHADOW DOPPEL-GANGER ITSELF...!
HE BEAT ME TO IT... KAKASHI, YOU...!
NO MORE ESCAPING !!
WHO...
GAH...

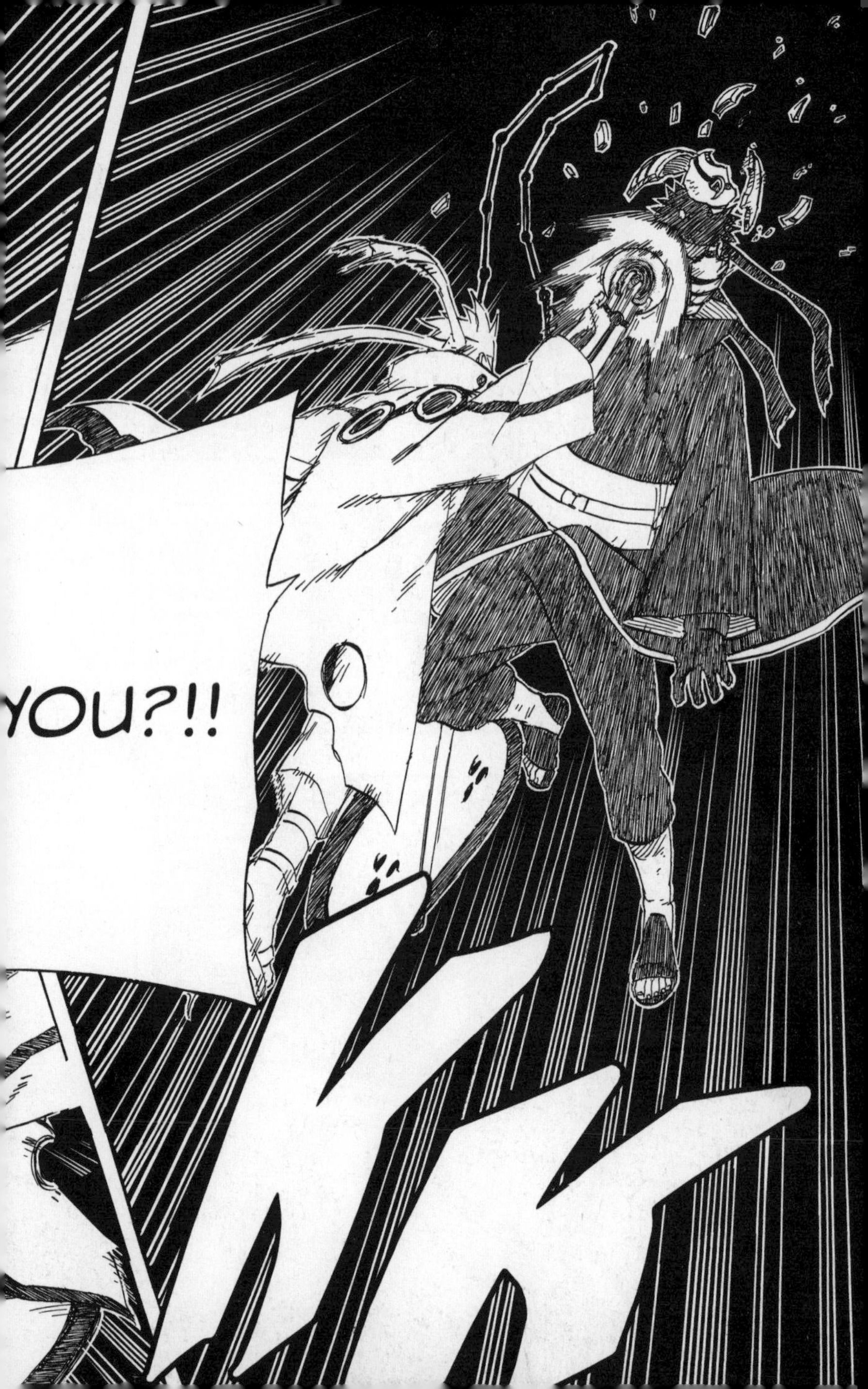
YOU?!!

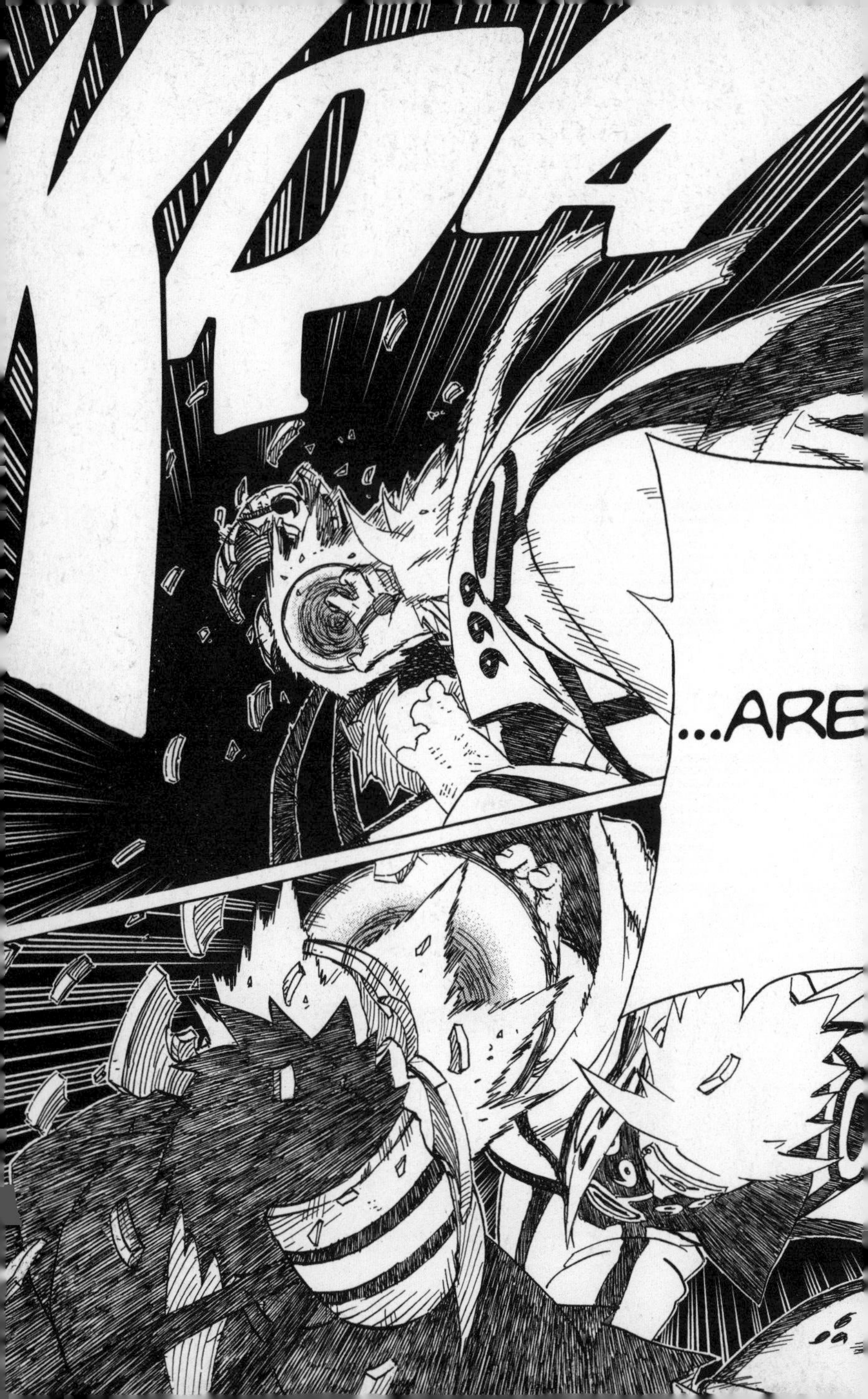
...ARE

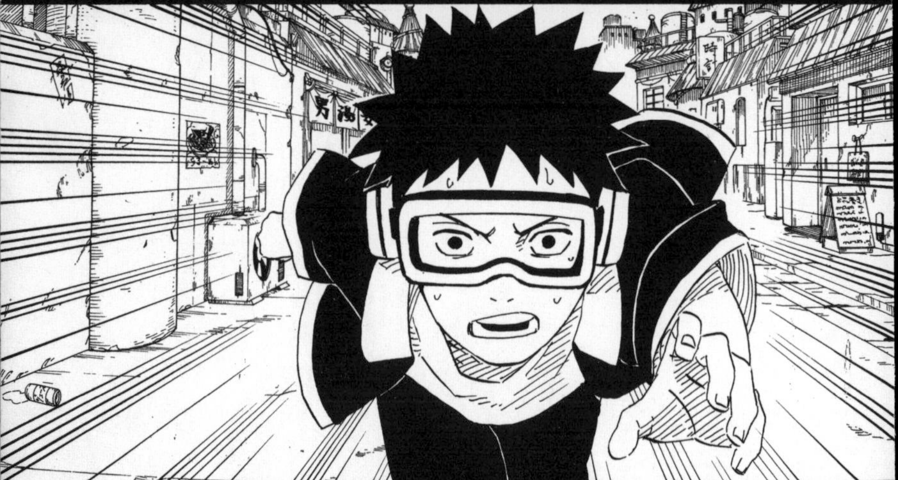

Number 599: Uchiha Obito

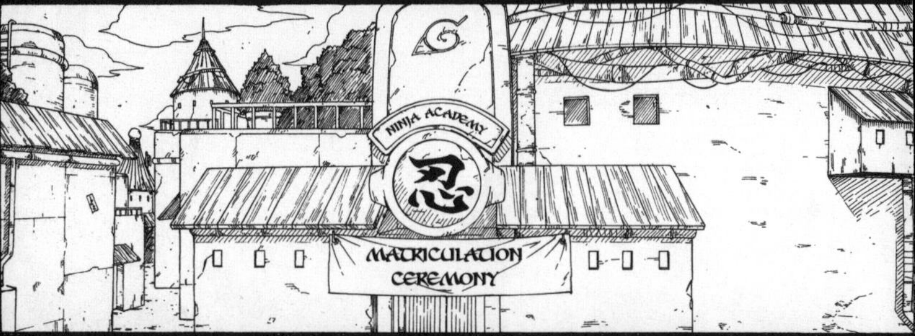
NINJA ACADEMY
忍
MATRICULATION CEREMONY

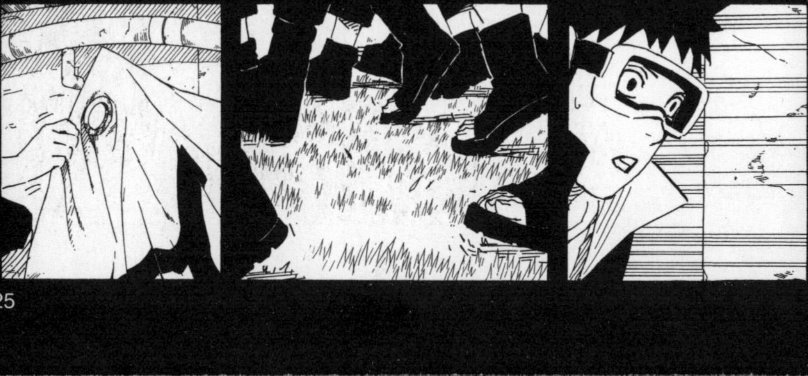

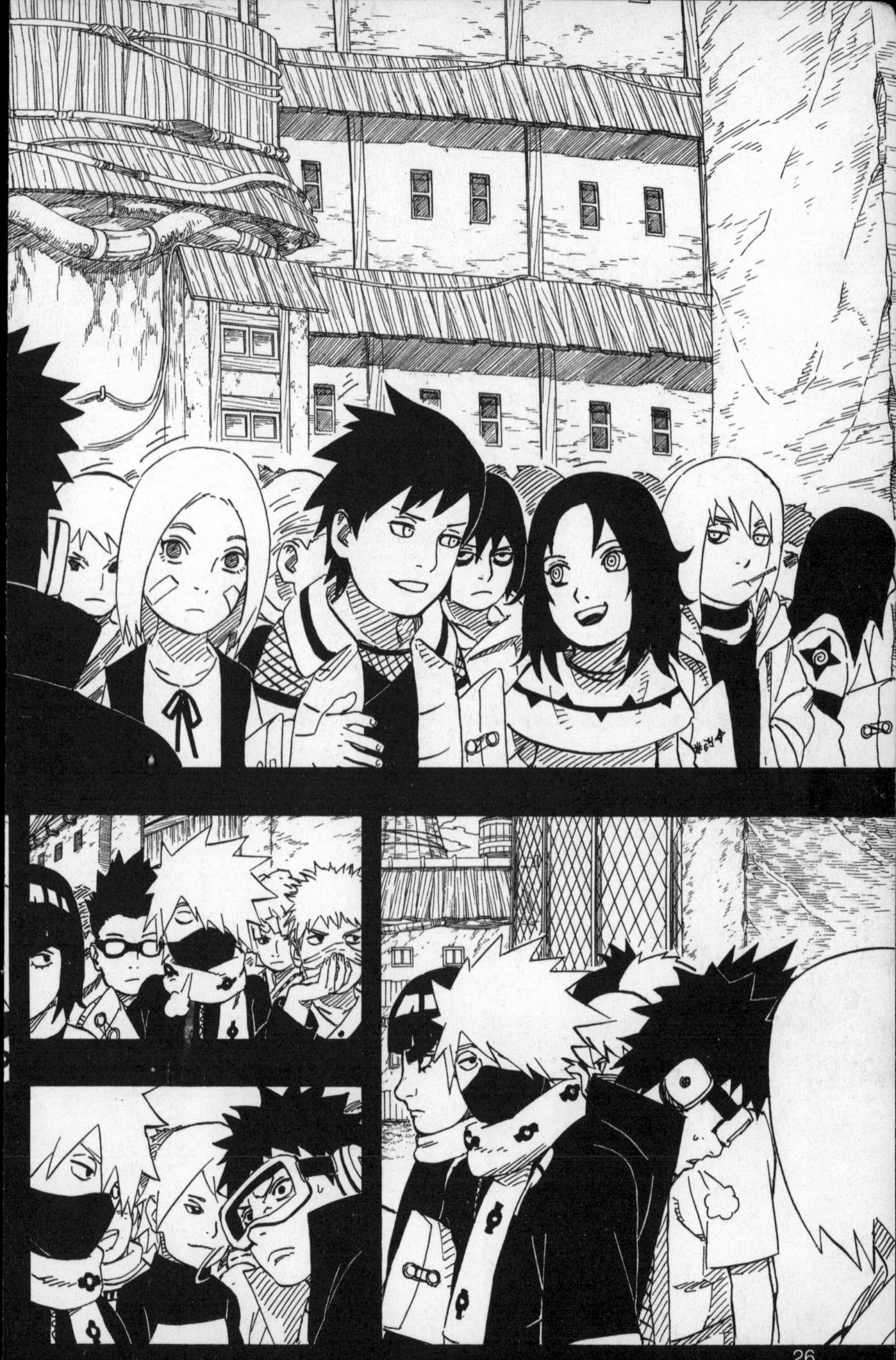

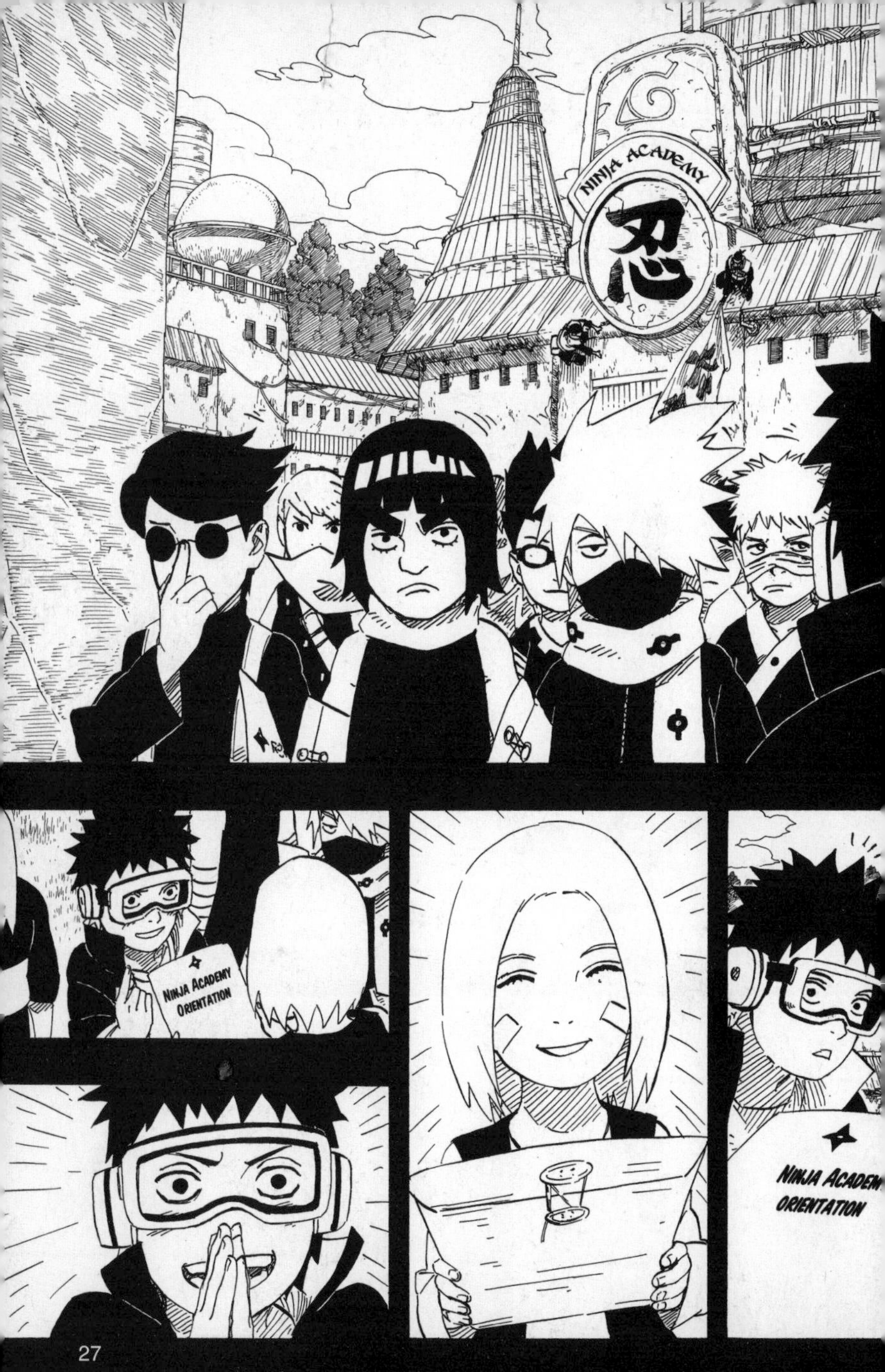
NINJA ACADEMY
忍
NINJA ACADEM
ORIENTATION
NINJA ACADEMY
ORIENTATION

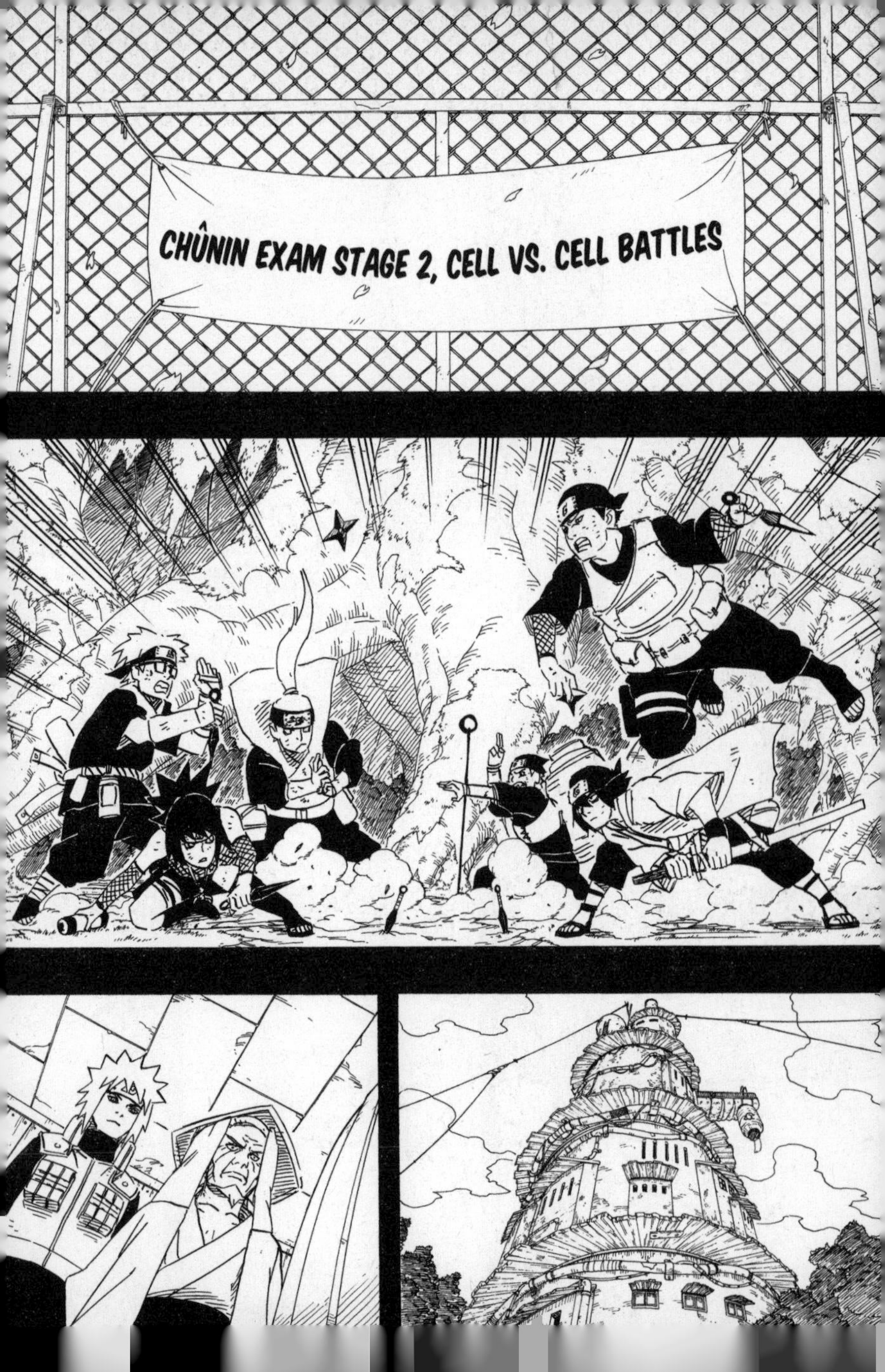
CHÛNIN EXAM STAGE 2, CELL VS. CELL BATTLES

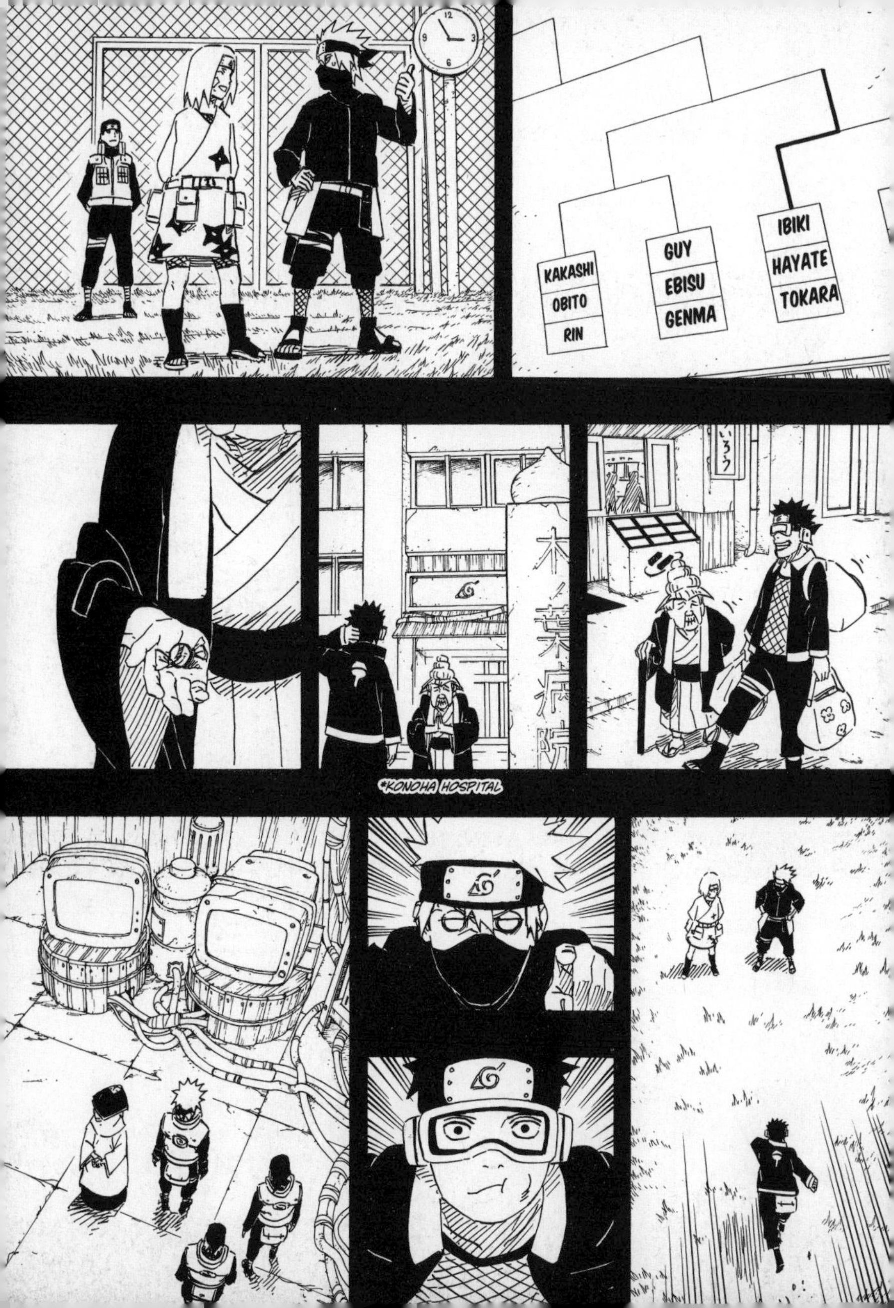
IBIKI
HAYATE
TOKARA
GUY
EBISU
GENMA
KAKASHI
OBITO
RIN
木ノ葉病院
*KONOHA HOSPITAL

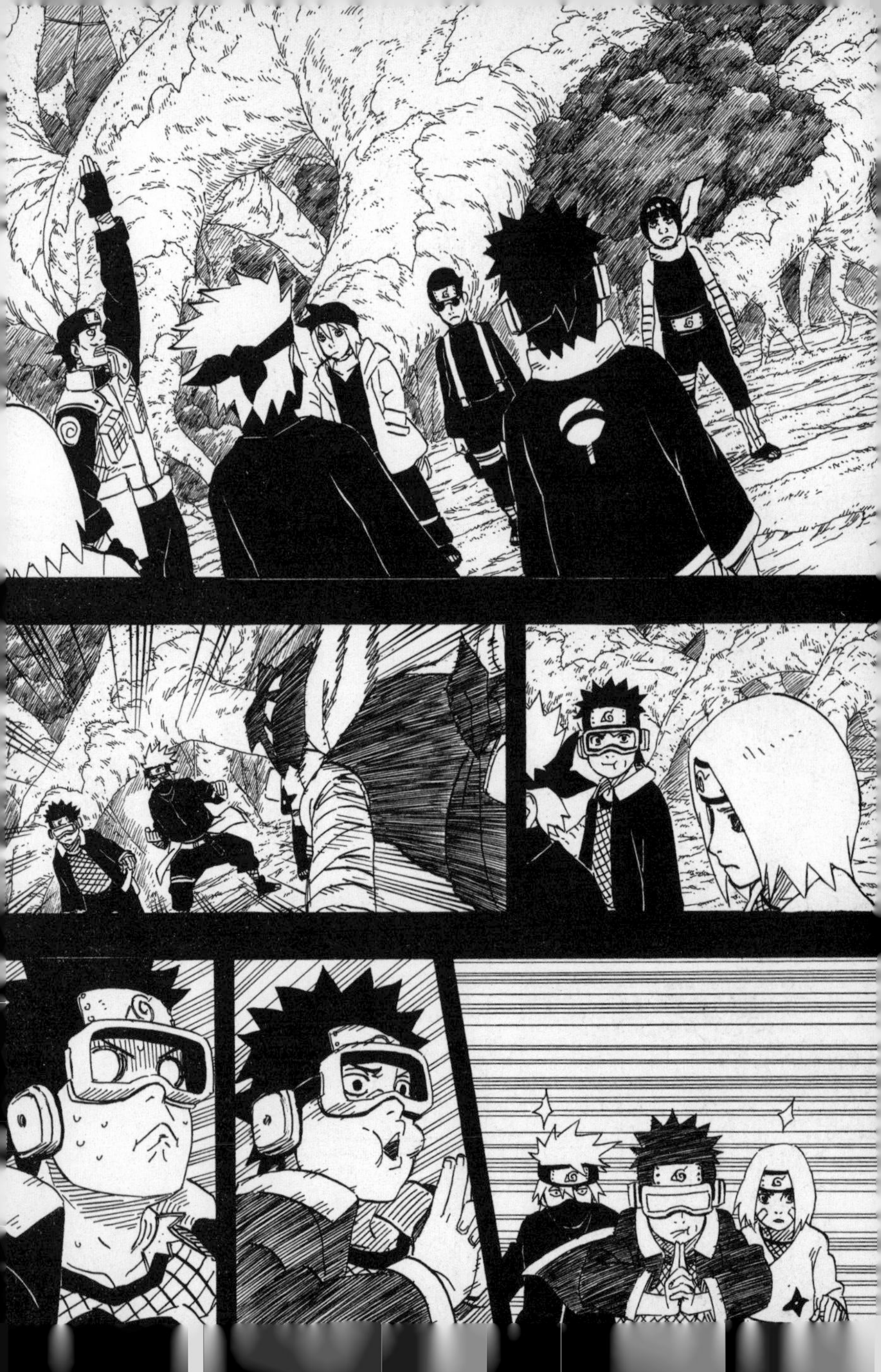

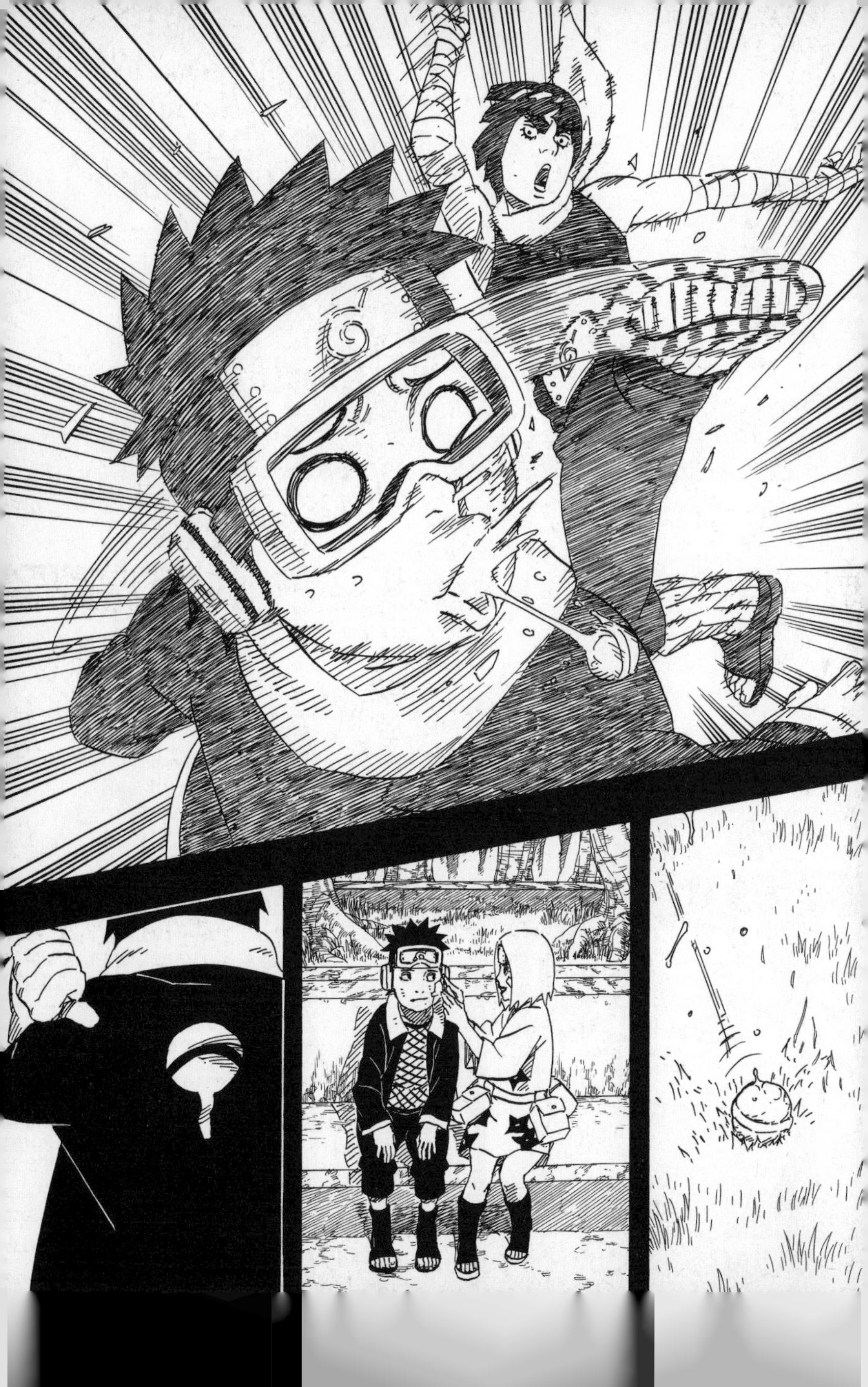

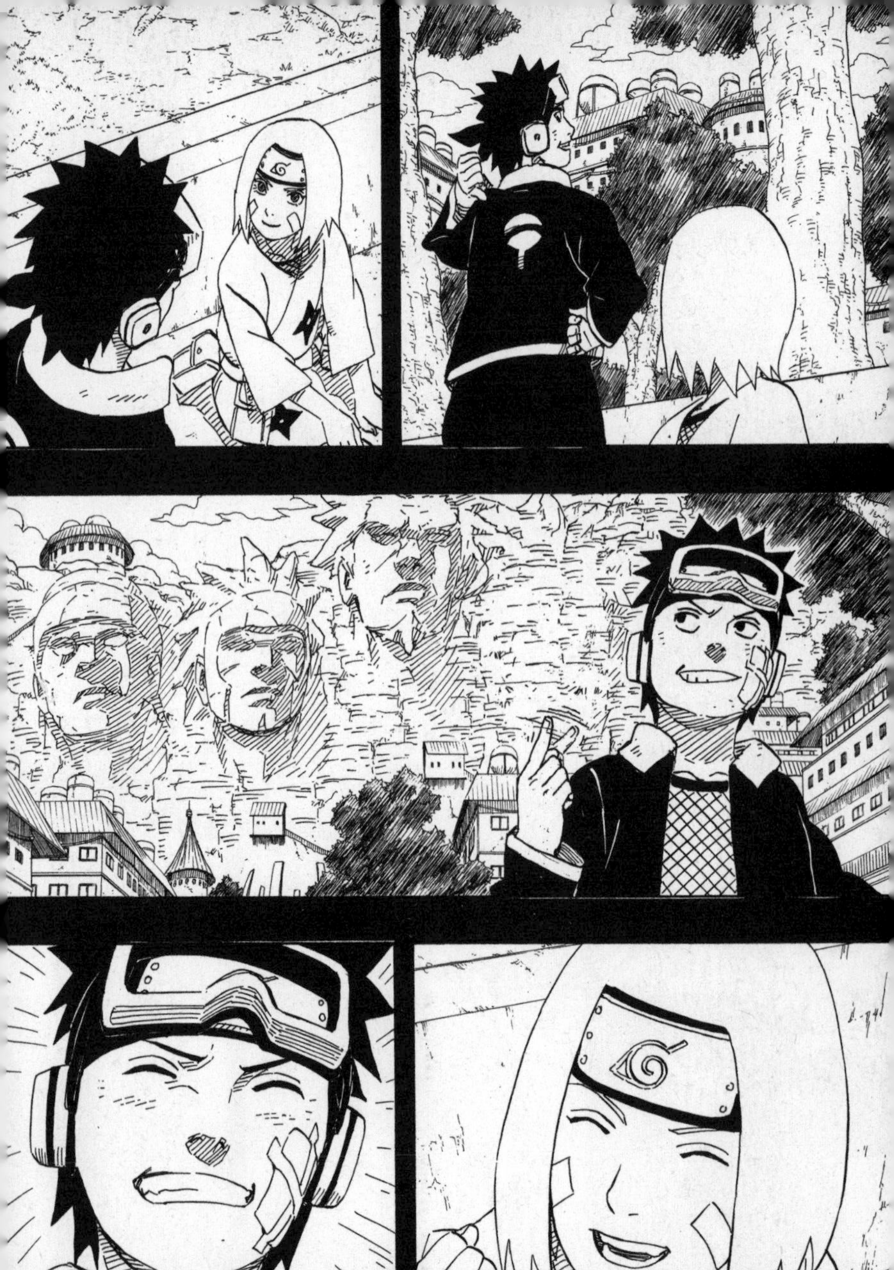

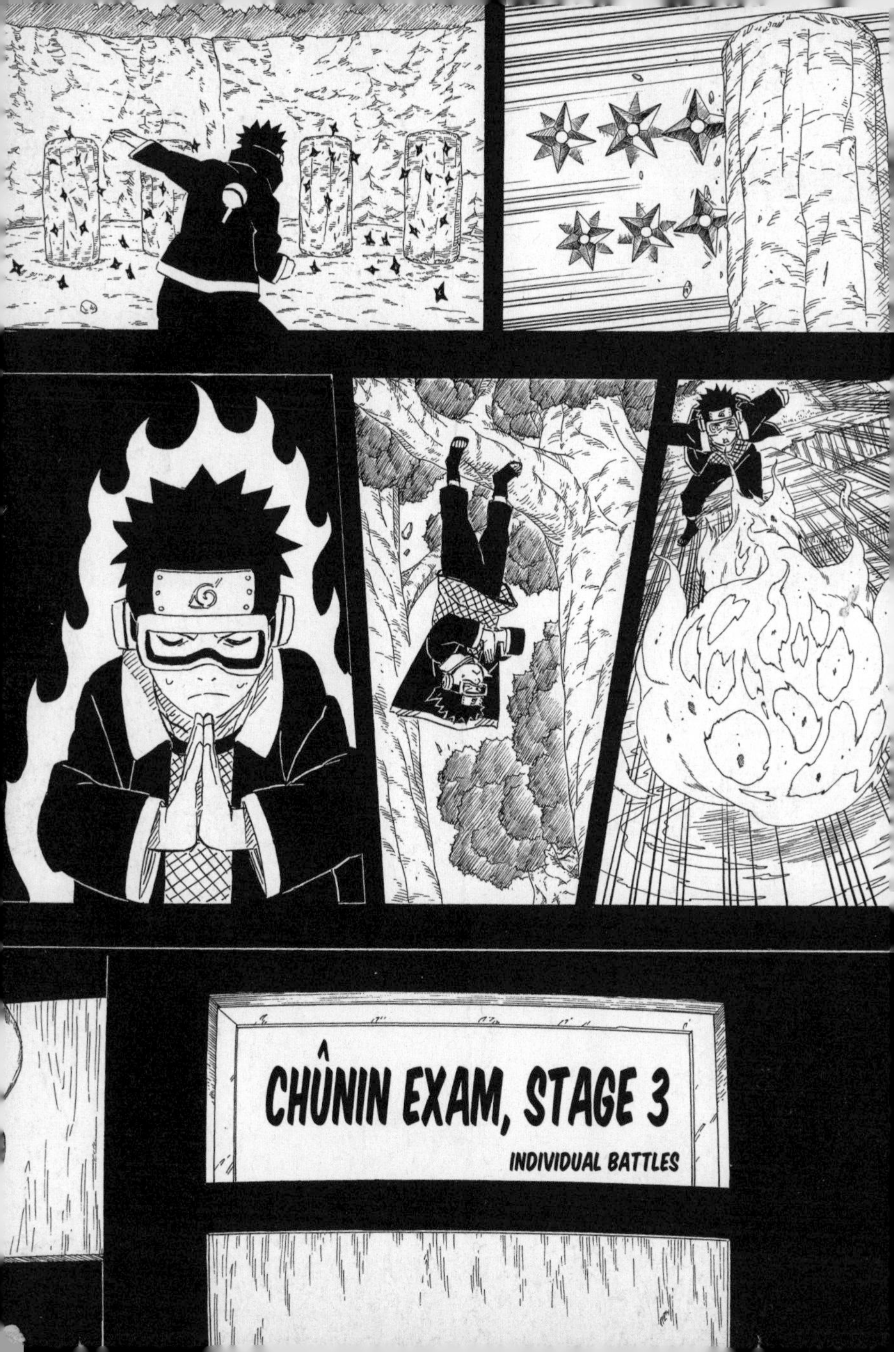
CHÛNIN EXAM, STAGE 3
INDIVIDUAL BATTLES

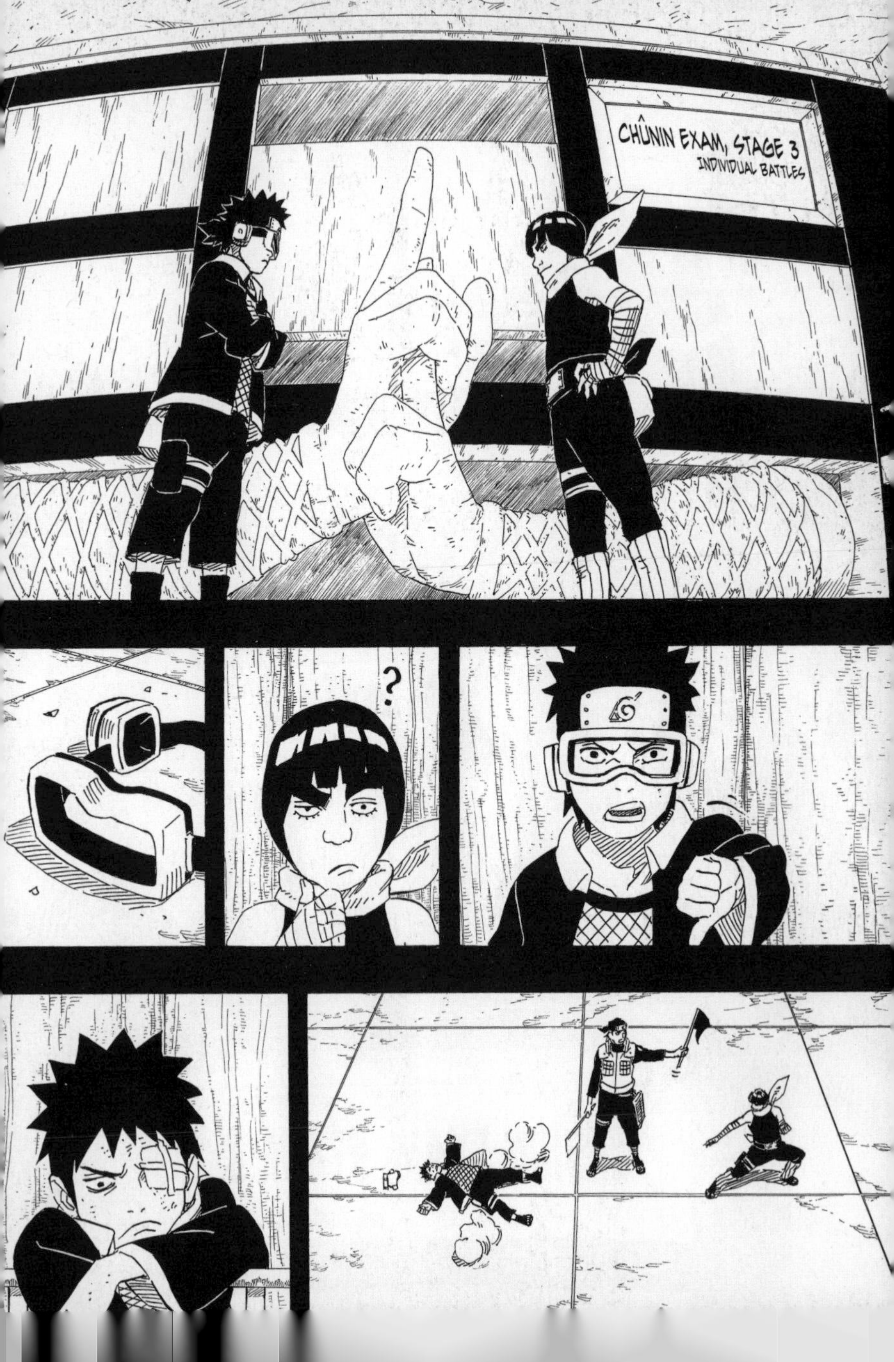
CHÛNIN EXAM, STAGE 3
INDIVIDUAL BATTLES
?

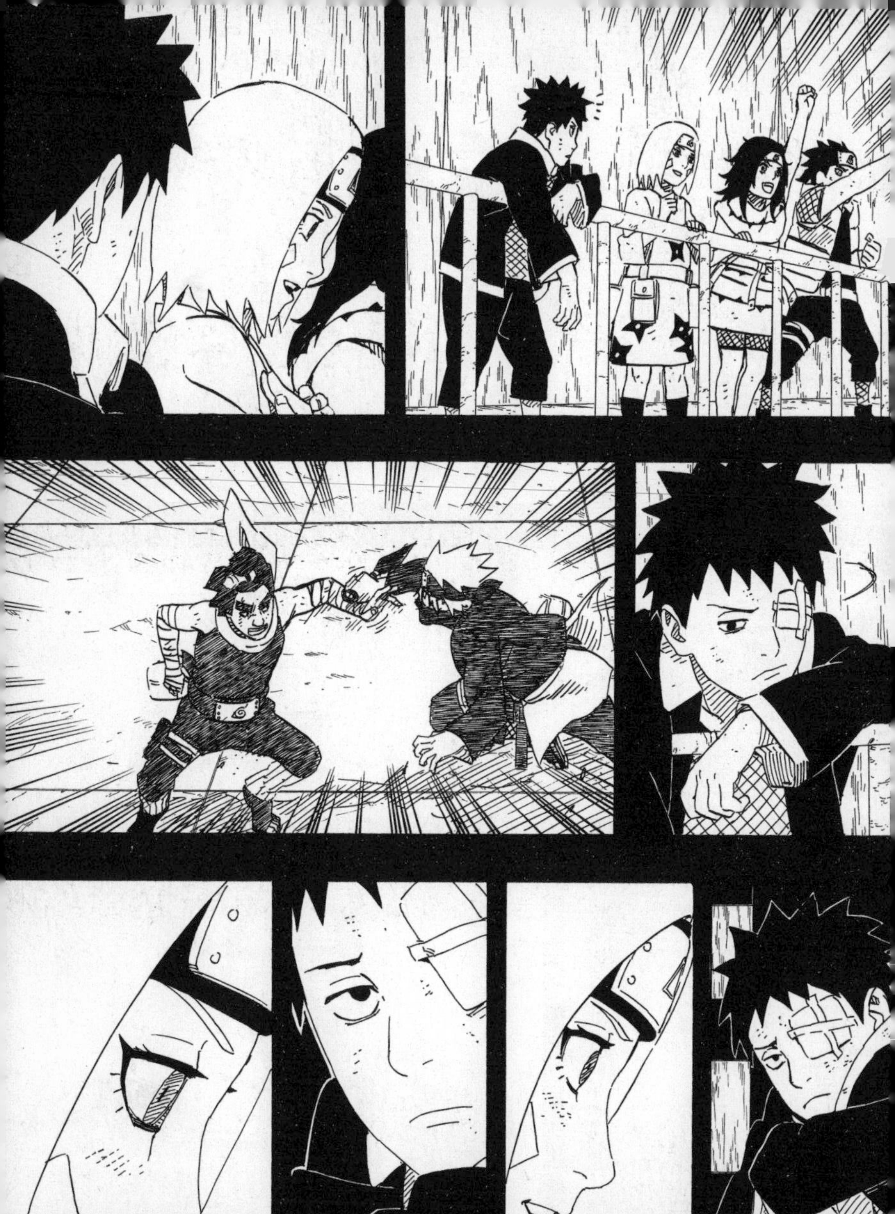

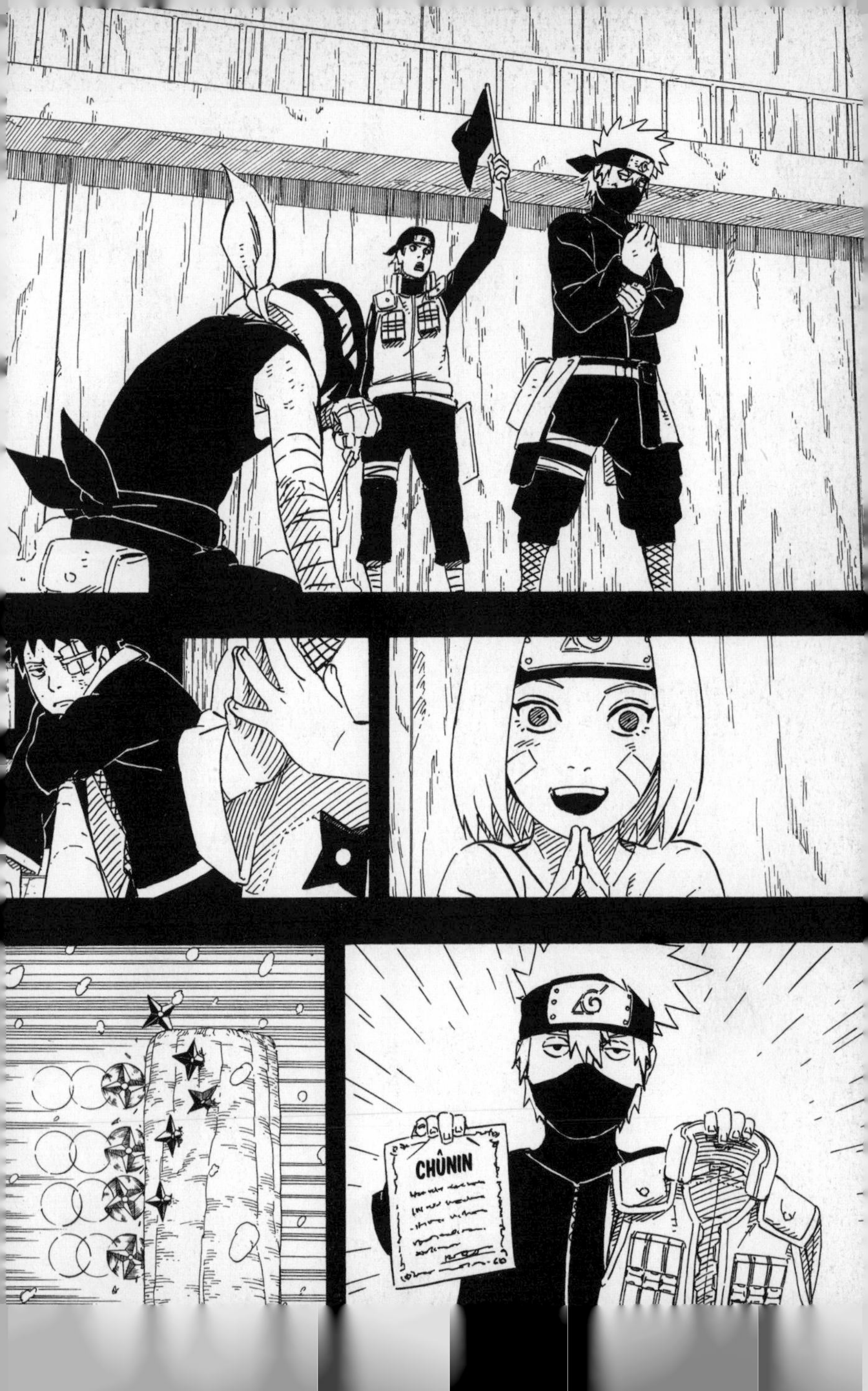
CHÛNIN

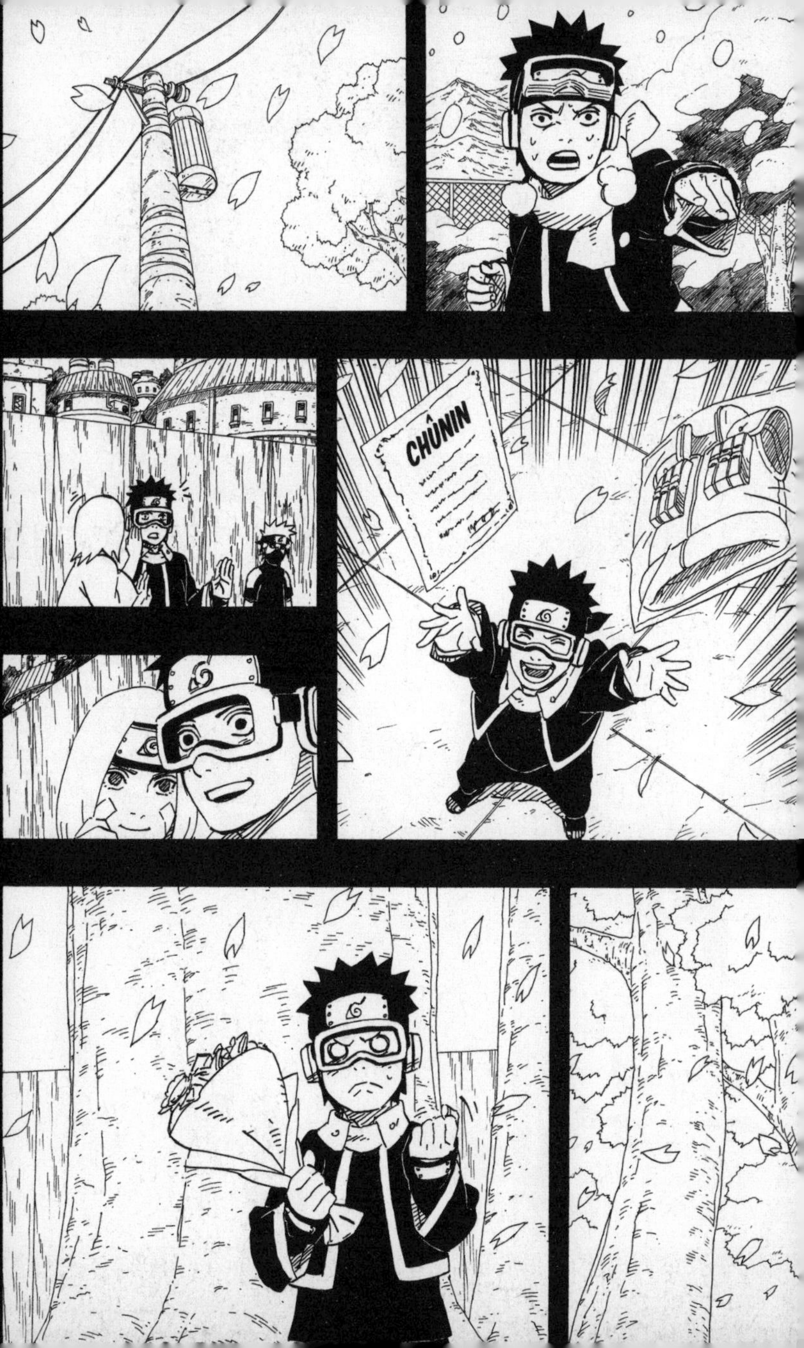
CHÛNIN

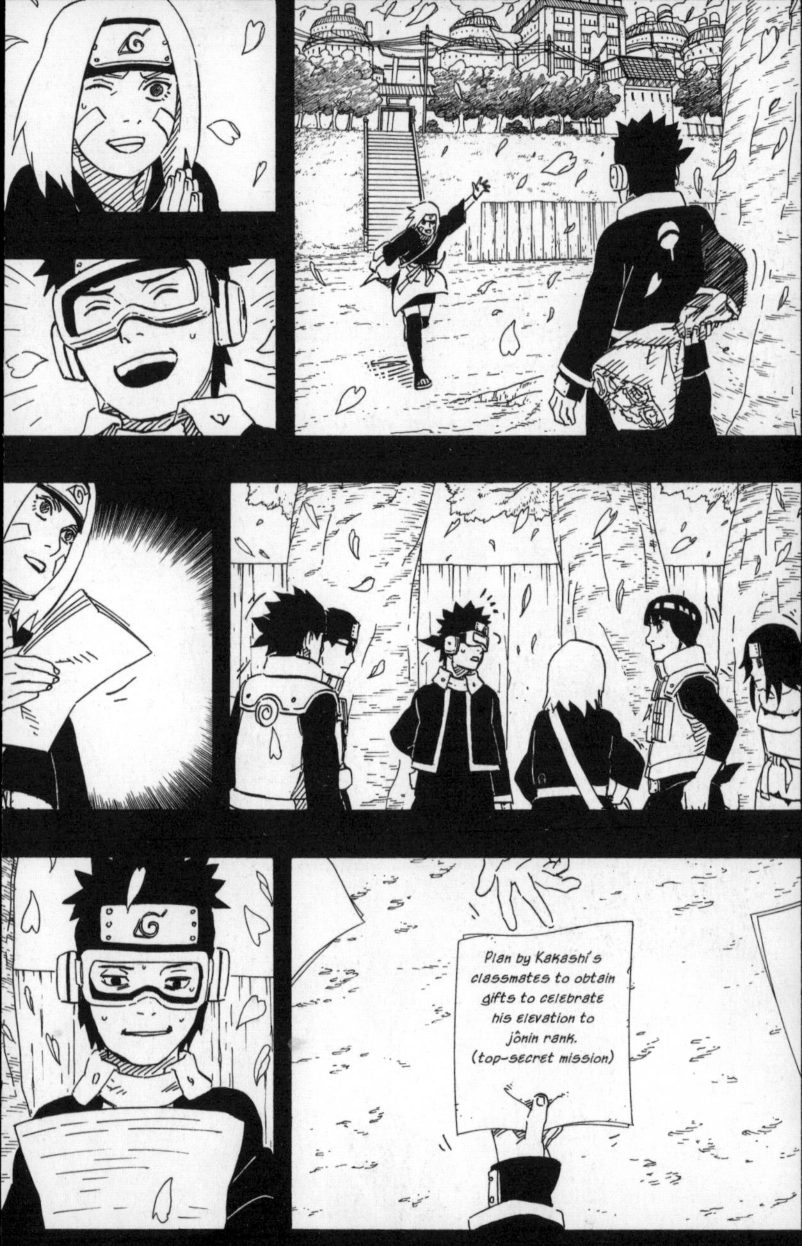
Plan by Kakashi's classmates to obtain gifts to celebrate his elevation to jônin rank. (top-secret mission)

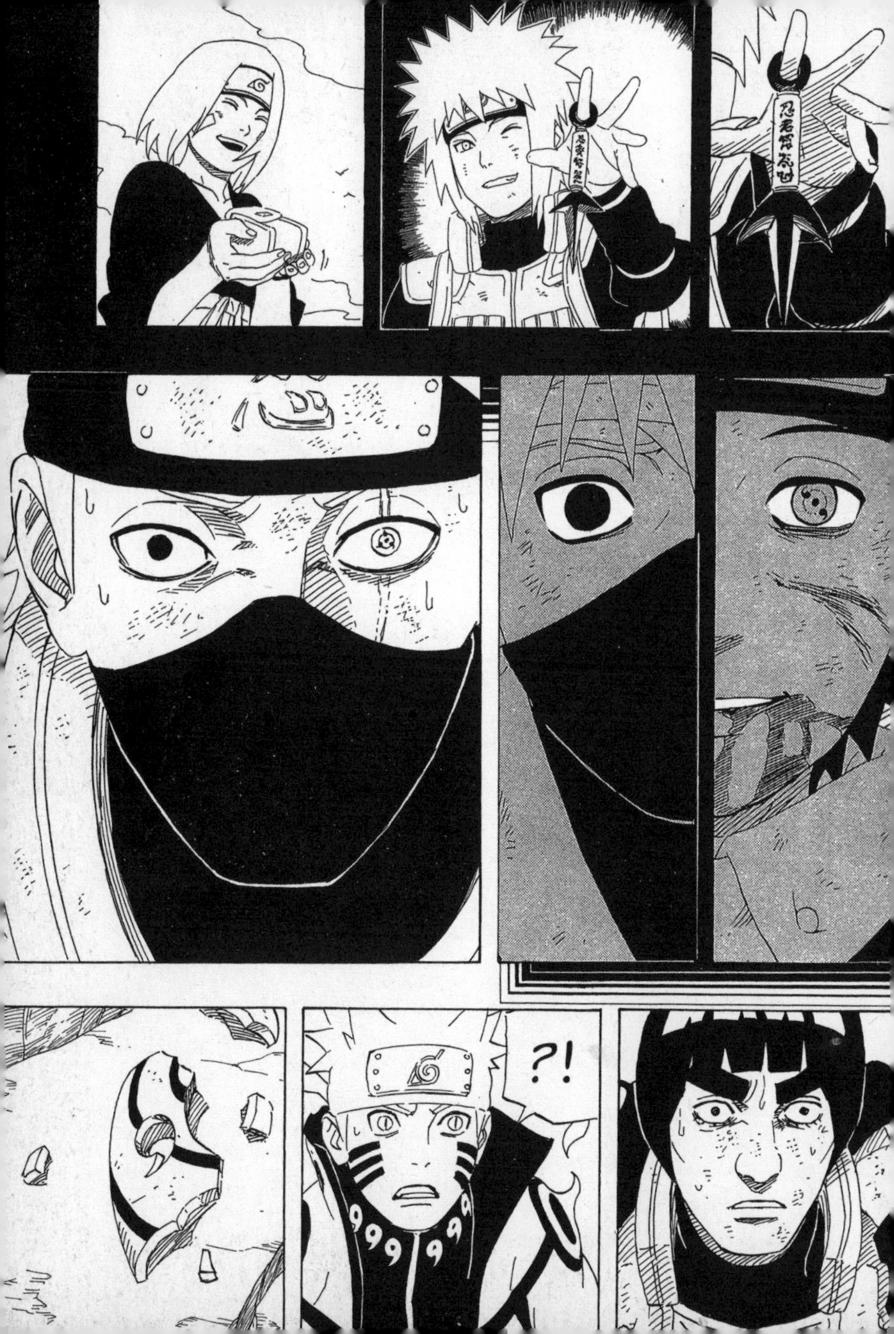
?!

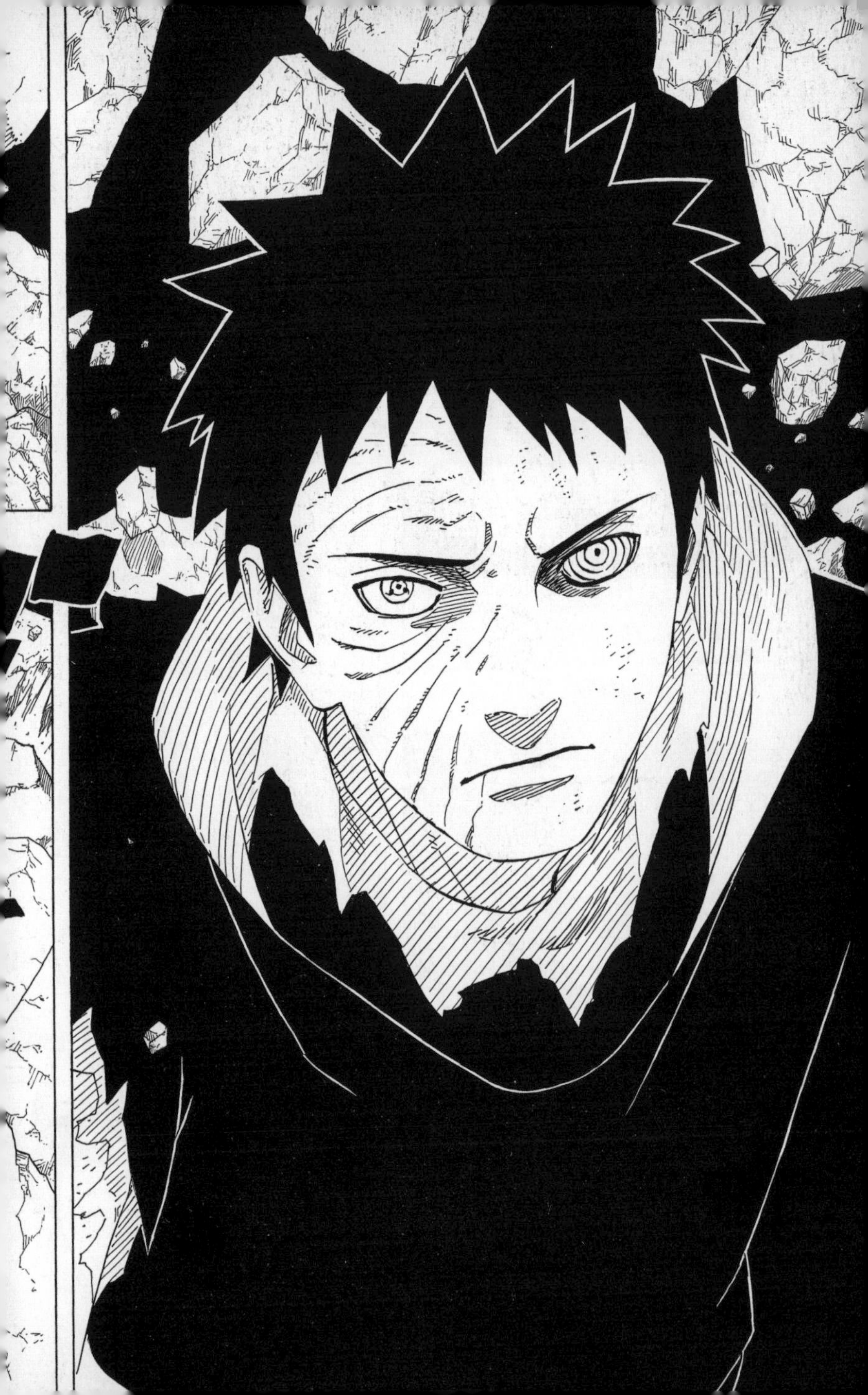

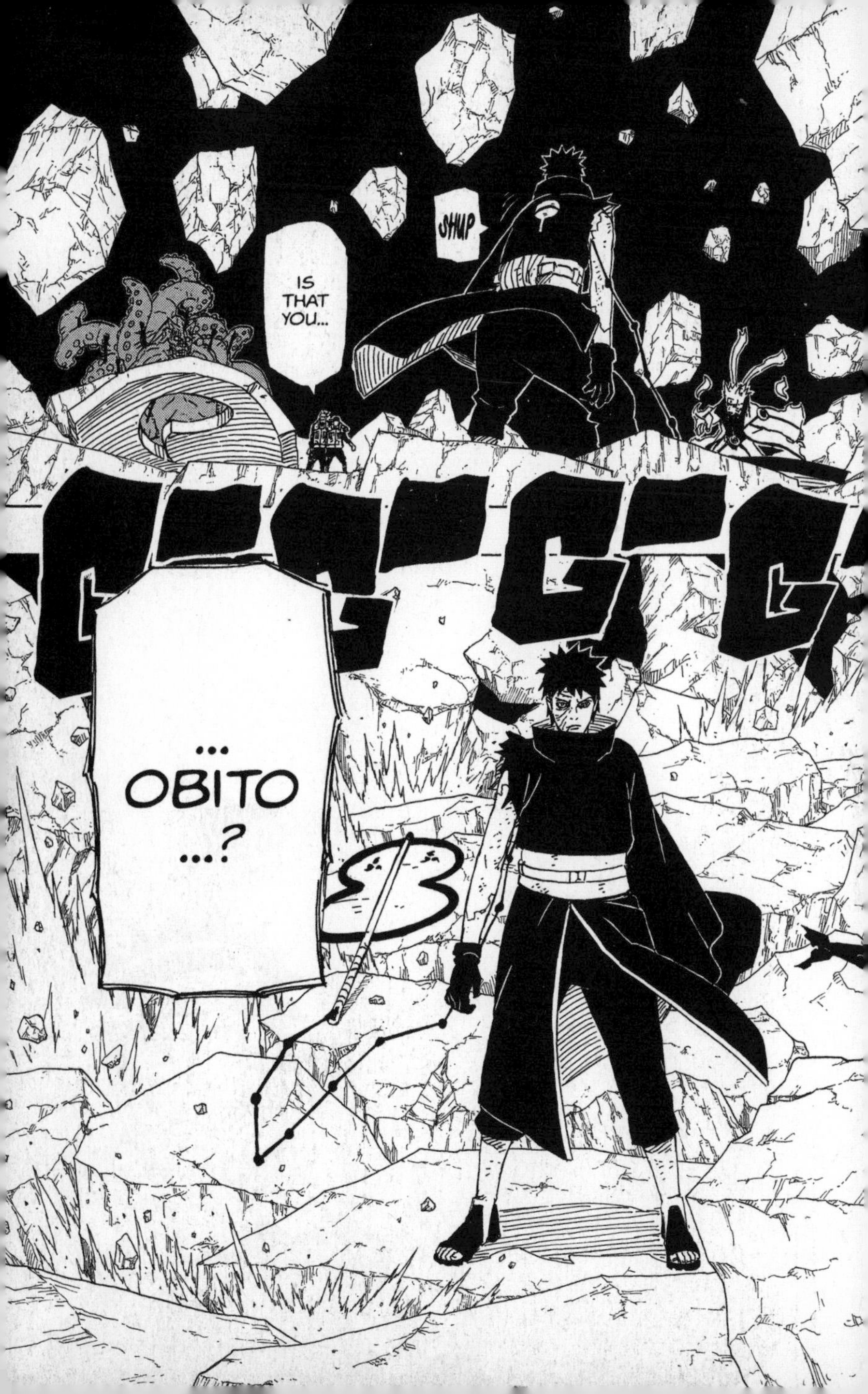
SHUP
IS THAT YOU...
...OBITO ...?

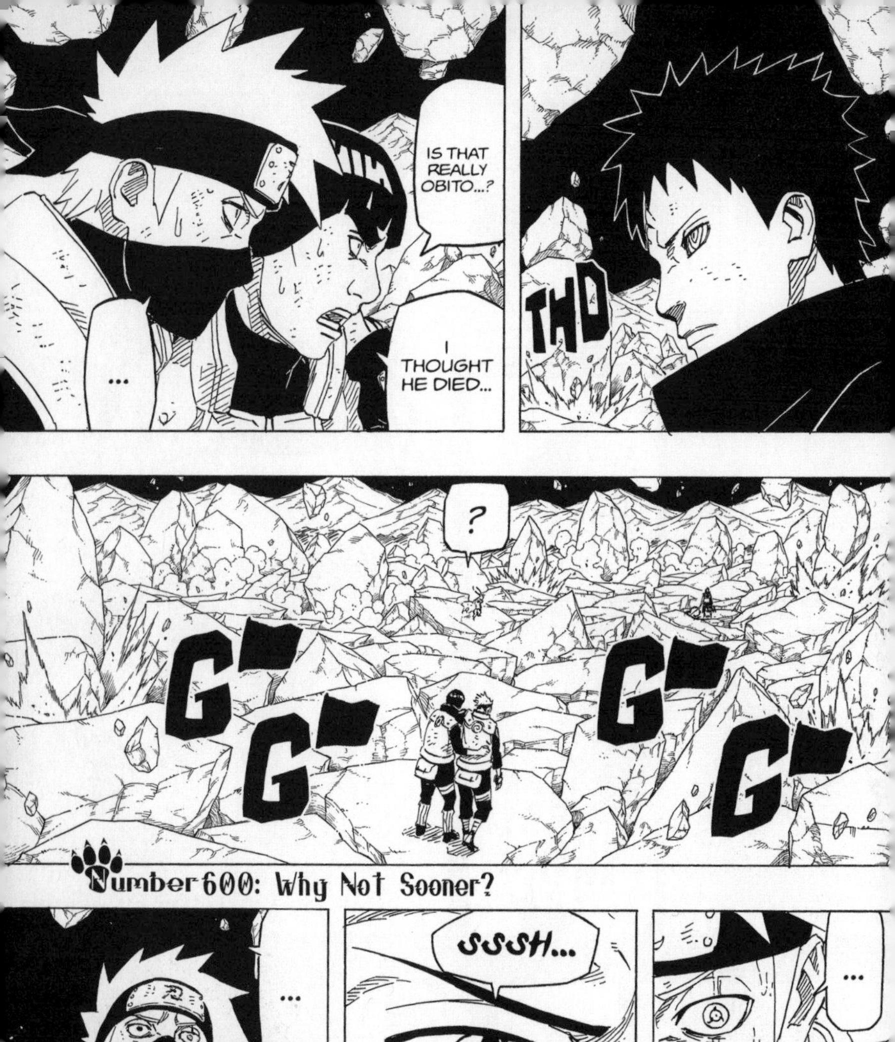
THD
IS THAT REALLY OBITO...?
I THOUGHT HE DIED...
...
?
G' G'
G' G'

Number 600: Why Not Sooner?

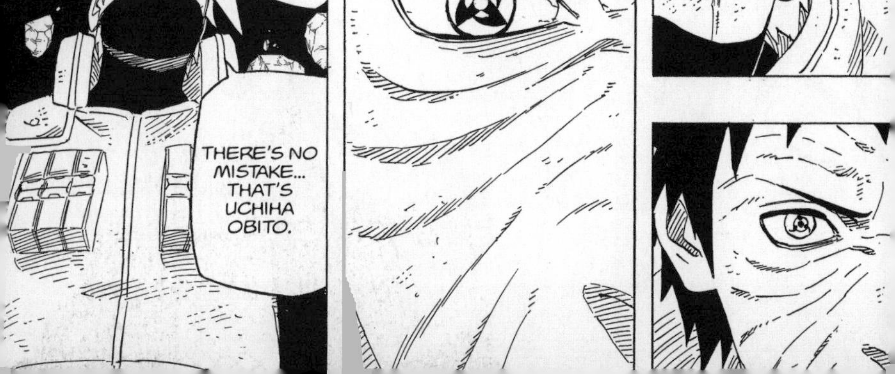
...
SSSH...
...
THERE'S NO MISTAKE... THAT'S UCHIHA OBITO.

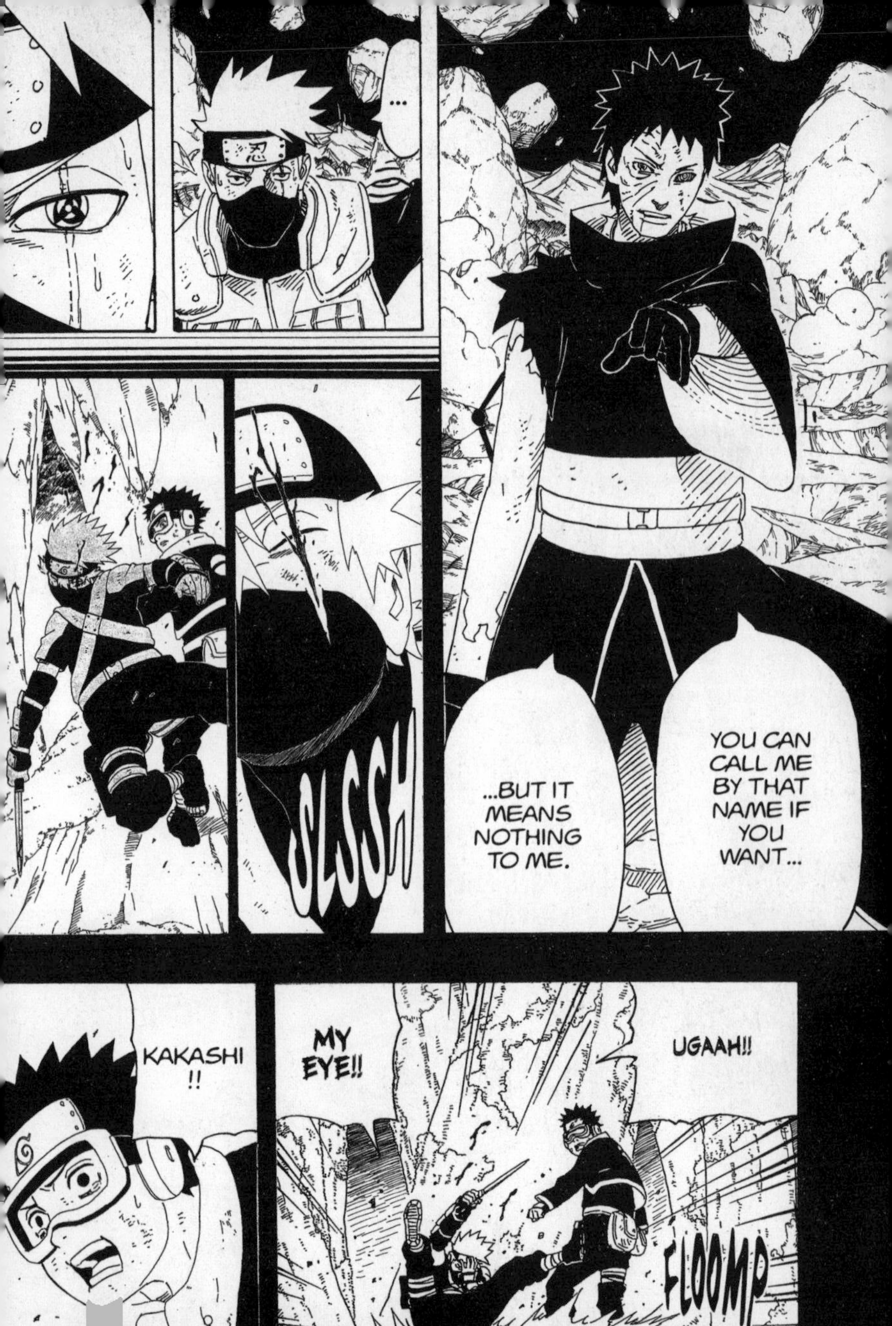
YOU CAN CALL ME BY THAT NAME IF YOU WANT...
...BUT IT MEANS NOTHING TO ME.
...
SLSSH
UGAAH!!
MY EYE!!
FLOOMP
KAKASHI !!

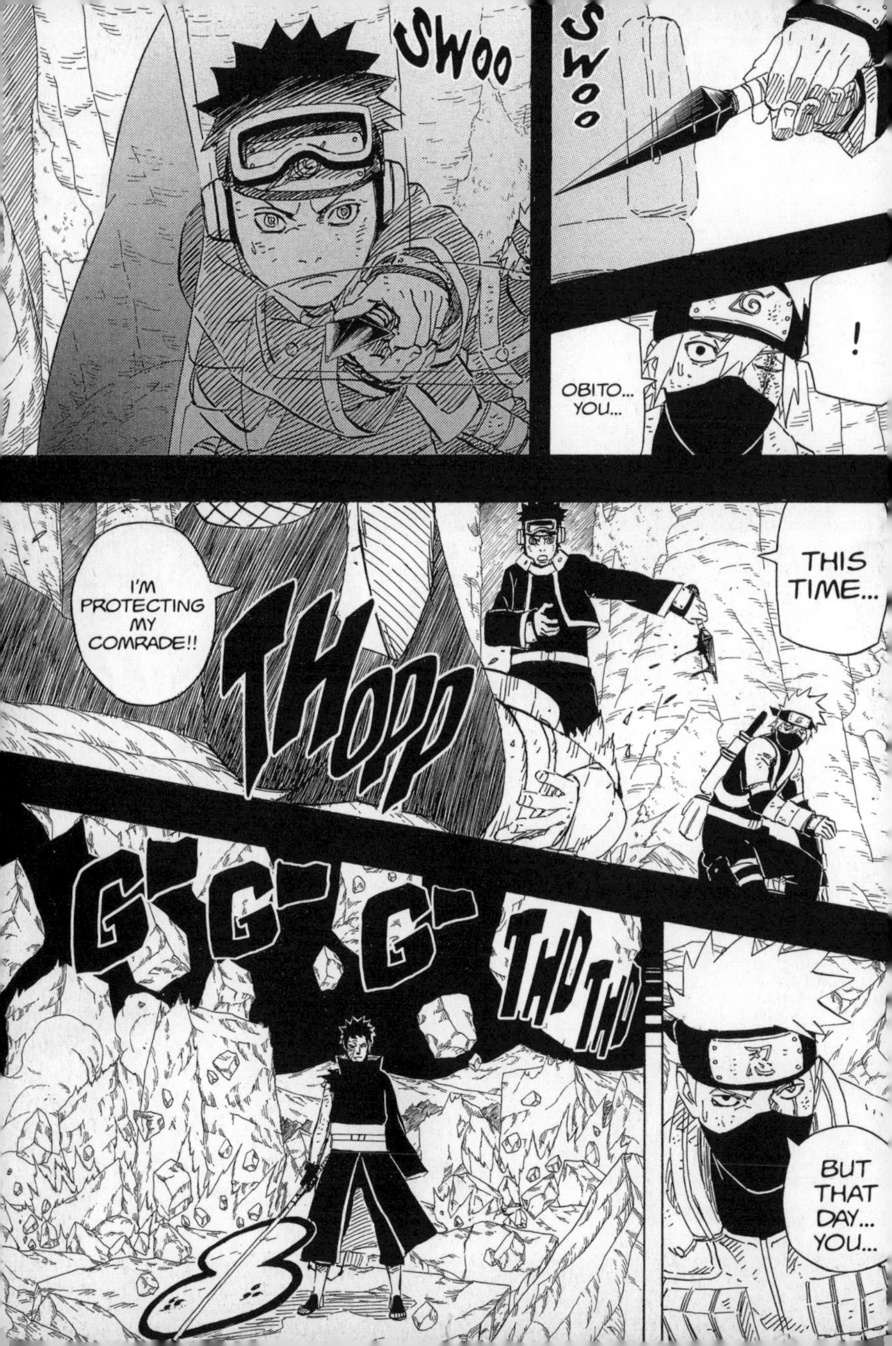
SWOO
!
OBITO... YOU...
SWOO
THIS TIME...
I'M PROTECTING MY COMRADE!!
THOPP
BUT THAT DAY... YOU...
G G G
THD THD

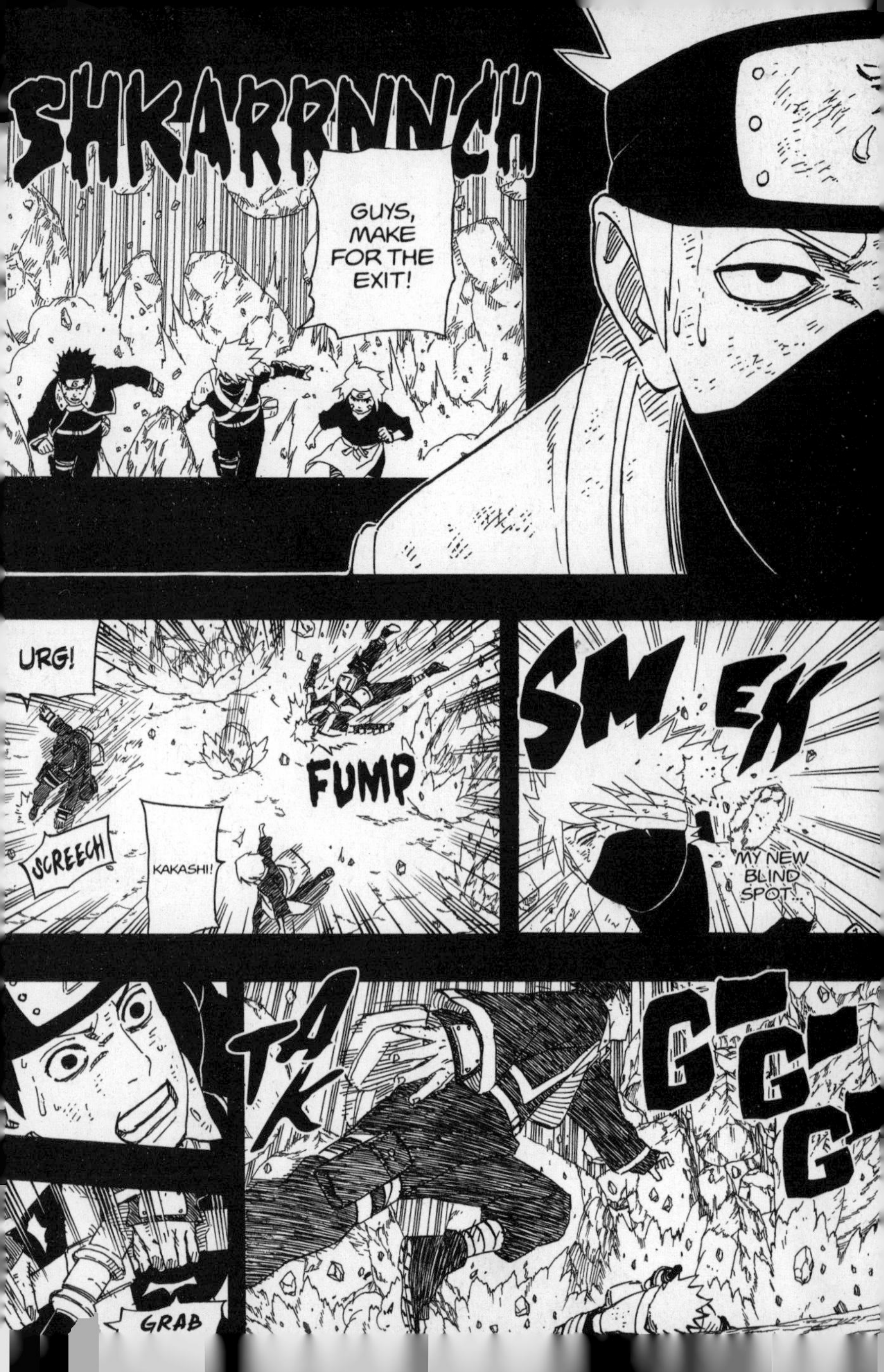
SHKARRNNCH
GUYS, MAKE FOR THE EXIT!
SMEK
MY NEW BLIND SPOT...
URG!
FUMP
KAKASHI!
SCREECH
GGG
TAK
GRAB

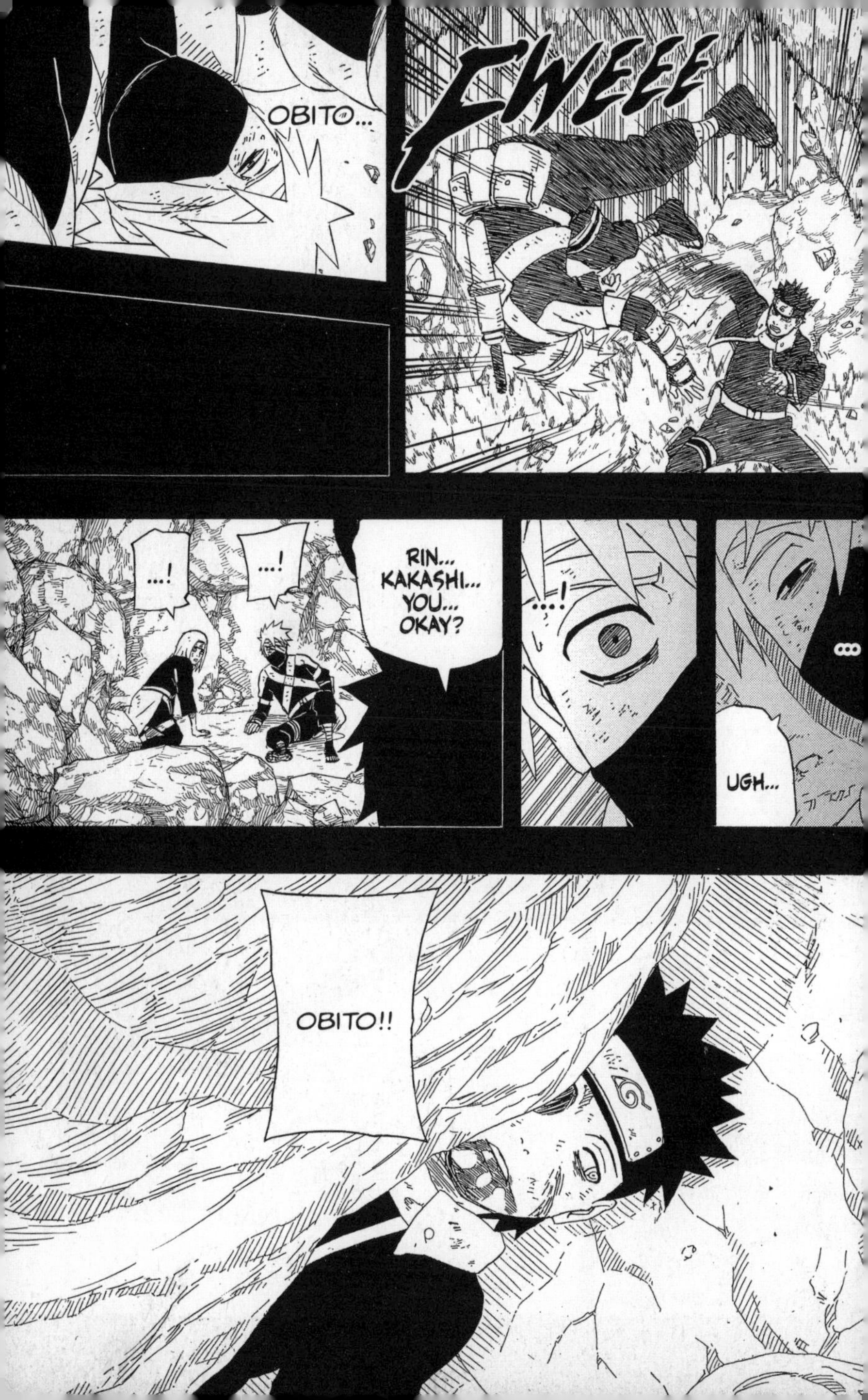
FWEEE
OBITO...
...
UGH...
...!
RIN... KAKASHI... YOU... OKAY?
...!
...!
OBITO!!

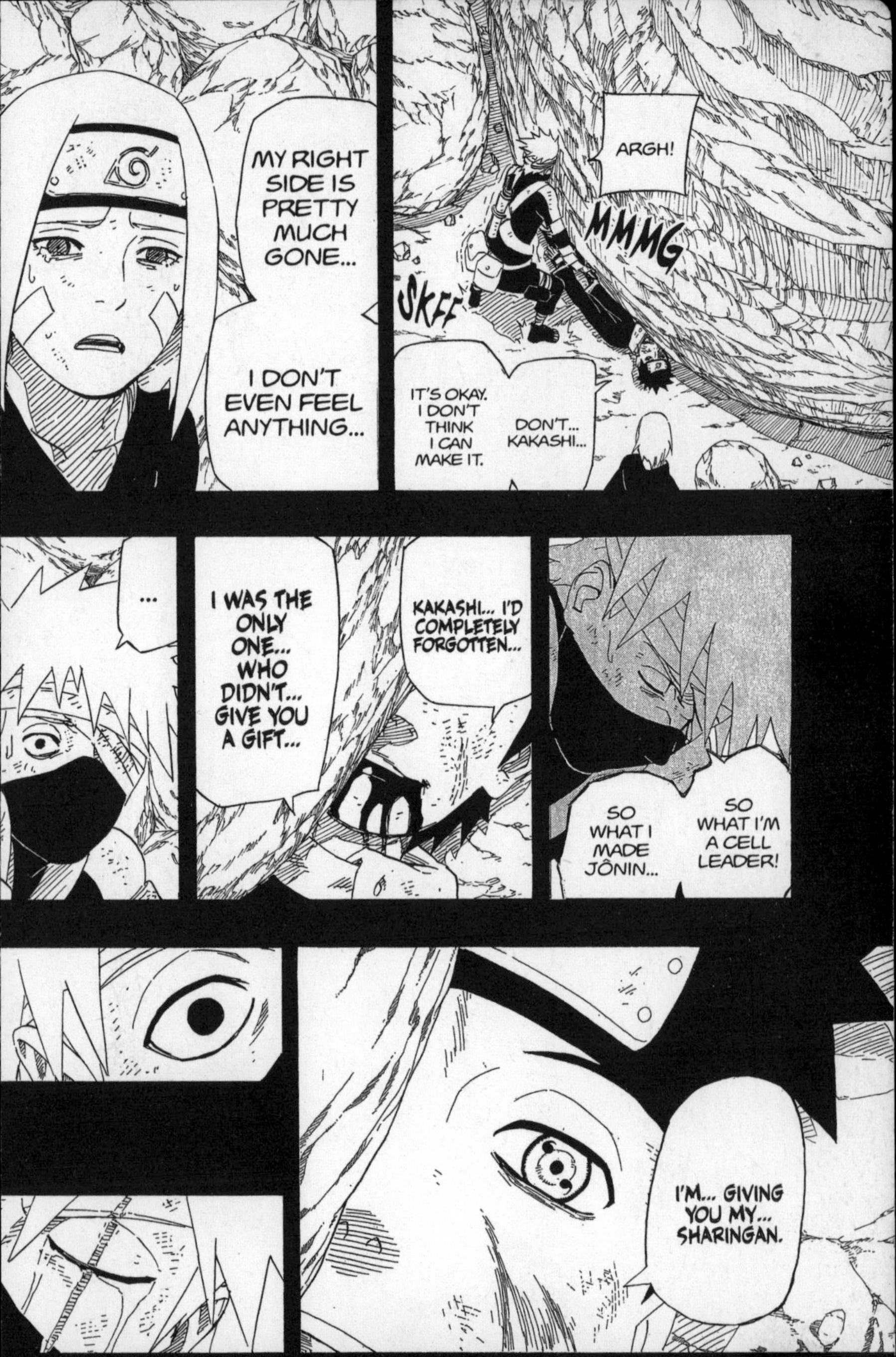
ARGH!
MMMG
SKFF
DON'T... KAKASHI...
IT'S OKAY. I DON'T THINK I CAN MAKE IT.
MY RIGHT SIDE IS PRETTY MUCH GONE...
I DON'T EVEN FEEL ANYTHING...
SO WHAT I'M A CELL LEADER!
SO WHAT I MADE JÔNIN...
KAKASHI... I'D COMPLETELY FORGOTTEN...
I WAS THE ONLY ONE... WHO DIDN'T... GIVE YOU A GIFT...
...
I'M... GIVING YOU MY... SHARINGAN.

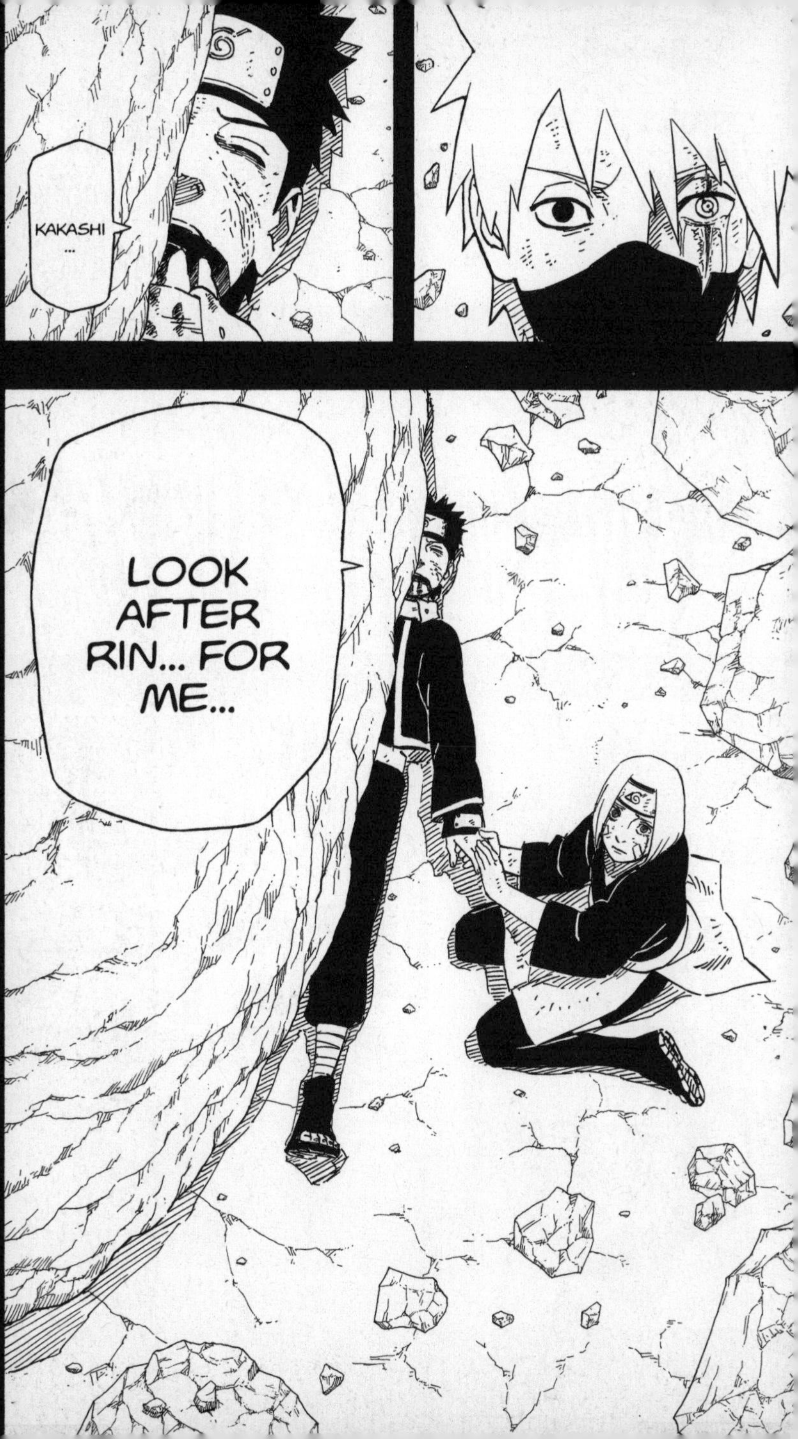
KAKASHI ...
LOOK AFTER RIN... FOR ME...

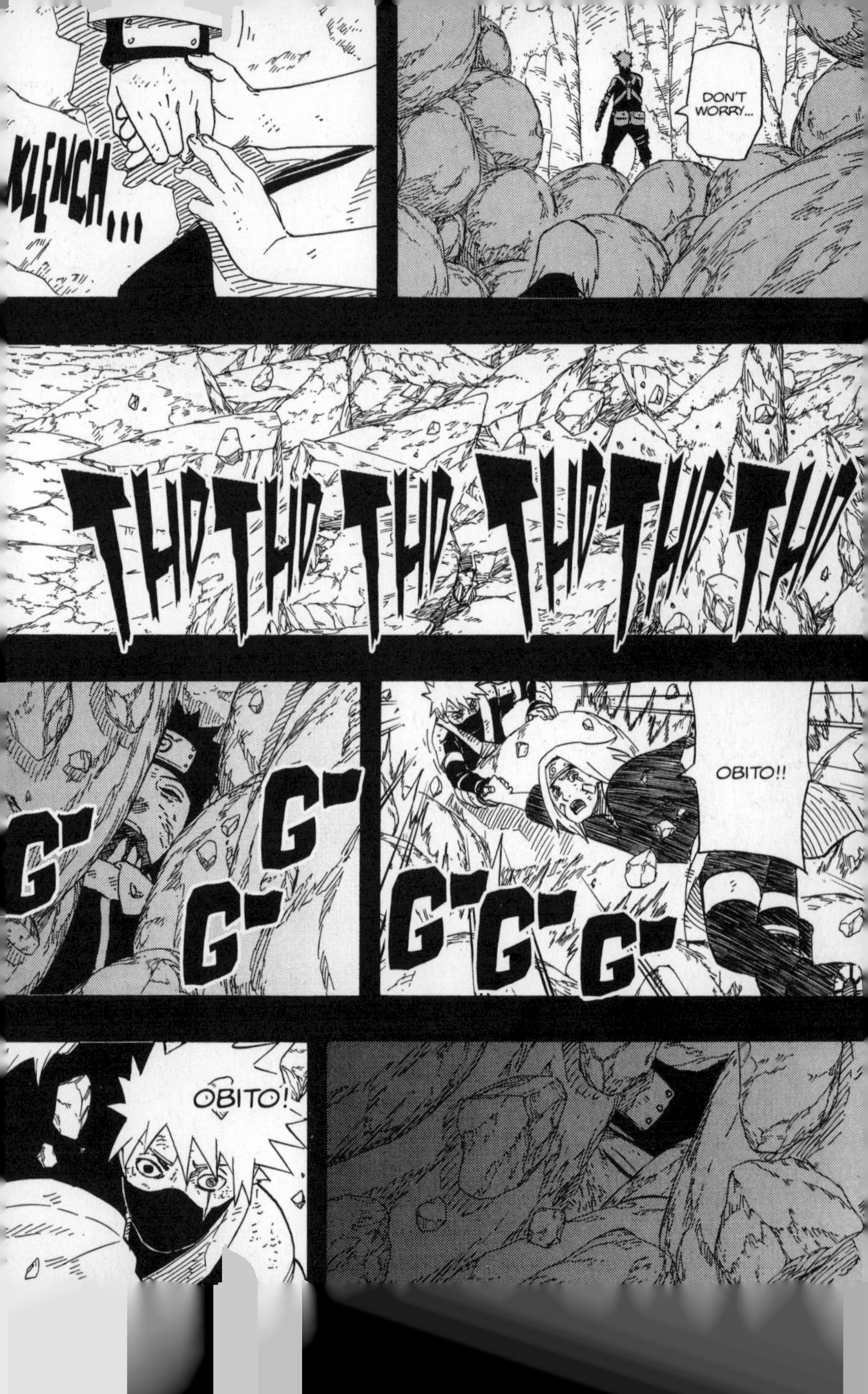
DON'T WORRY...
KLENCH...
THD THD THD THD THD THD
OBITO!!
G- G- G-
G- G G-
OBITO!

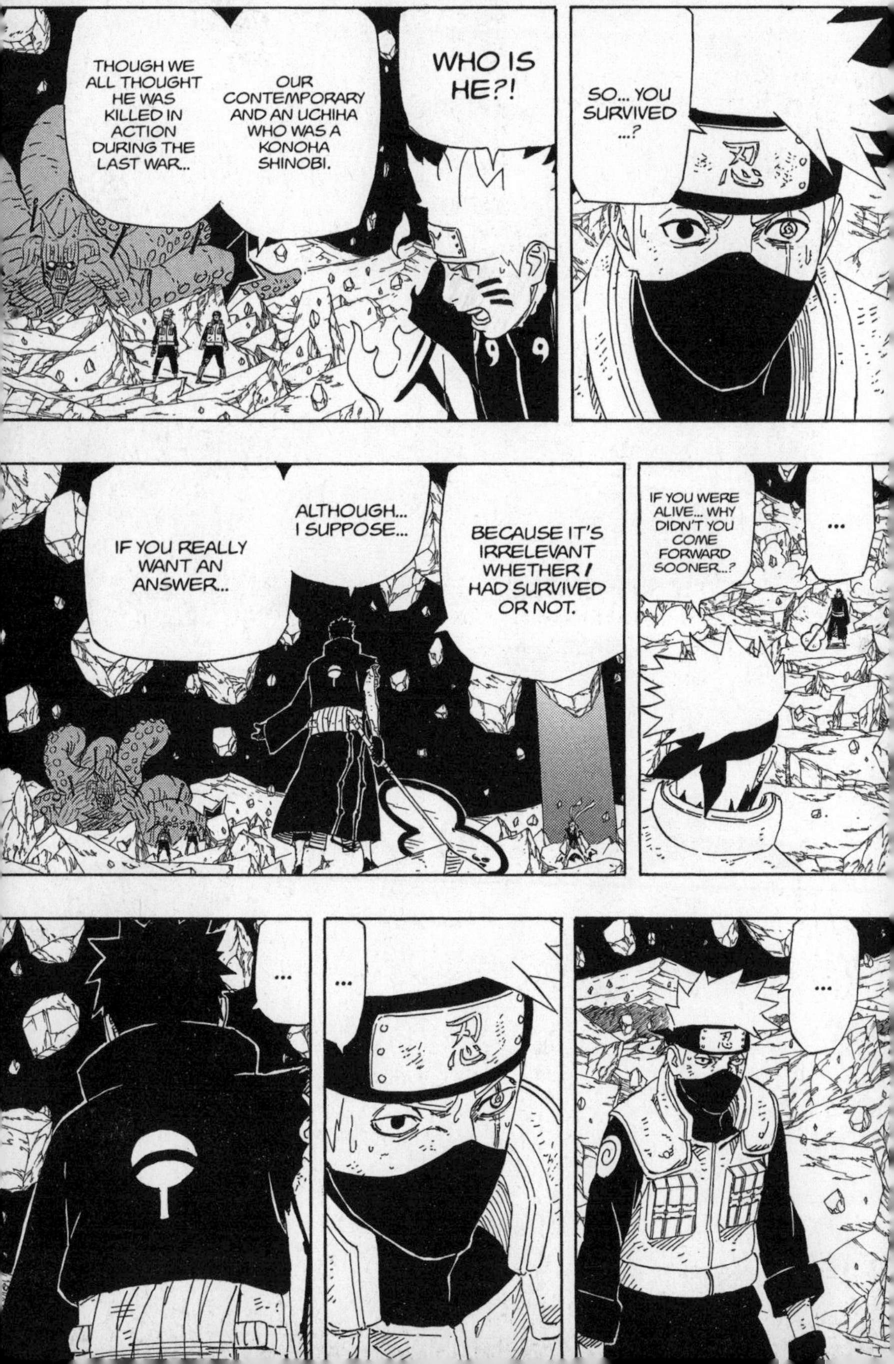
SO... YOU SURVIVED ...?
WHO IS HE?!
OUR CONTEMPORARY AND AN UCHIHA WHO WAS A KONOHA SHINOBI.
THOUGH WE ALL THOUGHT HE WAS KILLED IN ACTION DURING THE LAST WAR...
...
IF YOU WERE ALIVE... WHY DIDN'T YOU COME FORWARD SOONER...?
BECAUSE IT'S IRRELEVANT WHETHER I HAD SURVIVED OR NOT.
ALTHOUGH... I SUPPOSE...
IF YOU REALLY WANT AN ANSWER...
...
...
...

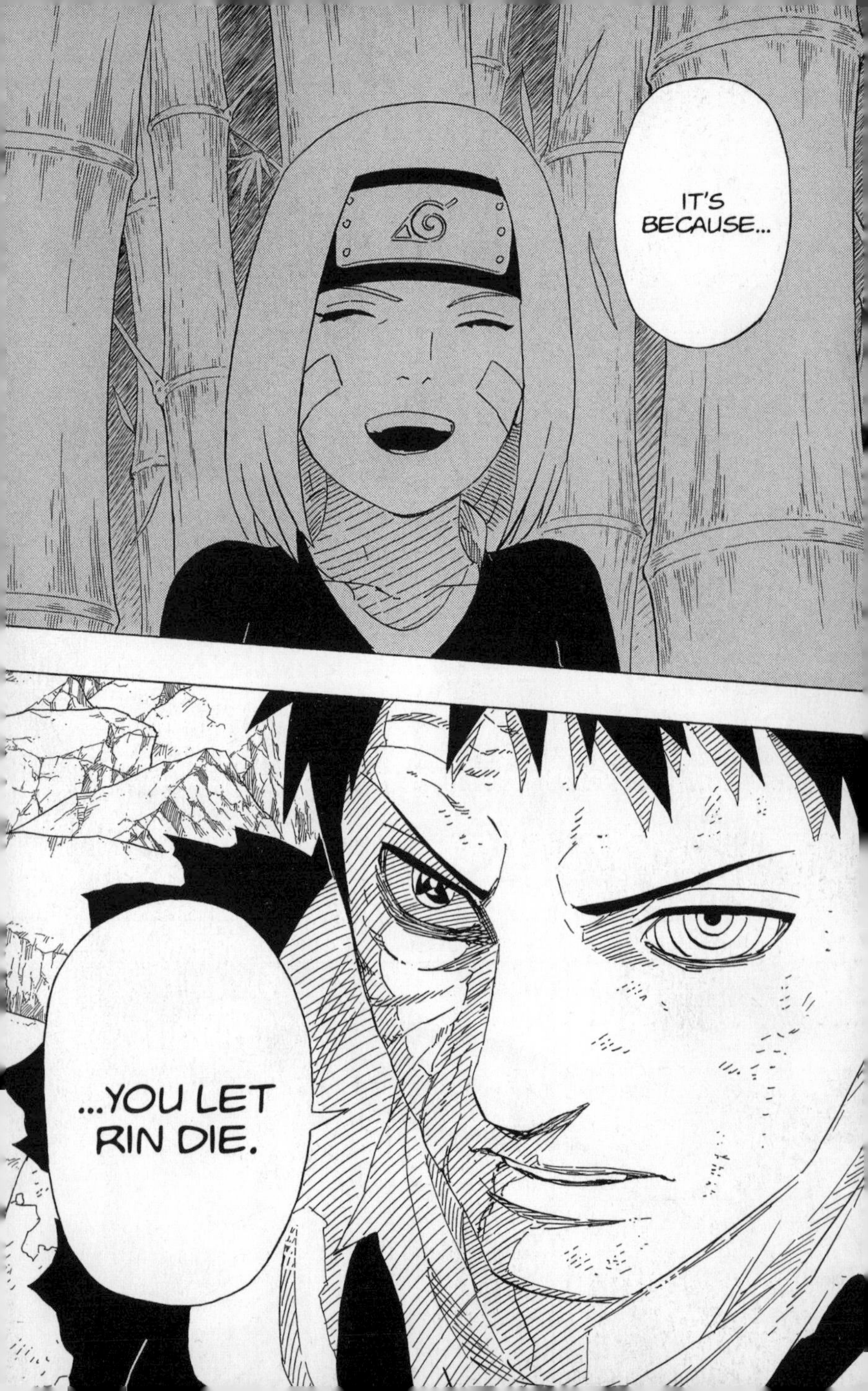
IT'S BECAUSE...
...YOU LET RIN DIE.

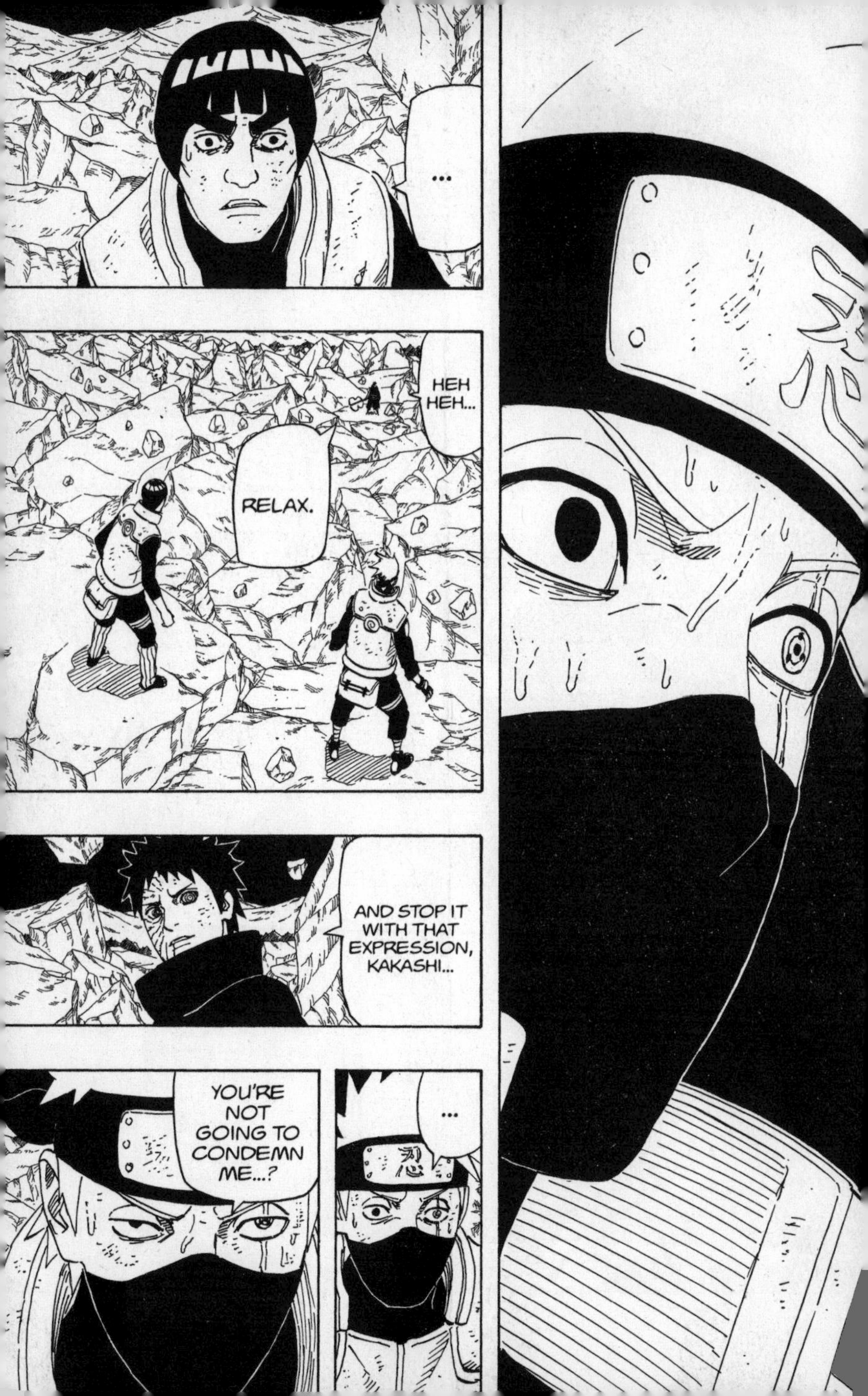
...
HEH HEH...
RELAX.
AND STOP IT WITH THAT EXPRESSION, KAKASHI...
...
YOU'RE NOT GOING TO CONDEMN ME...?

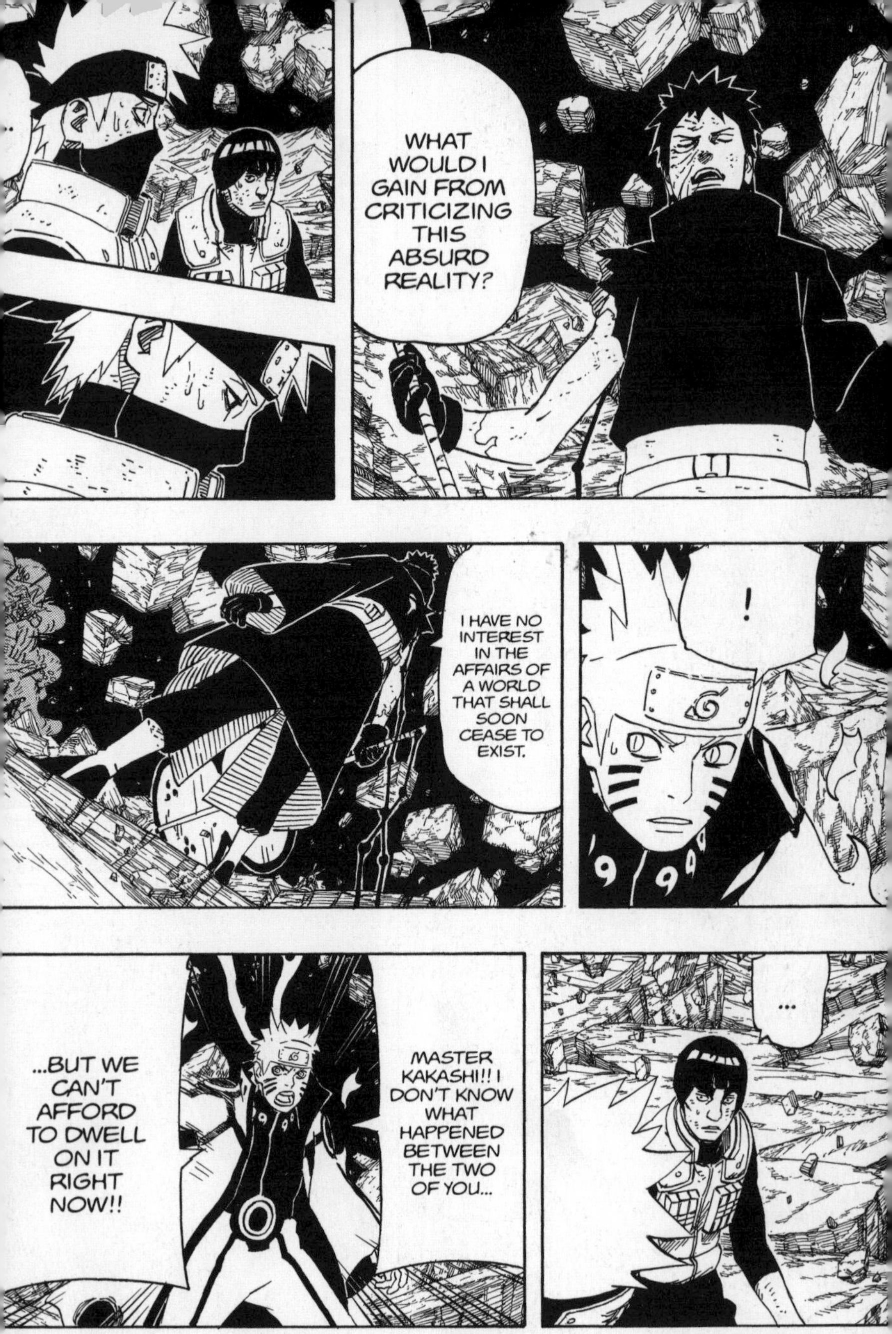
WHAT WOULD I GAIN FROM CRITICIZING THIS ABSURD REALITY?
!
I HAVE NO INTEREST IN THE AFFAIRS OF A WORLD THAT SHALL SOON CEASE TO EXIST.
...
MASTER KAKASHI!! I DON'T KNOW WHAT HAPPENED BETWEEN THE TWO OF YOU...
...BUT WE CAN'T AFFORD TO DWELL ON IT RIGHT NOW!!

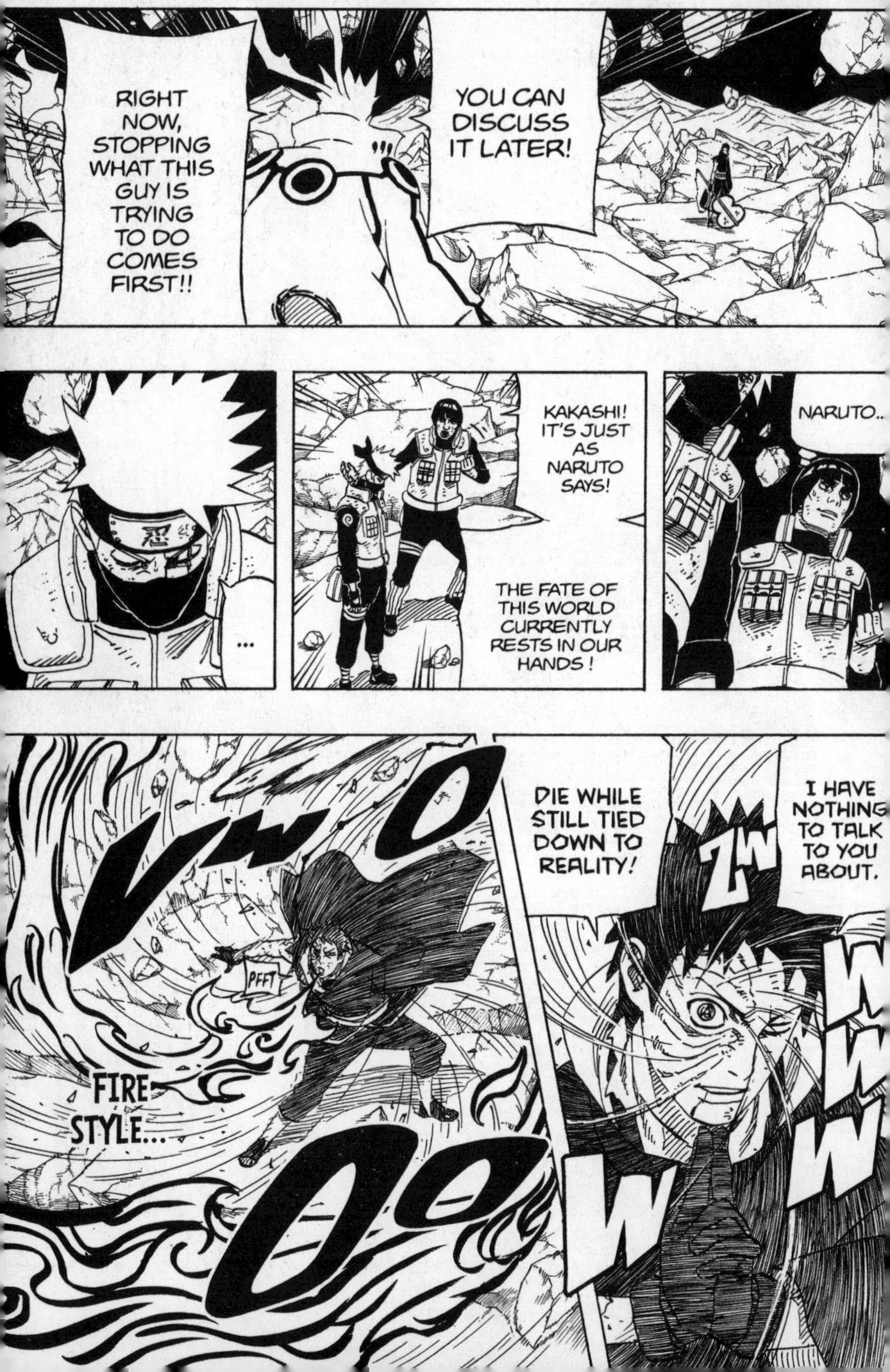
YOU CAN DISCUSS IT LATER!
RIGHT NOW, STOPPING WHAT THIS GUY IS TRYING TO DO COMES FIRST!!
NARUTO..
KAKASHI! IT'S JUST AS NARUTO SAYS!
THE FATE OF THIS WORLD CURRENTLY RESTS IN OUR HANDS!
...
I HAVE NOTHING TO TALK TO YOU ABOUT.
DIE WHILE STILL TIED DOWN TO REALITY!
PFFT
FIRE STYLE...

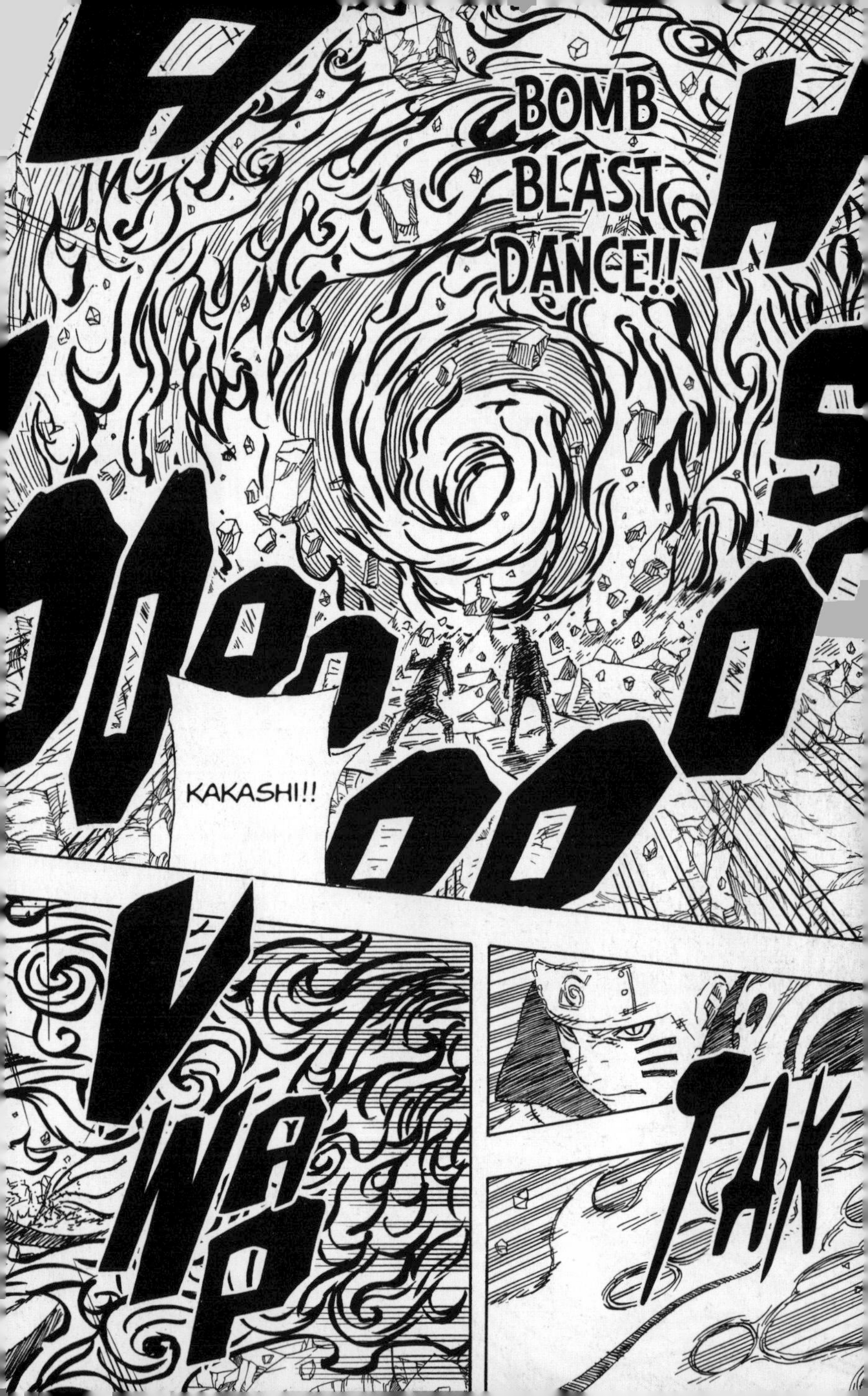
BOMB BLAST DANCE!!
KAKASHI!!
TAK

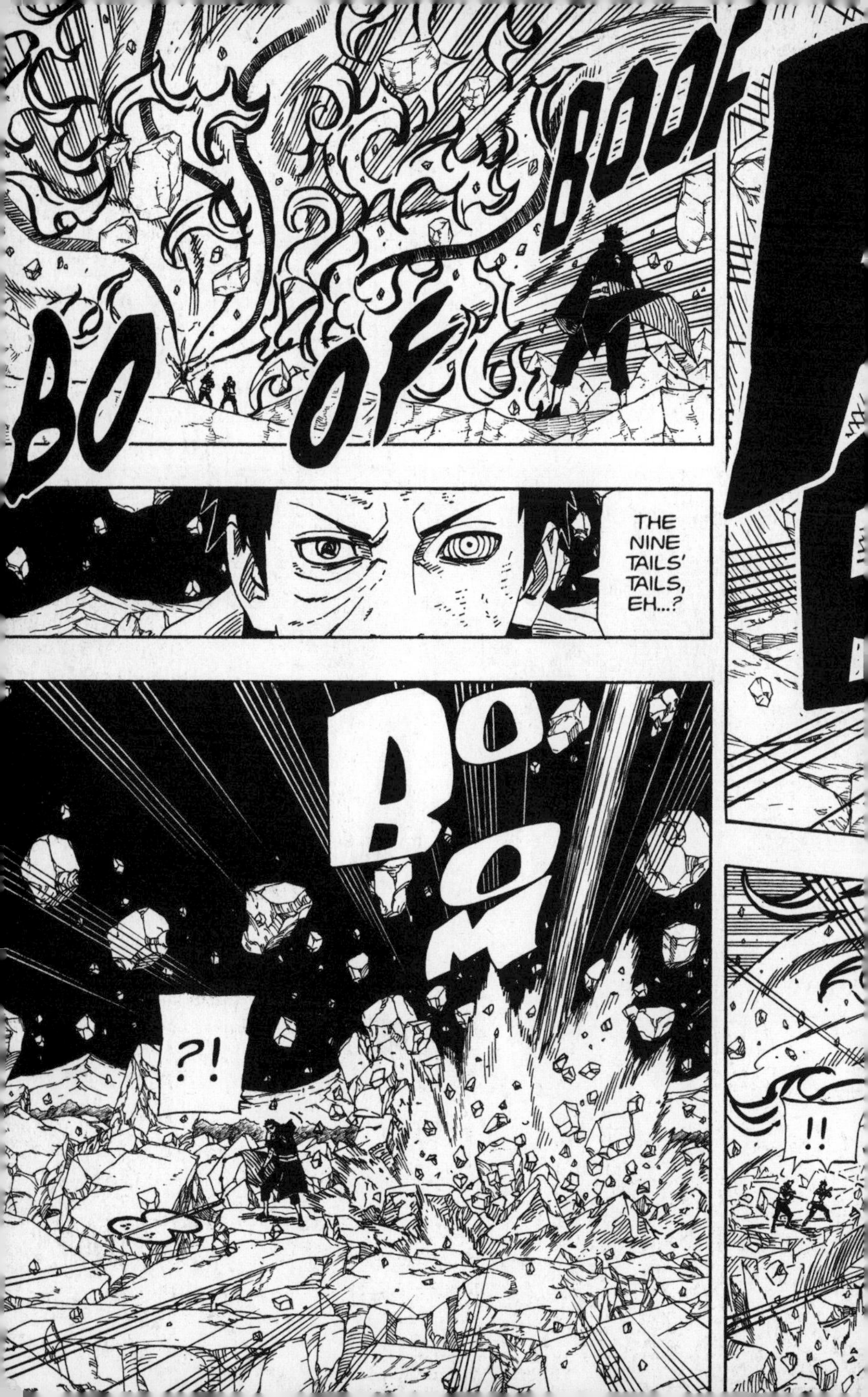

BOOM
THE NINE TAILS' TAILS, EH...?
!!
BOOM
?!

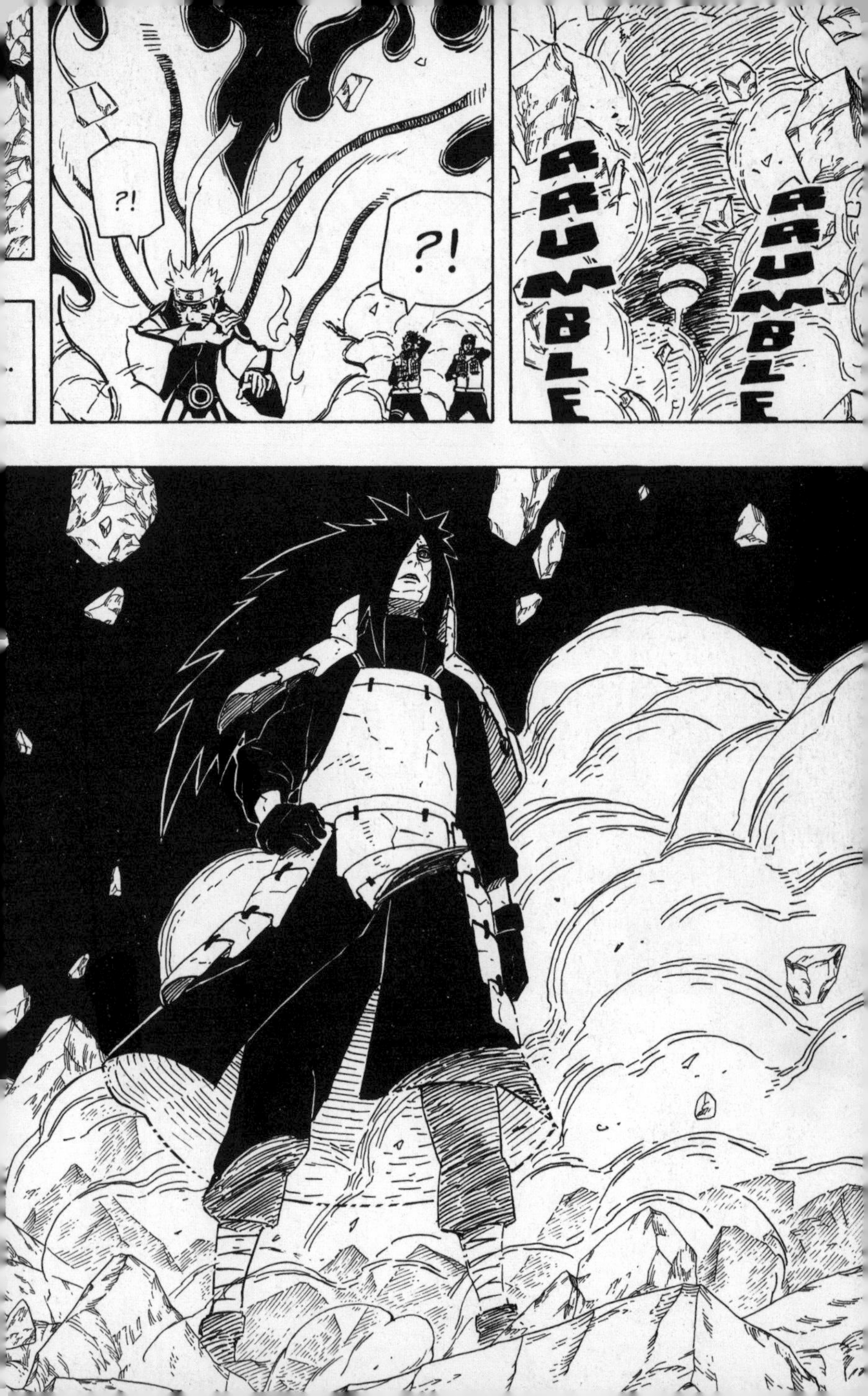
RUMBLE
RUMBLE
?!
?!

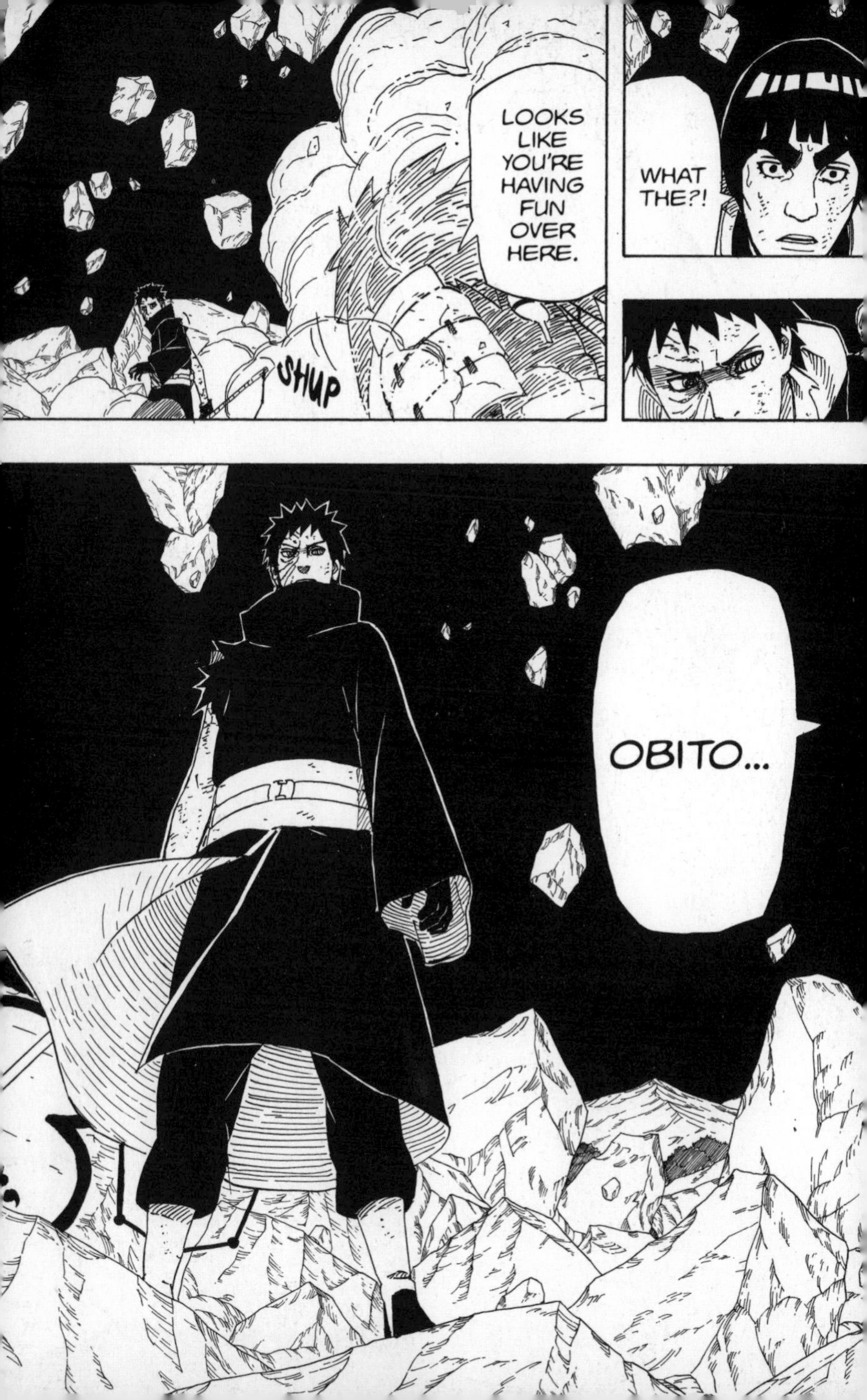
WHAT THE?!
LOOKS LIKE YOU'RE HAVING FUN OVER HERE.
SHUP
OBITO...

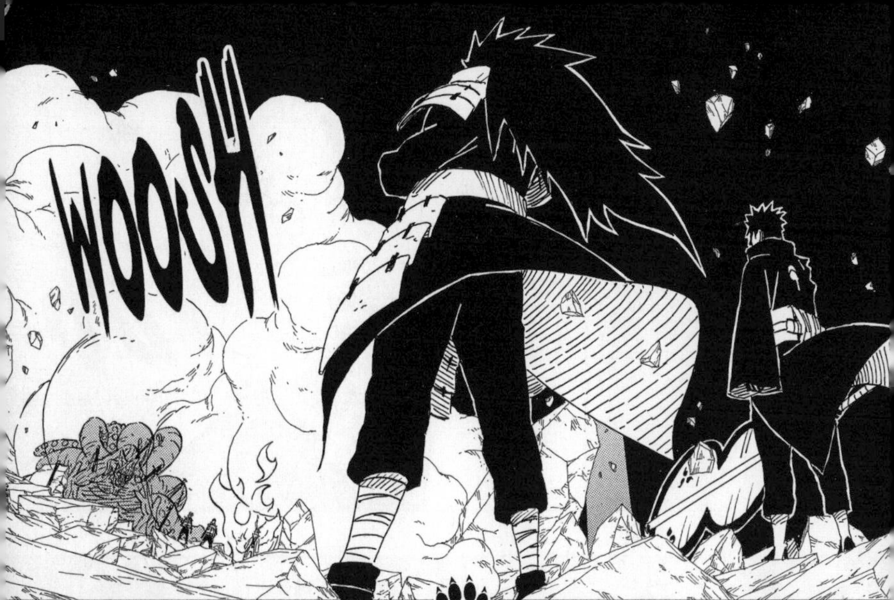
WOOSH

Number 601: Obito and Madara

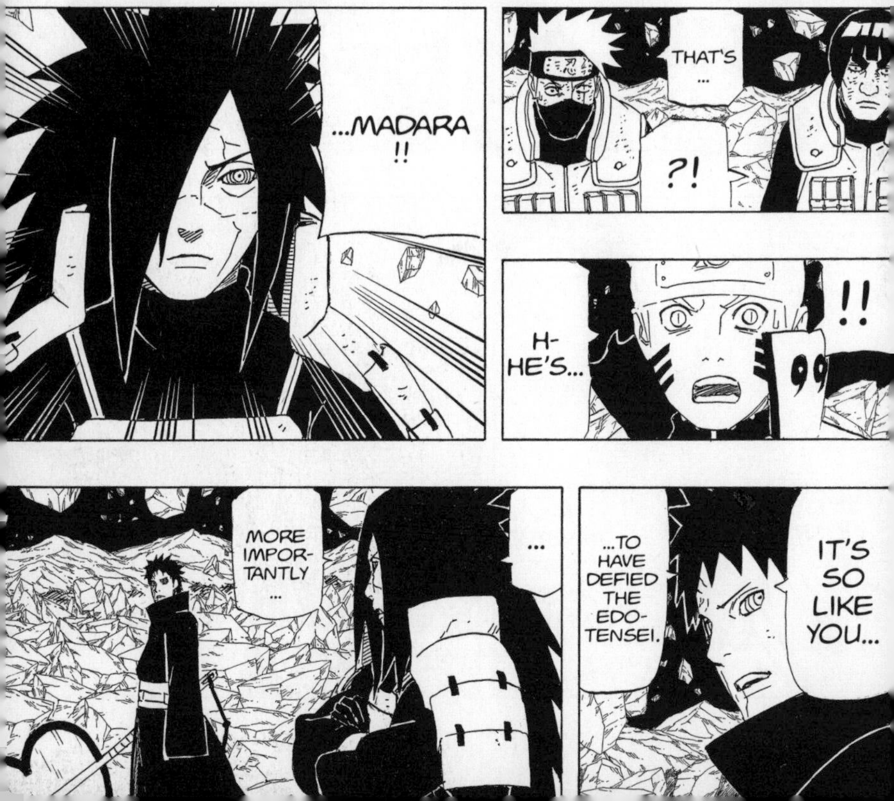
THAT'S ...
?!
H- HE'S...
!!
...MADARA !!
IT'S SO LIKE YOU...
...TO HAVE DEFIED THE EDO-TENSEI.
...
MORE IMPORTANTLY ...

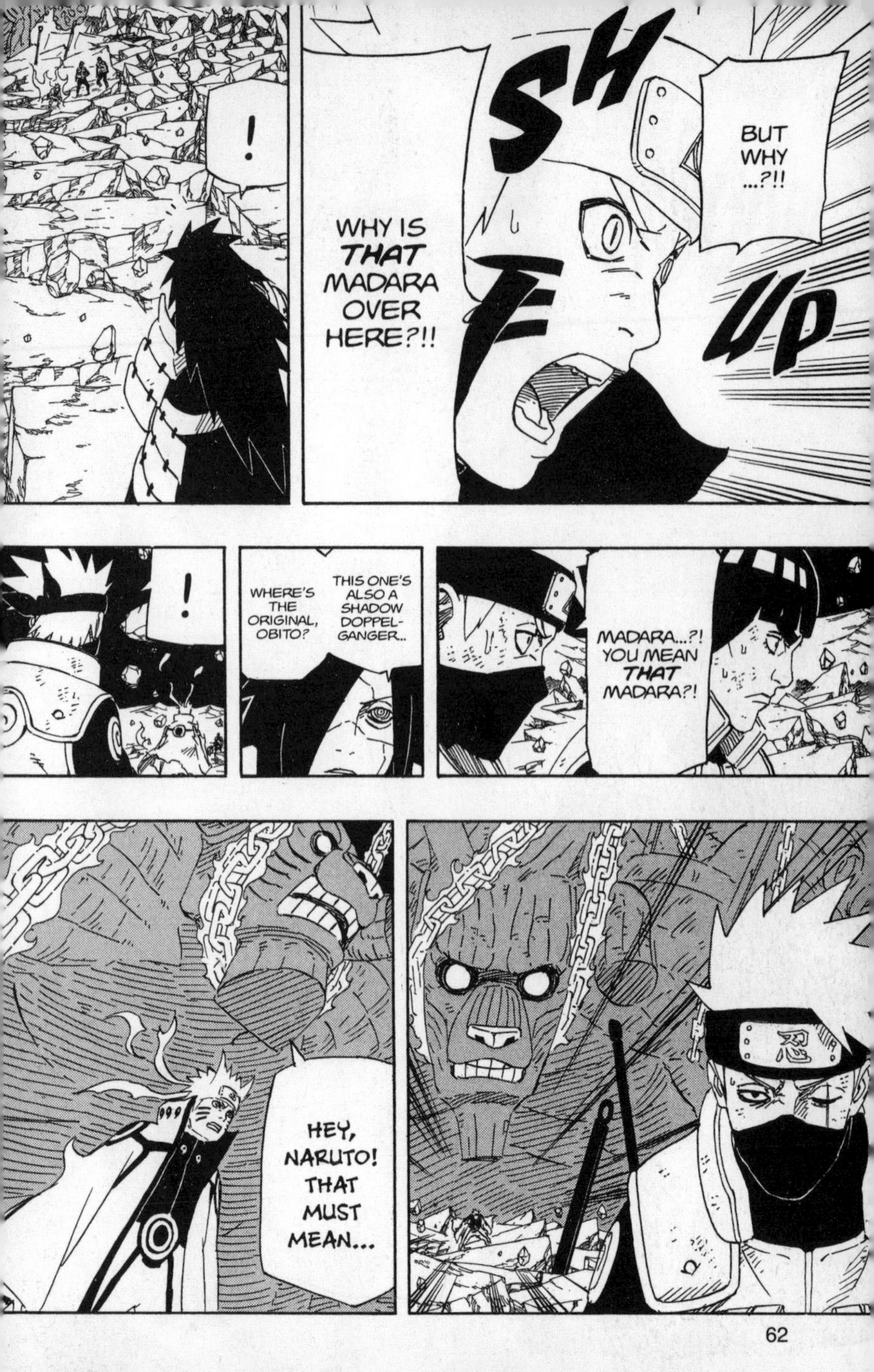
BUT WHY ...?!!
SH
UP
WHY IS THAT MADARA OVER HERE?!!
!
MADARA...?! YOU MEAN THAT MADARA?!
THIS ONE'S ALSO A SHADOW DOPPEL-GANGER...
WHERE'S THE ORIGINAL, OBITO?
!
HEY, NARUTO! THAT MUST MEAN...

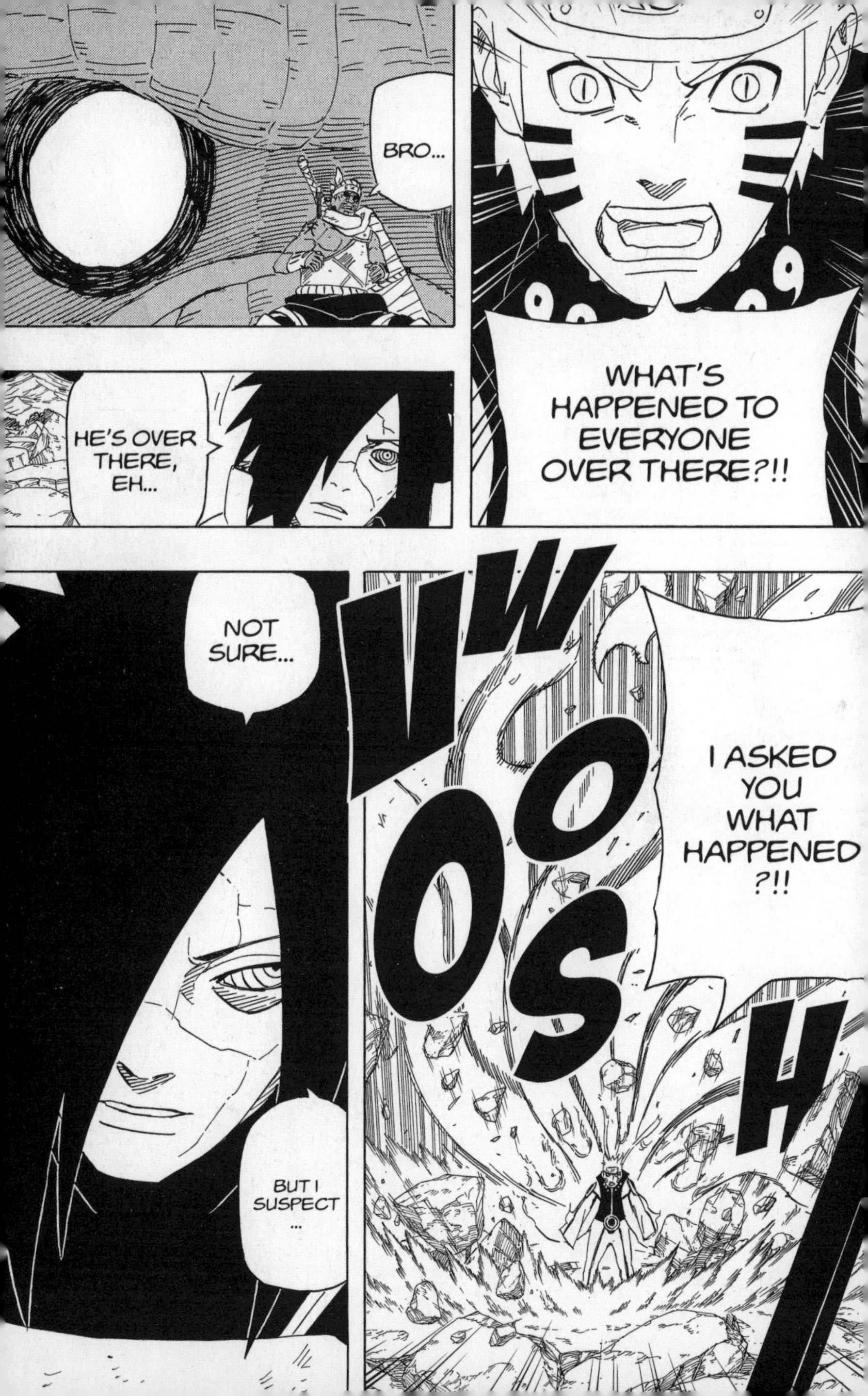
WHAT'S HAPPENED TO EVERYONE OVER THERE?!!
BRO...
HE'S OVER THERE, EH...
I ASKED YOU WHAT HAPPENED ?!!
WHOOSH
NOT SURE...
BUT I SUSPECT ...

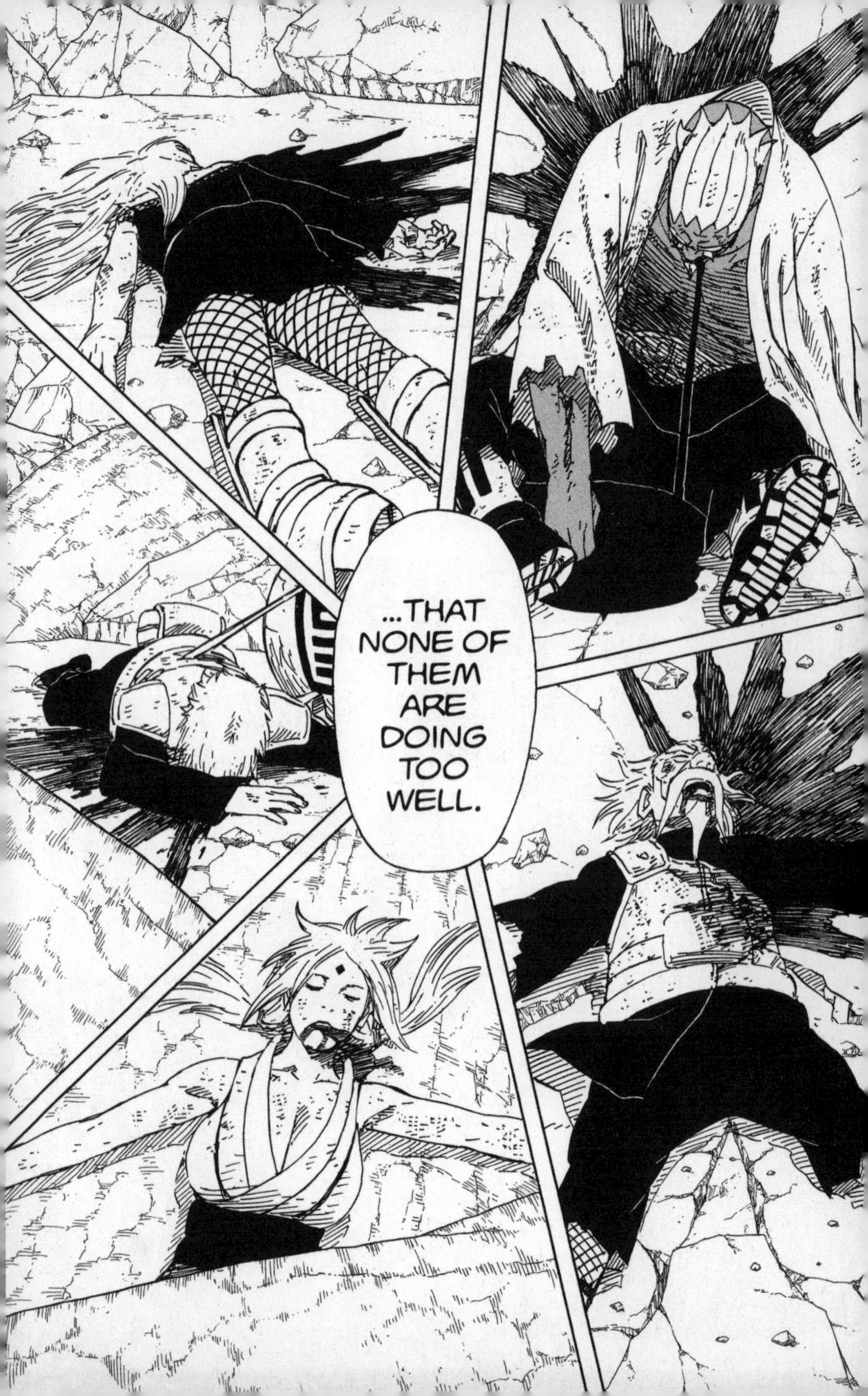
...THAT NONE OF THEM ARE DOING TOO WELL.

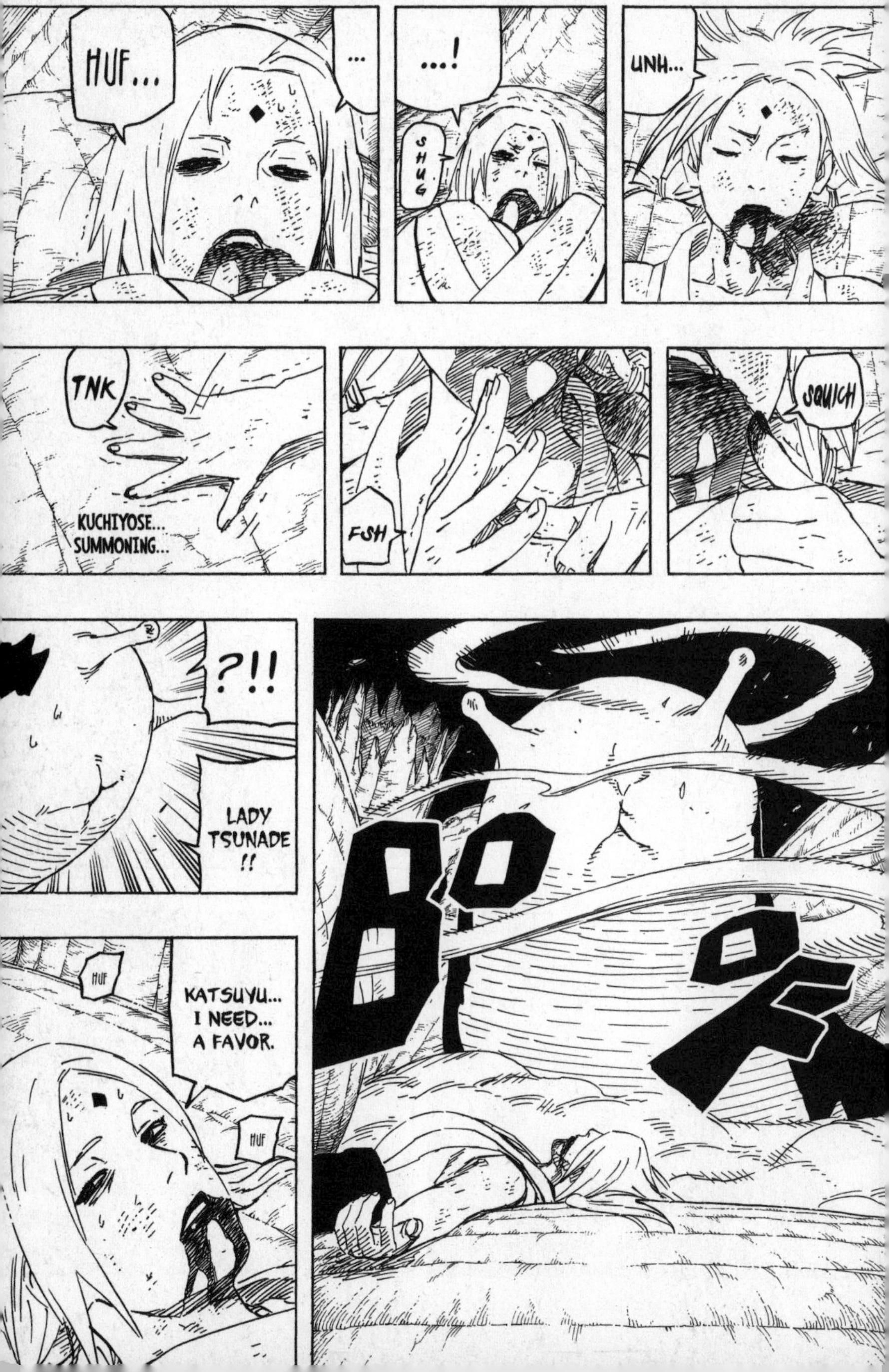
UNH...
...!
SHUG
...
HUF...
SQUICH
FSH
TNK
KUCHIYOSE... SUMMONING...
BOOF
?!!
LADY TSUNADE !!
HUF
KATSUYU... I NEED... A FAVOR.
HUF

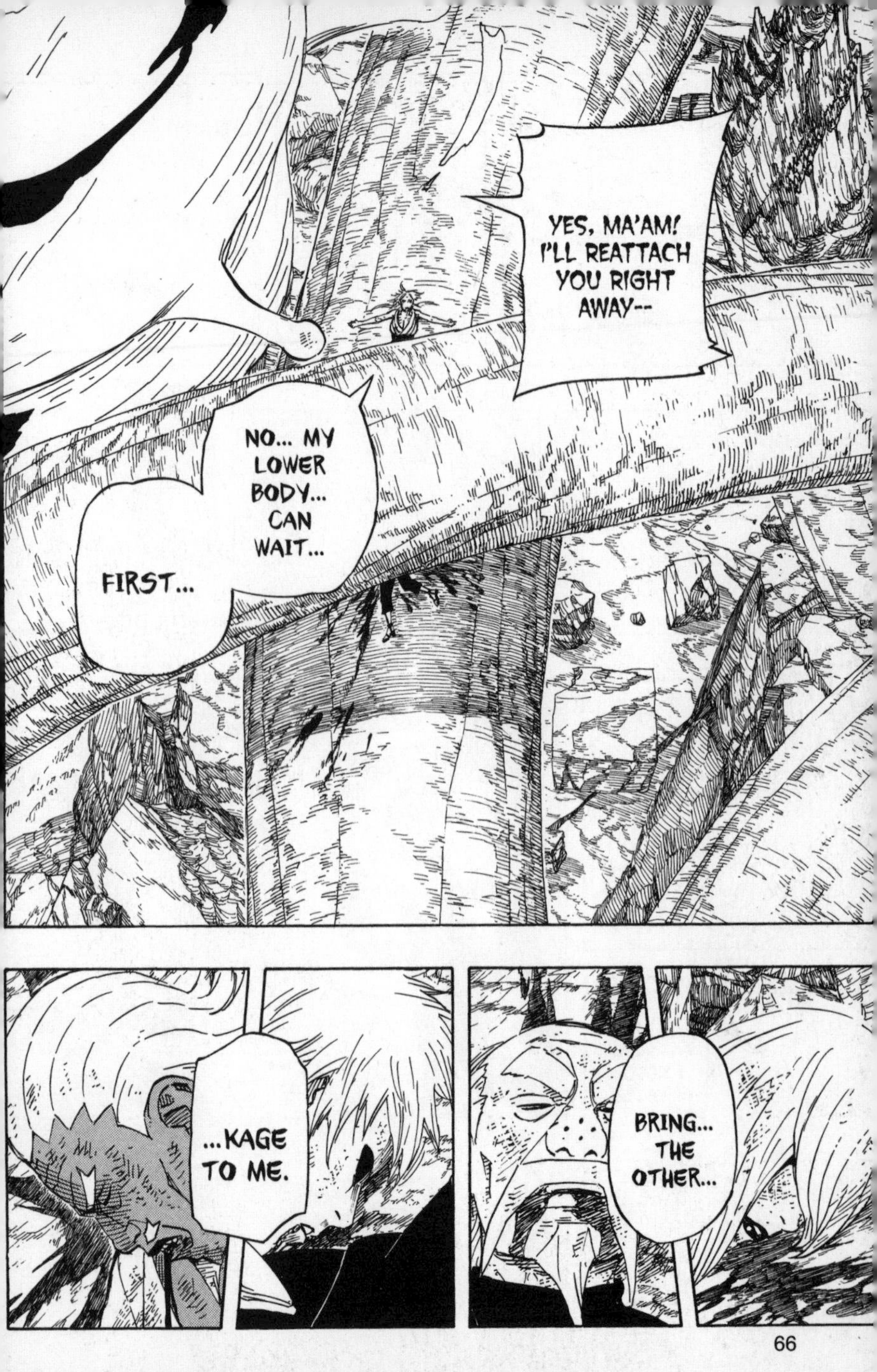
YES, MA'AM! I'LL REATTACH YOU RIGHT AWAY--
NO... MY LOWER BODY... CAN WAIT...
FIRST...
BRING... THE OTHER...
...KAGE TO ME.

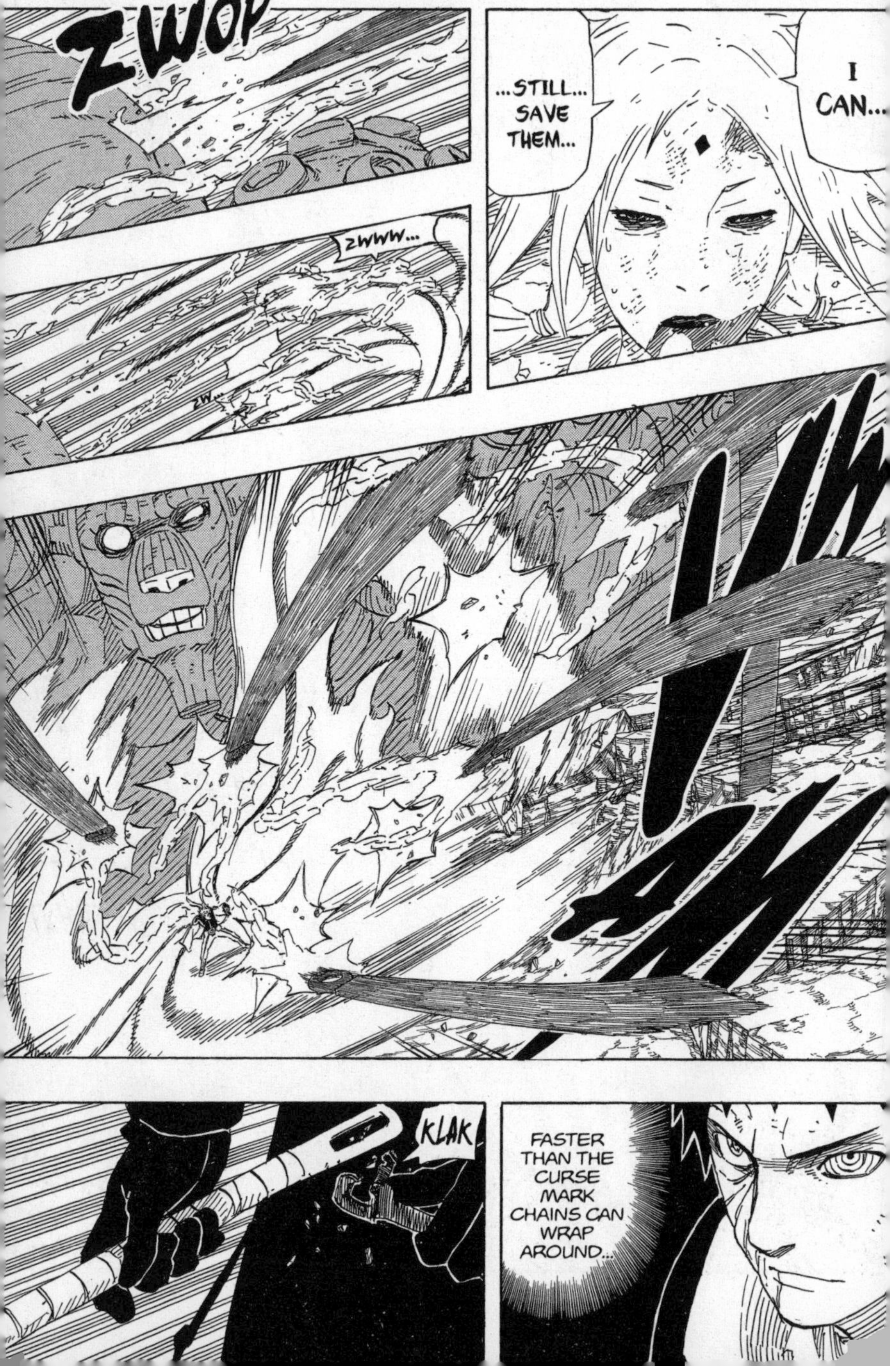
I CAN...
...STILL... SAVE THEM...
ZWOP
ZWWW...
ZW...
FASTER THAN THE CURSE MARK CHAINS CAN WRAP AROUND...
KLAK

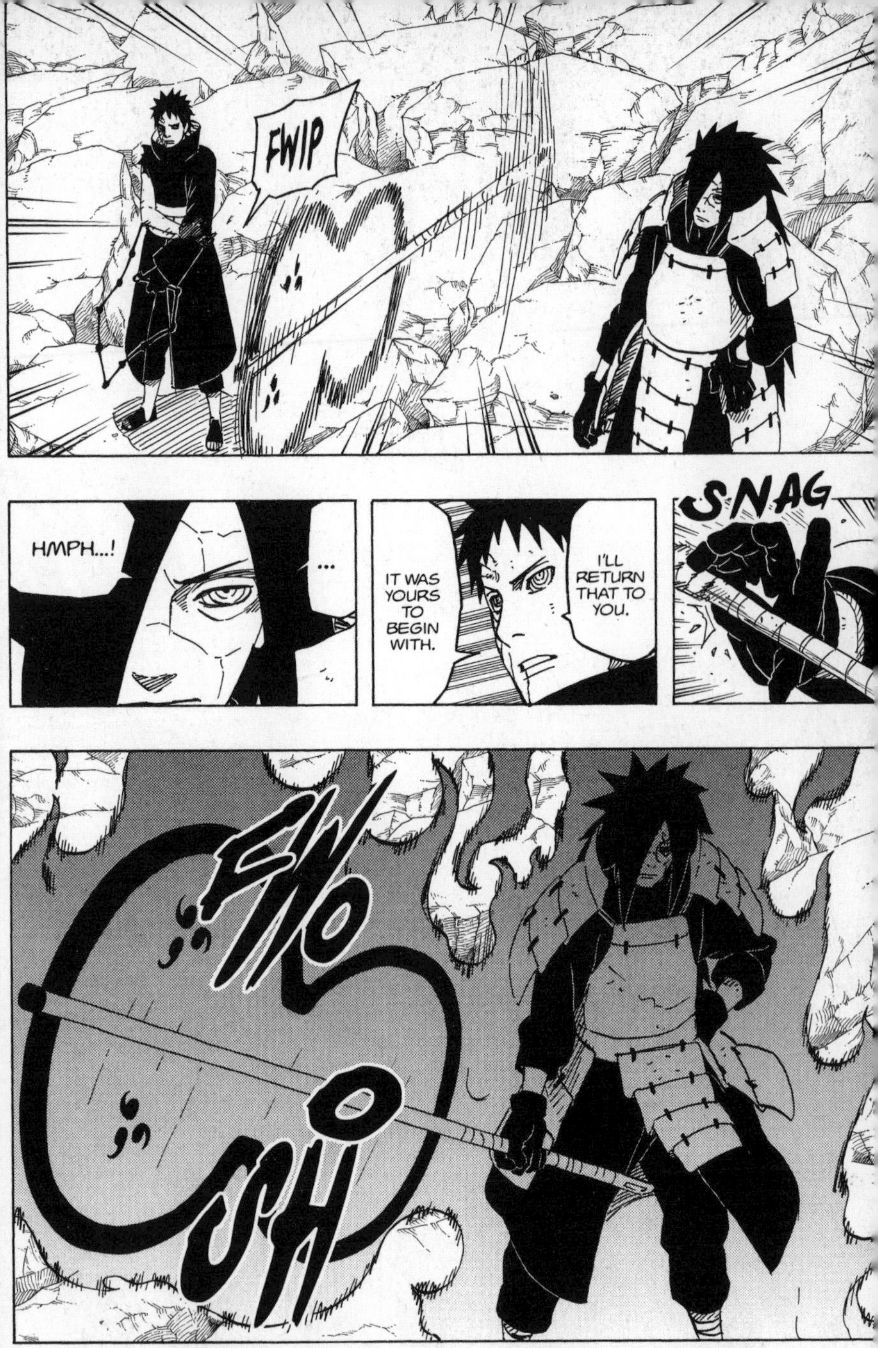
FWIP
SNAG
I'LL RETURN THAT TO YOU.
IT WAS YOURS TO BEGIN WITH.
...
HMPH...!

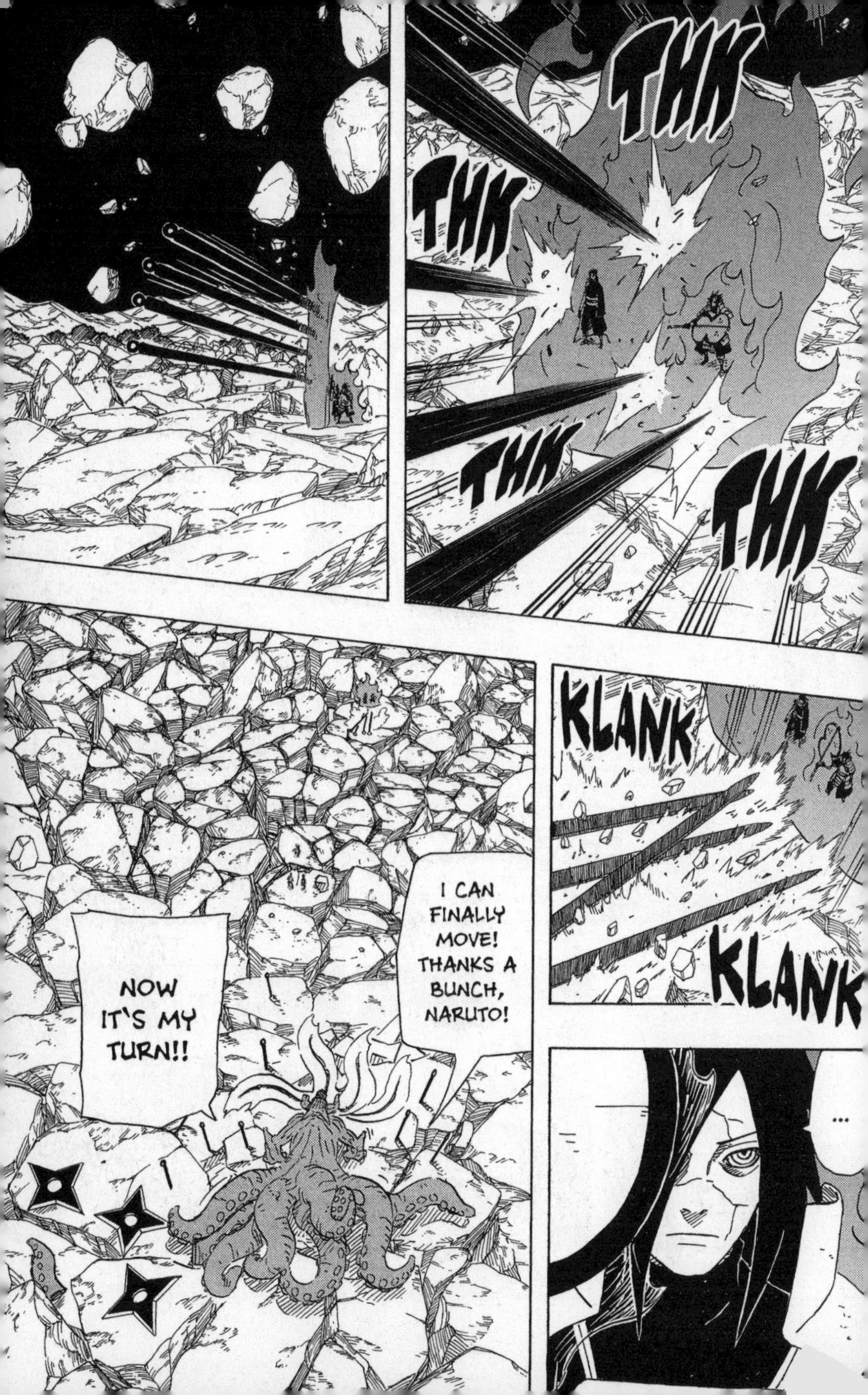
THK
THK
THK
THK
KLANK
KLANK
...
I CAN FINALLY MOVE! THANKS A BUNCH, NARUTO!
NOW IT'S MY TURN!!

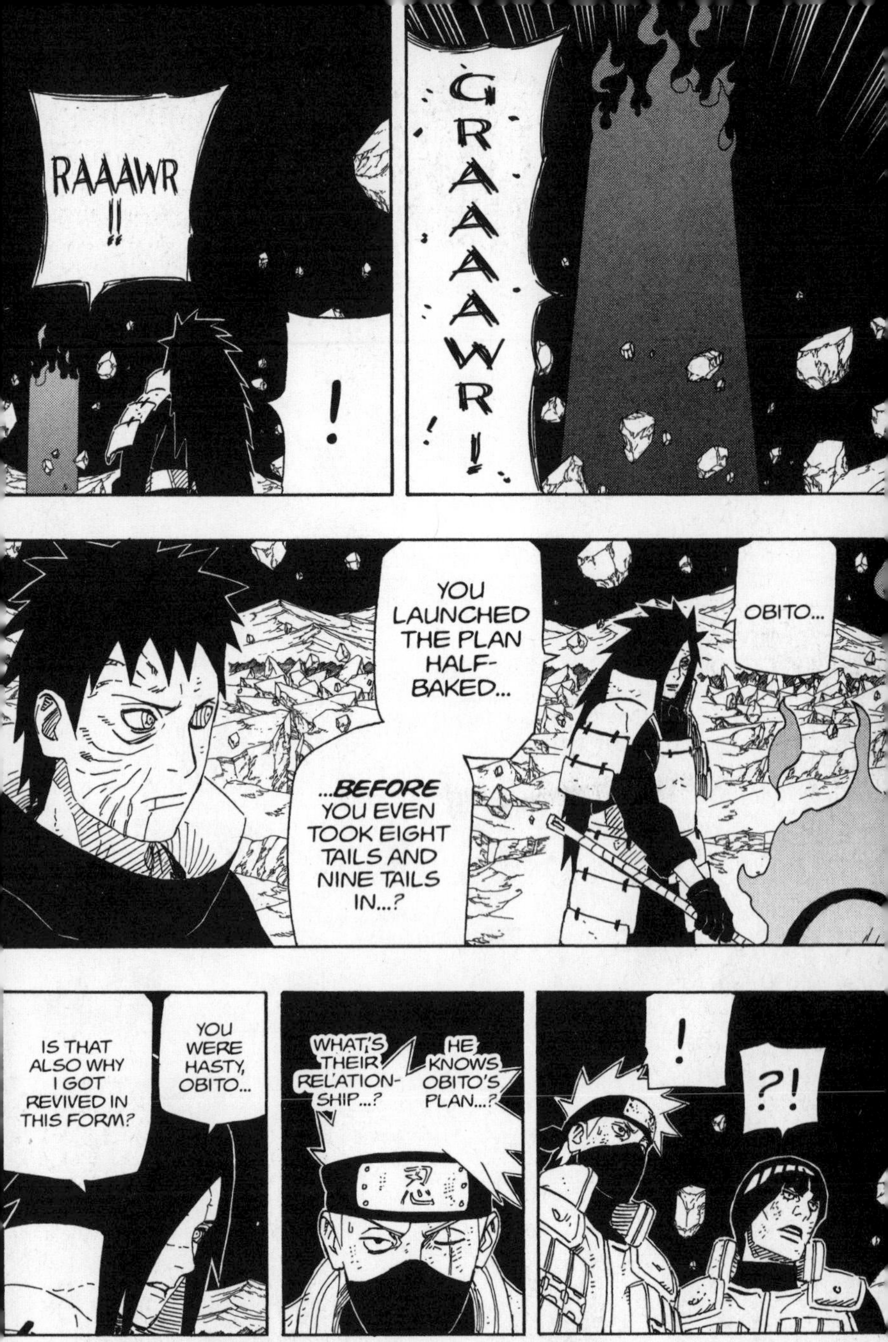
GRAAAAWR!!
RAAAWR!!
!
OBITO...
YOU LAUNCHED THE PLAN HALF-BAKED...
...*BEFORE* YOU EVEN TOOK EIGHT TAILS AND NINE TAILS IN...?
!
?!
HE KNOWS OBITO'S PLAN...?
WHAT'S THEIR RELATIONSHIP...?
YOU WERE HASTY, OBITO...
IS THAT ALSO WHY I GOT REVIVED IN THIS FORM?

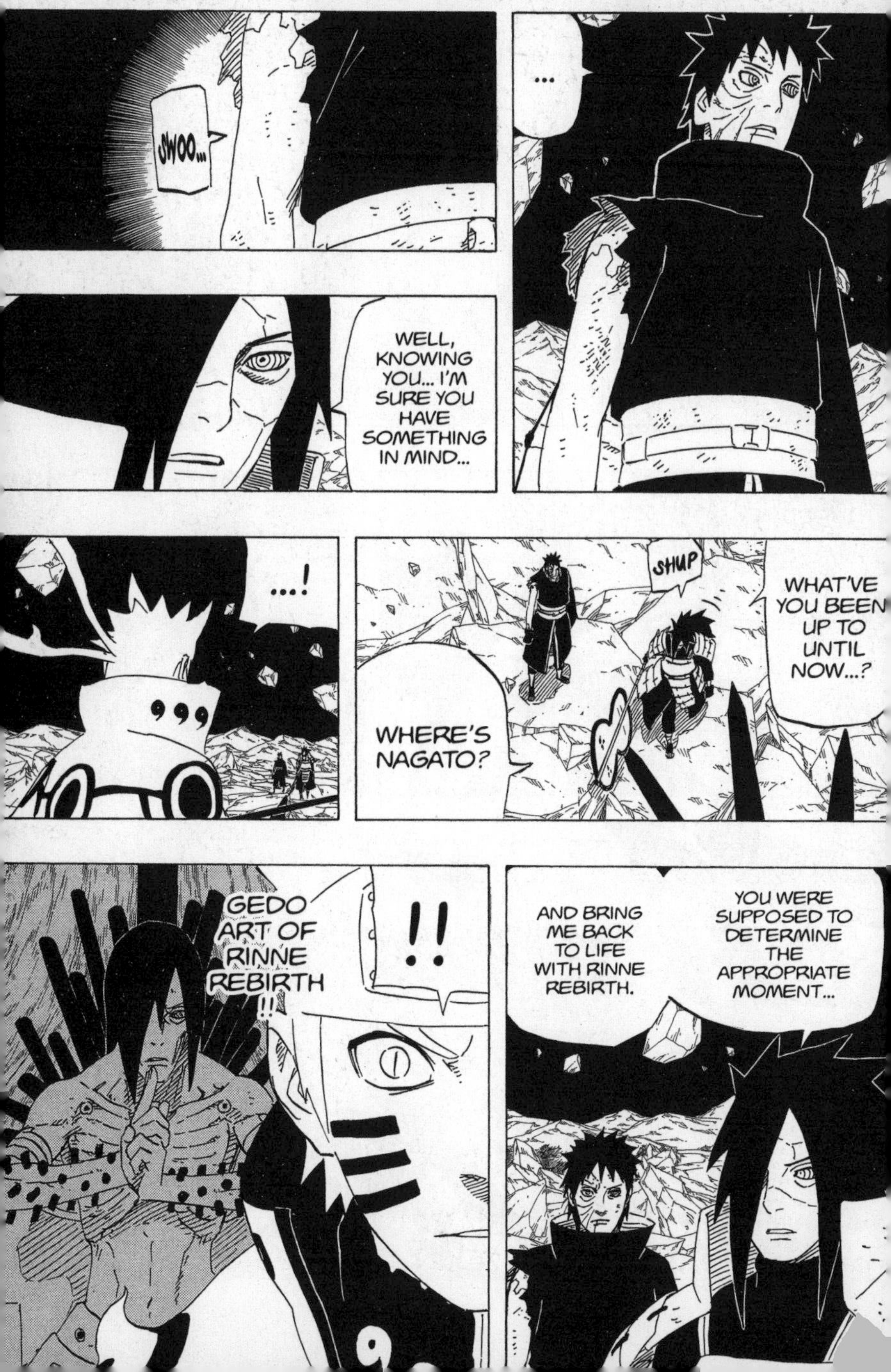
...
SWOO...
WELL, KNOWING YOU... I'M SURE YOU HAVE SOMETHING IN MIND...
SHUP
WHAT'VE YOU BEEN UP TO UNTIL NOW...?
WHERE'S NAGATO?
...!
YOU WERE SUPPOSED TO DETERMINE THE APPROPRIATE MOMENT...
AND BRING ME BACK TO LIFE WITH RINNE REBIRTH.
!!
GEDO ART OF RINNE REBIRTH!!

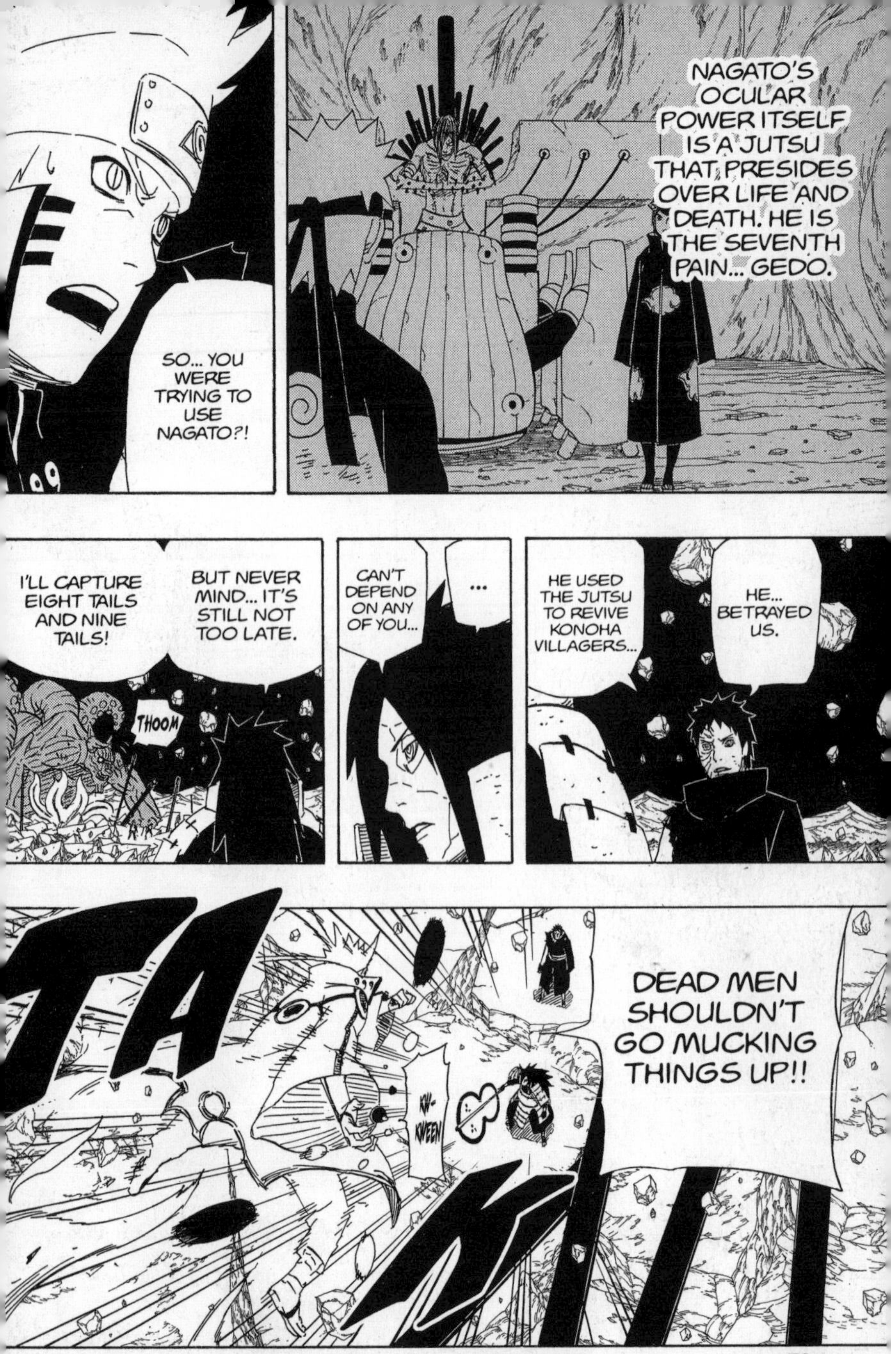
NAGATO'S OCULAR POWER ITSELF IS A JUTSU THAT PRESIDES OVER LIFE AND DEATH. HE IS THE SEVENTH PAIN... GEDO.
SO... YOU WERE TRYING TO USE NAGATO?!
HE... BETRAYED US.
HE USED THE JUTSU TO REVIVE KONOHA VILLAGERS...
...
CAN'T DEPEND ON ANY OF YOU...
BUT NEVER MIND... IT'S STILL NOT TOO LATE.
I'LL CAPTURE EIGHT TAILS AND NINE TAILS!
THOOM
DEAD MEN SHOULDN'T GO MUCKING THINGS UP!!
KW-KWEEN
TA

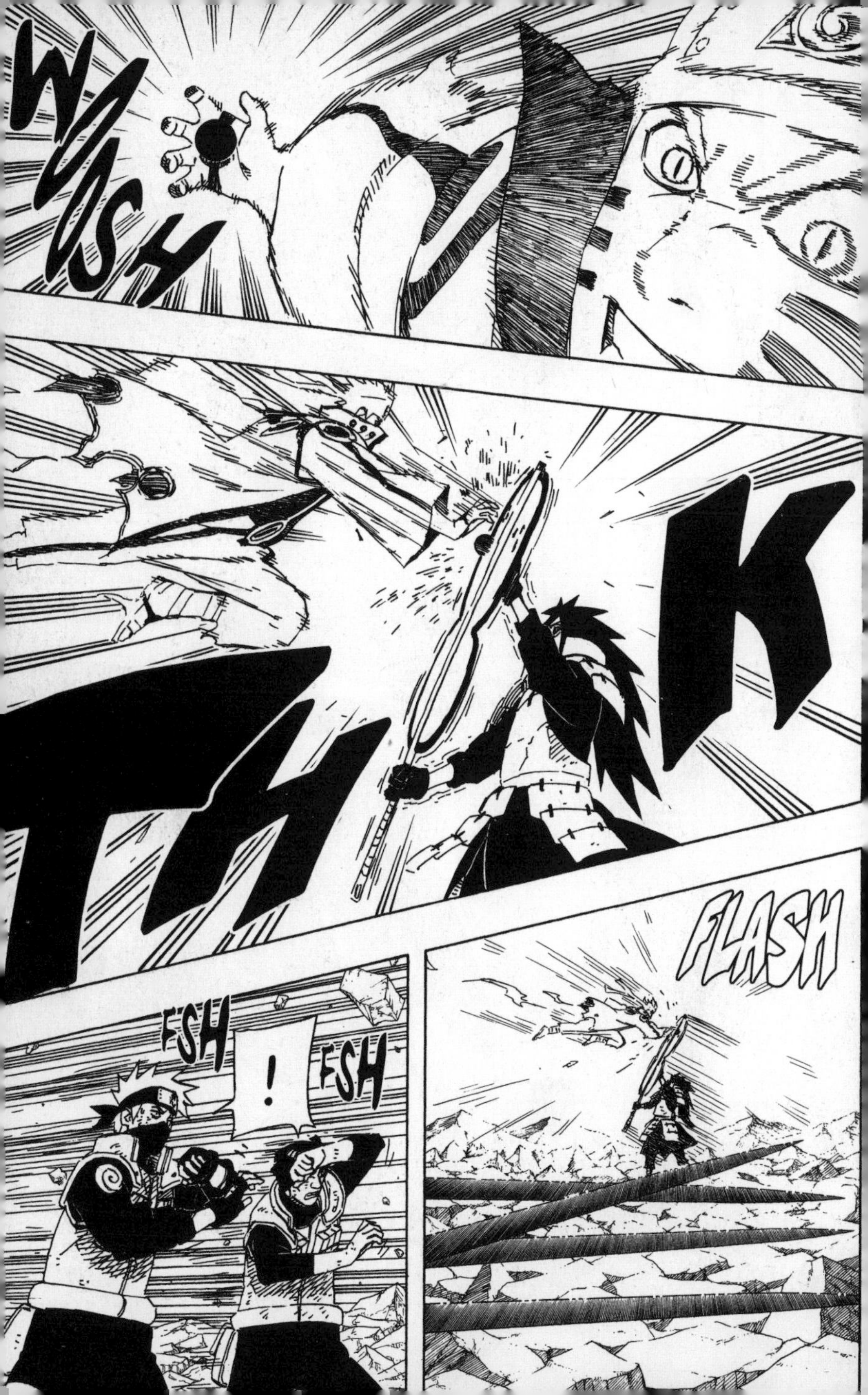

WHOSH
THUK
FLASH
FSH
FSH
!

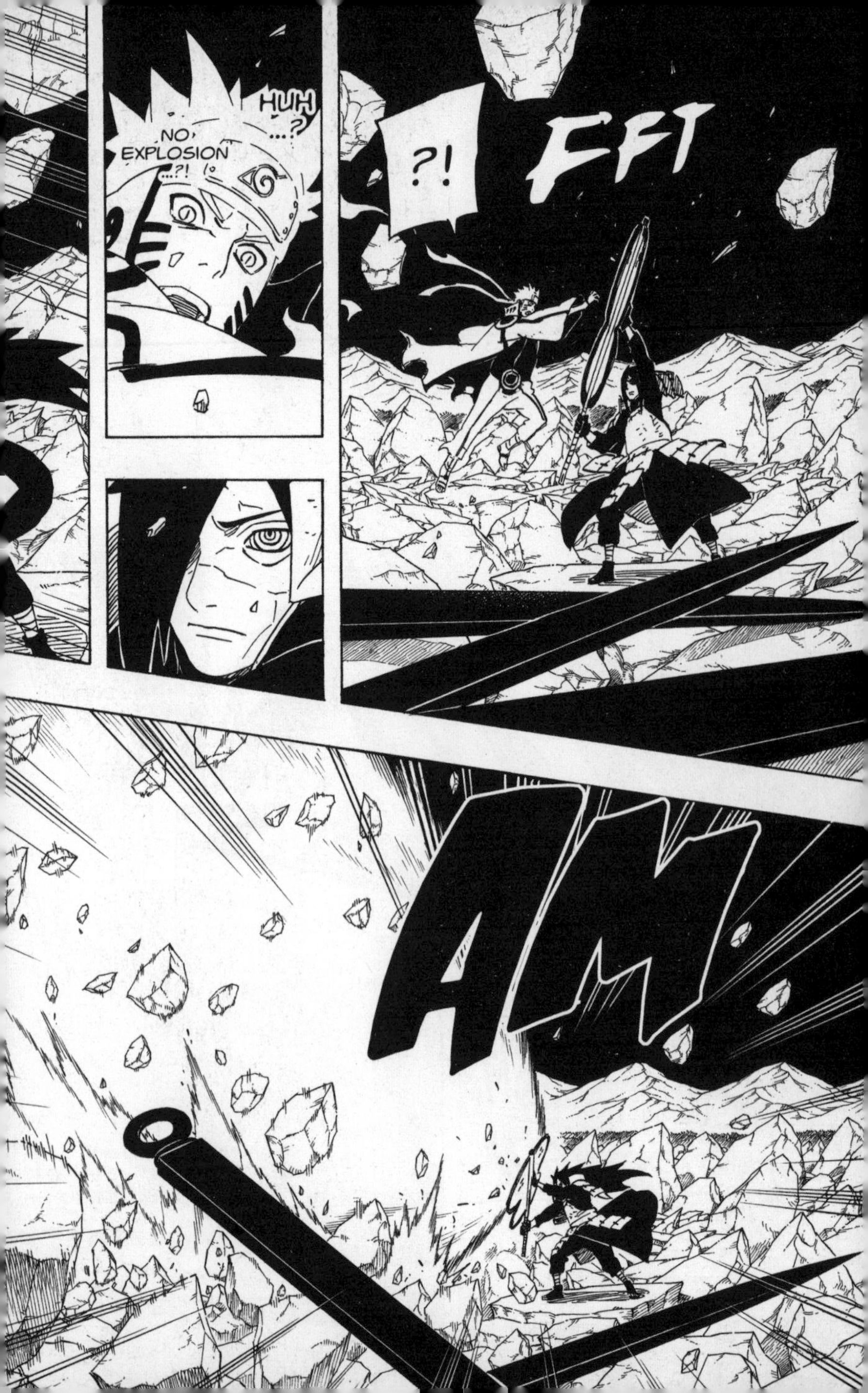
FFT
?!
HUH ...?
NO EXPLOSION ...?!
AM

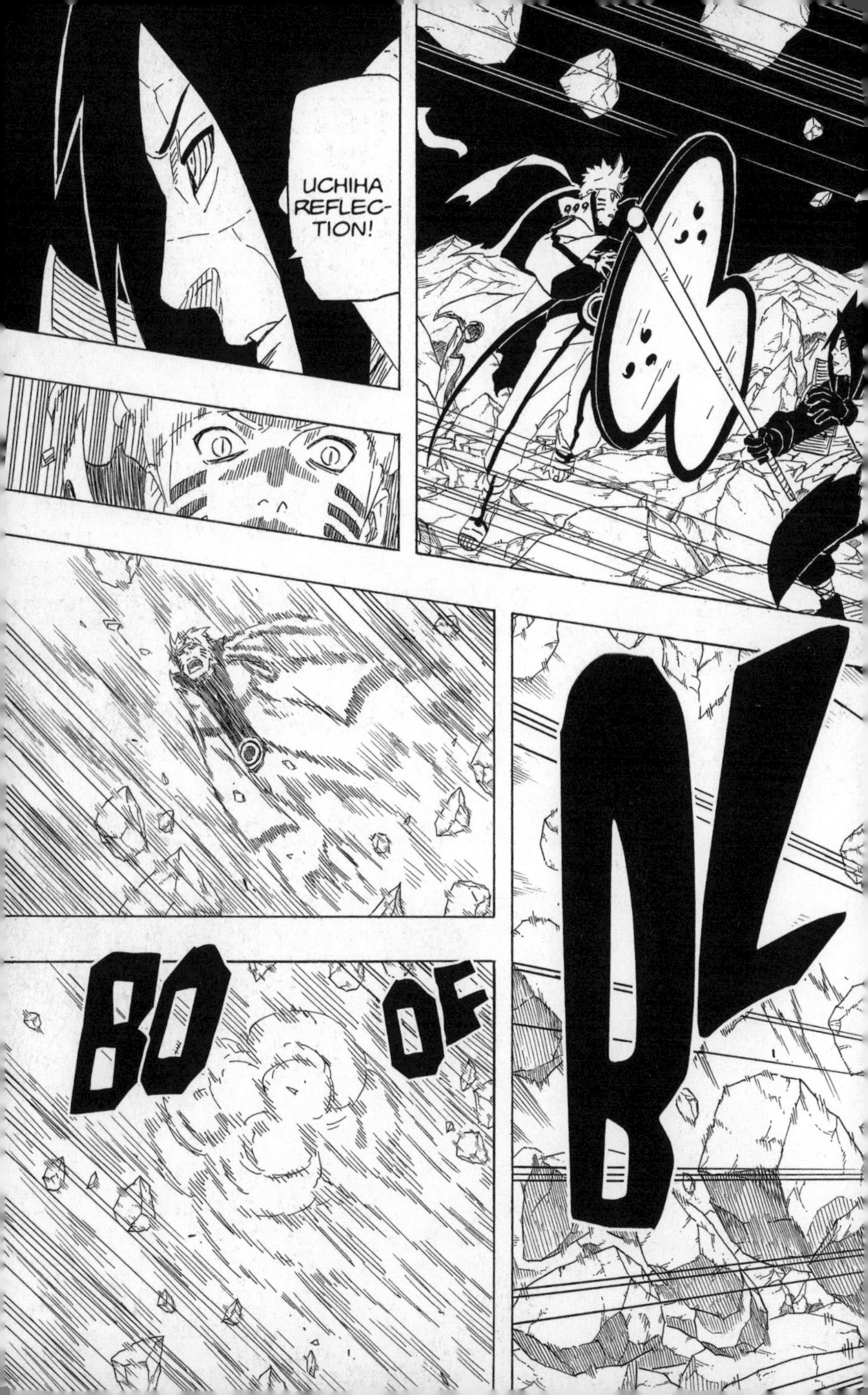
UCHIHA REFLECTION!
BOOF

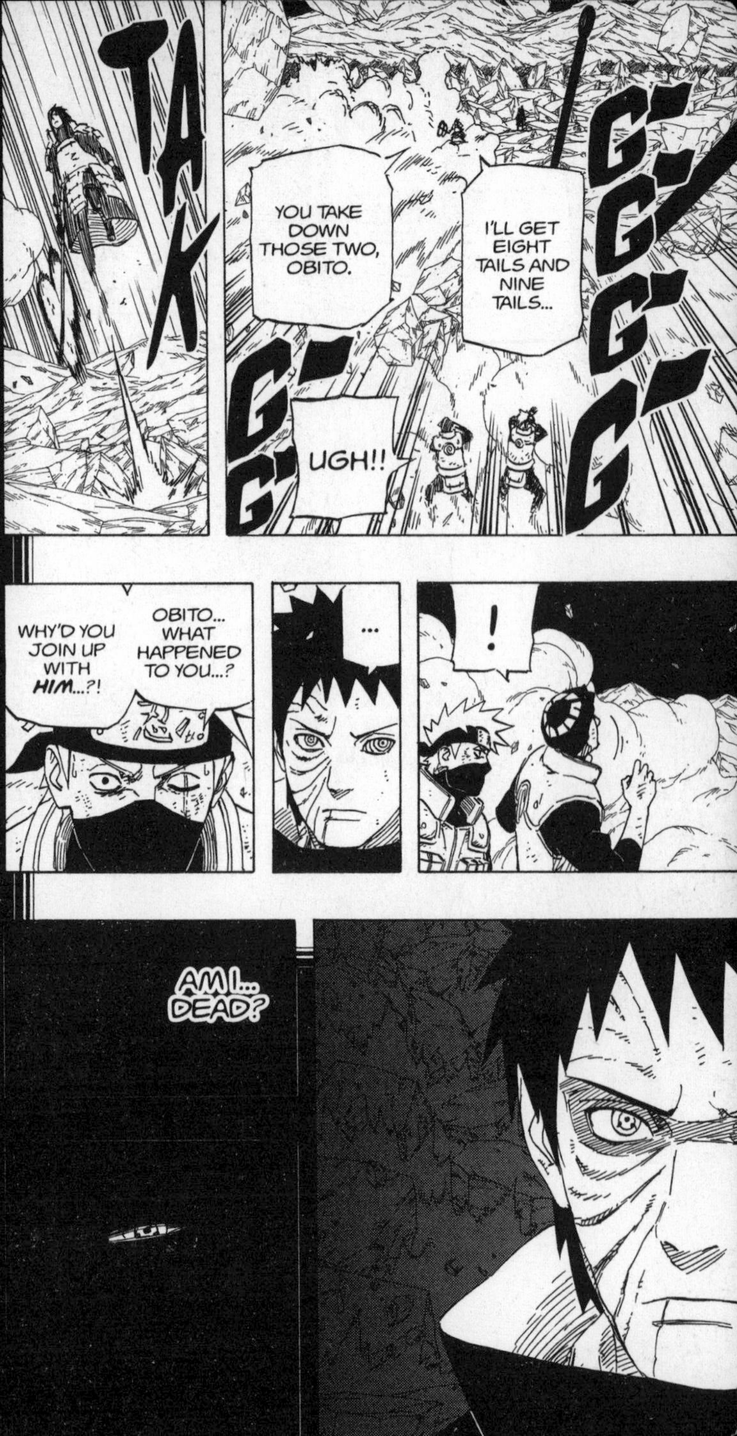
G-G-G-G-G
I'LL GET EIGHT TAILS AND NINE TAILS...
YOU TAKE DOWN THOSE TWO, OBITO.
G-G
UGH!!
TAK
!
...
OBITO... WHAT HAPPENED TO YOU...?
WHY'D YOU JOIN UP WITH *HIM*...?!
AM I... DEAD?

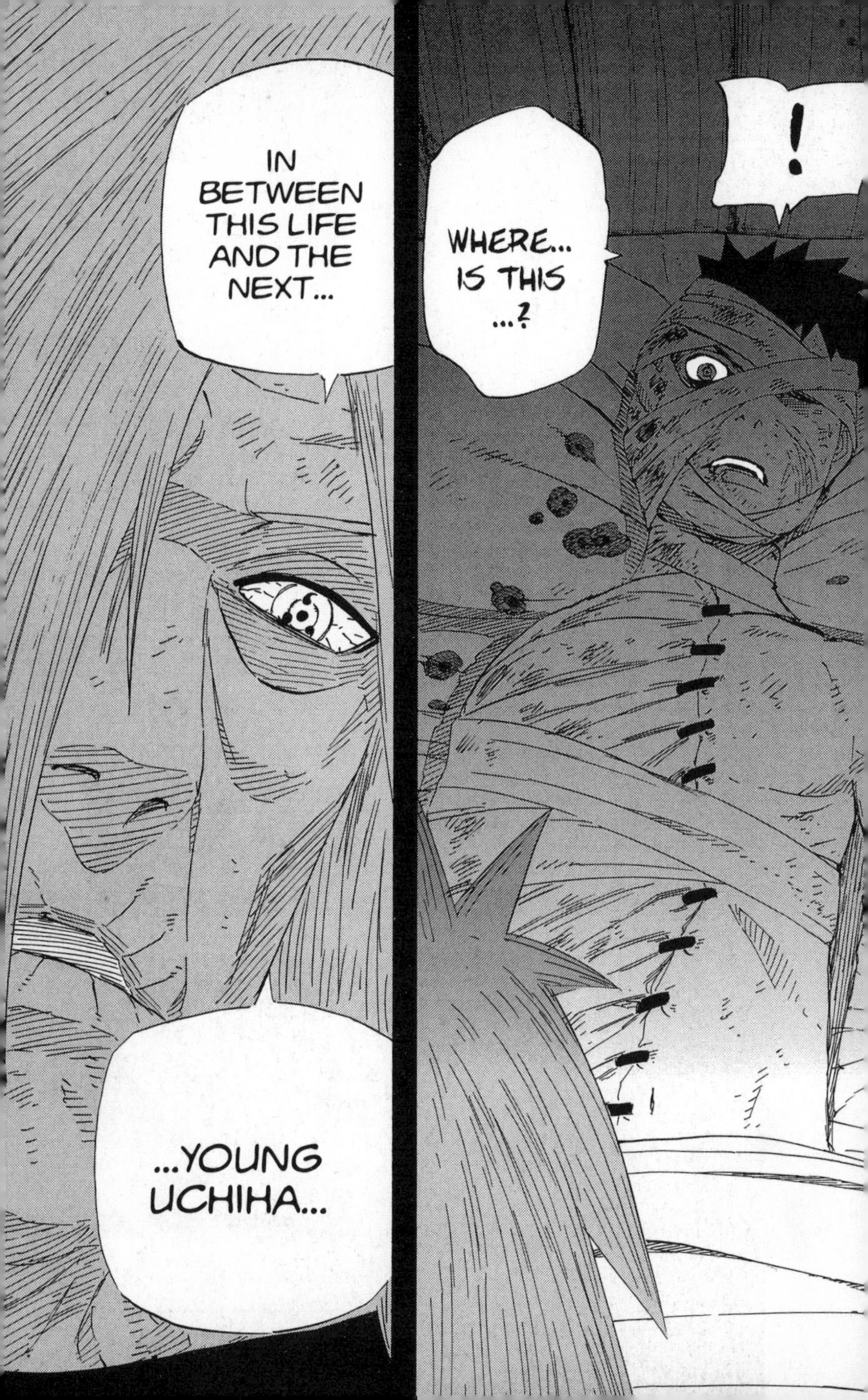
!
WHERE... IS THIS ...?
IN BETWEEN THIS LIFE AND THE NEXT...
...YOUNG UCHIHA...

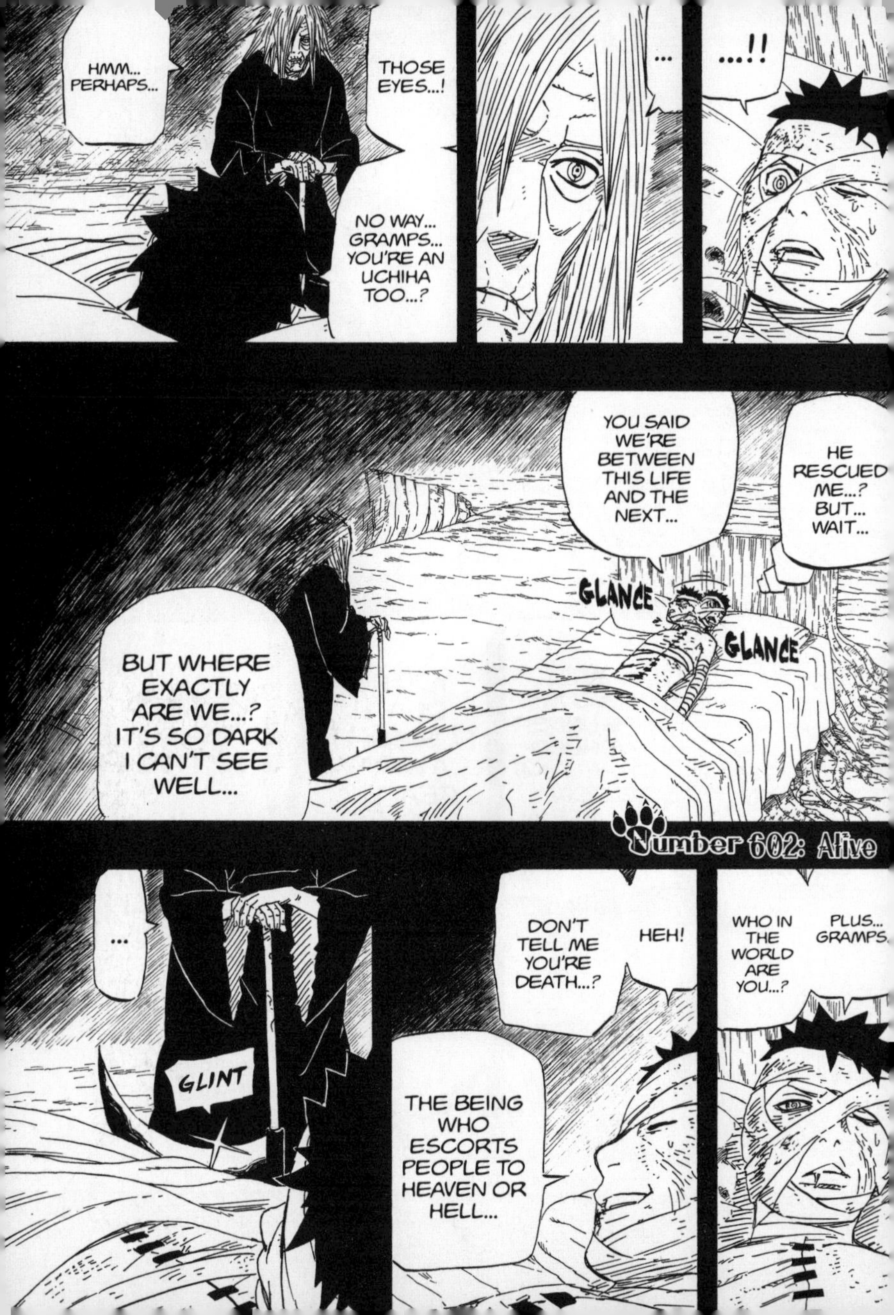
...!!
...
THOSE EYES...!
NO WAY... GRAMPS... YOU'RE AN UCHIHA TOO...?
HMM... PERHAPS...
HE RESCUED ME...? BUT... WAIT...
YOU SAID WE'RE BETWEEN THIS LIFE AND THE NEXT...
GLANCE
GLANCE
BUT WHERE EXACTLY ARE WE...? IT'S SO DARK I CAN'T SEE WELL...
Number 602: Alive
PLUS... GRAMPS.
WHO IN THE WORLD ARE YOU...?
HEH!
DON'T TELL ME YOU'RE DEATH...?
THE BEING WHO ESCORTS PEOPLE TO HEAVEN OR HELL...
...
GLINT

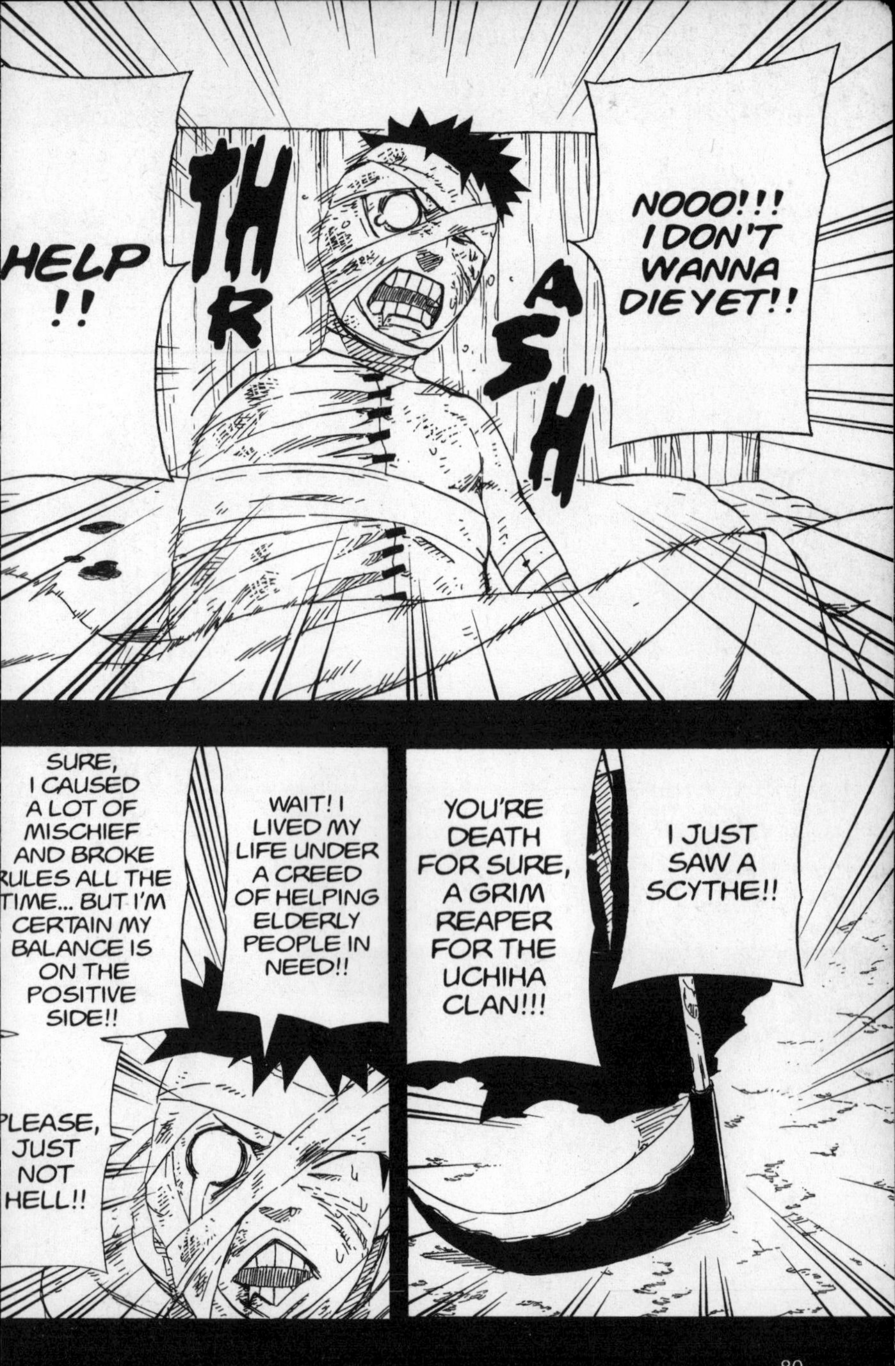
NOOO!!! I DON'T WANNA DIE YET!!
THRASH
HELP !!
I JUST SAW A SCYTHE!!
YOU'RE DEATH FOR SURE, A GRIM REAPER FOR THE UCHIHA CLAN!!!
WAIT! I LIVED MY LIFE UNDER A CREED OF HELPING ELDERLY PEOPLE IN NEED!!
SURE, I CAUSED A LOT OF MISCHIEF AND BROKE RULES ALL THE TIME... BUT I'M CERTAIN MY BALANCE IS ON THE POSITIVE SIDE!!
PLEASE, JUST NOT HELL!!

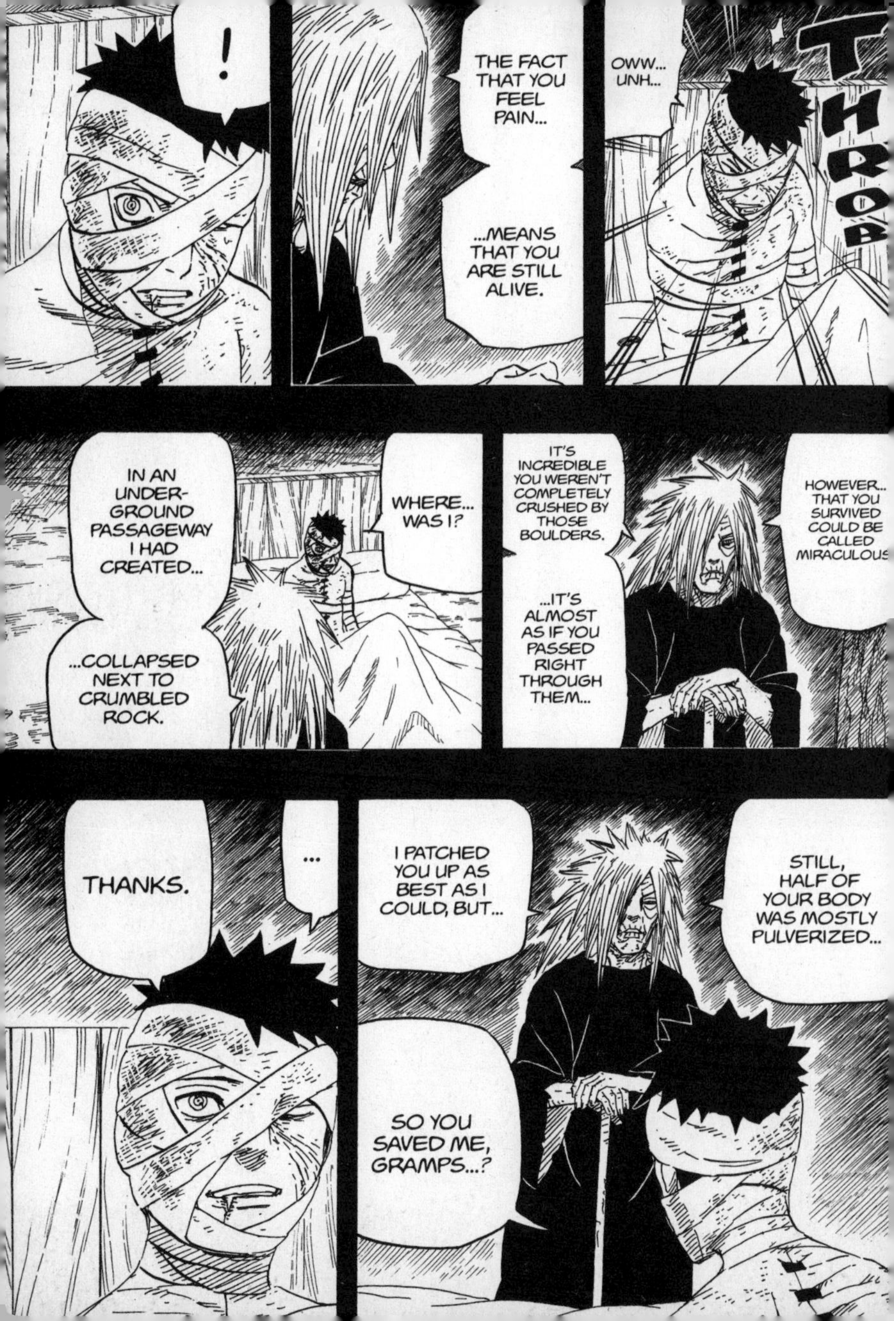
THROB
OWW... UNH...
THE FACT THAT YOU FEEL PAIN...
...MEANS THAT YOU ARE STILL ALIVE.
!
HOWEVER... THAT YOU SURVIVED COULD BE CALLED MIRACULOUS
IT'S INCREDIBLE YOU WEREN'T COMPLETELY CRUSHED BY THOSE BOULDERS.
...IT'S ALMOST AS IF YOU PASSED RIGHT THROUGH THEM...
WHERE... WAS I?
IN AN UNDER-GROUND PASSAGEWAY I HAD CREATED...
...COLLAPSED NEXT TO CRUMBLED ROCK.
STILL, HALF OF YOUR BODY WAS MOSTLY PULVERIZED...
I PATCHED YOU UP AS BEST AS I COULD, BUT...
SO YOU SAVED ME, GRAMPS...?
...
THANKS.

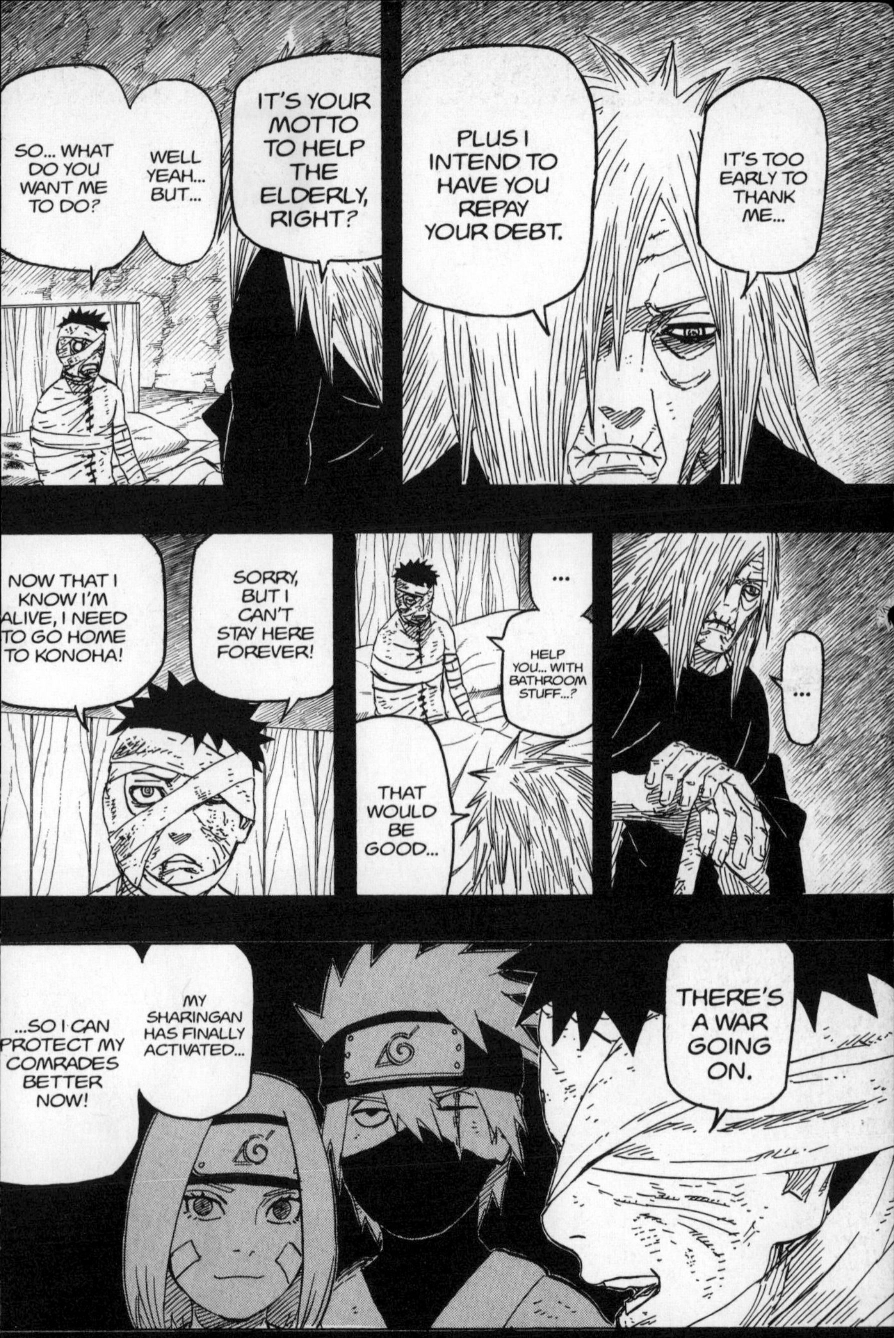

IT'S TOO EARLY TO THANK ME...
PLUS I INTEND TO HAVE YOU REPAY YOUR DEBT.
IT'S YOUR MOTTO TO HELP THE ELDERLY, RIGHT?
WELL YEAH... BUT...
SO... WHAT DO YOU WANT ME TO DO?
...
...
HELP YOU... WITH BATHROOM STUFF...?
THAT WOULD BE GOOD...
SORRY, BUT I CAN'T STAY HERE FOREVER!
NOW THAT I KNOW I'M ALIVE, I NEED TO GO HOME TO KONOHA!
THERE'S A WAR GOING ON.
MY SHARINGAN HAS FINALLY ACTIVATED...
...SO I CAN PROTECT MY COMRADES BETTER NOW!

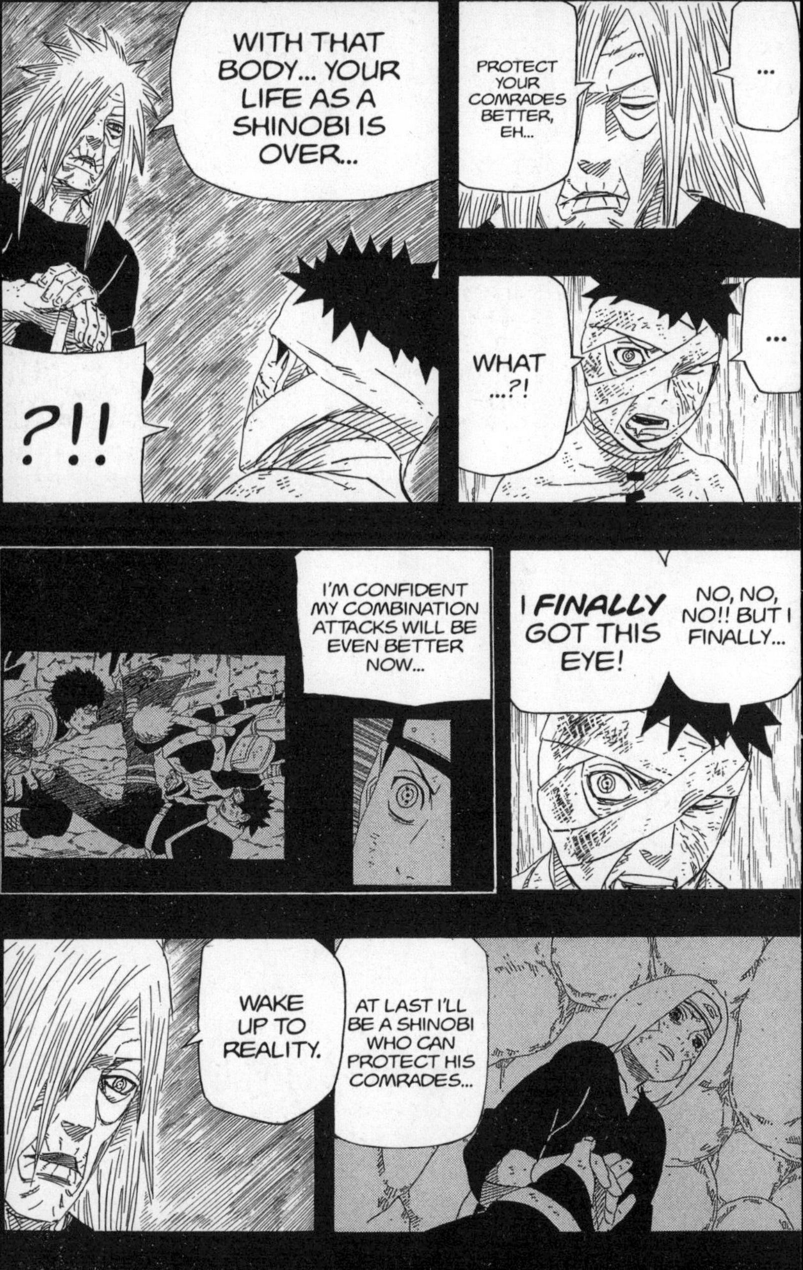
...
PROTECT YOUR COMRADES BETTER, EH...
...
WHAT ...?!
WITH THAT BODY... YOUR LIFE AS A SHINOBI IS OVER...
?!!
NO, NO, NO!! BUT I FINALLY...
I FINALLY GOT THIS EYE!
I'M CONFIDENT MY COMBINATION ATTACKS WILL BE EVEN BETTER NOW...
AT LAST I'LL BE A SHINOBI WHO CAN PROTECT HIS COMRADES...
WAKE UP TO REALITY.

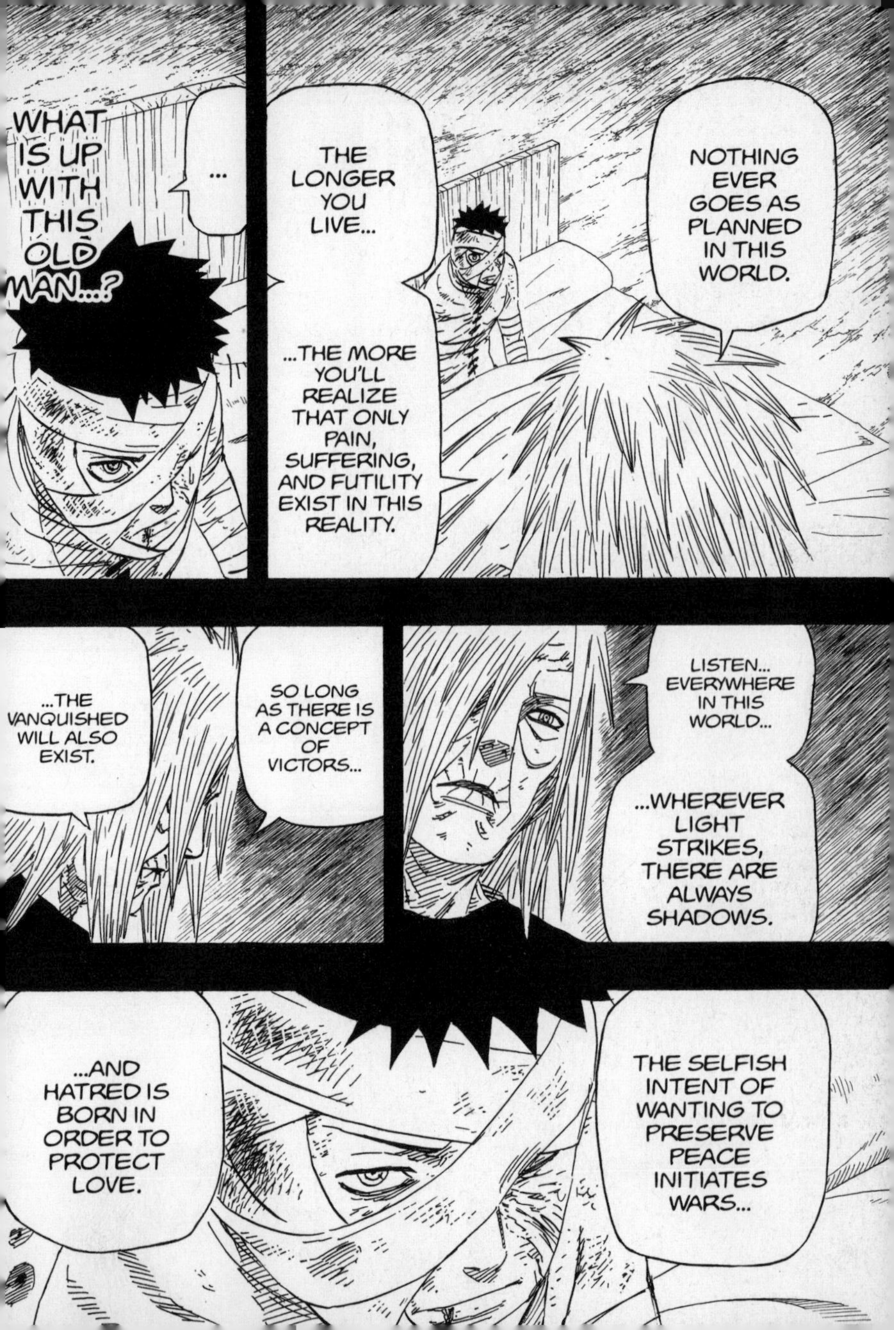
NOTHING EVER GOES AS PLANNED IN THIS WORLD.
THE LONGER YOU LIVE...
...THE MORE YOU'LL REALIZE THAT ONLY PAIN, SUFFERING, AND FUTILITY EXIST IN THIS REALITY.
...
WHAT IS UP WITH THIS OLD MAN...?
LISTEN... EVERYWHERE IN THIS WORLD...
...WHEREVER LIGHT STRIKES, THERE ARE ALWAYS SHADOWS.
SO LONG AS THERE IS A CONCEPT OF VICTORS...
...THE VANQUISHED WILL ALSO EXIST.
THE SELFISH INTENT OF WANTING TO PRESERVE PEACE INITIATES WARS...
...AND HATRED IS BORN IN ORDER TO PROTECT LOVE.

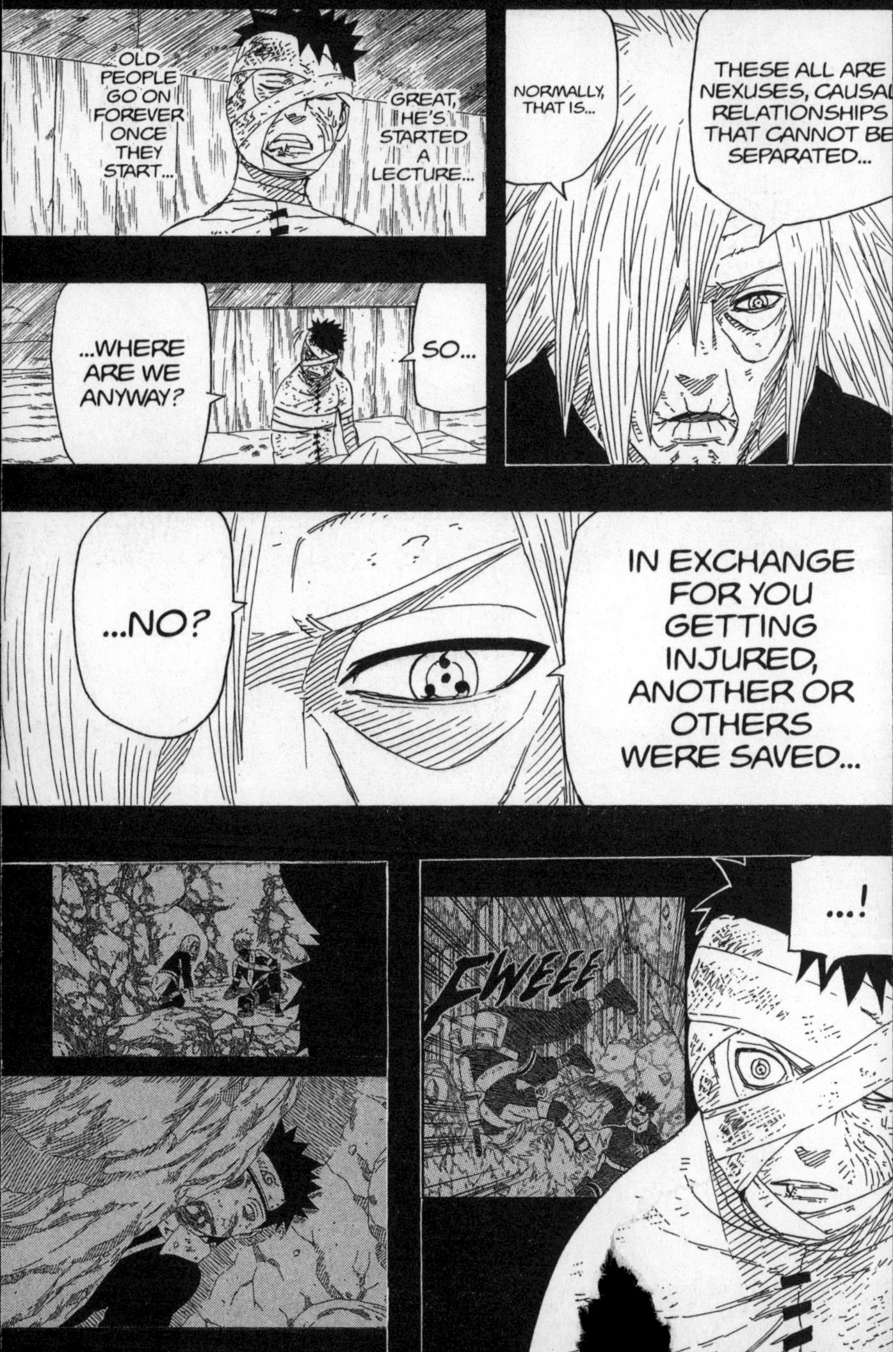
THESE ALL ARE NEXUSES, CAUSAL RELATIONSHIPS THAT CANNOT BE SEPARATED...
NORMALLY, THAT IS...
GREAT, HE'S STARTED A LECTURE...
OLD PEOPLE GO ON FOREVER ONCE THEY START...
SO...
...WHERE ARE WE ANYWAY?
IN EXCHANGE FOR YOU GETTING INJURED, ANOTHER OR OTHERS WERE SAVED...
...NO?
...!
CWEEE

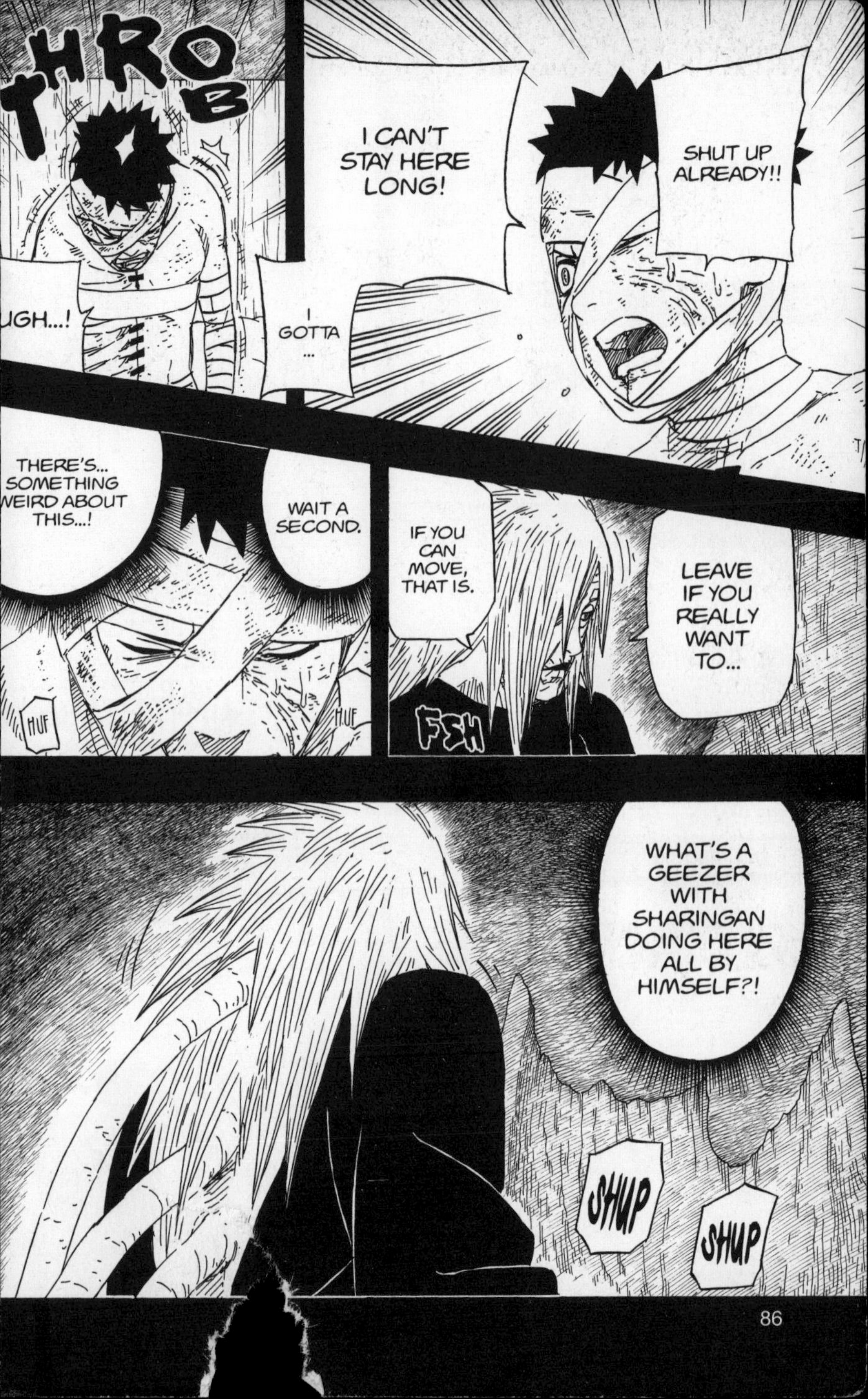
SHUT UP ALREADY!!
I CAN'T STAY HERE LONG!
I GOTTA ...
THROB
UGH...!
LEAVE IF YOU REALLY WANT TO...
IF YOU CAN MOVE, THAT IS.
FSH
WAIT A SECOND.
THERE'S... SOMETHING WEIRD ABOUT THIS...!
HUF
HUF
WHAT'S A GEEZER WITH SHARINGAN DOING HERE ALL BY HIMSELF?!
SHUP
SHUP

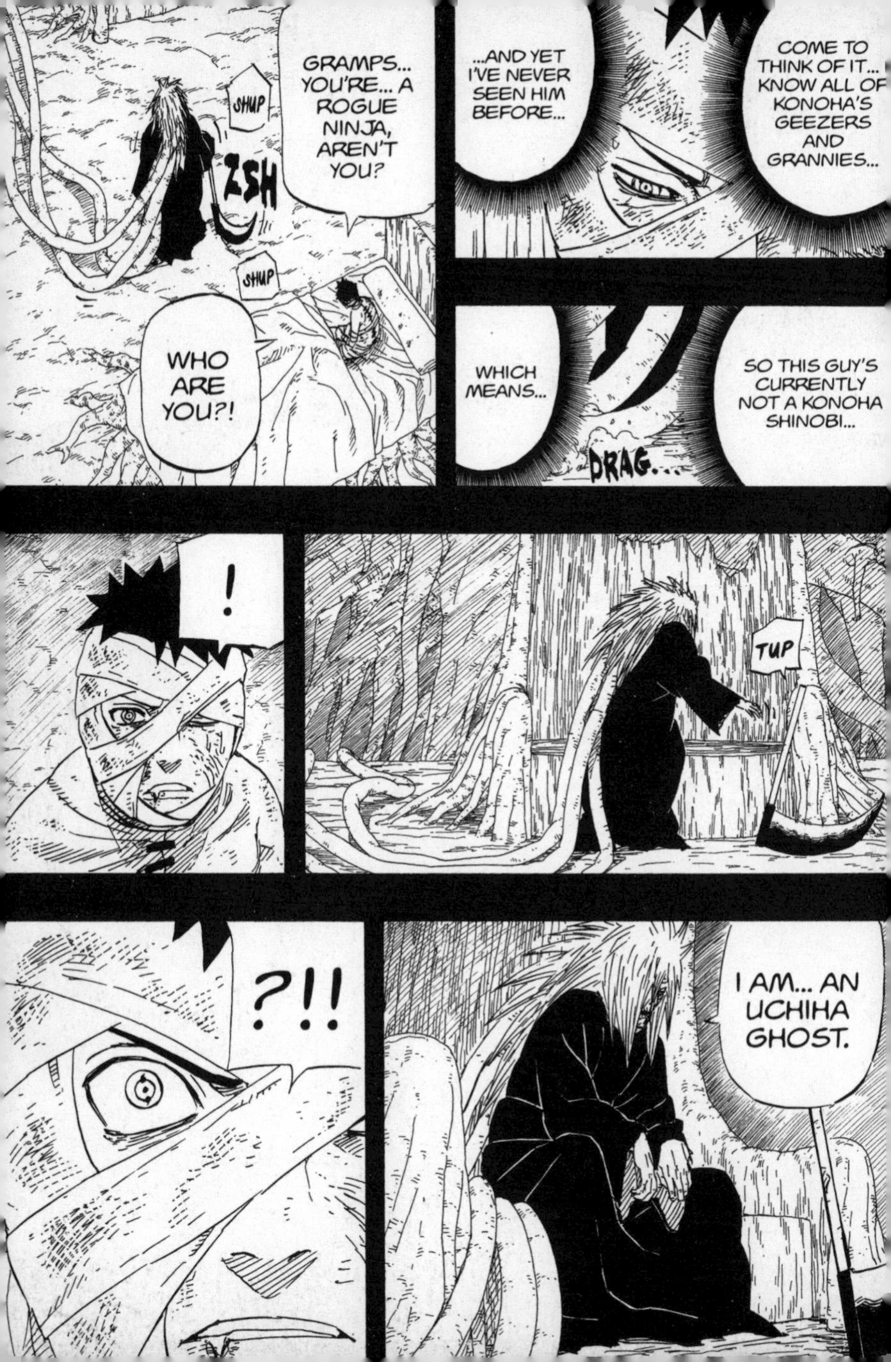
COME TO THINK OF IT... KNOW ALL OF KONOHA'S GEEZERS AND GRANNIES...
...AND YET I'VE NEVER SEEN HIM BEFORE...
SO THIS GUY'S CURRENTLY NOT A KONOHA SHINOBI...
WHICH MEANS...
DRAG...
GRAMPS... YOU'RE... A ROGUE NINJA, AREN'T YOU?
SHUP
ZSH
SHUP
WHO ARE YOU?!
TUP
!
I AM... AN UCHIHA GHOST.
?!!

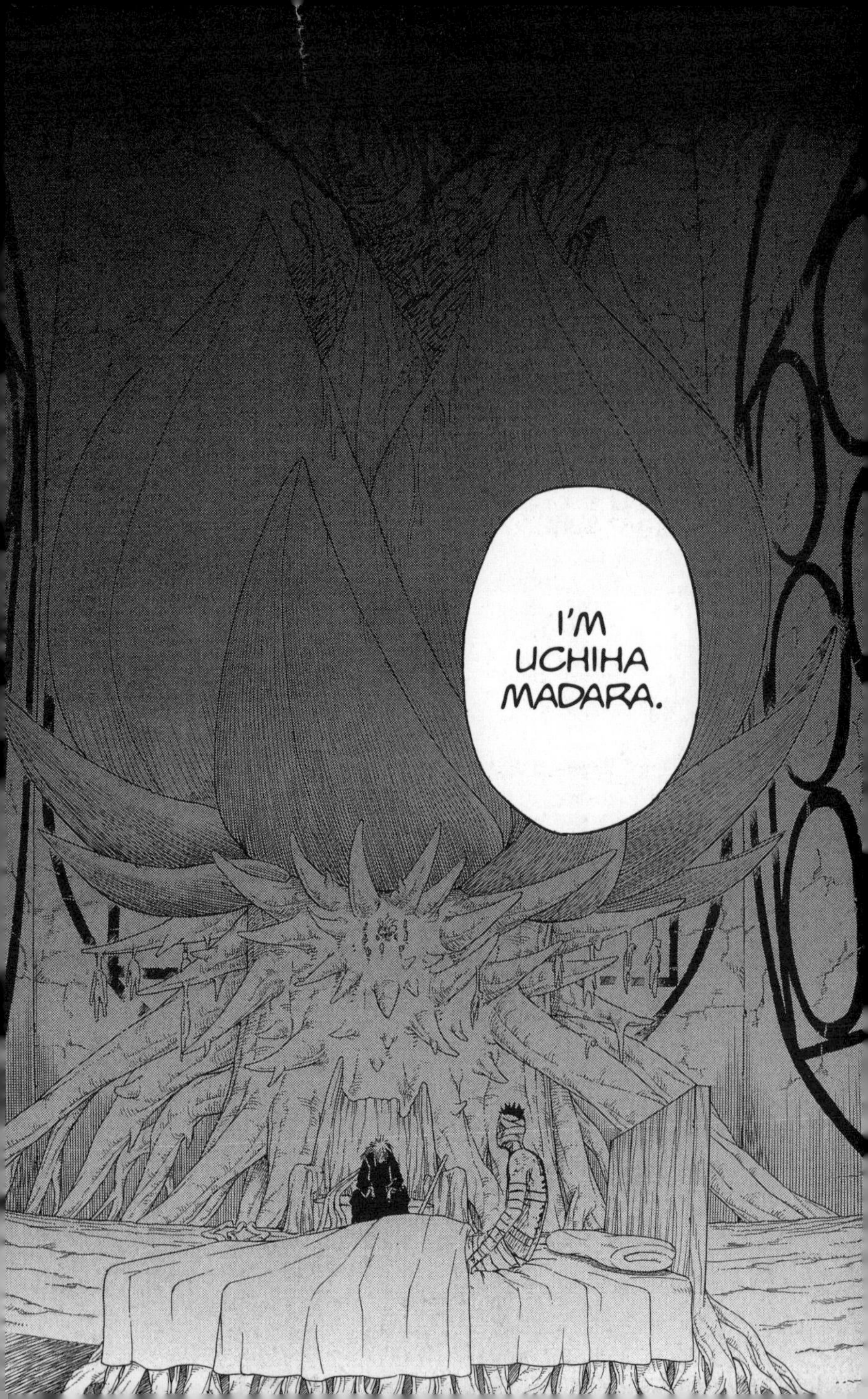
I'M UCHIHA MADARA.

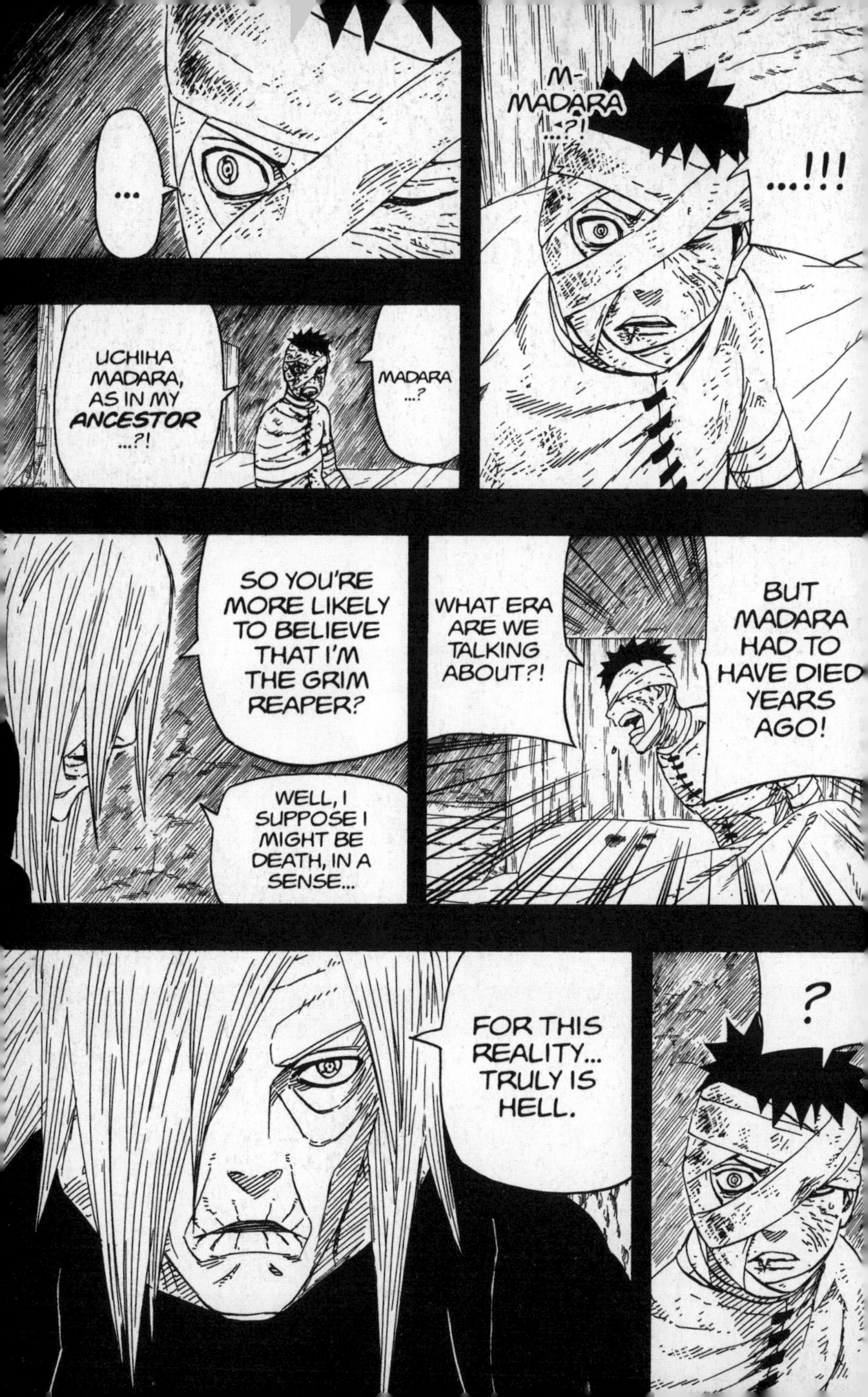
M- MADARA ...?!
...!!!
...
MADARA ...?
UCHIHA MADARA, AS IN MY ANCESTOR ...?!
BUT MADARA HAD TO HAVE DIED YEARS AGO!
WHAT ERA ARE WE TALKING ABOUT?!
SO YOU'RE MORE LIKELY TO BELIEVE THAT I'M THE GRIM REAPER?
WELL, I SUPPOSE I MIGHT BE DEATH, IN A SENSE...
?
FOR THIS REALITY... TRULY IS HELL.

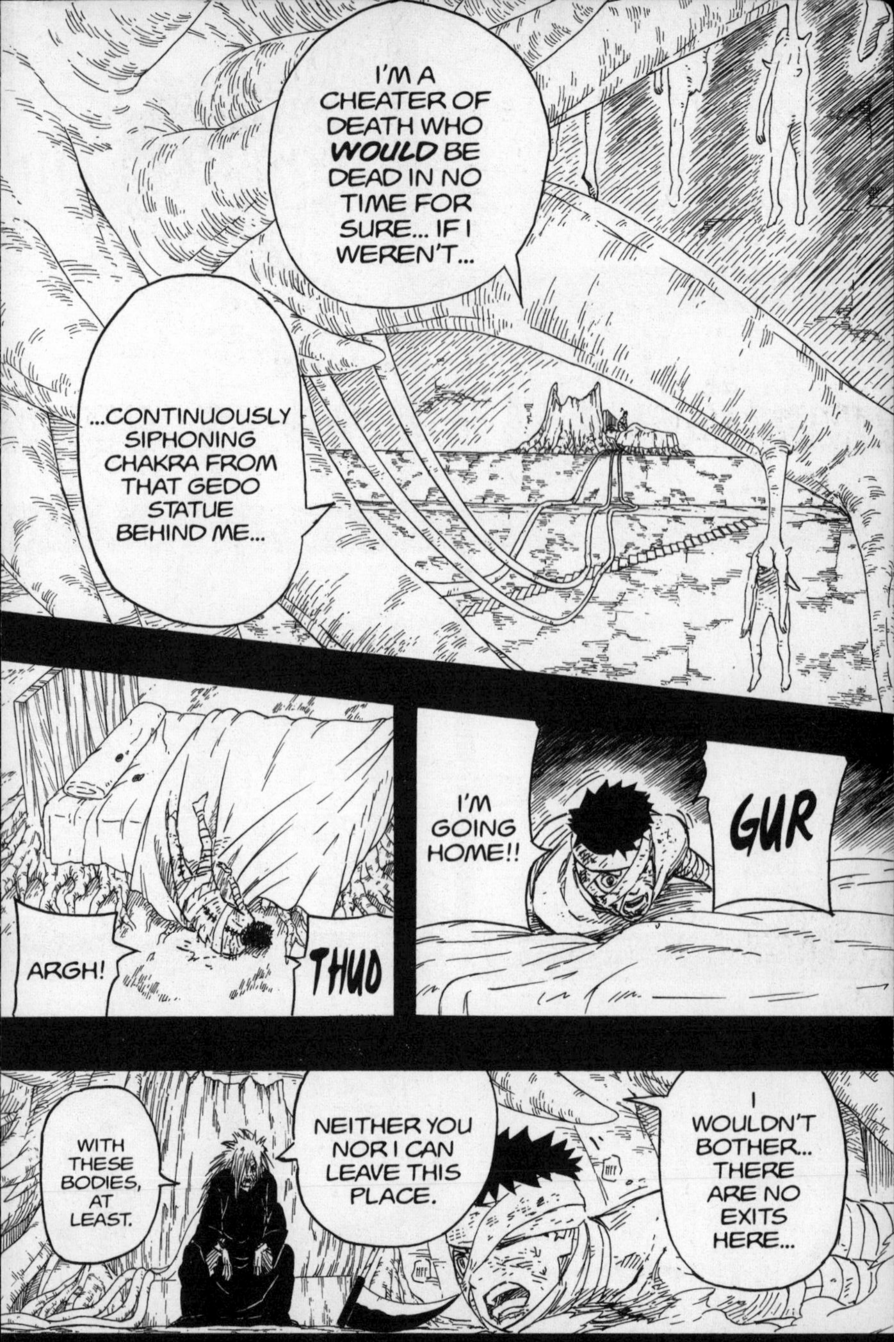
I'M A CHEATER OF DEATH WHO WOULD BE DEAD IN NO TIME FOR SURE... IF I WEREN'T...
...CONTINUOUSLY SIPHONING CHAKRA FROM THAT GEDO STATUE BEHIND ME...
GUR
I'M GOING HOME!!
THUD
ARGH!
I WOULDN'T BOTHER... THERE ARE NO EXITS HERE...
NEITHER YOU NOR I CAN LEAVE THIS PLACE.
WITH THESE BODIES, AT LEAST.

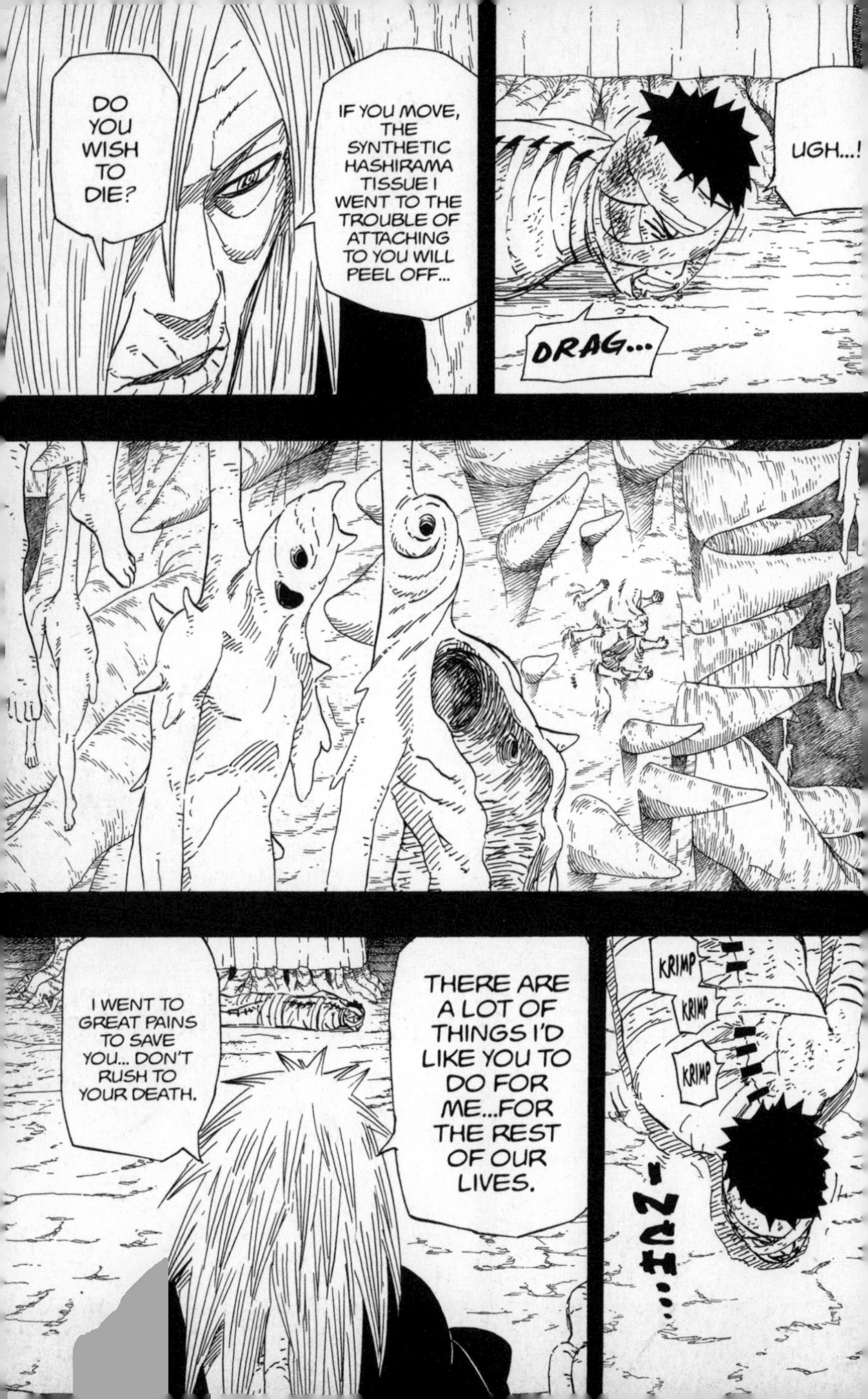
UGH...!
DRAG...
IF YOU MOVE, THE SYNTHETIC HASHIRAMA TISSUE I WENT TO THE TROUBLE OF ATTACHING TO YOU WILL PEEL OFF...
DO YOU WISH TO DIE?
KRIMP
KRIMP
KRIMP
NGH...
THERE ARE A LOT OF THINGS I'D LIKE YOU TO DO FOR ME...FOR THE REST OF OUR LIVES.
I WENT TO GREAT PAINS TO SAVE YOU... DON'T RUSH TO YOUR DEATH.

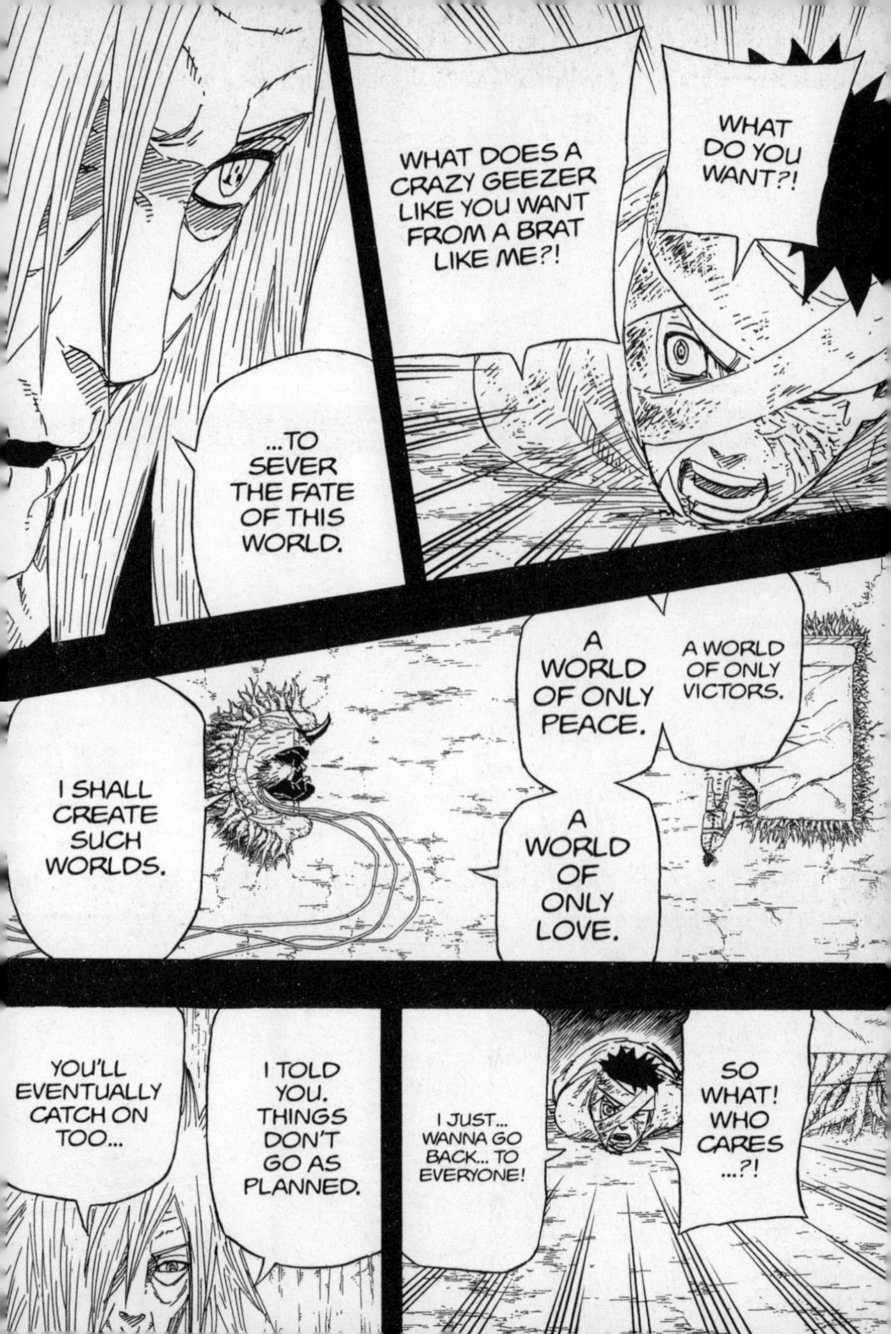
WHAT DO YOU WANT?!
WHAT DOES A CRAZY GEEZER LIKE YOU WANT FROM A BRAT LIKE ME?!
...TO SEVER THE FATE OF THIS WORLD.
A WORLD OF ONLY VICTORS.
A WORLD OF ONLY PEACE.
A WORLD OF ONLY LOVE.
I SHALL CREATE SUCH WORLDS.
SO WHAT! WHO CARES ...?!
I JUST... WANNA GO BACK... TO EVERYONE!
I TOLD YOU. THINGS DON'T GO AS PLANNED.
YOU'LL EVENTUALLY CATCH ON TOO...

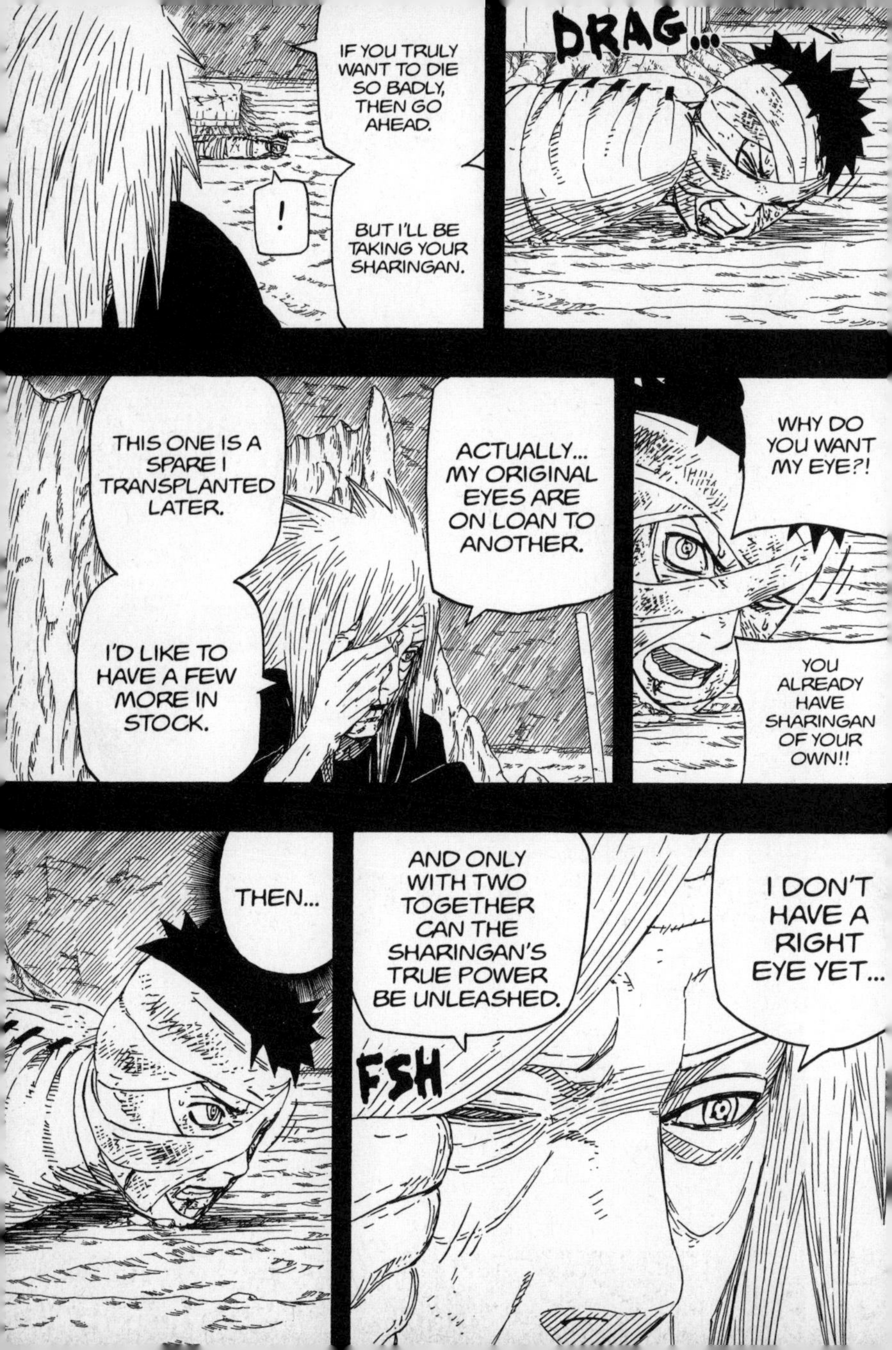
DRAG...
IF YOU TRULY WANT TO DIE SO BADLY, THEN GO AHEAD.
!
BUT I'LL BE TAKING YOUR SHARINGAN.
WHY DO YOU WANT MY EYE?!
YOU ALREADY HAVE SHARINGAN OF YOUR OWN!!
ACTUALLY... MY ORIGINAL EYES ARE ON LOAN TO ANOTHER.
THIS ONE IS A SPARE I TRANSPLANTED LATER.
I'D LIKE TO HAVE A FEW MORE IN STOCK.
I DON'T HAVE A RIGHT EYE YET...
AND ONLY WITH TWO TOGETHER CAN THE SHARINGAN'S TRUE POWER BE UNLEASHED.
FSH
THEN...

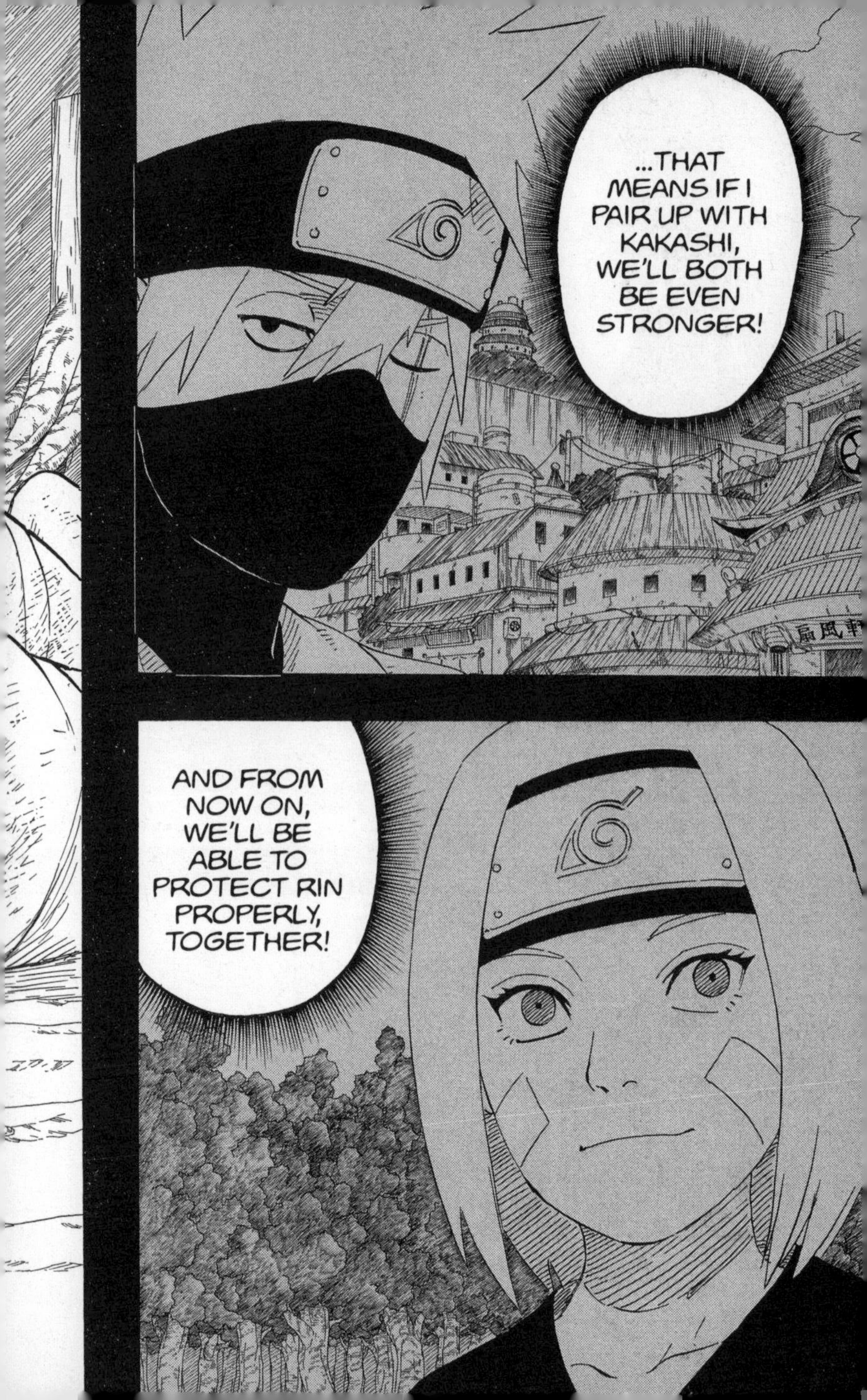
...THAT MEANS IF I PAIR UP WITH KAKASHI, WE'LL BOTH BE EVEN STRONGER!
AND FROM NOW ON, WE'LL BE ABLE TO PROTECT RIN PROPERLY, TOGETHER!

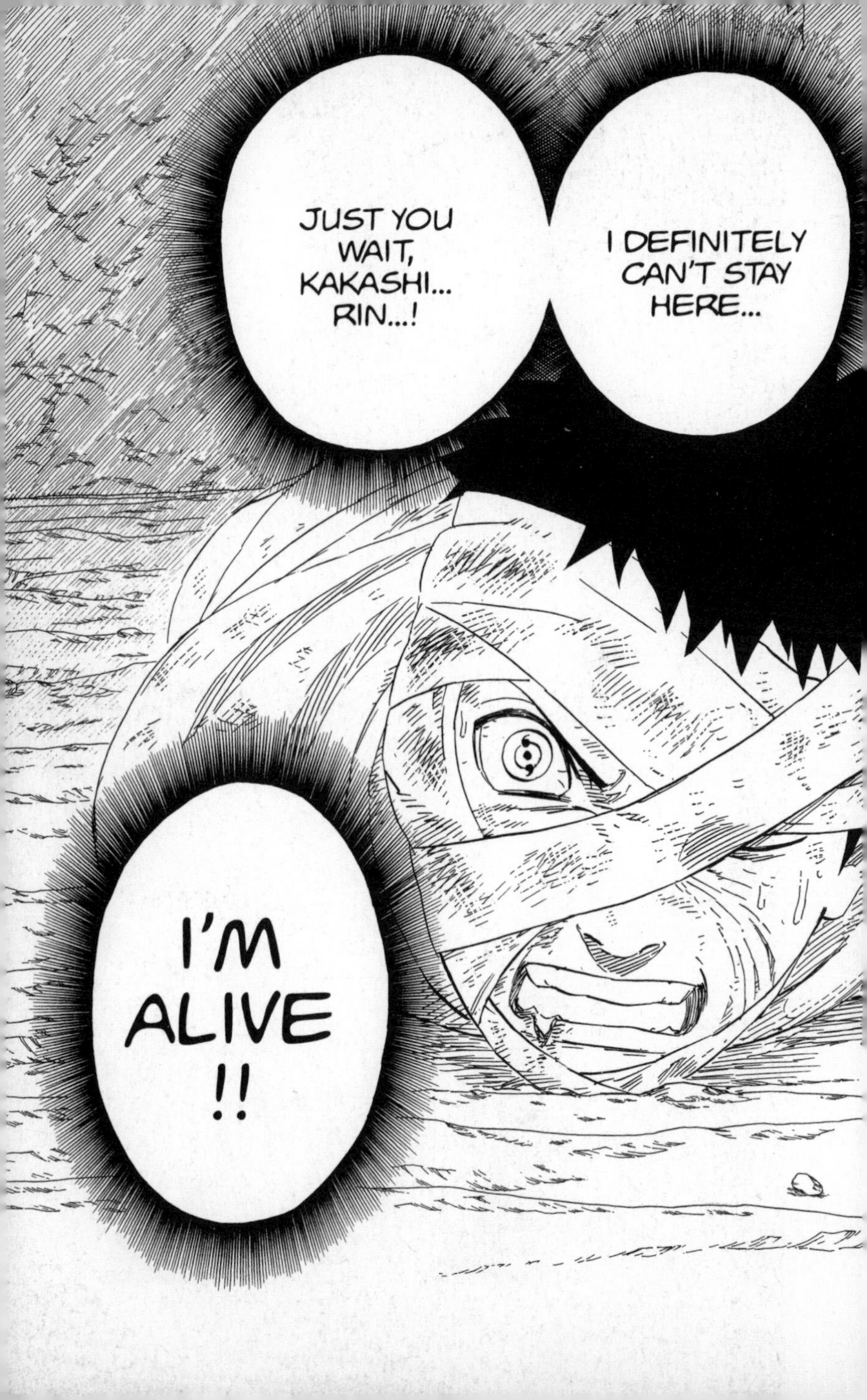
I DEFINITELY CAN'T STAY HERE...
JUST YOU WAIT, KAKASHI... RIN...!
I'M ALIVE !!

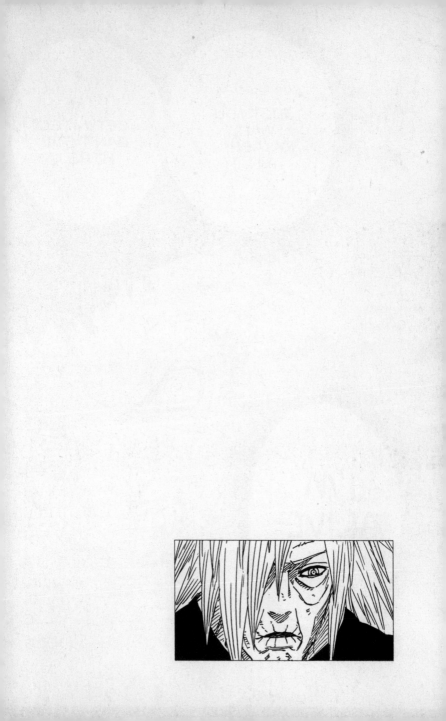

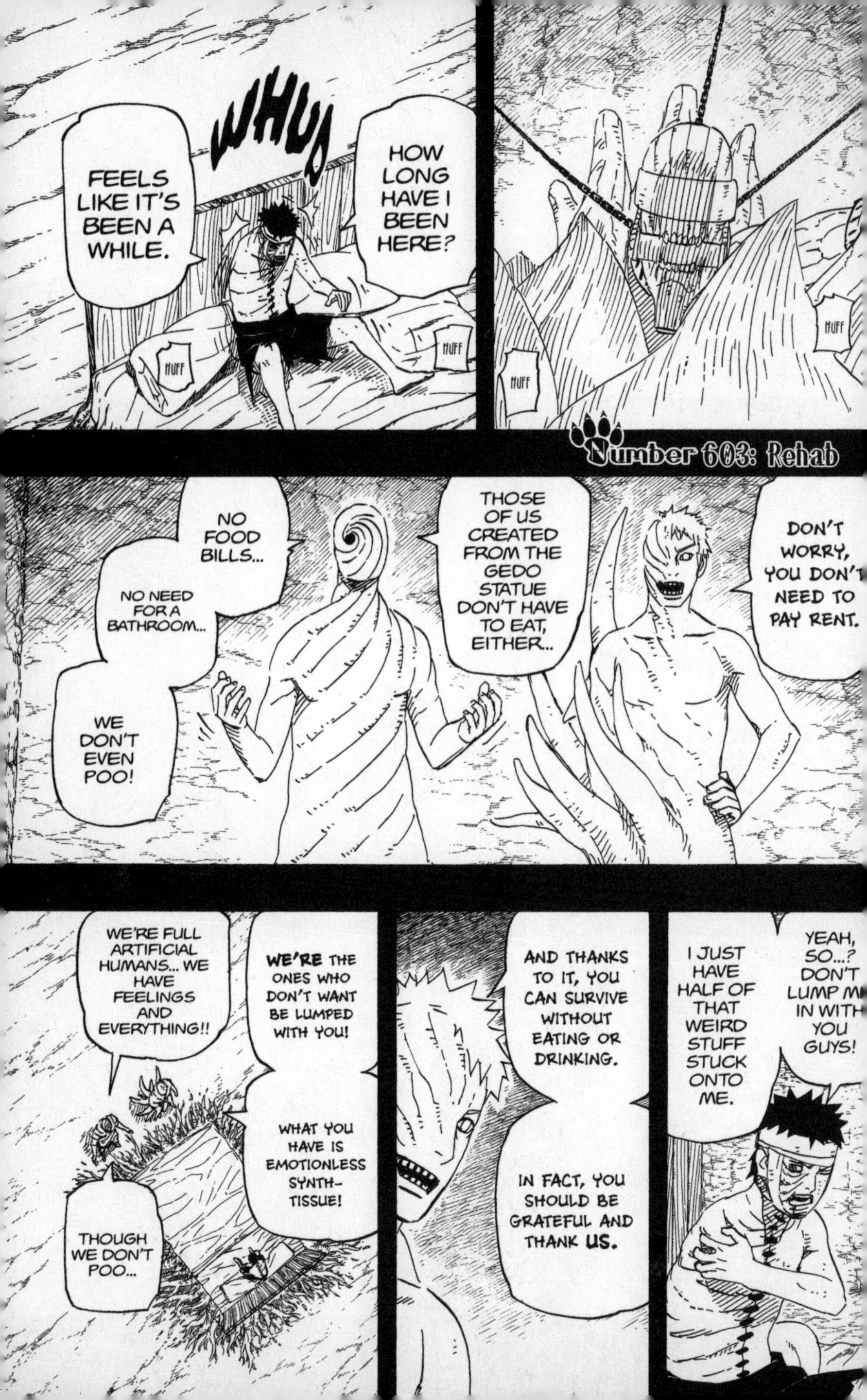
HUFF
HUFF
WHUD
HOW LONG HAVE I BEEN HERE?
FEELS LIKE IT'S BEEN A WHILE.
HUFF
HUFF
Number 603: Rehab
DON'T WORRY, YOU DON'T NEED TO PAY RENT.
THOSE OF US CREATED FROM THE GEDO STATUE DON'T HAVE TO EAT, EITHER...
NO FOOD BILLS...
NO NEED FOR A BATHROOM...
WE DON'T EVEN POO!
YEAH, SO...? DON'T LUMP ME IN WITH YOU GUYS!
I JUST HAVE HALF OF THAT WEIRD STUFF STUCK ONTO ME.
AND THANKS TO IT, YOU CAN SURVIVE WITHOUT EATING OR DRINKING.
IN FACT, YOU SHOULD BE GRATEFUL AND THANK US.
WE'RE THE ONES WHO DON'T WANT BE LUMPED WITH YOU!
WE'RE FULL ARTIFICIAL HUMANS... WE HAVE FEELINGS AND EVERYTHING!!
WHAT YOU HAVE IS EMOTIONLESS SYNTH-TISSUE!
THOUGH WE DON'T POO...

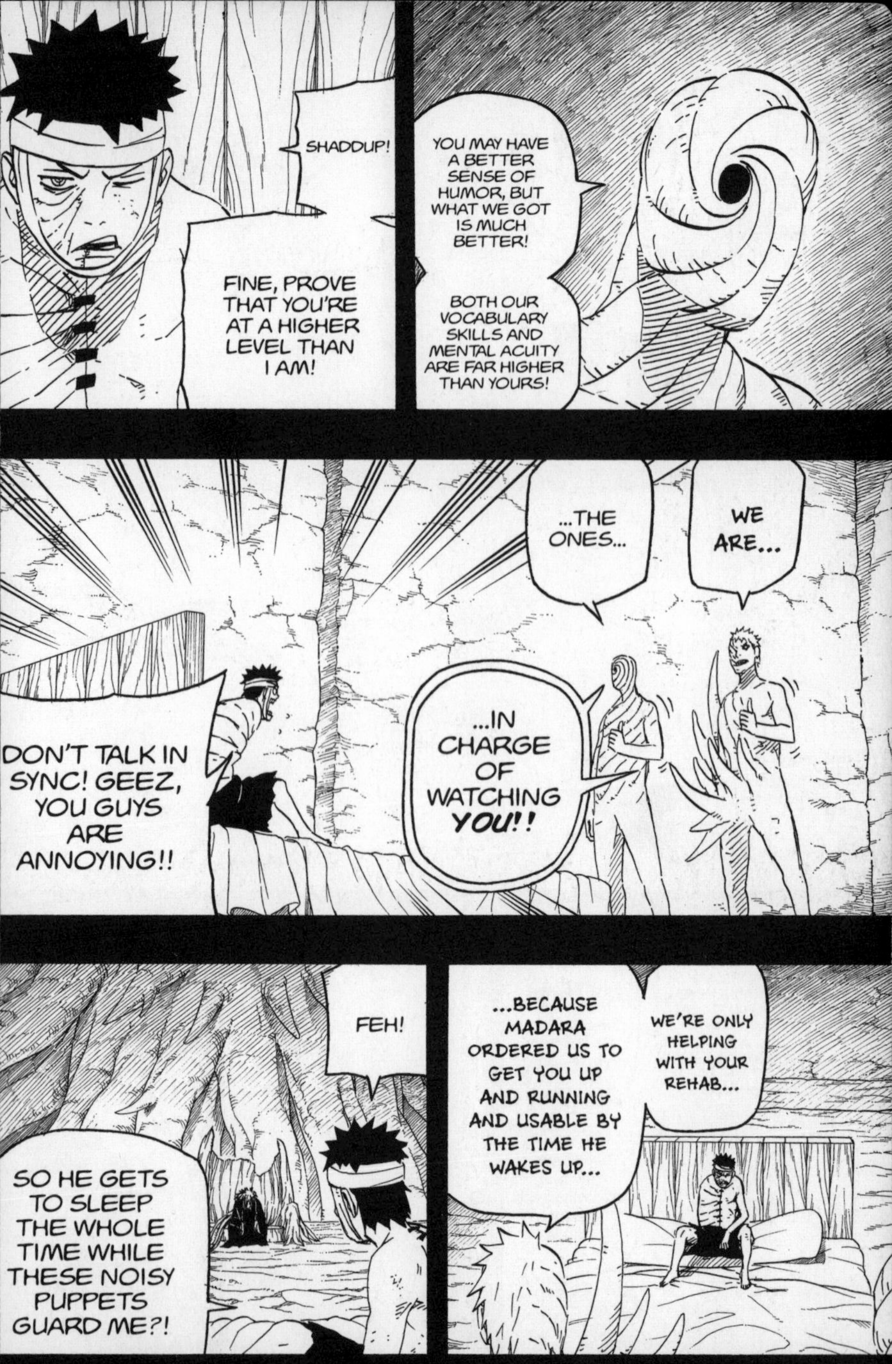
YOU MAY HAVE A BETTER SENSE OF HUMOR, BUT WHAT WE GOT IS MUCH BETTER!
BOTH OUR VOCABULARY SKILLS AND MENTAL ACUITY ARE FAR HIGHER THAN YOURS!
SHADDUP!
FINE, PROVE THAT YOU'RE AT A HIGHER LEVEL THAN I AM!
WE ARE...
...THE ONES...
...IN CHARGE OF WATCHING YOU!!
DON'T TALK IN SYNC! GEEZ, YOU GUYS ARE ANNOYING!!
WE'RE ONLY HELPING WITH YOUR REHAB...
...BECAUSE MADARA ORDERED US TO GET YOU UP AND RUNNING AND USABLE BY THE TIME HE WAKES UP...
FEH!
SO HE GETS TO SLEEP THE WHOLE TIME WHILE THESE NOISY PUPPETS GUARD ME?!

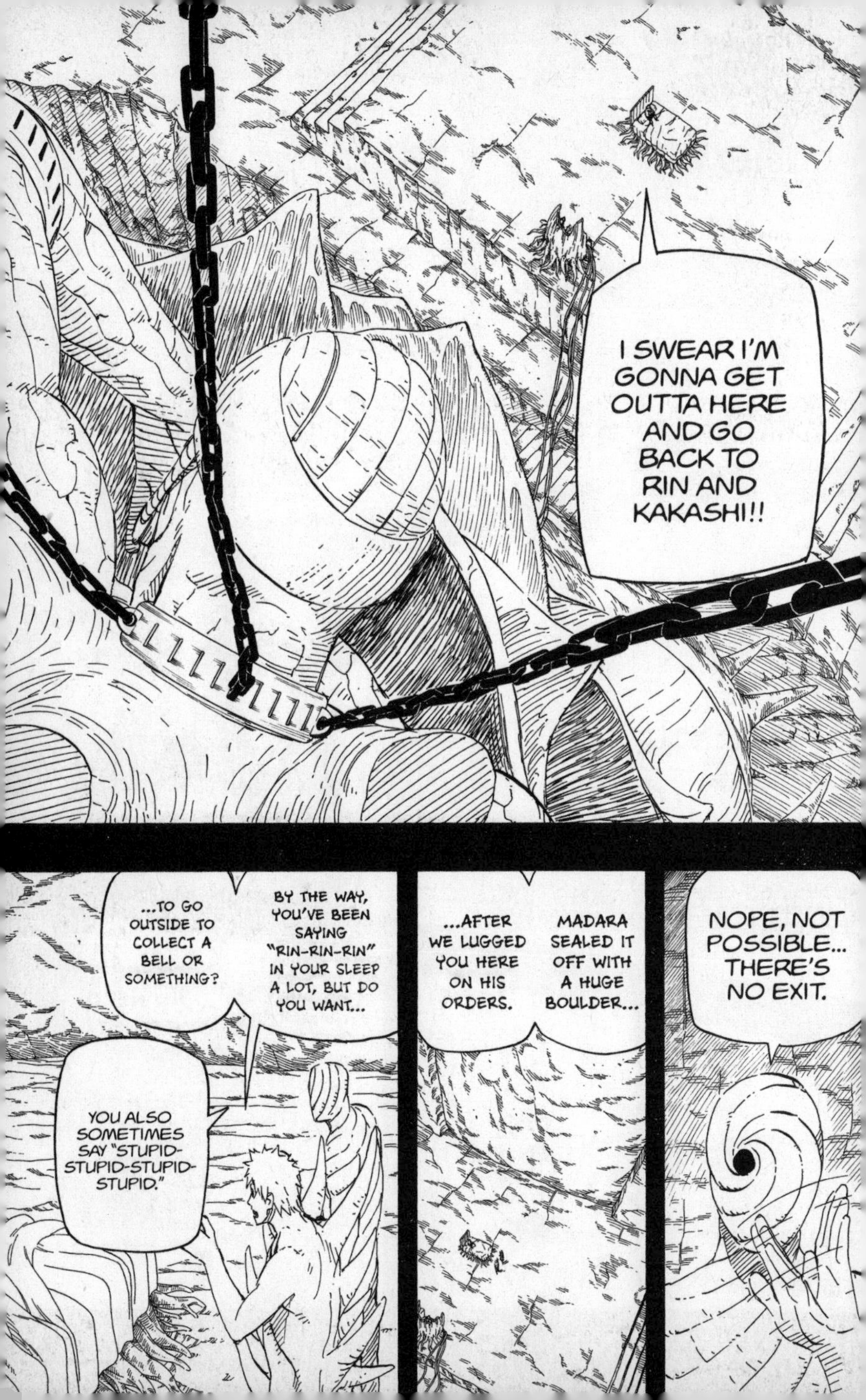
I SWEAR I'M GONNA GET OUTTA HERE AND GO BACK TO RIN AND KAKASHI!!
NOPE, NOT POSSIBLE... THERE'S NO EXIT.
MADARA SEALED IT OFF WITH A HUGE BOULDER...
...AFTER WE LUGGED YOU HERE ON HIS ORDERS.
BY THE WAY, YOU'VE BEEN SAYING "RIN-RIN-RIN" IN YOUR SLEEP A LOT, BUT DO YOU WANT...
...TO GO OUTSIDE TO COLLECT A BELL OR SOMETHING?
YOU ALSO SOMETIMES SAY "STUPID-STUPID-STUPID-STUPID."

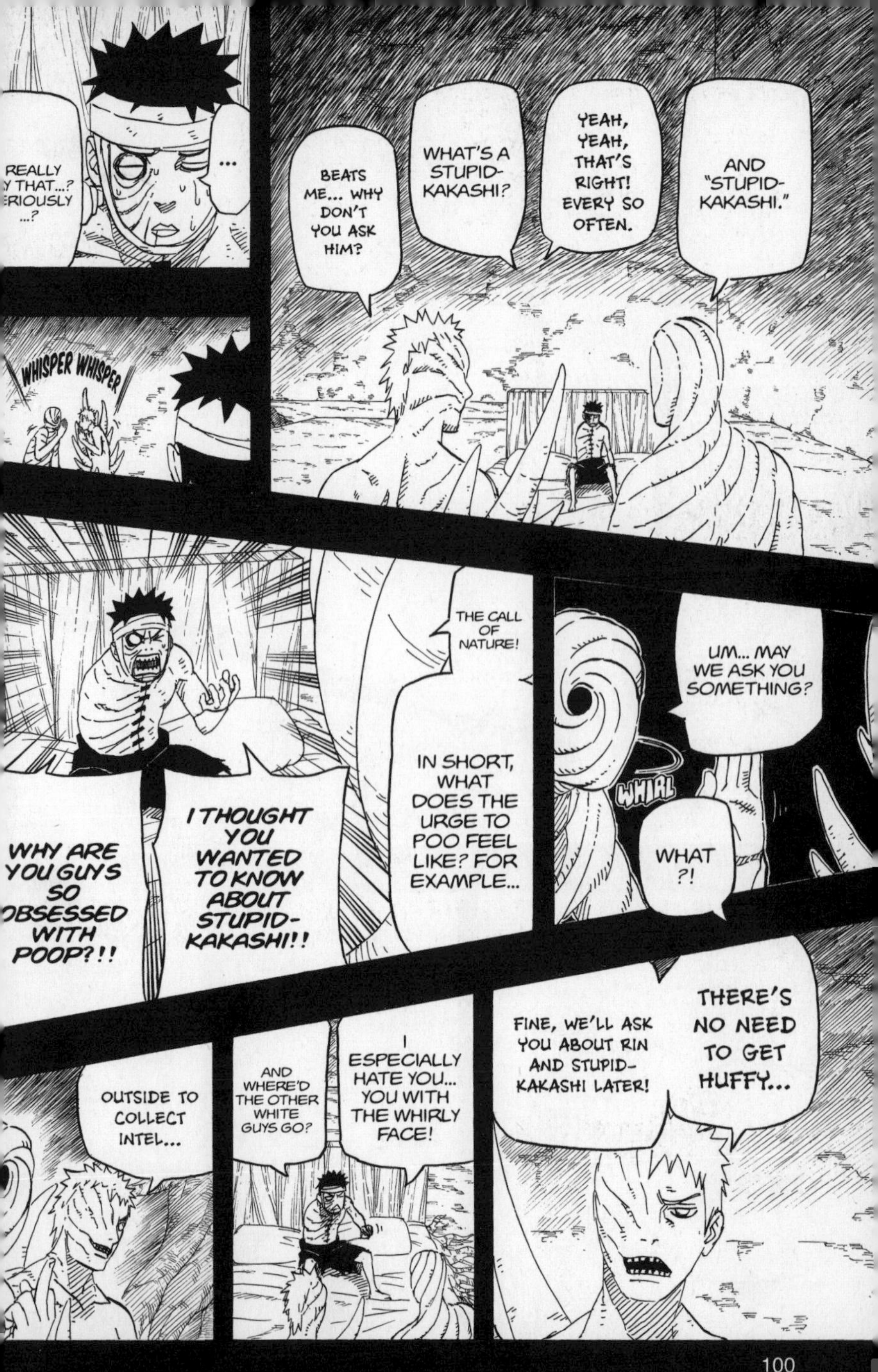
AND "STUPID-KAKASHI."
YEAH, YEAH, THAT'S RIGHT! EVERY SO OFTEN.
WHAT'S A STUPID-KAKASHI?
BEATS ME... WHY DON'T YOU ASK HIM?
...
REALLY Y THAT...? ERIOUSLY ...?
WHISPER WHISPER
UM... MAY WE ASK YOU SOMETHING?
WHIRL
WHAT ?!
THE CALL OF NATURE!
IN SHORT, WHAT DOES THE URGE TO POO FEEL LIKE? FOR EXAMPLE...
I THOUGHT YOU WANTED TO KNOW ABOUT STUPID-KAKASHI!!
WHY ARE YOU GUYS SO OBSESSED WITH POOP?!!
THERE'S NO NEED TO GET HUFFY...
FINE, WE'LL ASK YOU ABOUT RIN AND STUPID-KAKASHI LATER!
I ESPECIALLY HATE YOU... YOU WITH THE WHIRLY FACE!
AND WHERE'D THE OTHER WHITE GUYS GO?
OUTSIDE TO COLLECT INTEL...

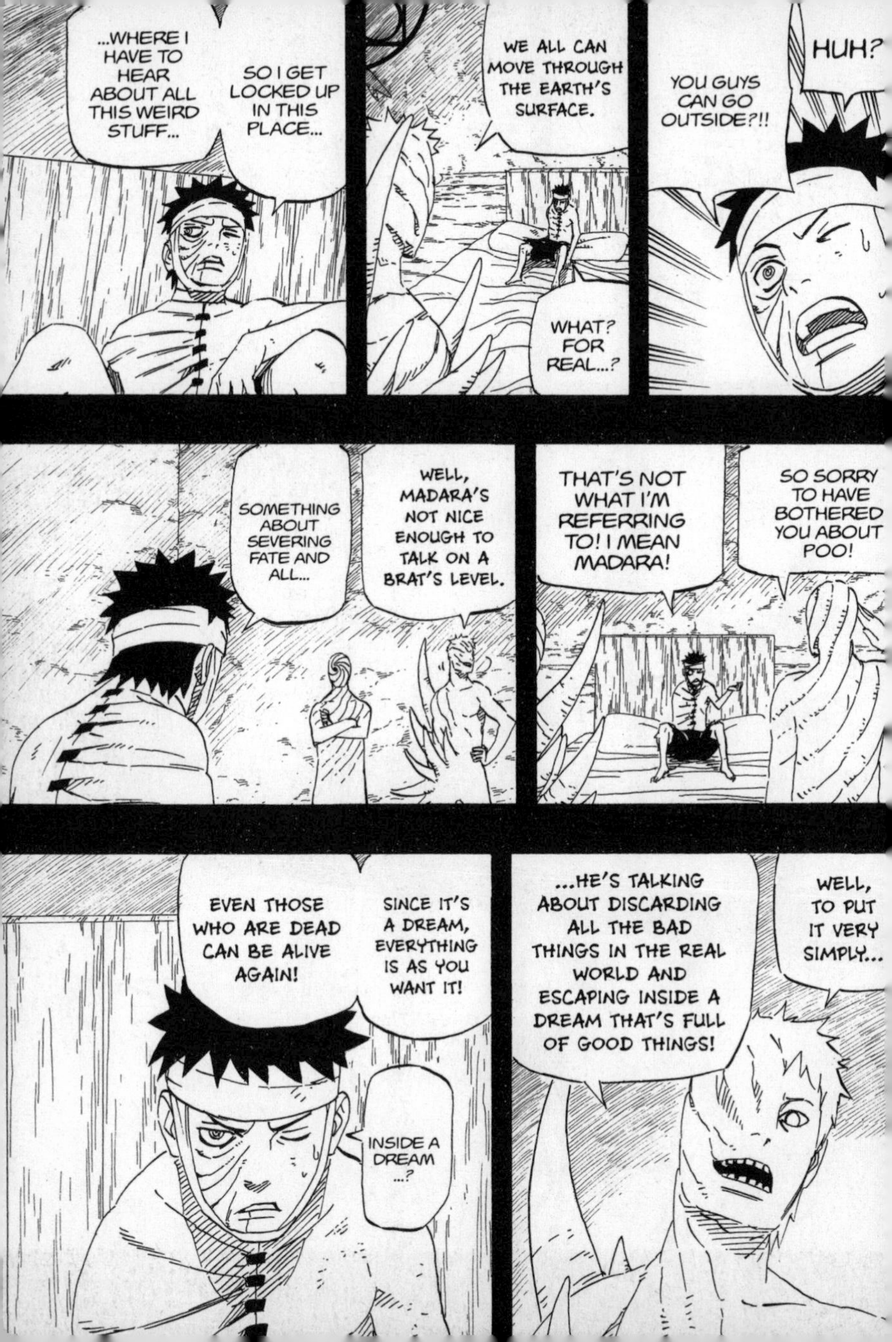
HUH?
YOU GUYS CAN GO OUTSIDE?!!
WE ALL CAN MOVE THROUGH THE EARTH'S SURFACE.
WHAT? FOR REAL...?
SO I GET LOCKED UP IN THIS PLACE...
...WHERE I HAVE TO HEAR ABOUT ALL THIS WEIRD STUFF...
SO SORRY TO HAVE BOTHERED YOU ABOUT POO!
THAT'S NOT WHAT I'M REFERRING TO! I MEAN MADARA!
WELL, MADARA'S NOT NICE ENOUGH TO TALK ON A BRAT'S LEVEL.
SOMETHING ABOUT SEVERING FATE AND ALL...
WELL, TO PUT IT VERY SIMPLY...
...HE'S TALKING ABOUT DISCARDING ALL THE BAD THINGS IN THE REAL WORLD AND ESCAPING INSIDE A DREAM THAT'S FULL OF GOOD THINGS!
SINCE IT'S A DREAM, EVERYTHING IS AS YOU WANT IT!
EVEN THOSE WHO ARE DEAD CAN BE ALIVE AGAIN!
INSIDE A DREAM ...?

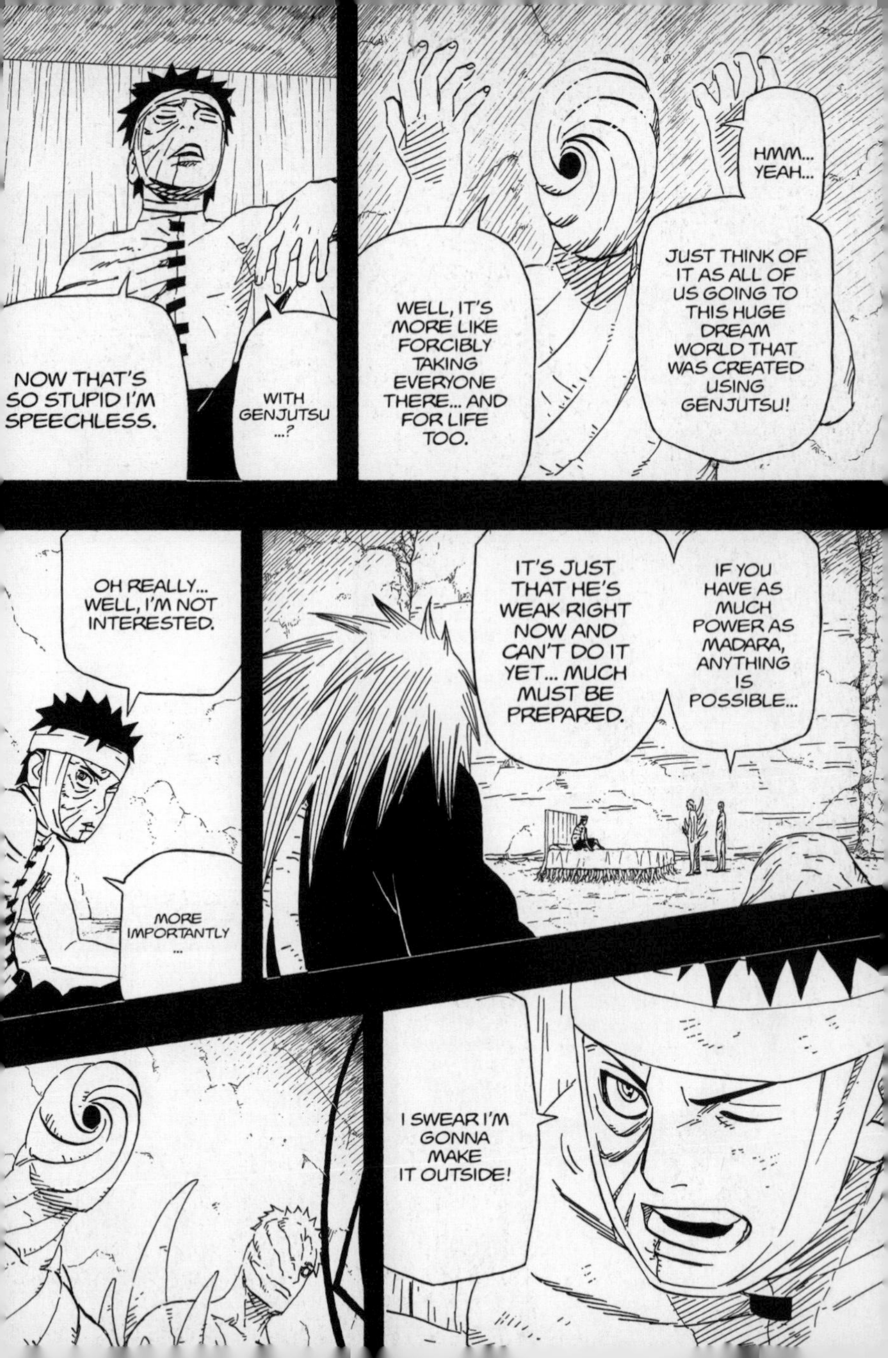
HMM... YEAH...
JUST THINK OF IT AS ALL OF US GOING TO THIS HUGE DREAM WORLD THAT WAS CREATED USING GENJUTSU!
WELL, IT'S MORE LIKE FORCIBLY TAKING EVERYONE THERE... AND FOR LIFE TOO.
WITH GENJUTSU ...?
NOW THAT'S SO STUPID I'M SPEECHLESS.
IF YOU HAVE AS MUCH POWER AS MADARA, ANYTHING IS POSSIBLE...
IT'S JUST THAT HE'S WEAK RIGHT NOW AND CAN'T DO IT YET... MUCH MUST BE PREPARED.
OH REALLY... WELL, I'M NOT INTERESTED.
MORE IMPORTANTLY ...
I SWEAR I'M GONNA MAKE IT OUTSIDE!

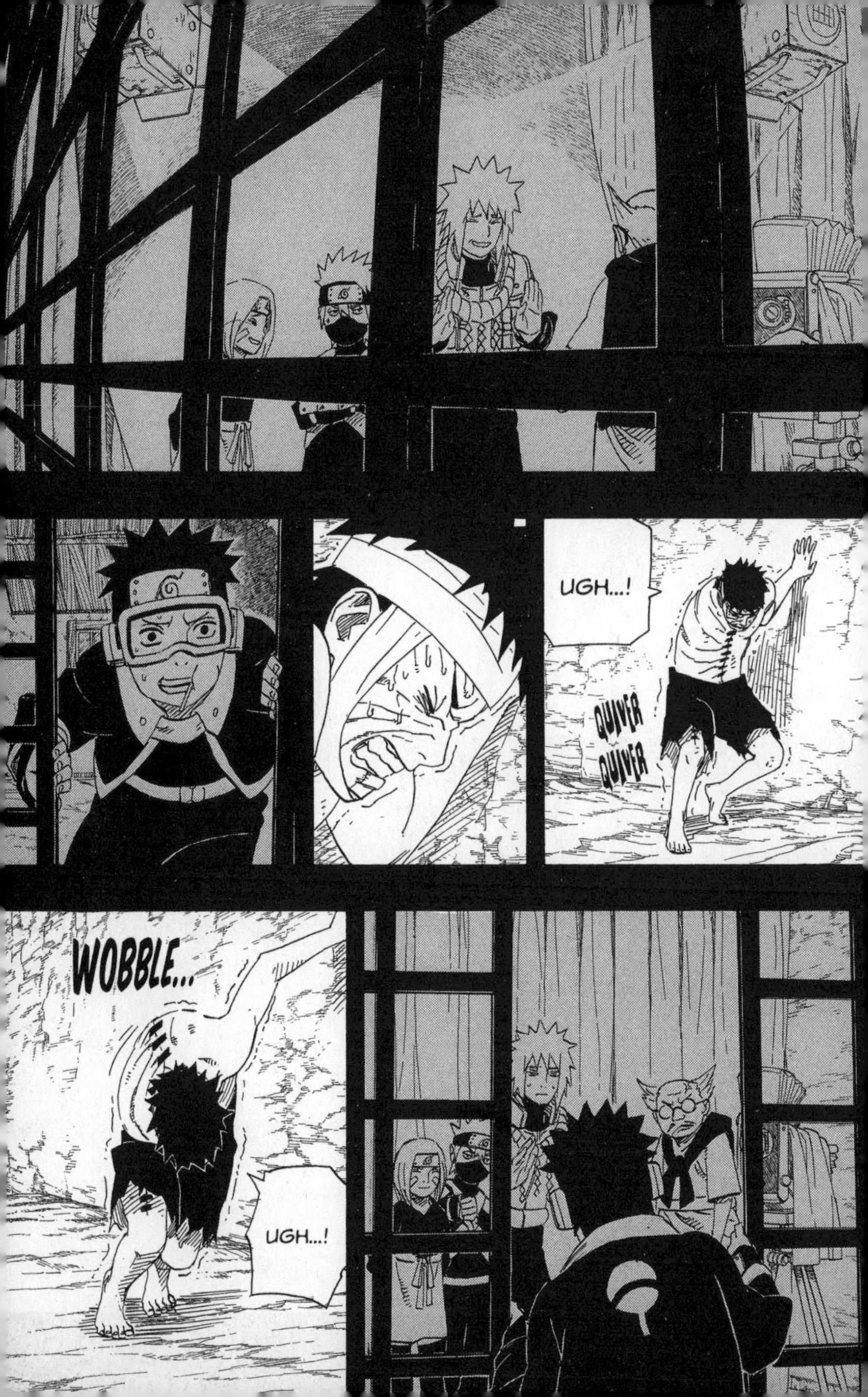
UGH...!
QUIVER QUIVER
WOBBLE...
UGH...!

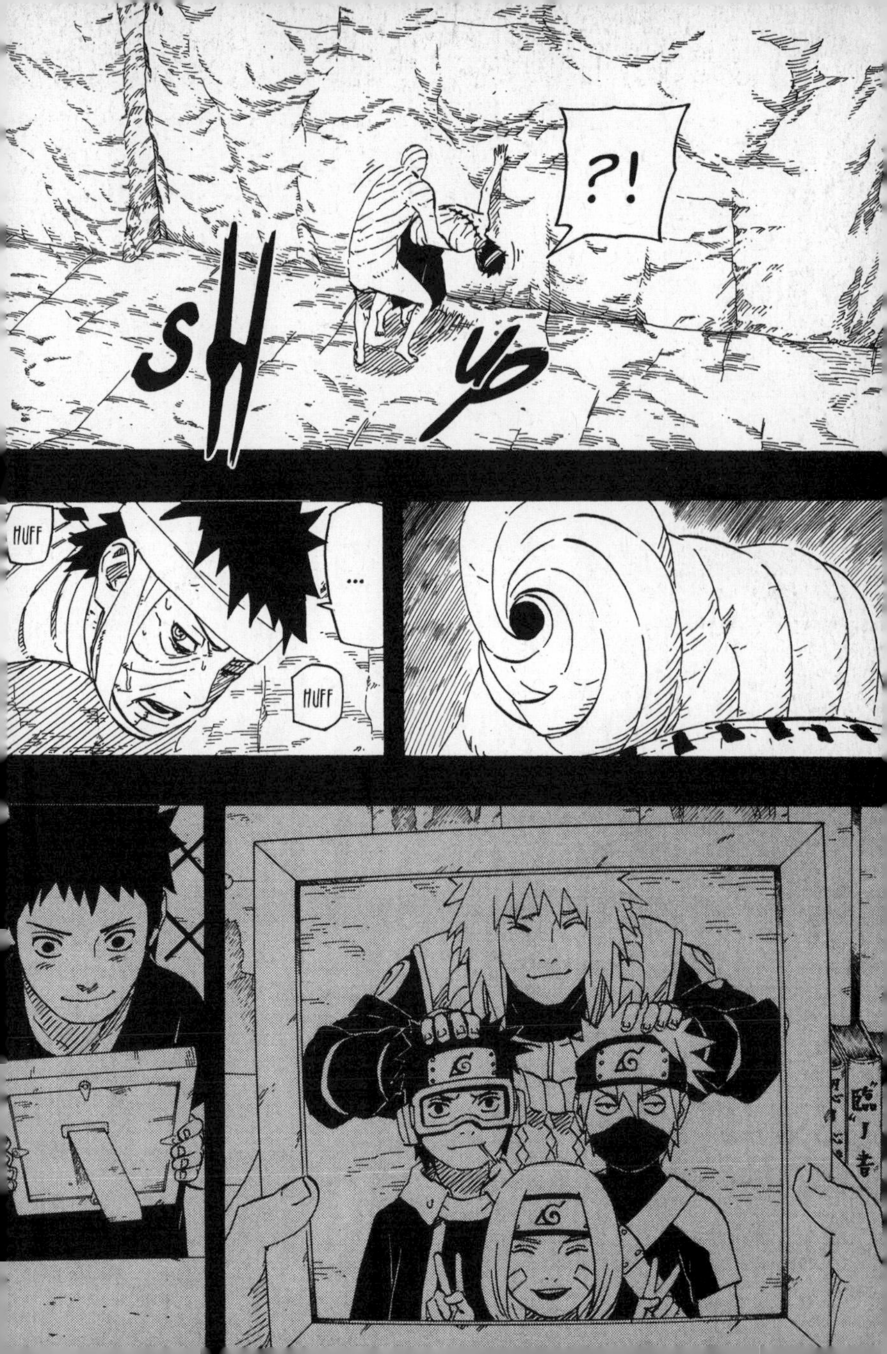
?!
SHUP
HUFF
...
HUFF

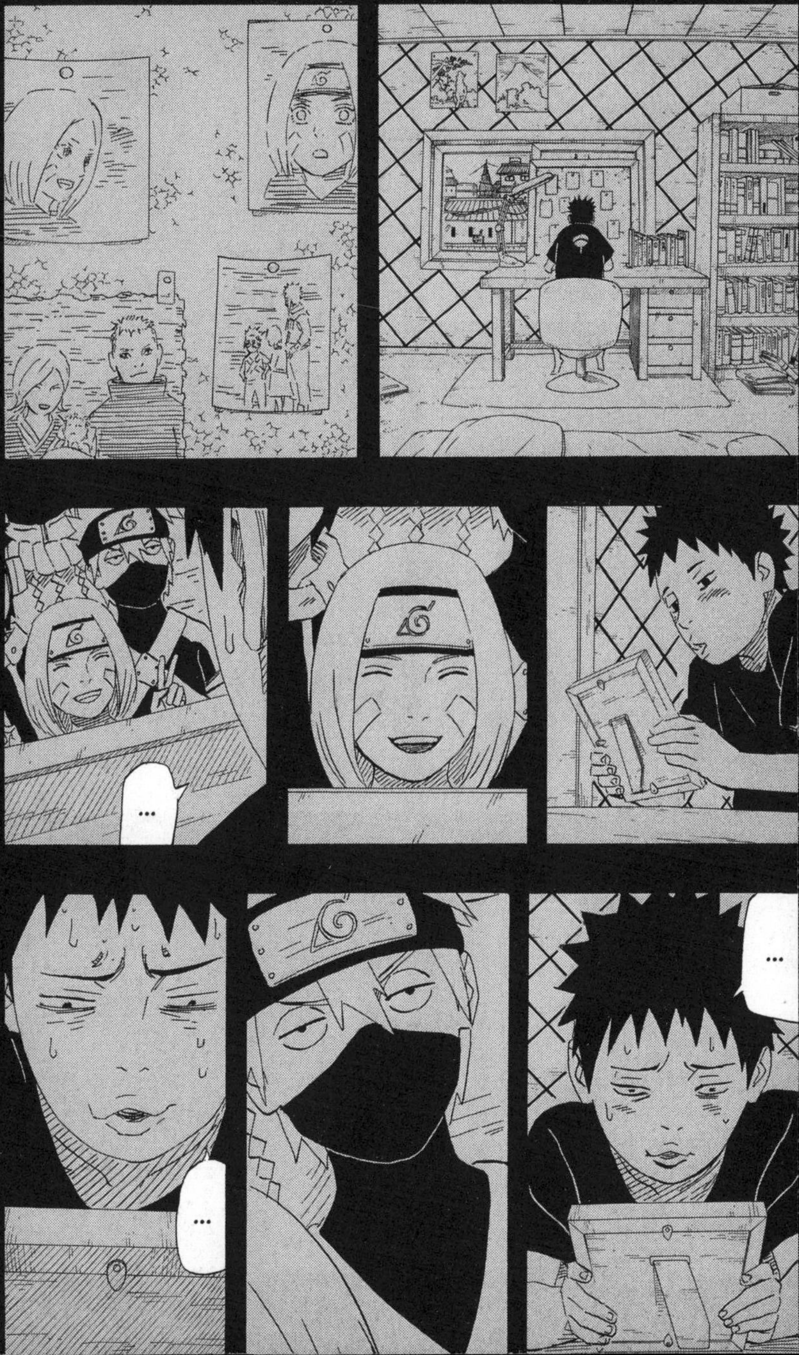
...
...
...

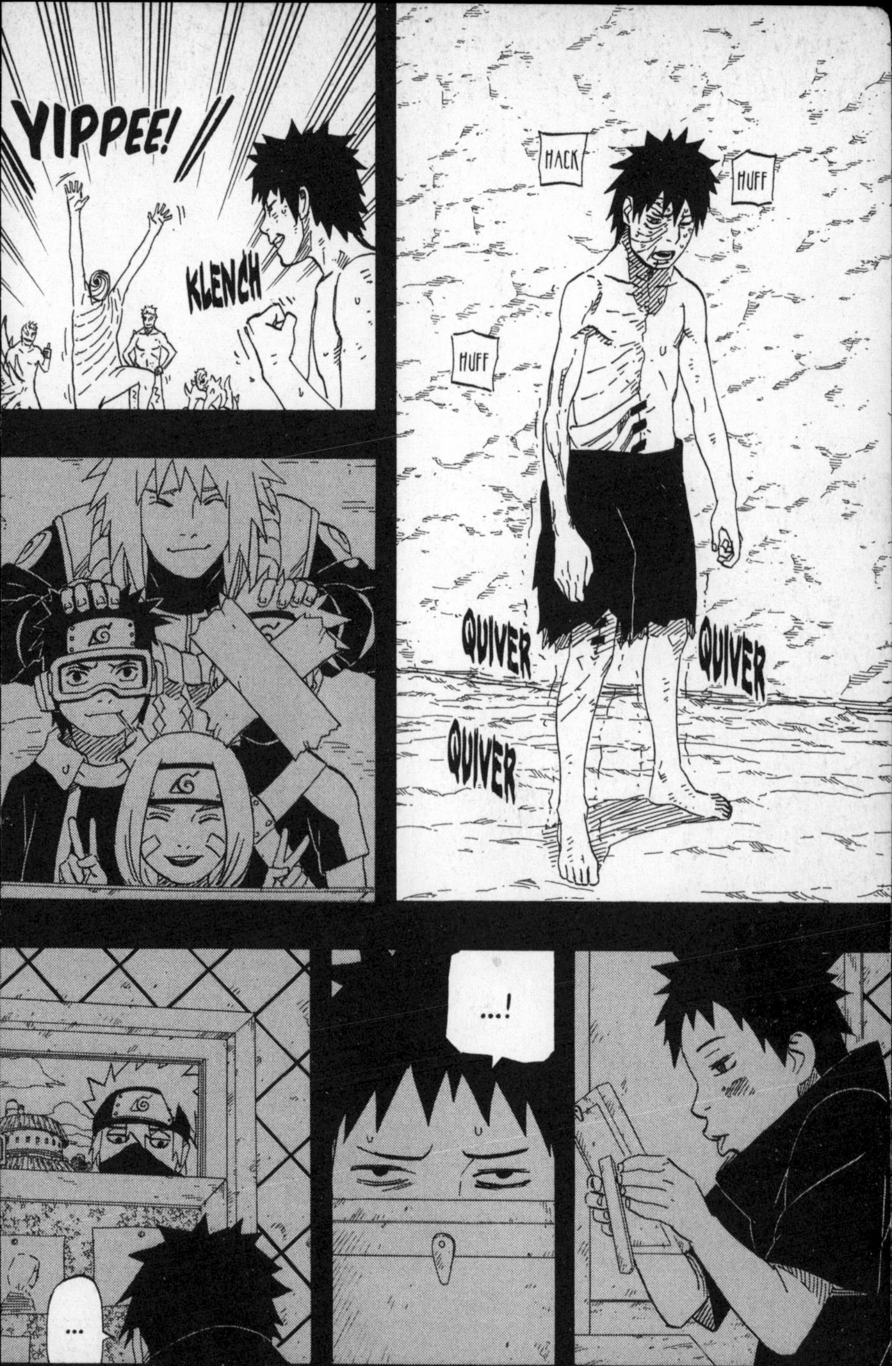
HUFF
HACK
HUFF
QUIVER
QUIVER
QUIVER
YIPPEE!
KLENCH
...!
...

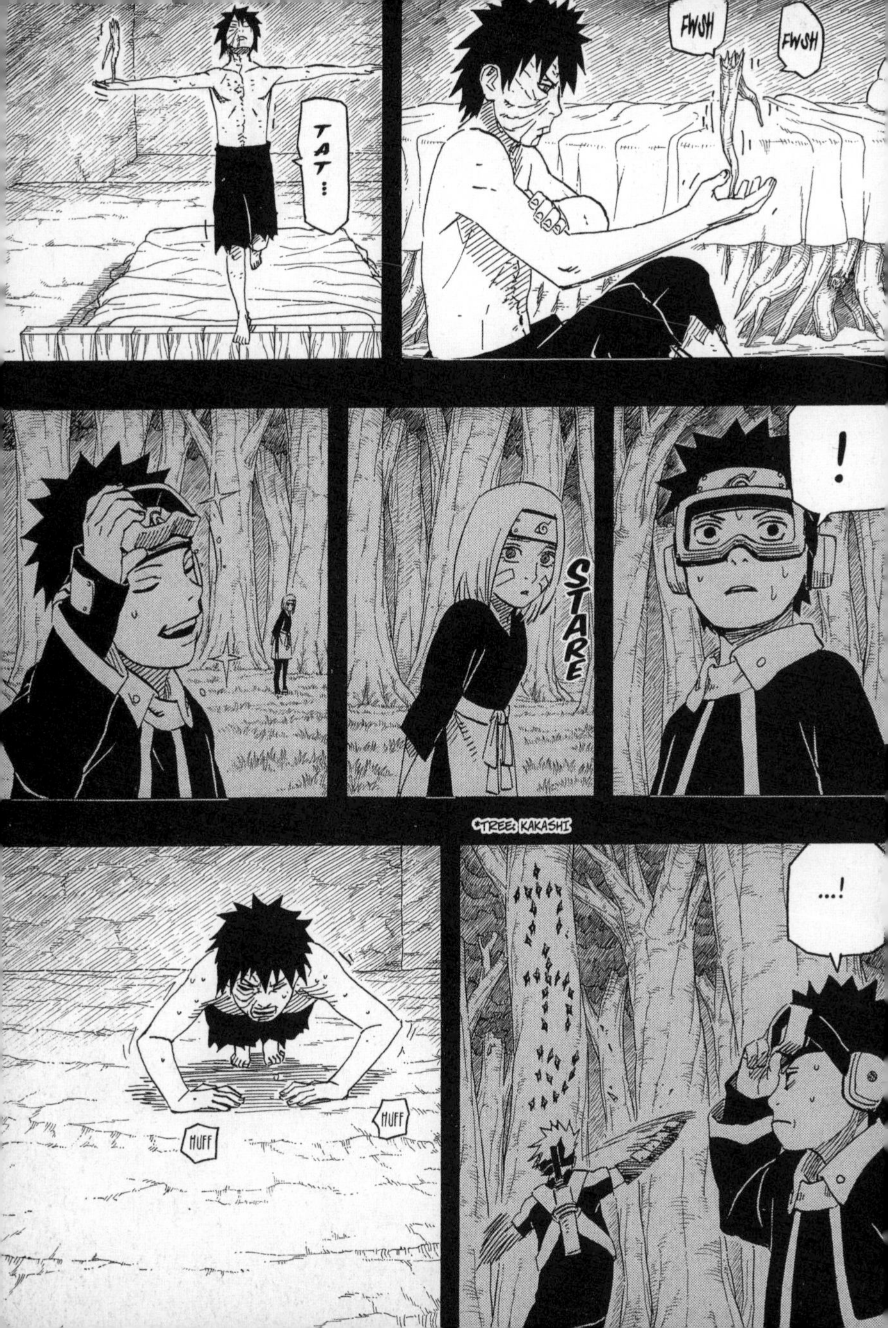
FWSH
FWSH
TAT...
!
STARE
*TREE: KAKASHI
...!
HUFF
HUFF

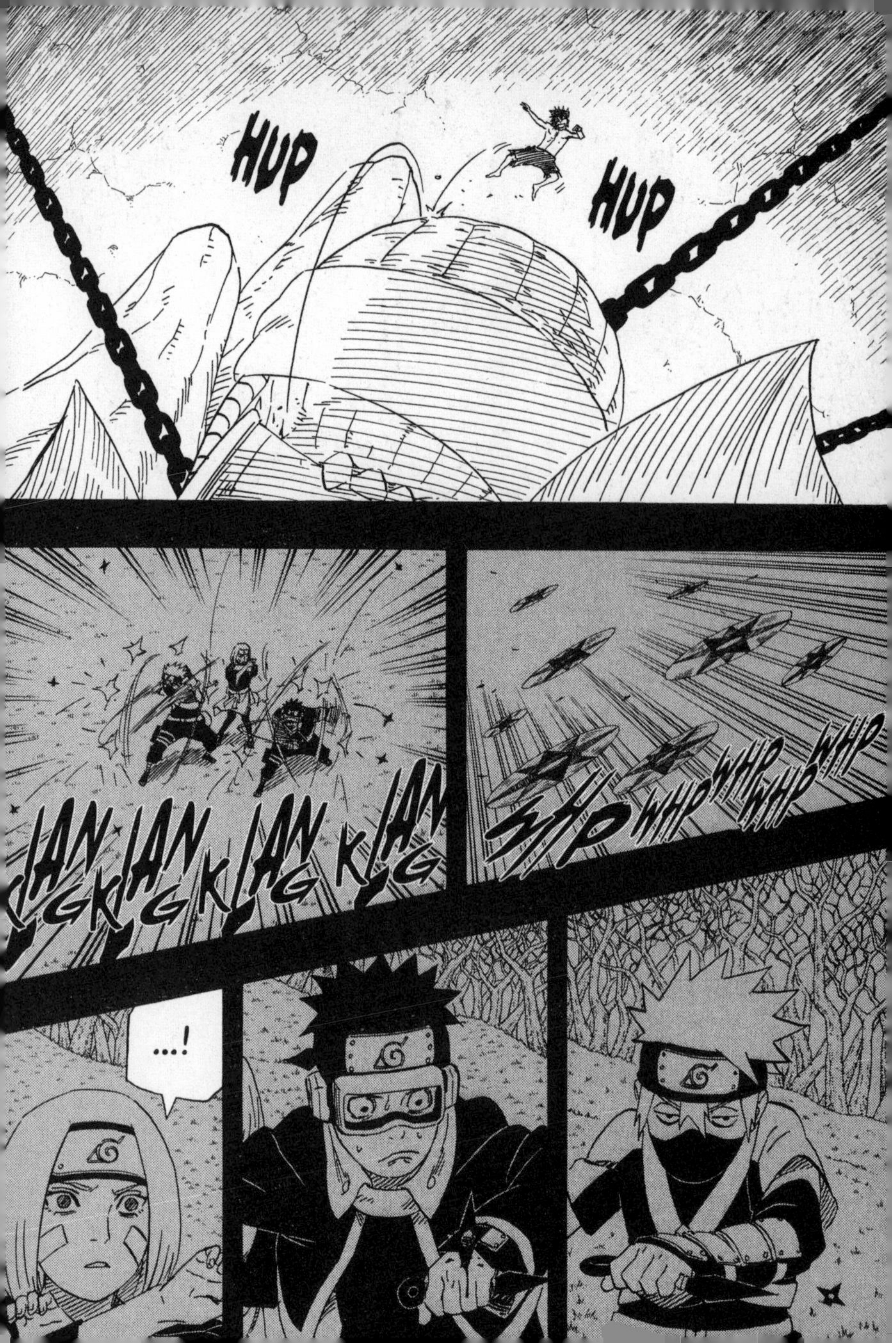
HUP
HUP
WHP WHP WHP WHP WHP
KLANG KLANG KLANG KLANG
...!

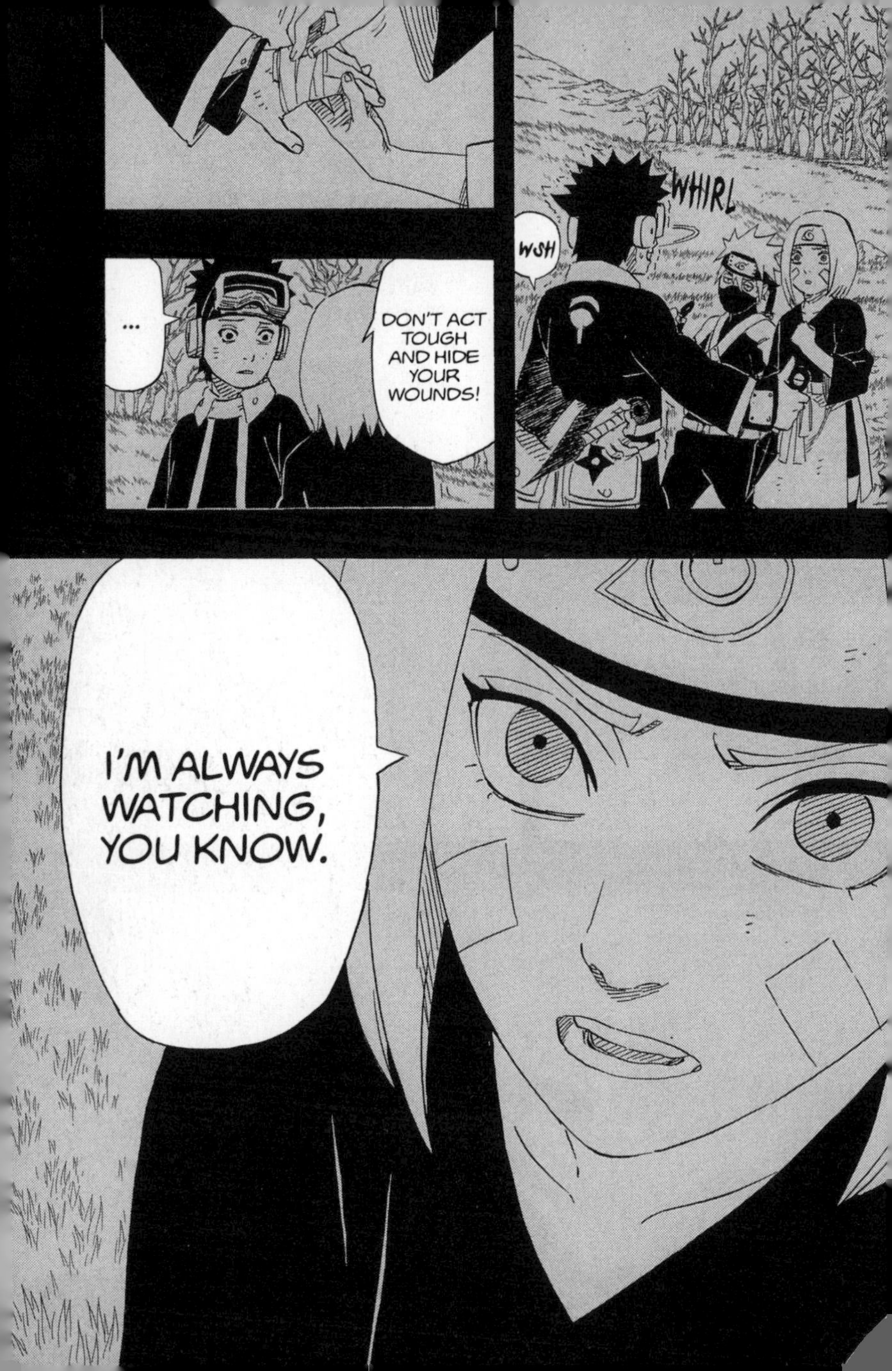
WHIRL
WSH
DON'T ACT TOUGH AND HIDE YOUR WOUNDS!
...
I'M ALWAYS WATCHING, YOU KNOW.

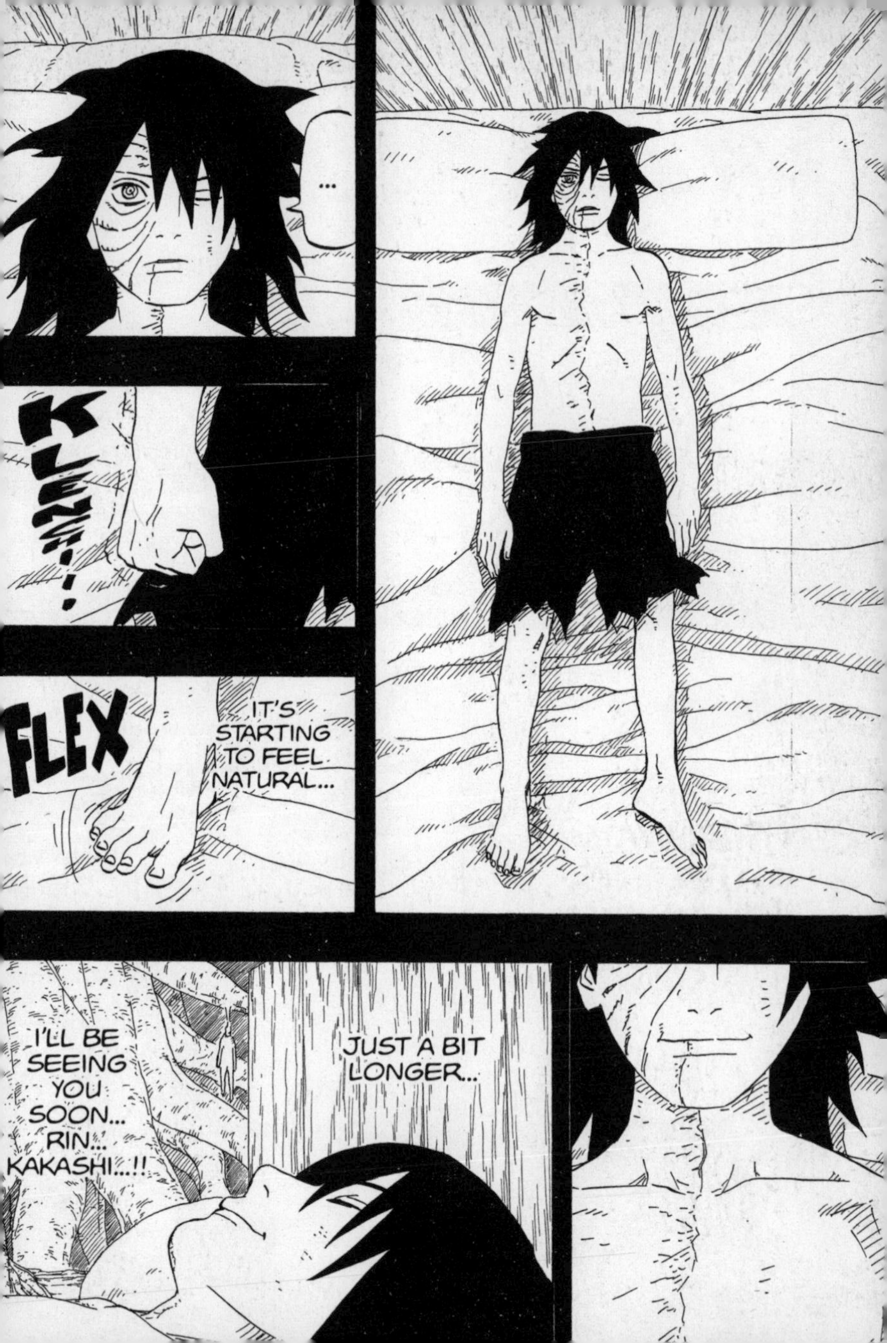
...
KLENCH!!
FLEX
IT'S STARTING TO FEEL NATURAL...
JUST A BIT LONGER...
I'LL BE SEEING YOU SOON... RIN... KAKASHI...!!

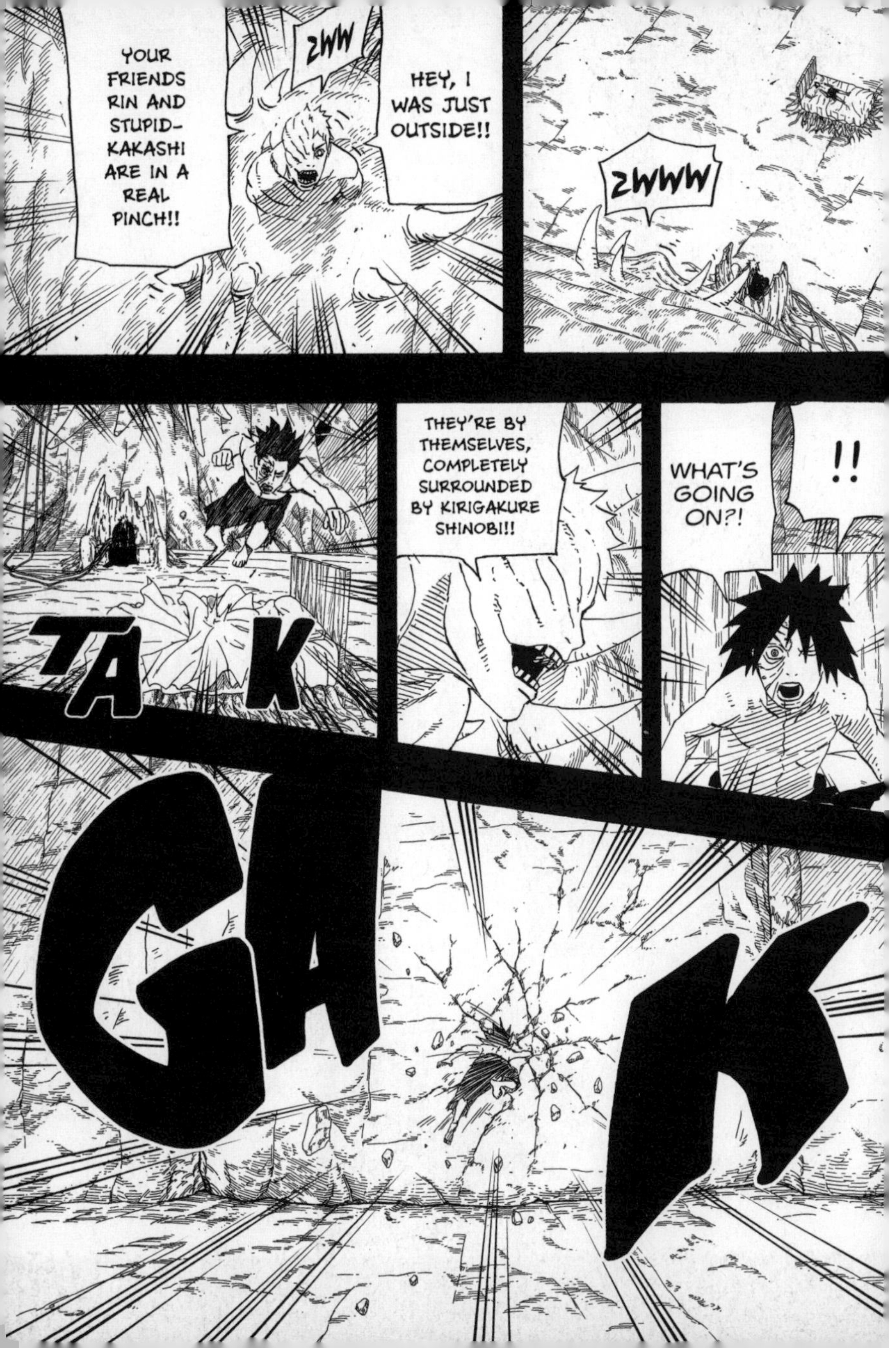
ZWWW
HEY, I WAS JUST OUTSIDE!!
ZWW
YOUR FRIENDS RIN AND STUPID-KAKASHI ARE IN A REAL PINCH!!
!!
WHAT'S GOING ON?!
THEY'RE BY THEMSELVES, COMPLETELY SURROUNDED BY KIRIGAKURE SHINOBI!!
TAK
GAK

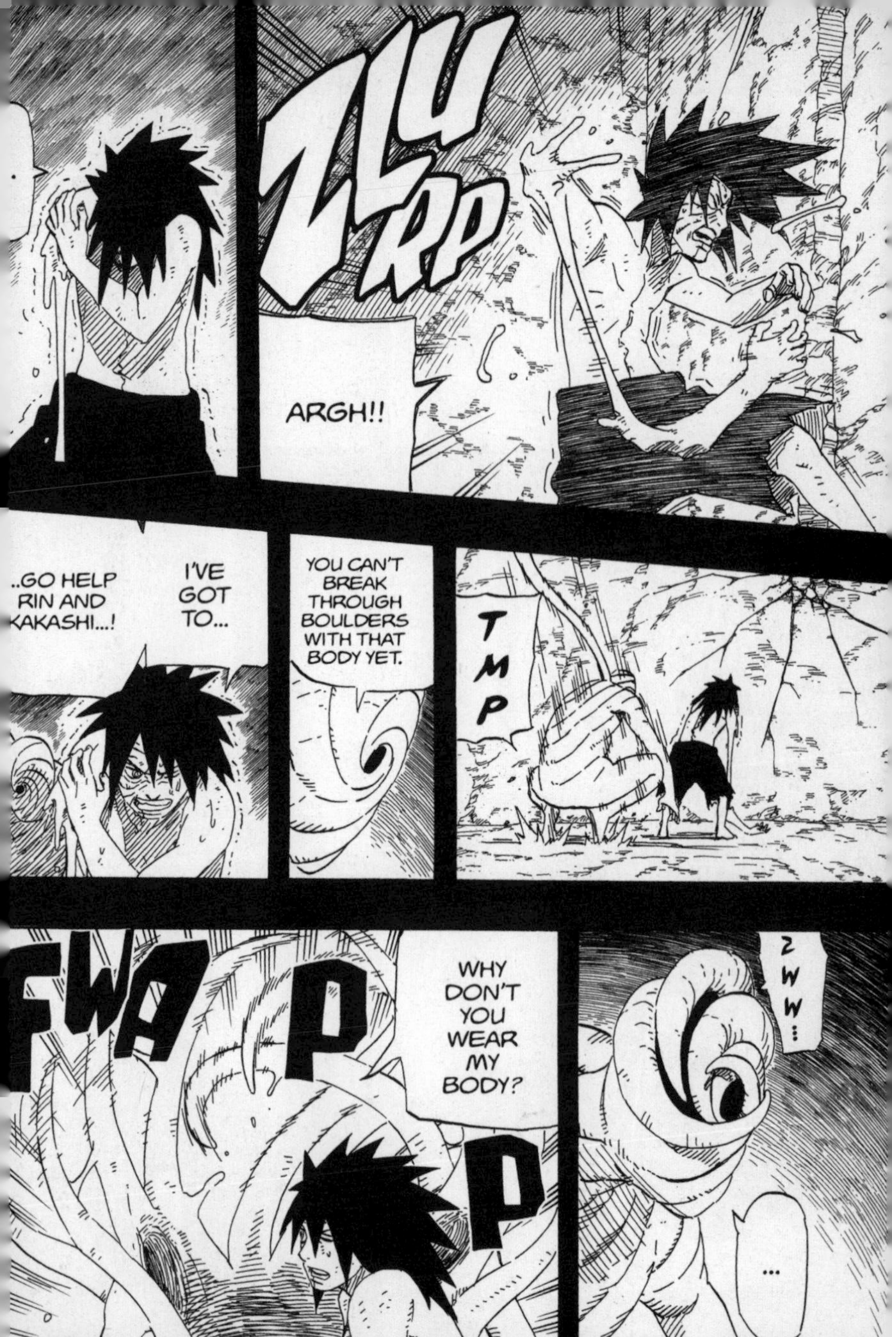
ZLURRP
ARGH!!
TMP
YOU CAN'T BREAK THROUGH BOULDERS WITH THAT BODY YET.
I'VE GOT TO...
...GO HELP RIN AND KAKASHI...!
ZWW...
...
FWAP
WHY DON'T YOU WEAR MY BODY?
P
P

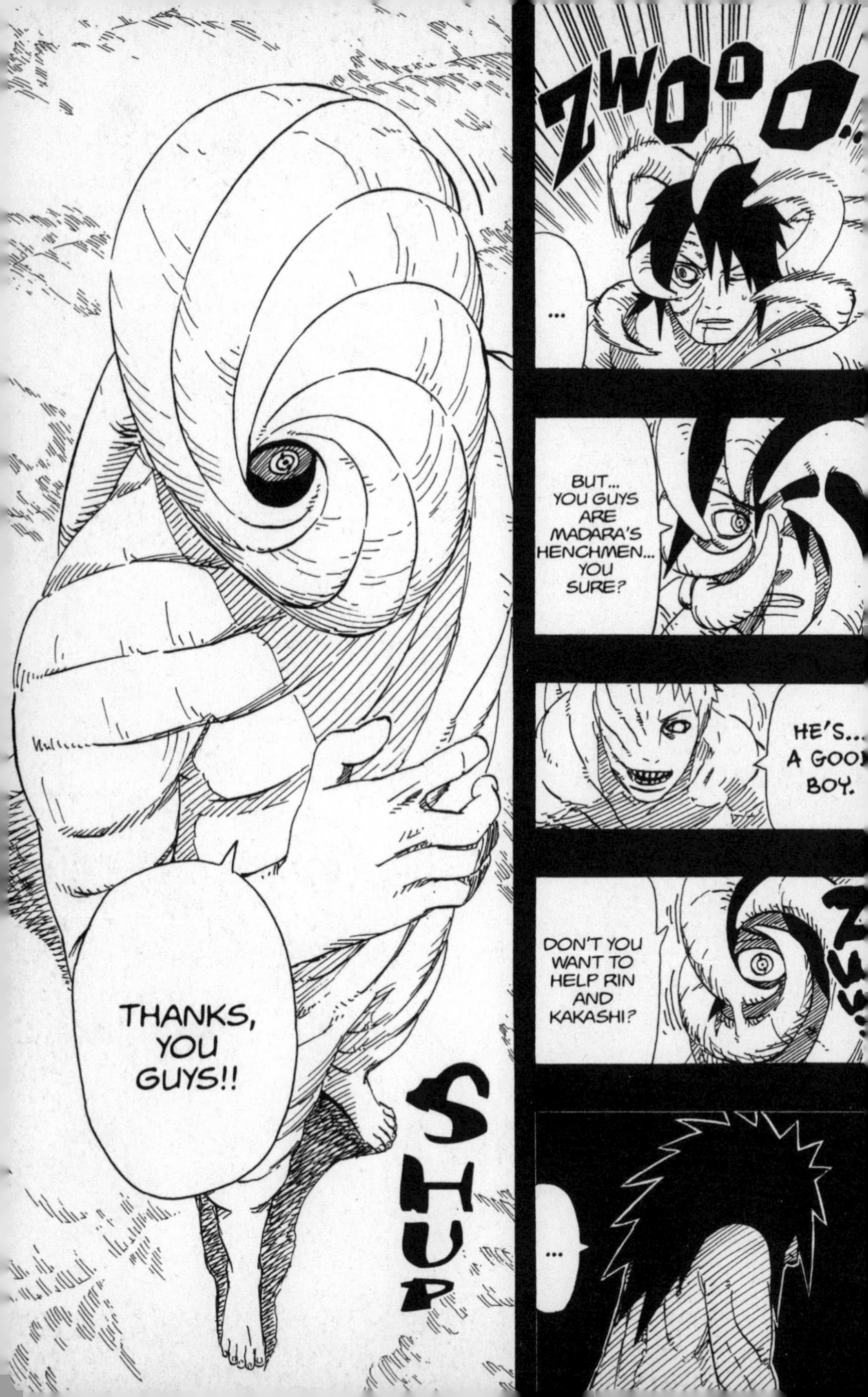
ZWOOO..
...
BUT... YOU GUYS ARE MADARA'S HENCHMEN... YOU SURE?
HE'S... A GOO BOY.
DON'T YOU WANT TO HELP RIN AND KAKASHI?
...
SHUP
THANKS, YOU GUYS!!

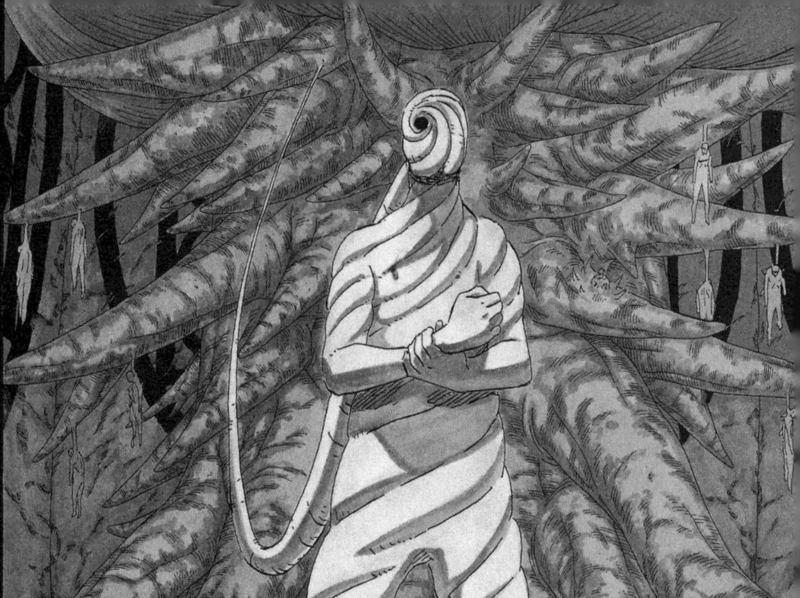

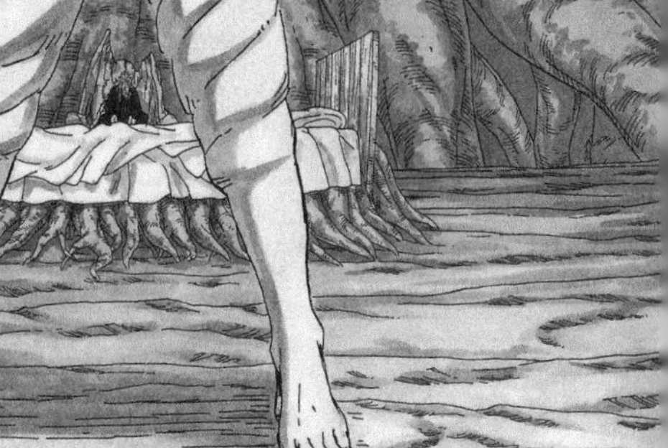

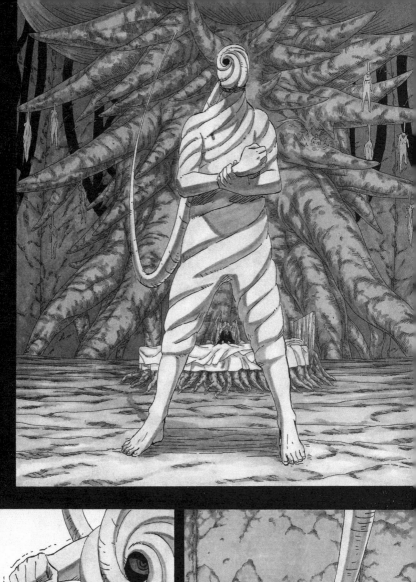

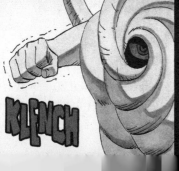

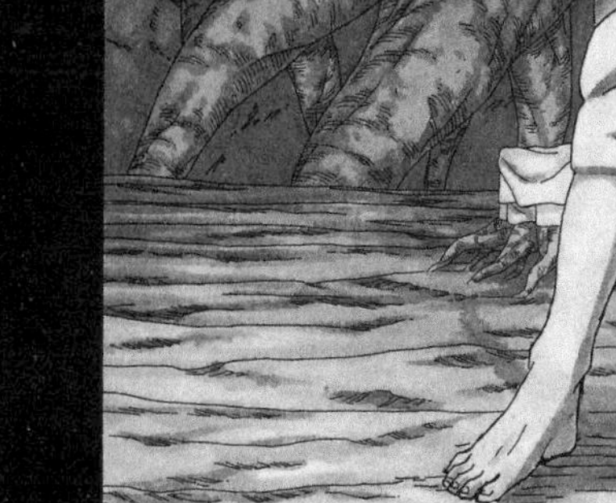
KLENCH

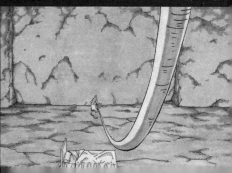

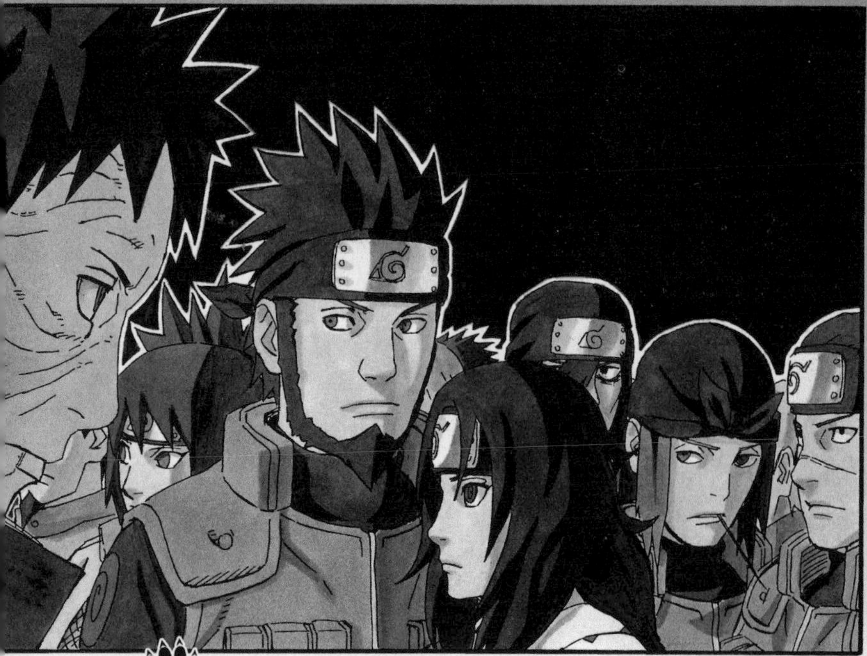

Number 604: Reunion, and Then...

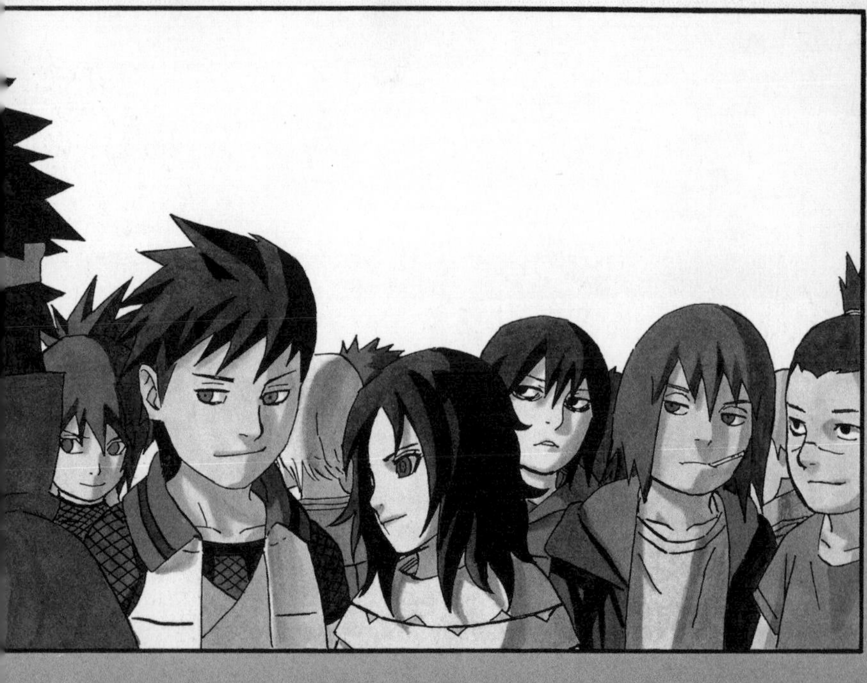

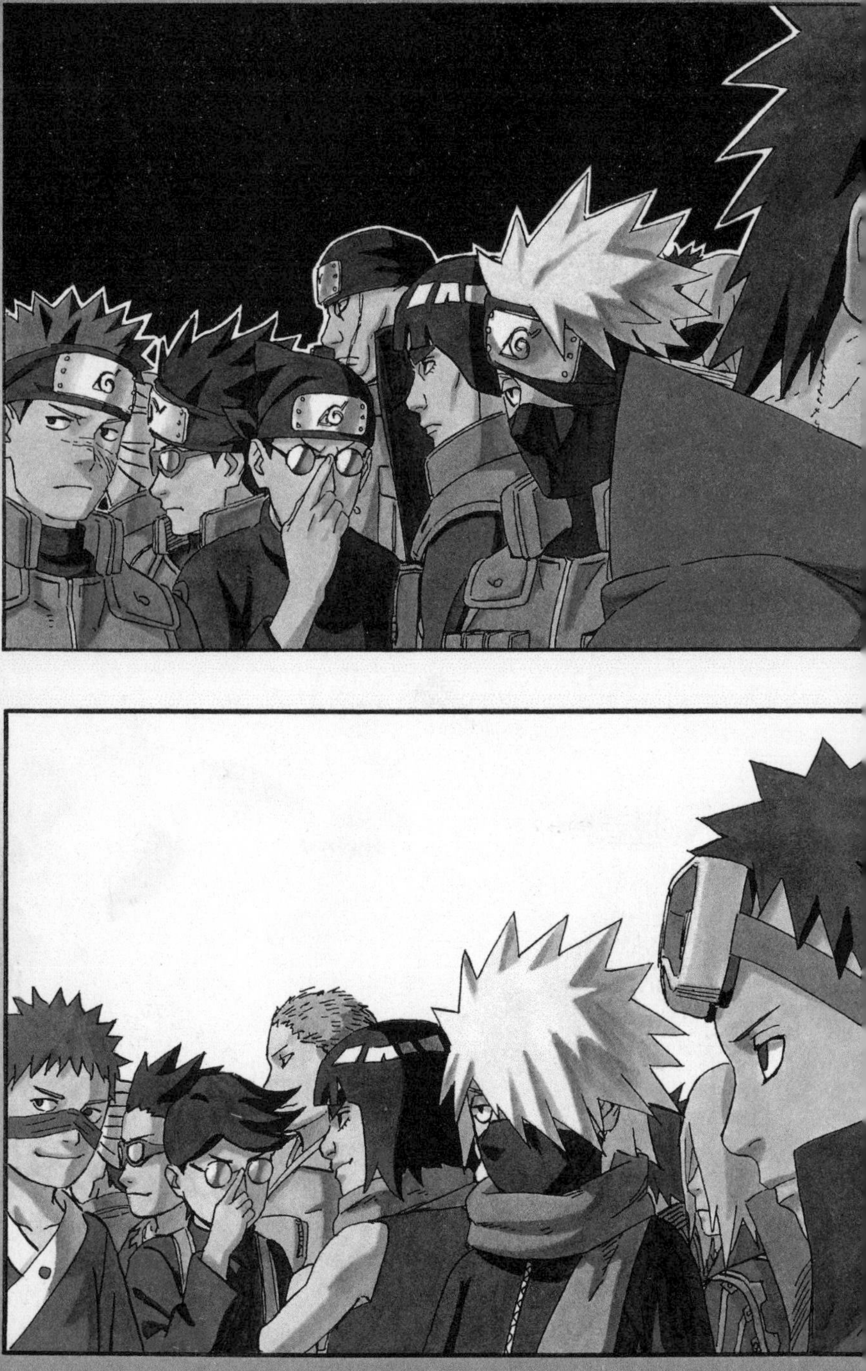

NARUTO

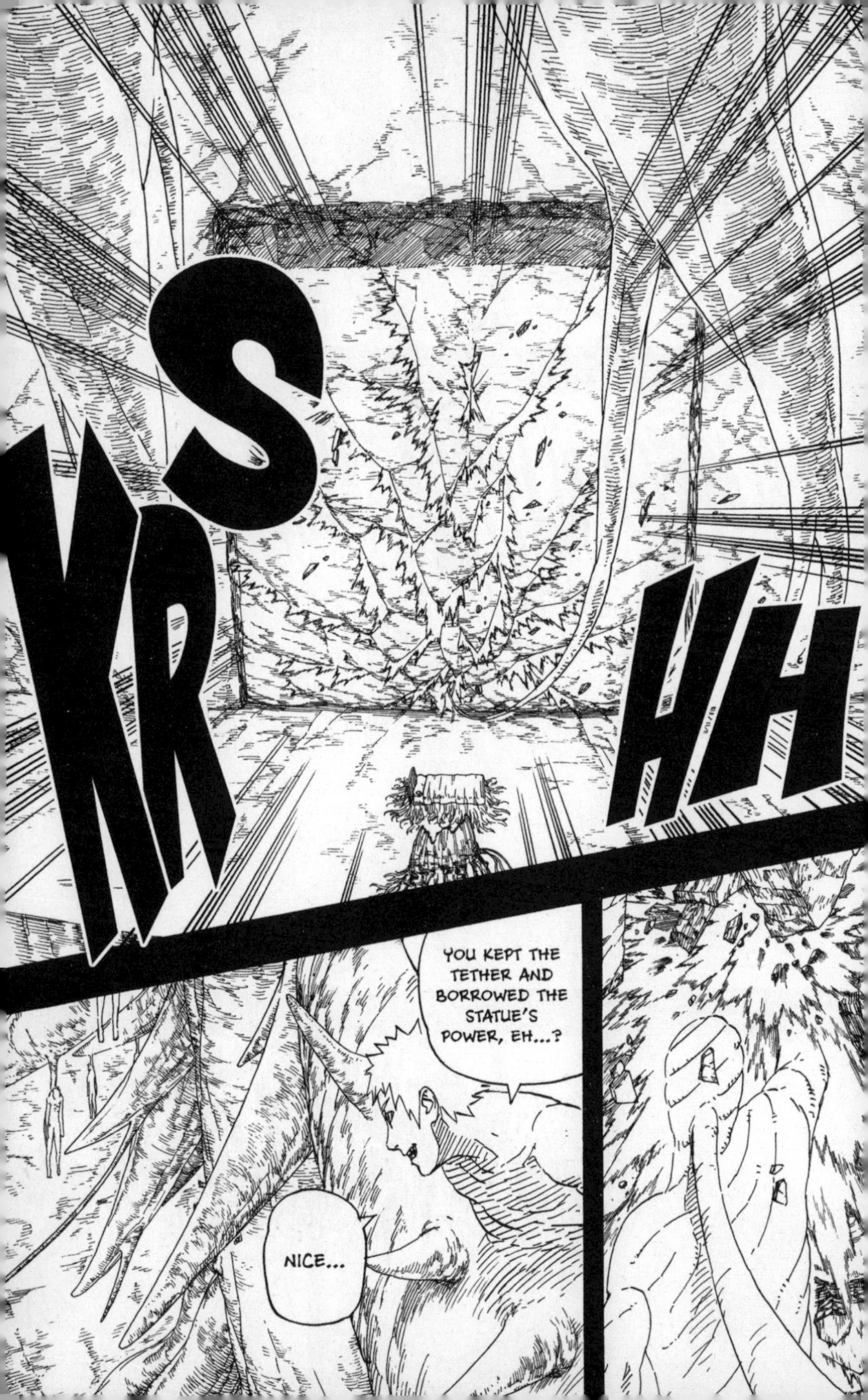
KRSHH
YOU KEPT THE TETHER AND BORROWED THE STATUE'S POWER, EH...?
NICE...

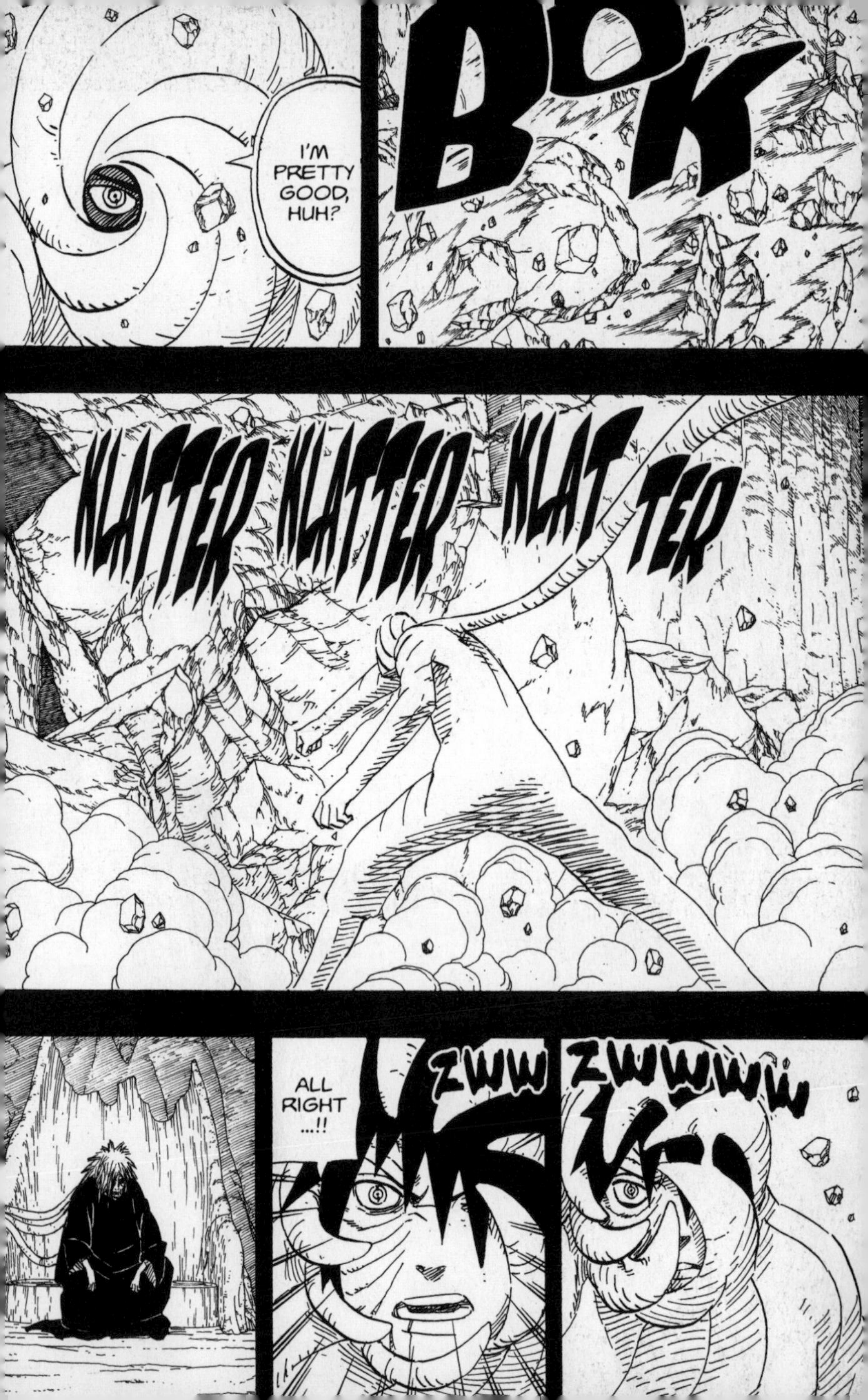
BDOK
I'M PRETTY GOOD, HUH?
KLATTER KLATTER KLAT TER
ZWWWWW
ALL RIGHT ...!!
ZWW

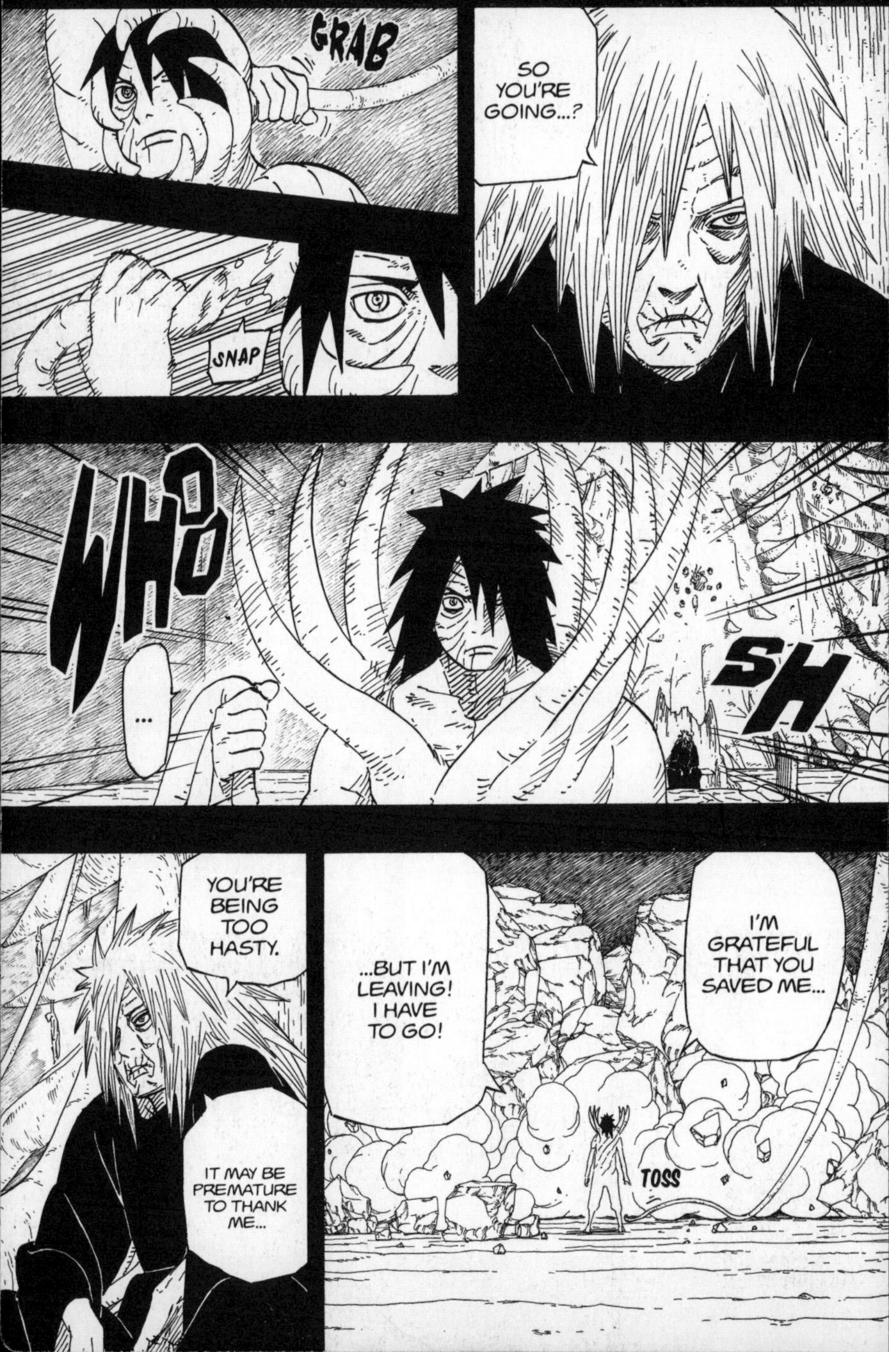
SO YOU'RE GOING...?
GRAB
SNAP
SH
WHO
...
I'M GRATEFUL THAT YOU SAVED ME...
...BUT I'M LEAVING! I HAVE TO GO!
TOSS
YOU'RE BEING TOO HASTY.
IT MAY BE PREMATURE TO THANK ME...

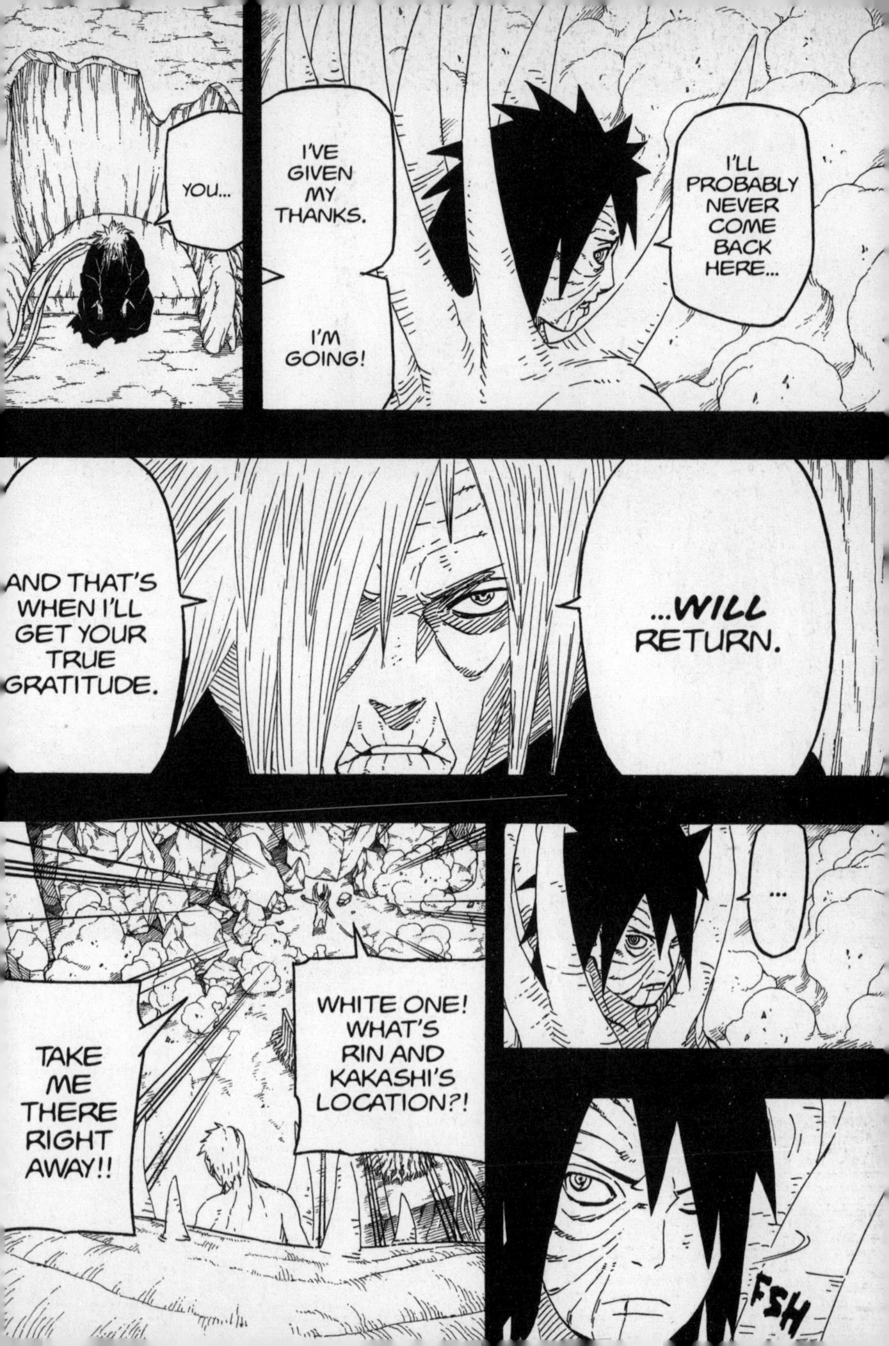
I'LL PROBABLY NEVER COME BACK HERE...
I'VE GIVEN MY THANKS.
I'M GOING!
YOU...
...WILL RETURN.
AND THAT'S WHEN I'LL GET YOUR TRUE GRATITUDE.
...
FSH
WHITE ONE! WHAT'S RIN AND KAKASHI'S LOCATION?!
TAKE ME THERE RIGHT AWAY!!

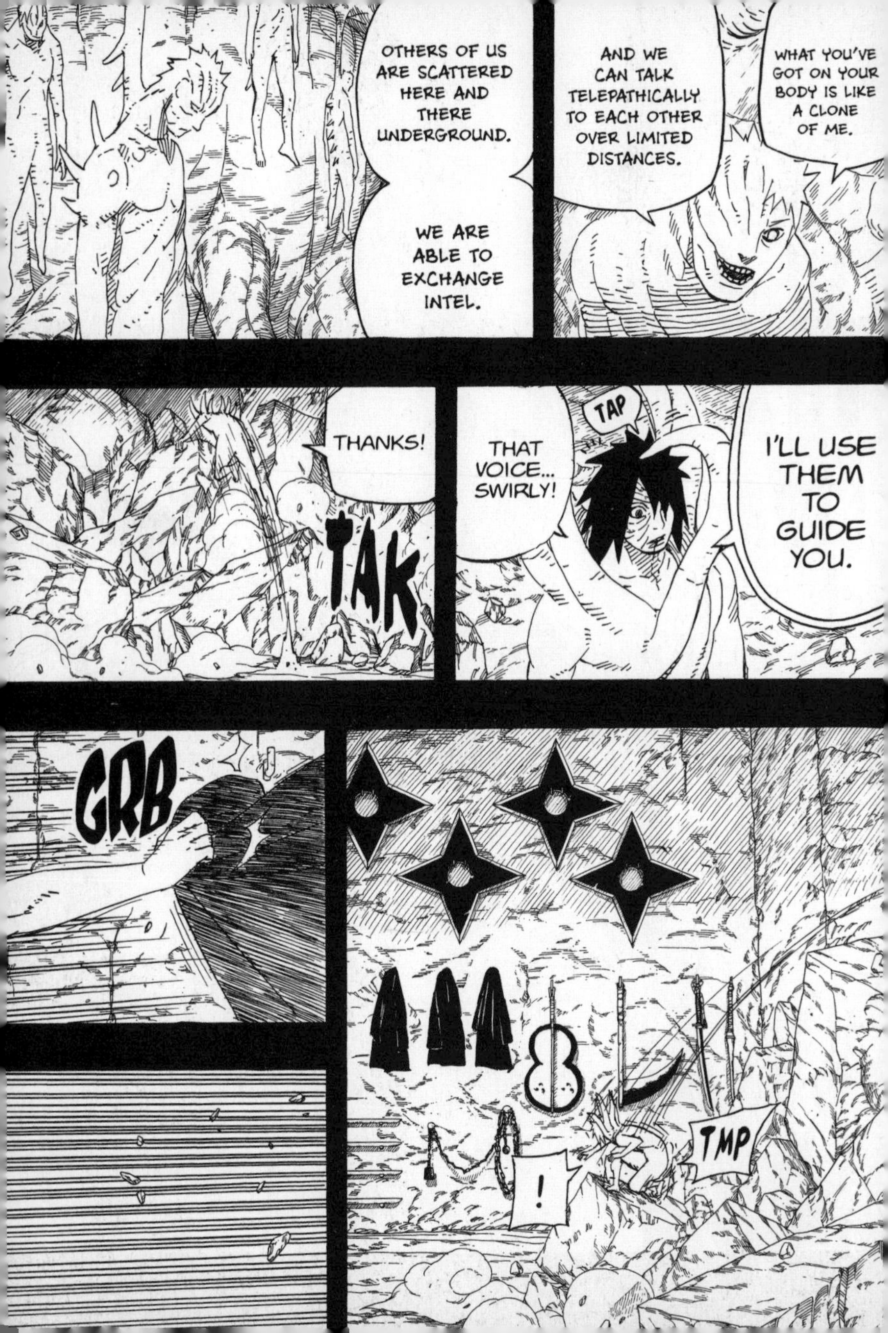
WHAT YOU'VE GOT ON YOUR BODY IS LIKE A CLONE OF ME.
AND WE CAN TALK TELEPATHICALLY TO EACH OTHER OVER LIMITED DISTANCES.
OTHERS OF US ARE SCATTERED HERE AND THERE UNDERGROUND.
WE ARE ABLE TO EXCHANGE INTEL.
I'LL USE THEM TO GUIDE YOU.
TAP
THAT VOICE... SWIRLY!
THANKS!
TAK
TMP
!
GRB

...

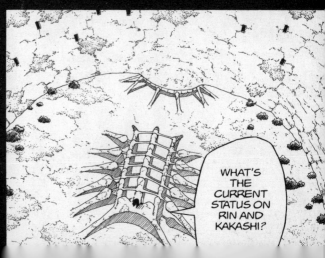

WHAT'S THE CURRENT STATUS ON RIN AND KAKASHI?

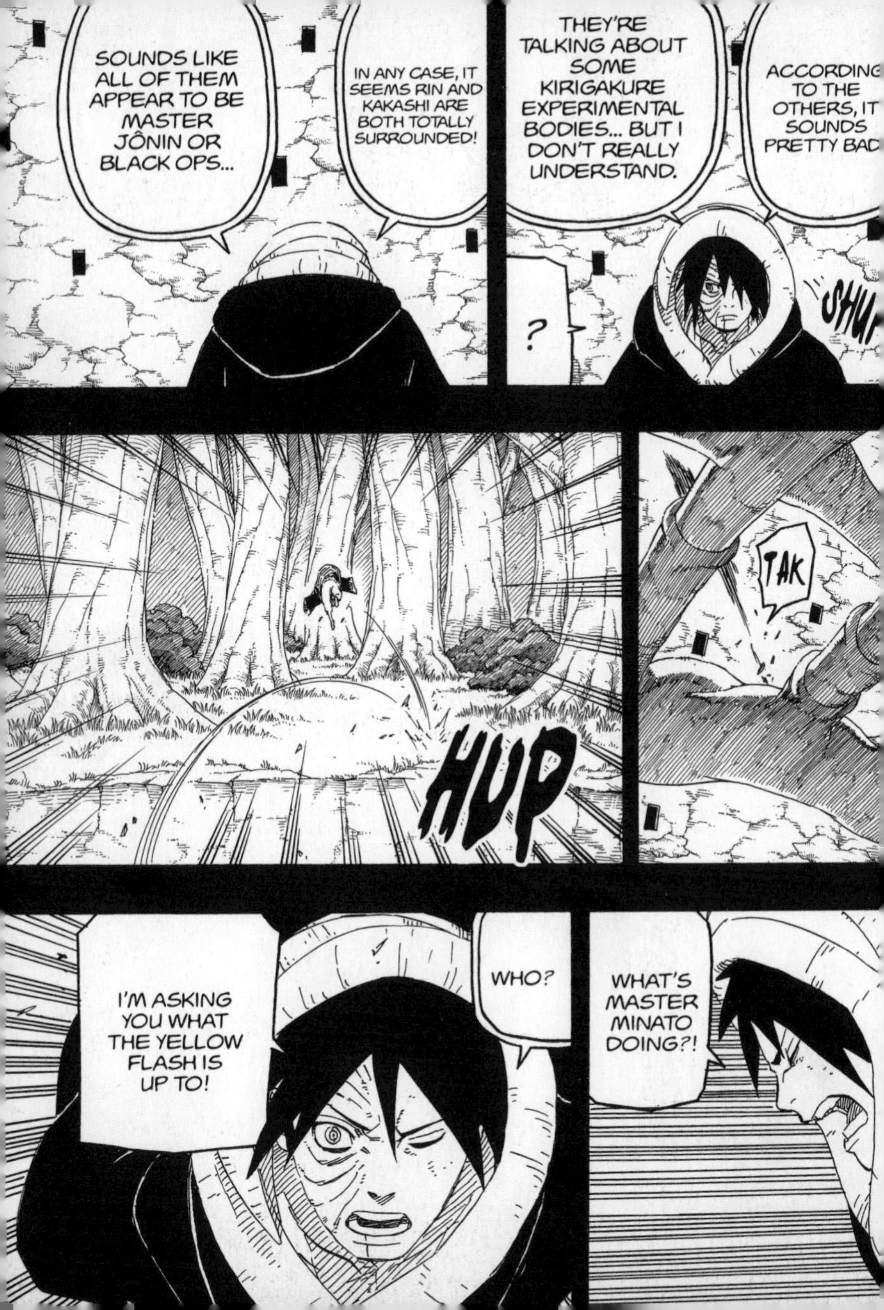
ACCORDIN TO THE OTHERS, IT SOUNDS PRETTY BAD
THEY'RE TALKING ABOUT SOME KIRIGAKURE EXPERIMENTAL BODIES... BUT I DON'T REALLY UNDERSTAND.
SHU
?
IN ANY CASE, IT SEEMS RIN AND KAKASHI ARE BOTH TOTALLY SURROUNDED!
SOUNDS LIKE ALL OF THEM APPEAR TO BE MASTER JÔNIN OR BLACK OPS...
TAK
HUP
WHAT'S MASTER MINATO DOING?!
WHO?
I'M ASKING YOU WHAT THE YELLOW FLASH IS UP TO!

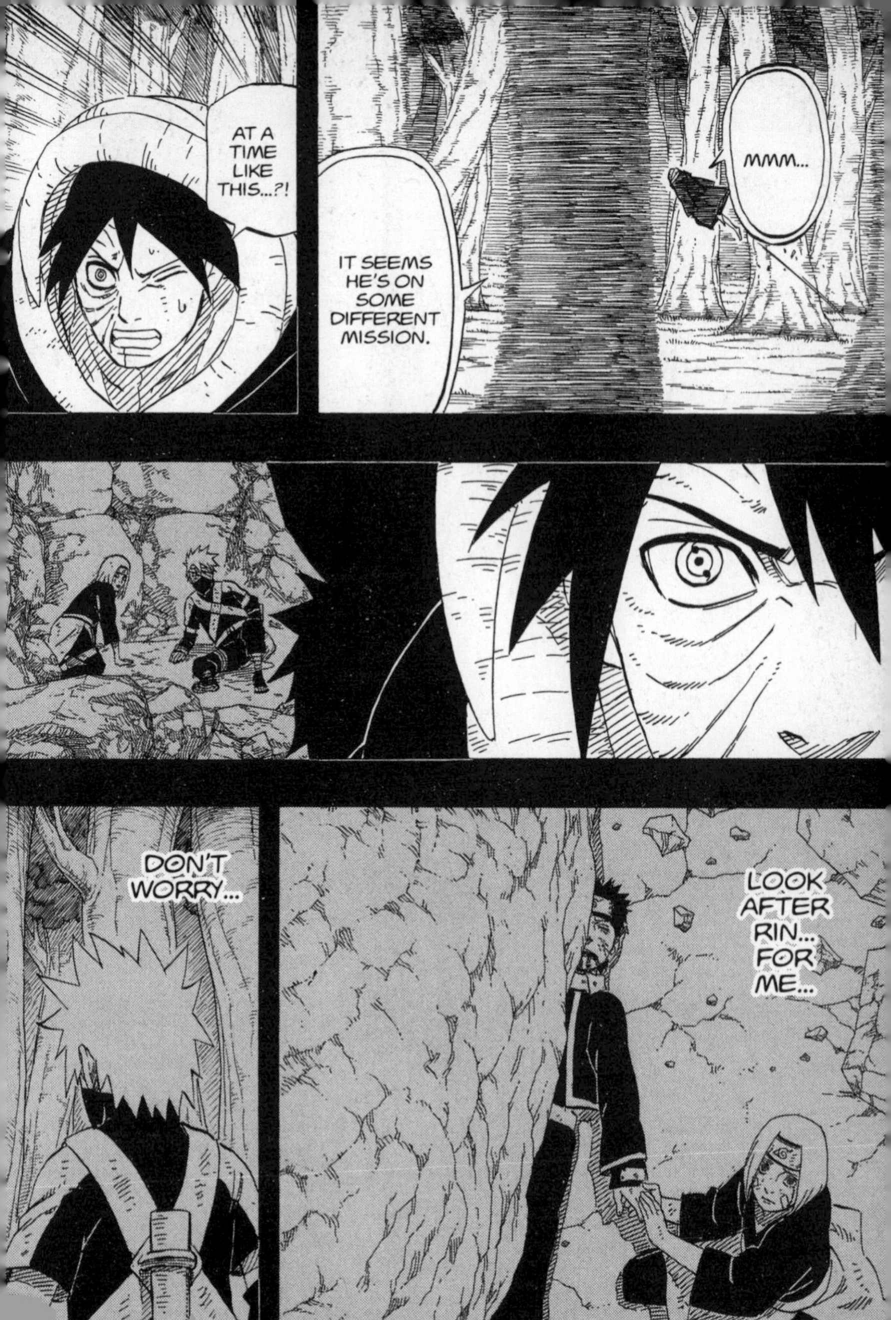
MMM...
IT SEEMS HE'S ON SOME DIFFERENT MISSION.
AT A TIME LIKE THIS...?!
LOOK AFTER RIN... FOR ME...
DON'T WORRY...

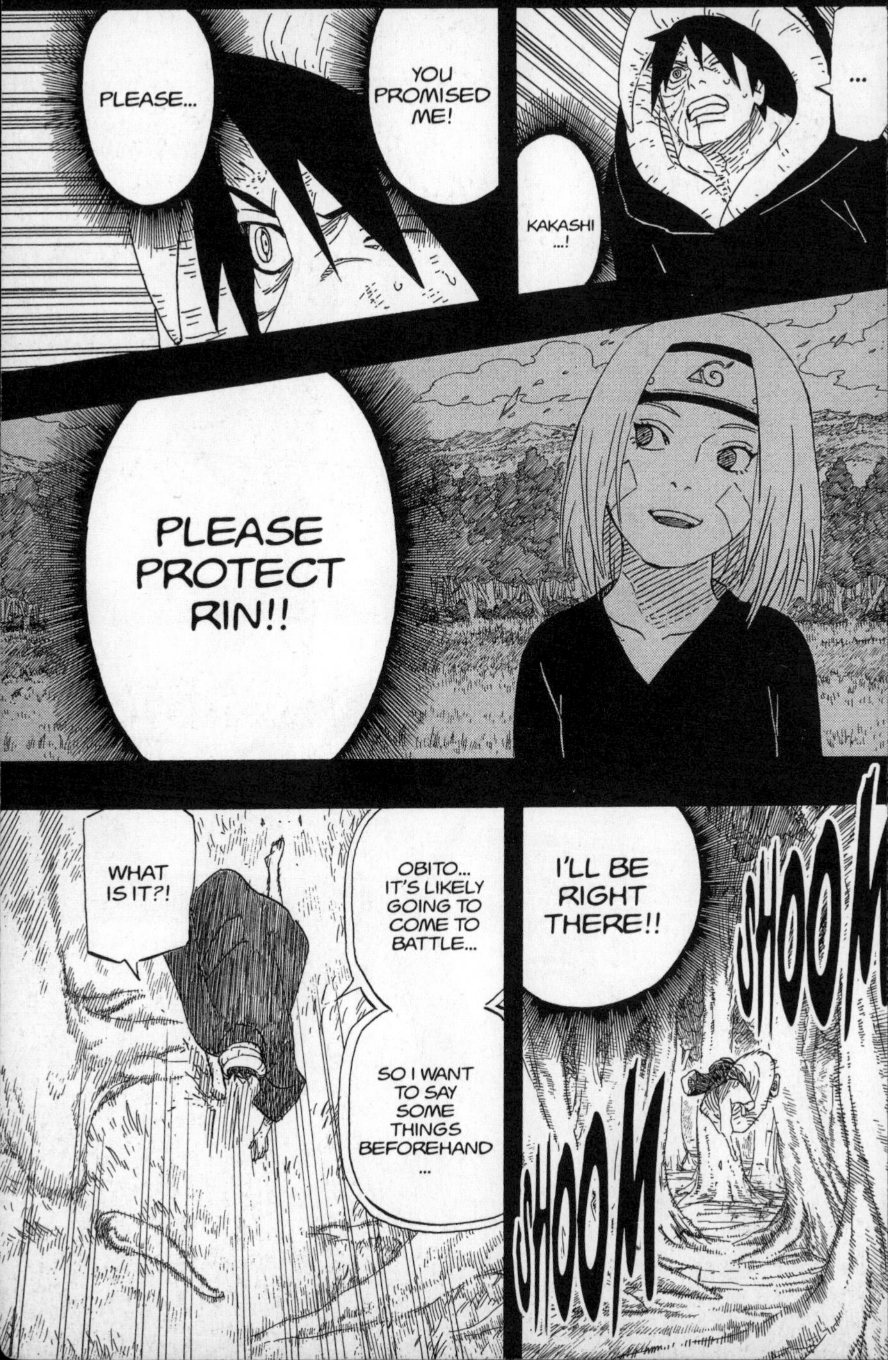
...
KAKASHI ...!
YOU PROMISED ME!
PLEASE...
PLEASE PROTECT RIN!!
I'LL BE RIGHT THERE!!
SHOOM
OBITO... IT'S LIKELY GOING TO COME TO BATTLE...
SO I WANT TO SAY SOME THINGS BEFOREHAND ...
WHAT IS IT?!

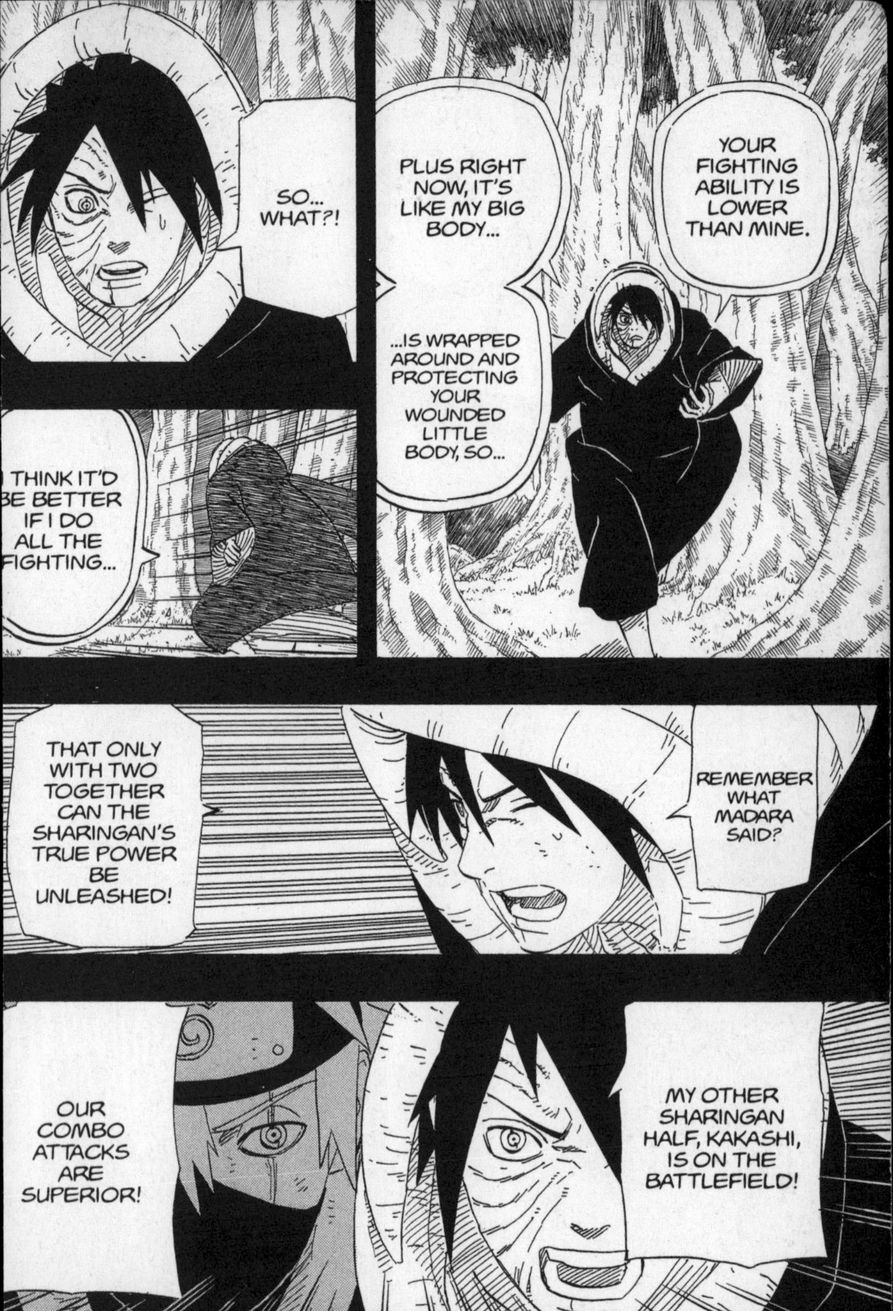
YOUR FIGHTING ABILITY IS LOWER THAN MINE.
PLUS RIGHT NOW, IT'S LIKE MY BIG BODY...
...IS WRAPPED AROUND AND PROTECTING YOUR WOUNDED LITTLE BODY, SO...
SO... WHAT?!
I THINK IT'D BE BETTER IF I DO ALL THE FIGHTING...
REMEMBER WHAT MADARA SAID?
THAT ONLY WITH TWO TOGETHER CAN THE SHARINGAN'S TRUE POWER BE UNLEASHED!
MY OTHER SHARINGAN HALF, KAKASHI, IS ON THE BATTLEFIELD!
OUR COMBO ATTACKS ARE SUPERIOR!

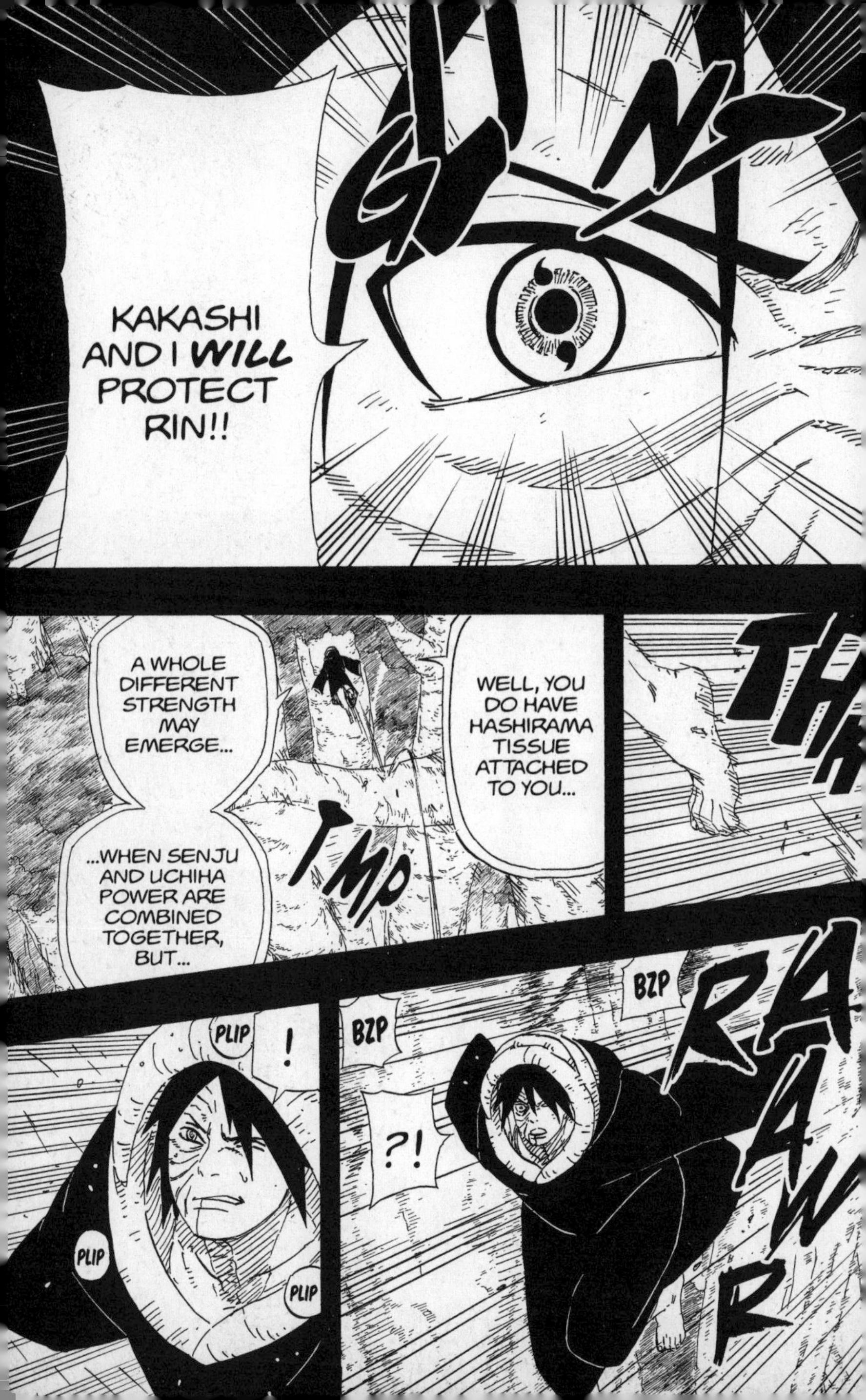
KAKASHI AND I WILL PROTECT RIN!!
WELL, YOU DO HAVE HASHIRAMA TISSUE ATTACHED TO YOU...
A WHOLE DIFFERENT STRENGTH MAY EMERGE...
...WHEN SENJU AND UCHIHA POWER ARE COMBINED TOGETHER, BUT...
TMP
BZP
BZP
?!
PLIP
!
PLIP
PLIP

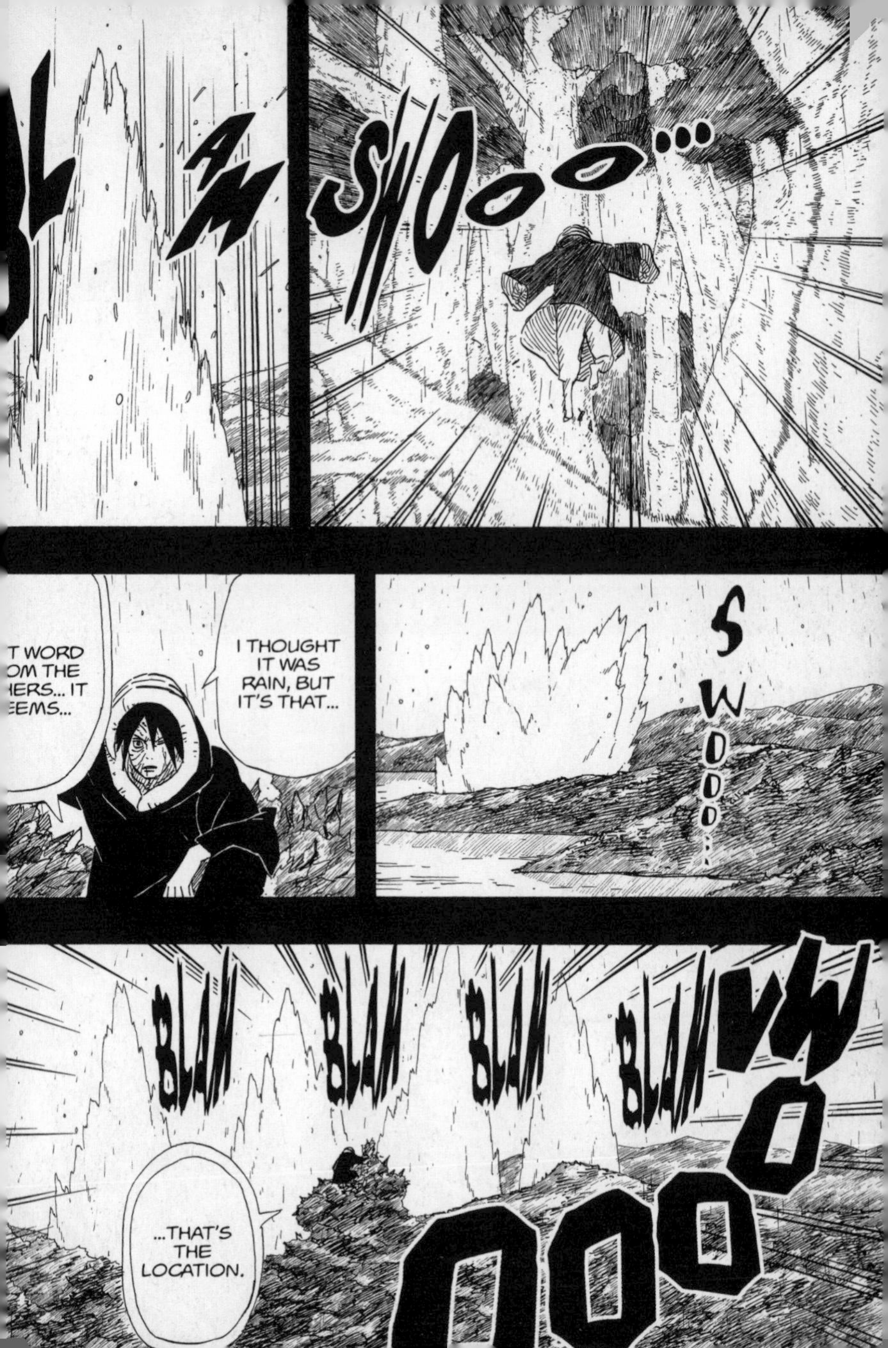
SHOOOO...
SWOOOO...
I THOUGHT IT WAS RAIN, BUT IT'S THAT...
T WORD OM THE HERS... IT EEMS...
VWOOOO
BLAM
BLAM
BLAM
BLAM
...THAT'S THE LOCATION.

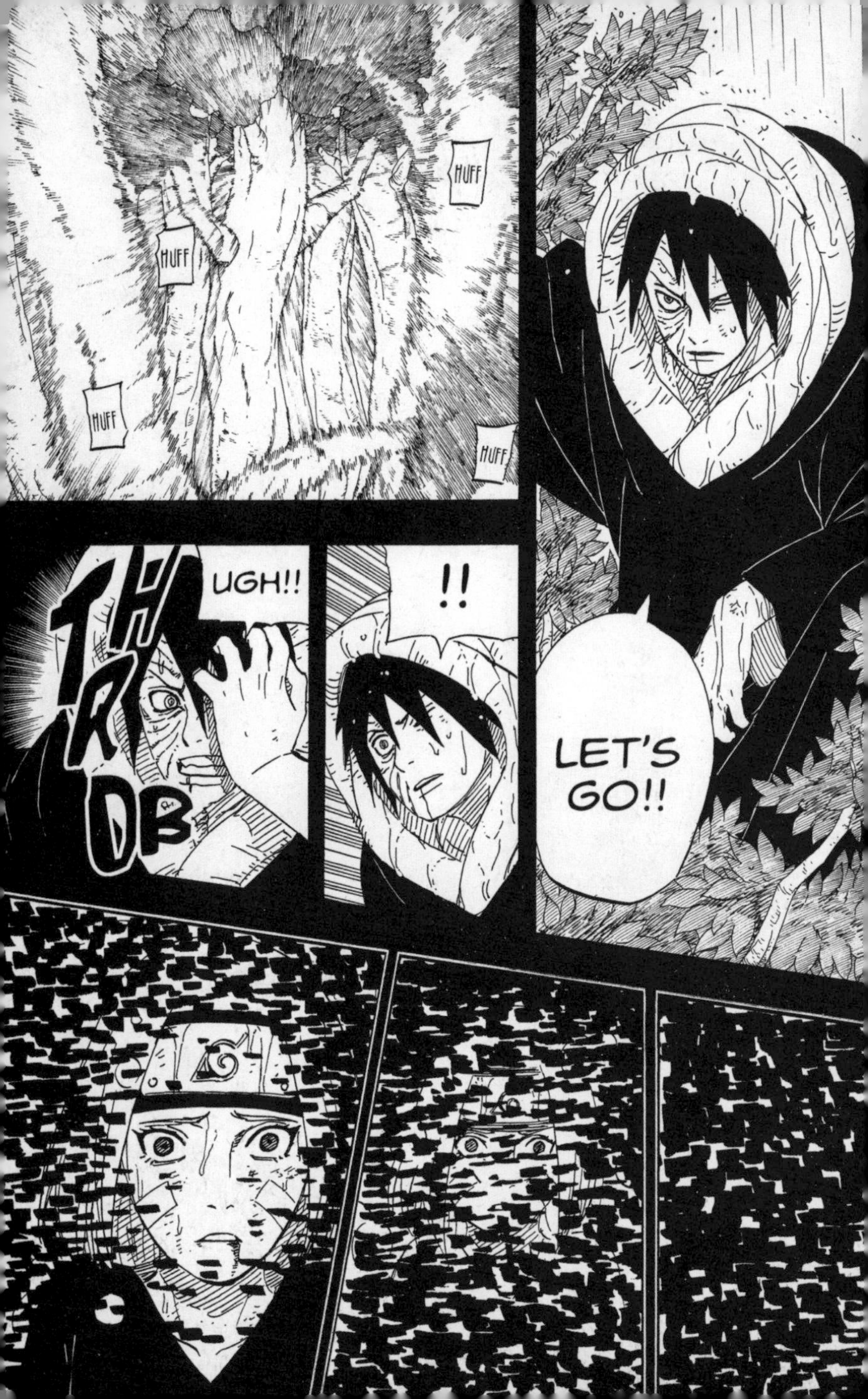
LET'S GO!!
HUFF
HUFF
HUFF
HUFF
!!
UGH!!
THROB

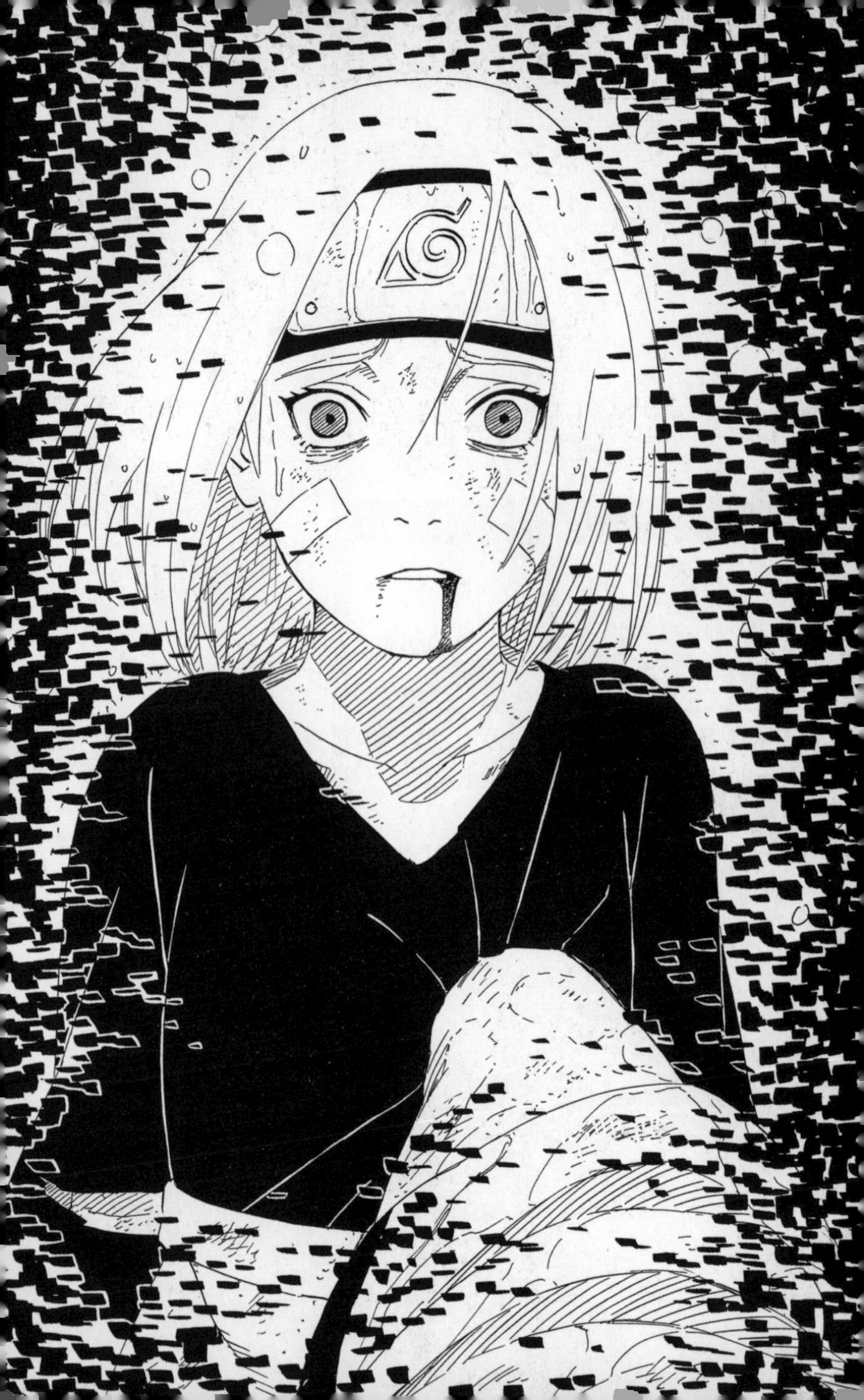

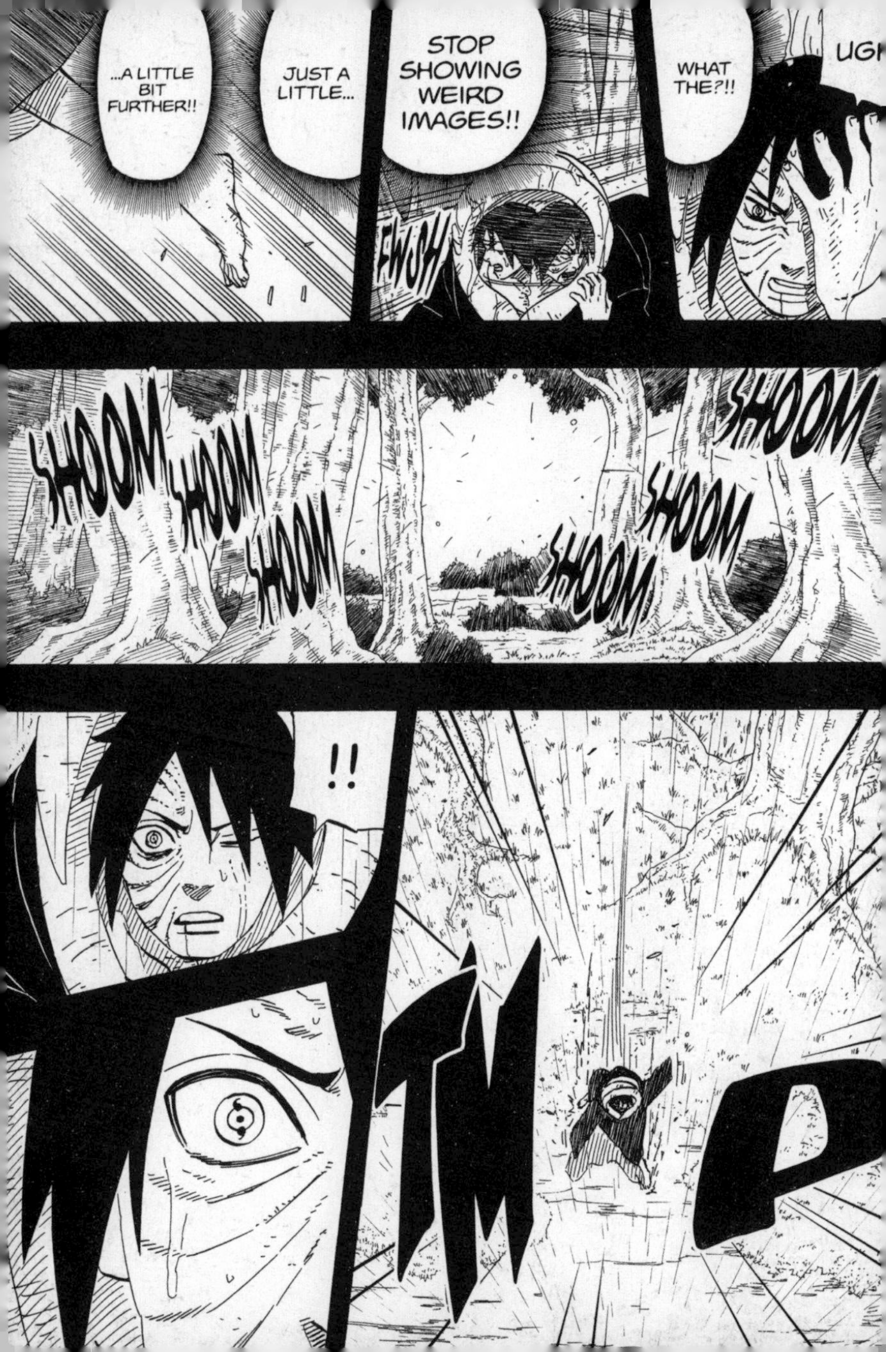

UG
WHAT THE?!!
STOP SHOWING WEIRD IMAGES!!
FWSH
JUST A LITTLE...
...A LITTLE BIT FURTHER!!
SHOOM
SHOOM
SHOOM
SHOOM
SHOOM
SHOOM
TMP
!!

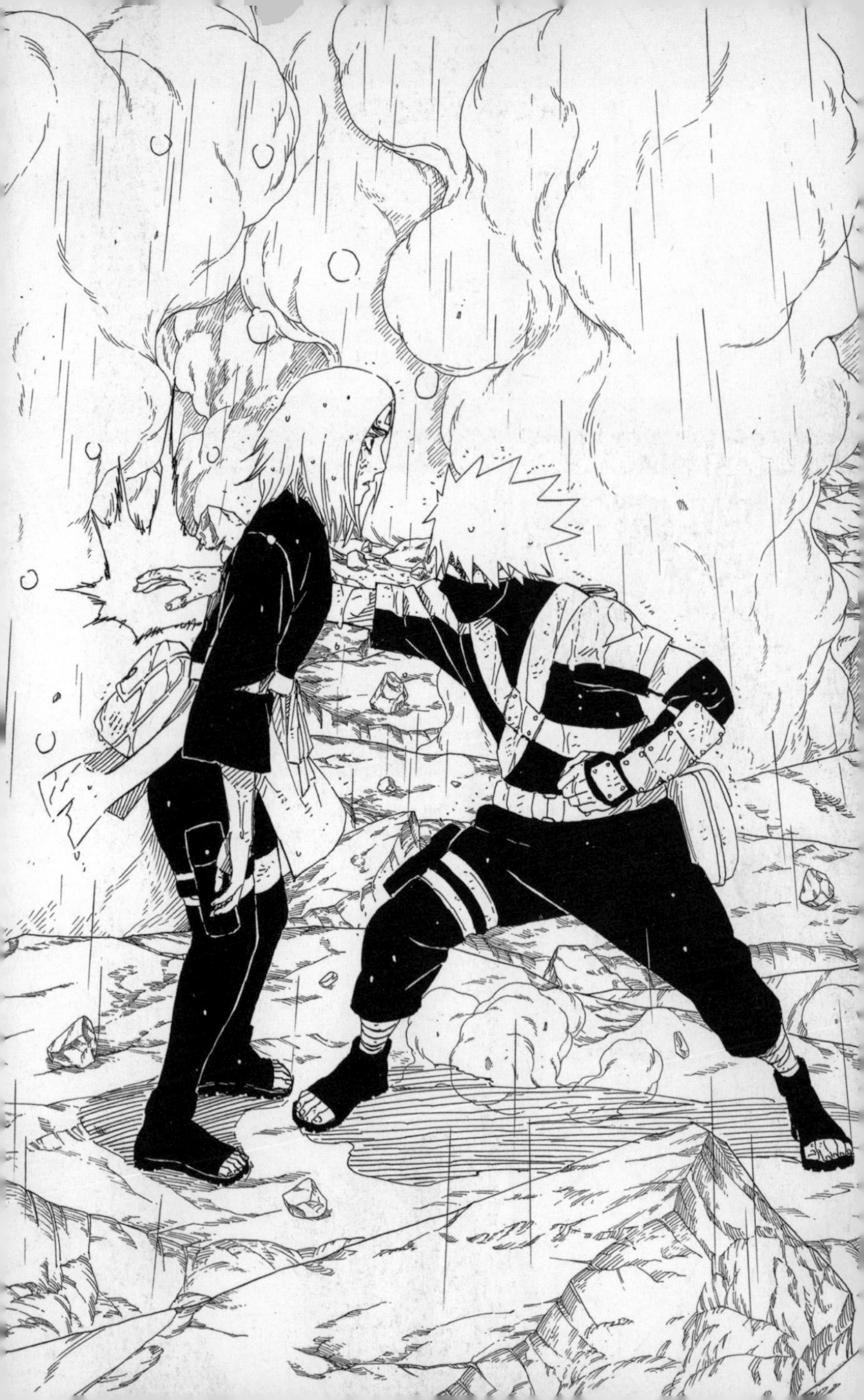

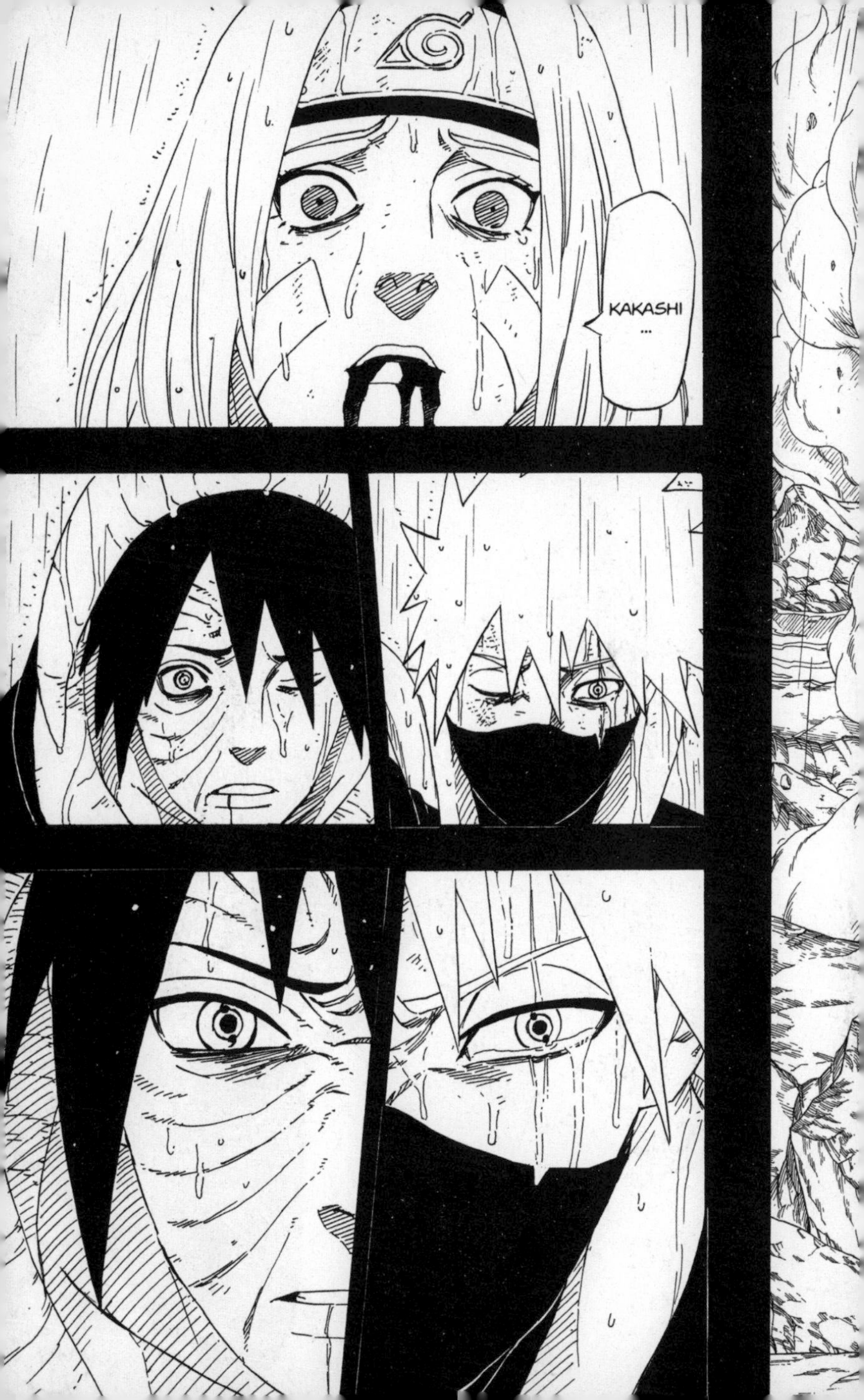
KAKASHI ...

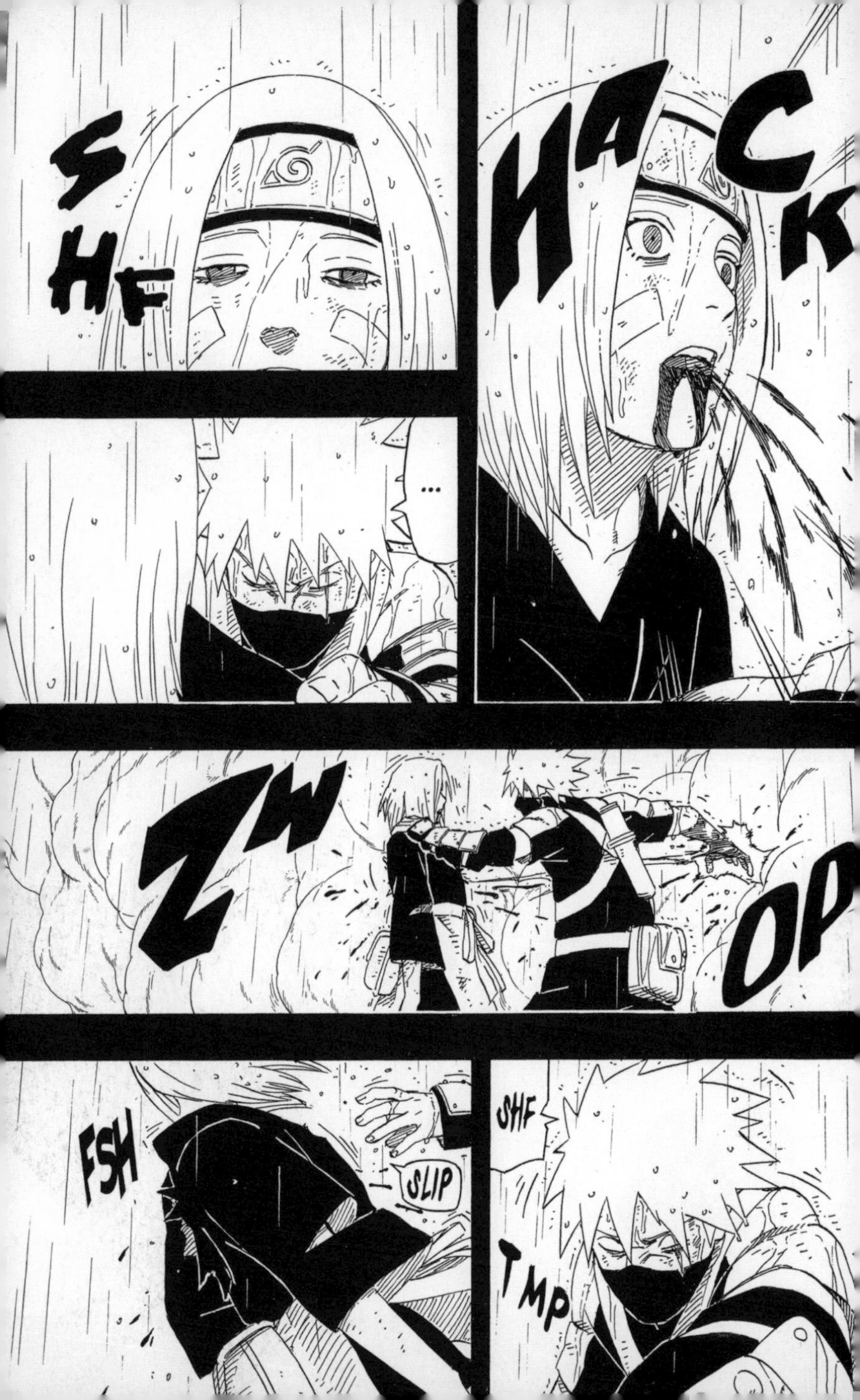
HACK
SHF
...
ZW OP
SHF
TMP
FSH
SLIP

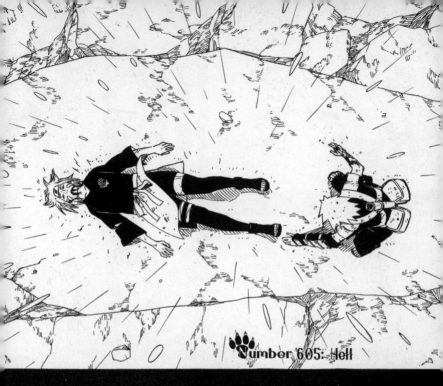

Number 605: Hell

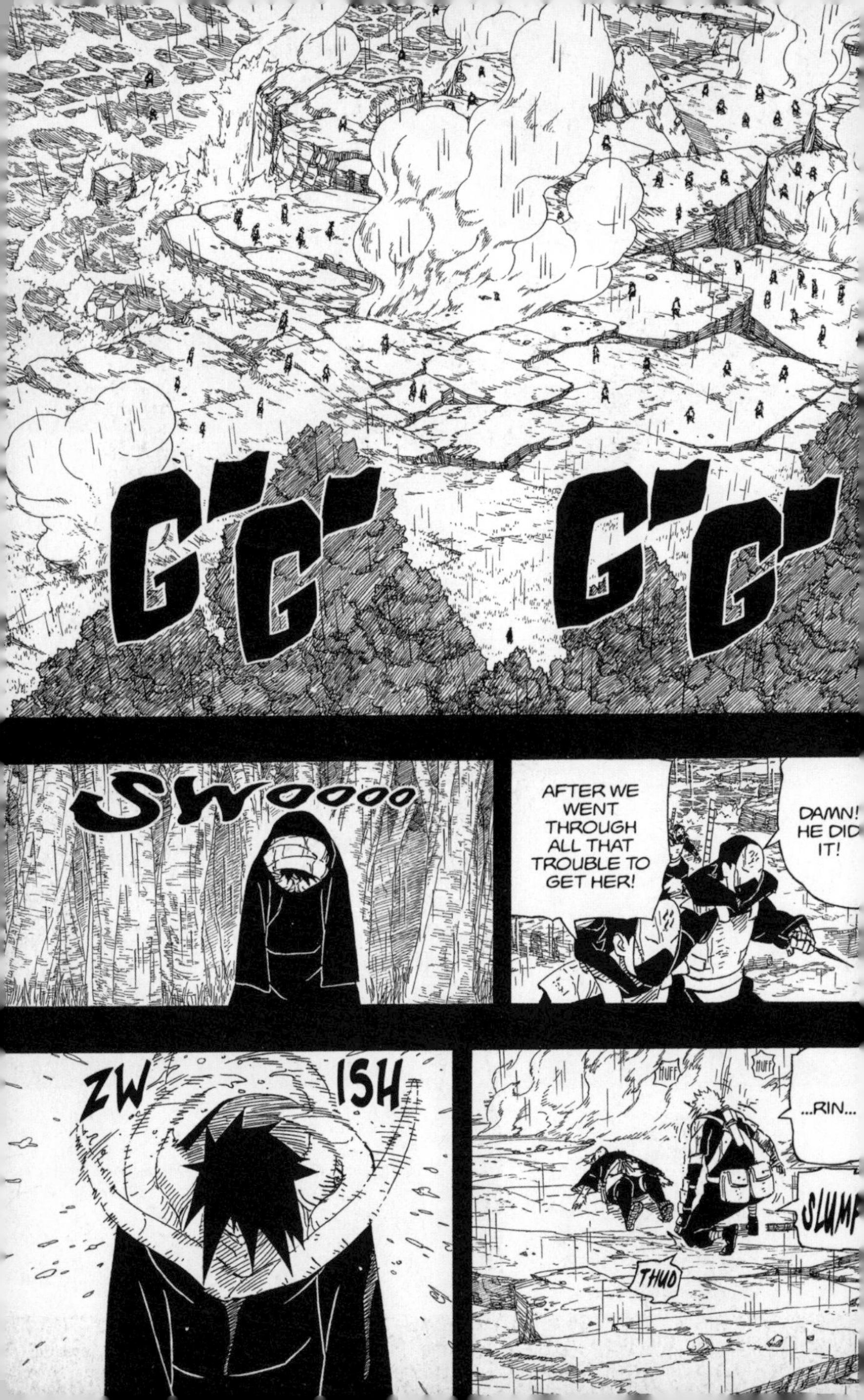
G'G'
G'G'
DAMN! HE DID IT!
AFTER WE WENT THROUGH ALL THAT TROUBLE TO GET HER!
SWOOOO
HUFF
HUFF
...RIN...
SLUMP
THUD
ZW
ISH

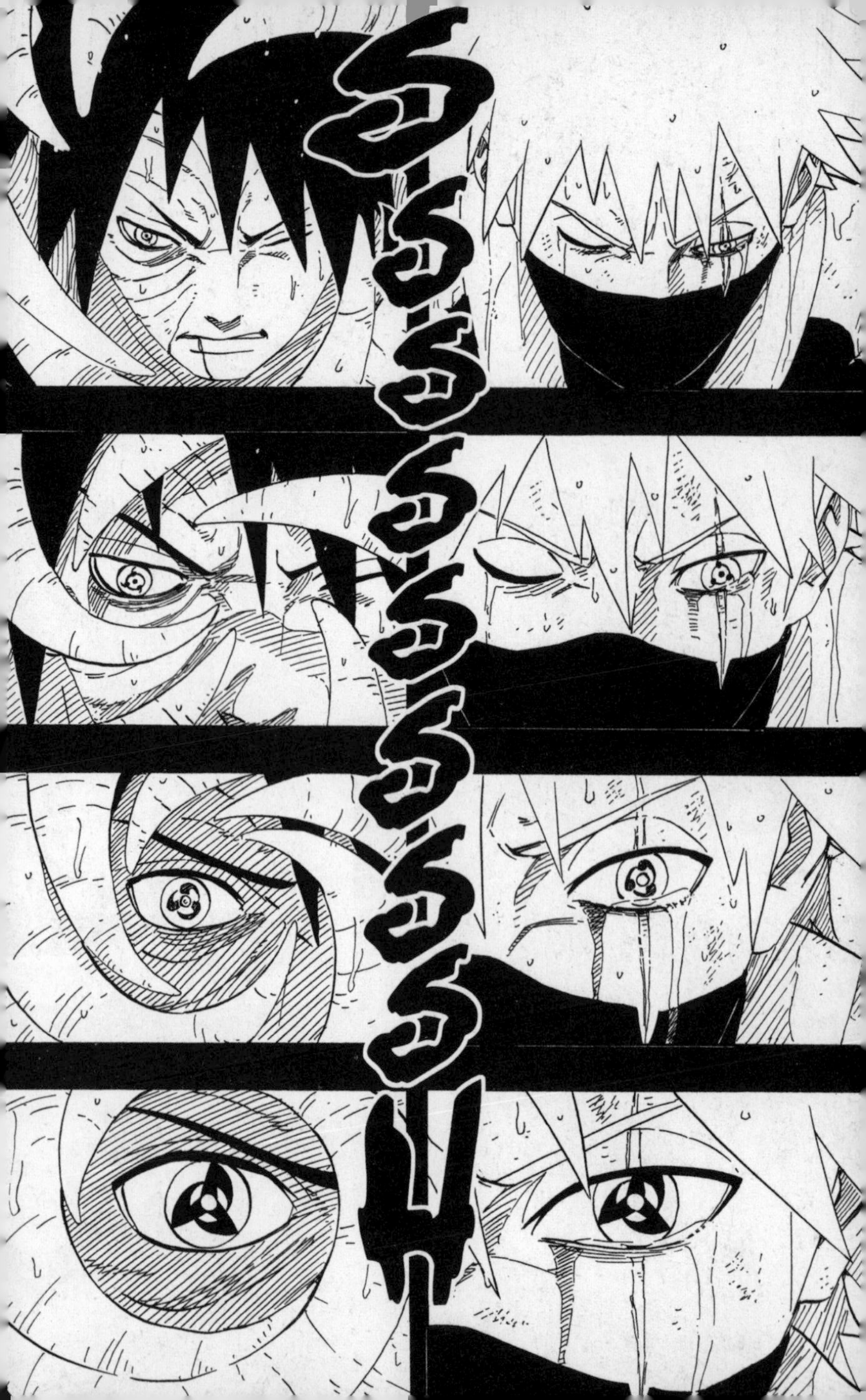

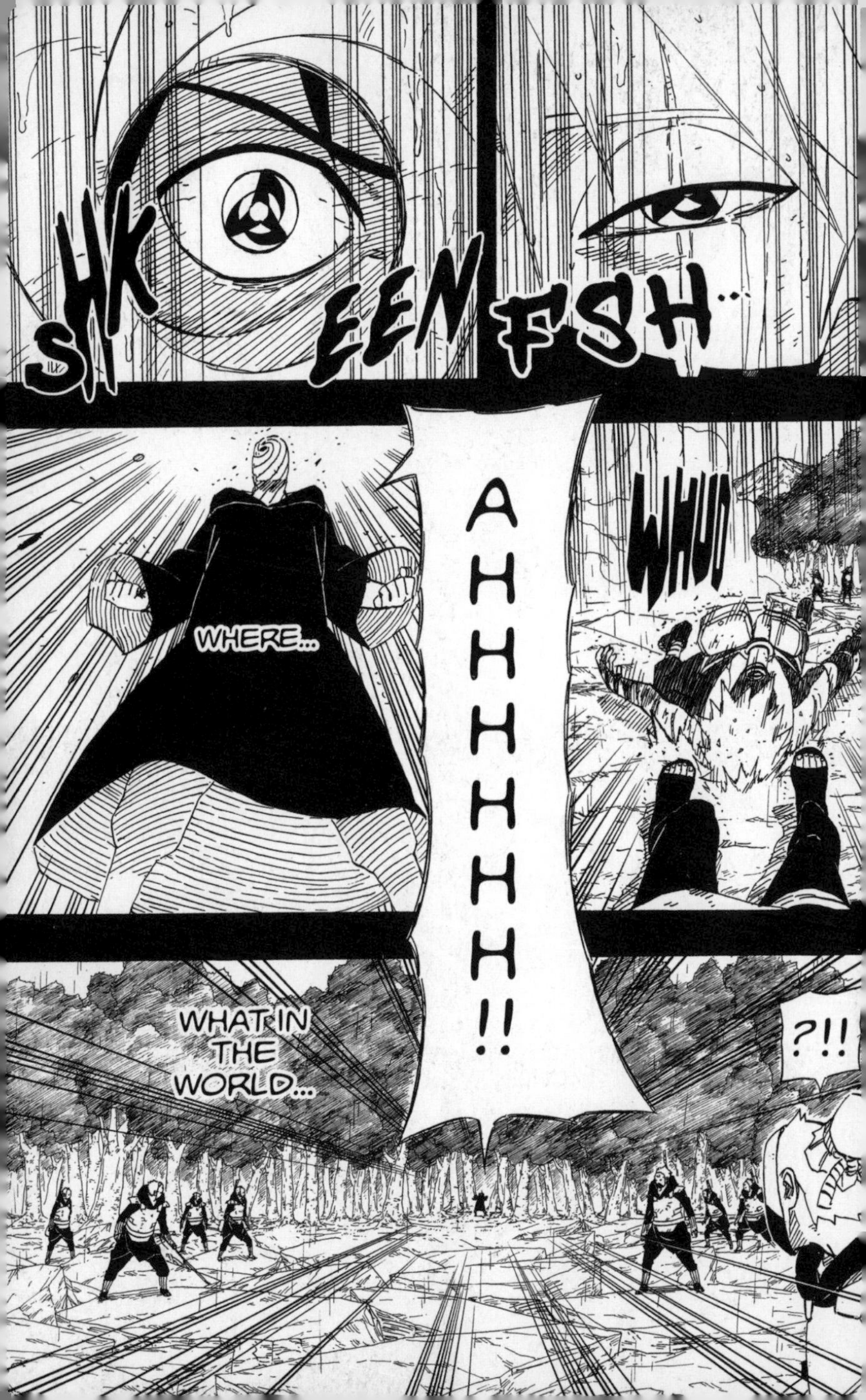

F'SH...
SHKEEN
WHUD
AHHHHHH!!
WHERE...
?!!
WHAT IN THE WORLD...

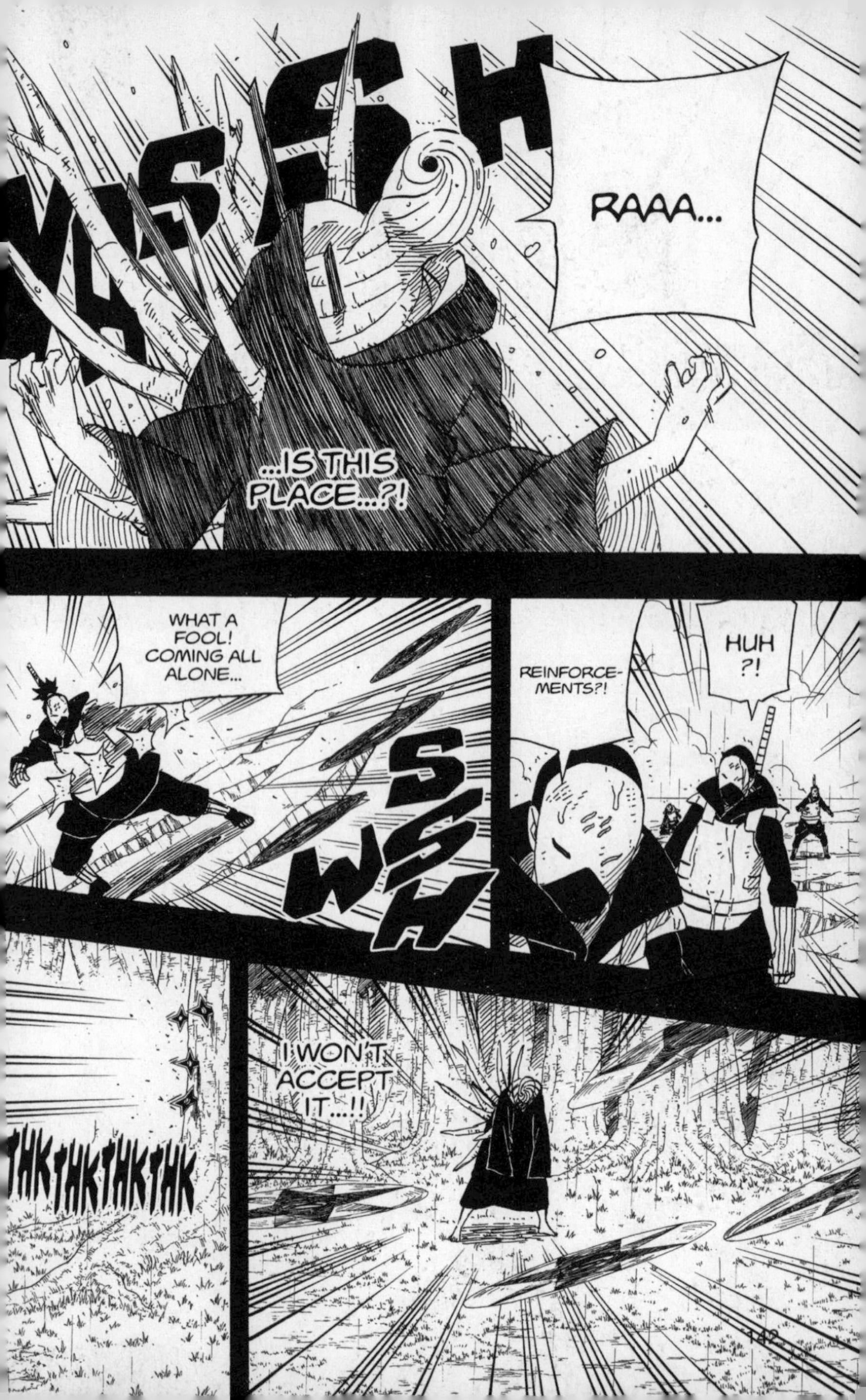
RAAA...
...IS THIS PLACE...?!
HUH ?!
REINFORCE-MENTS?!
WHAT A FOOL! COMING ALL ALONE...
I WON'T ACCEPT IT...!!
THKTHKTHKTHK

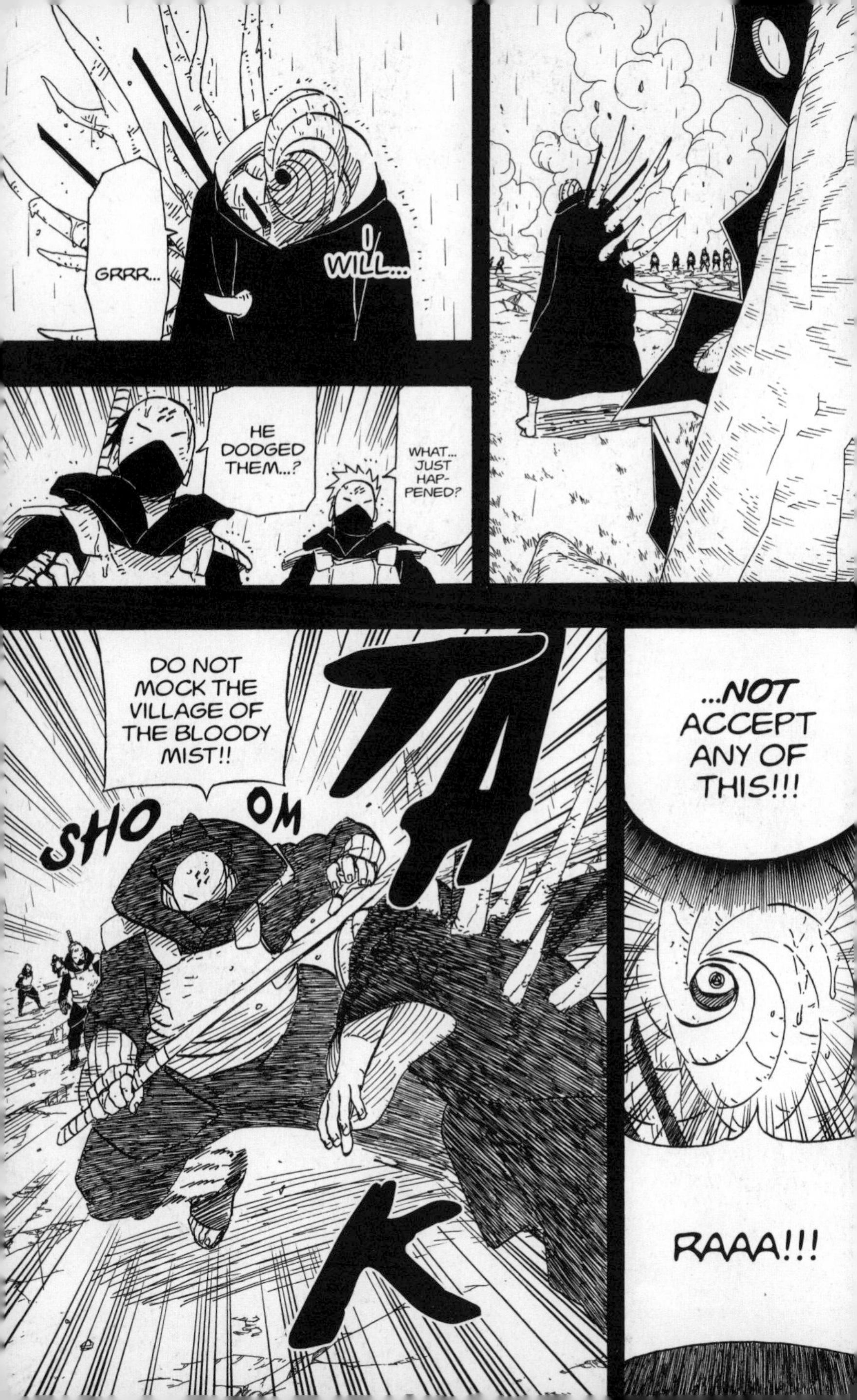
I WILL...
GRRR...
WHAT... JUST HAP-PENED?
HE DODGED THEM...?
...NOT ACCEPT ANY OF THIS!!!
RAAA!!!
DO NOT MOCK THE VILLAGE OF THE BLOODY MIST!!
SHOOM
TAK

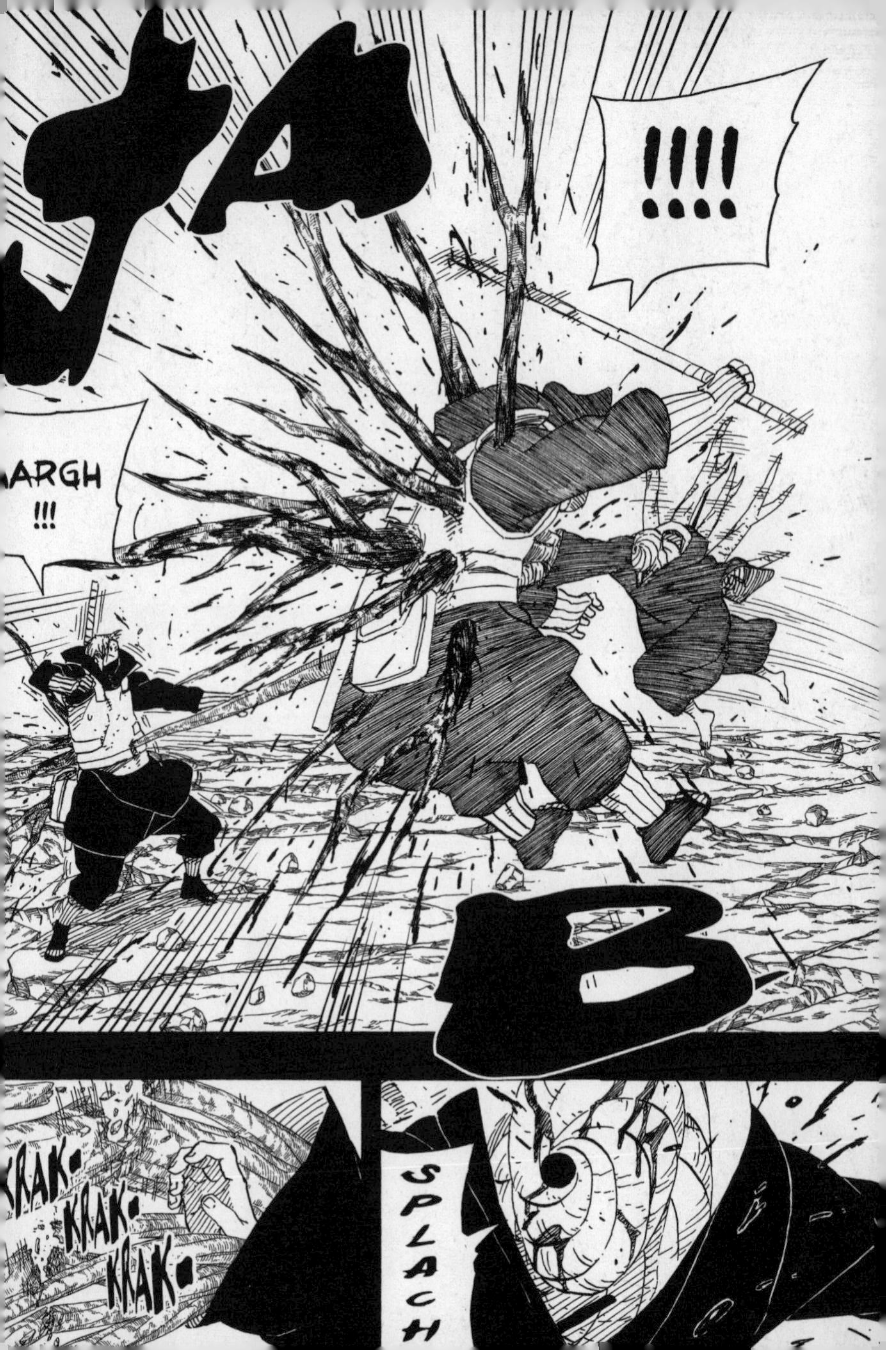
JAB
!!!!
ARGH !!!
SPLACH
KRAK- KRAK- KRAK-

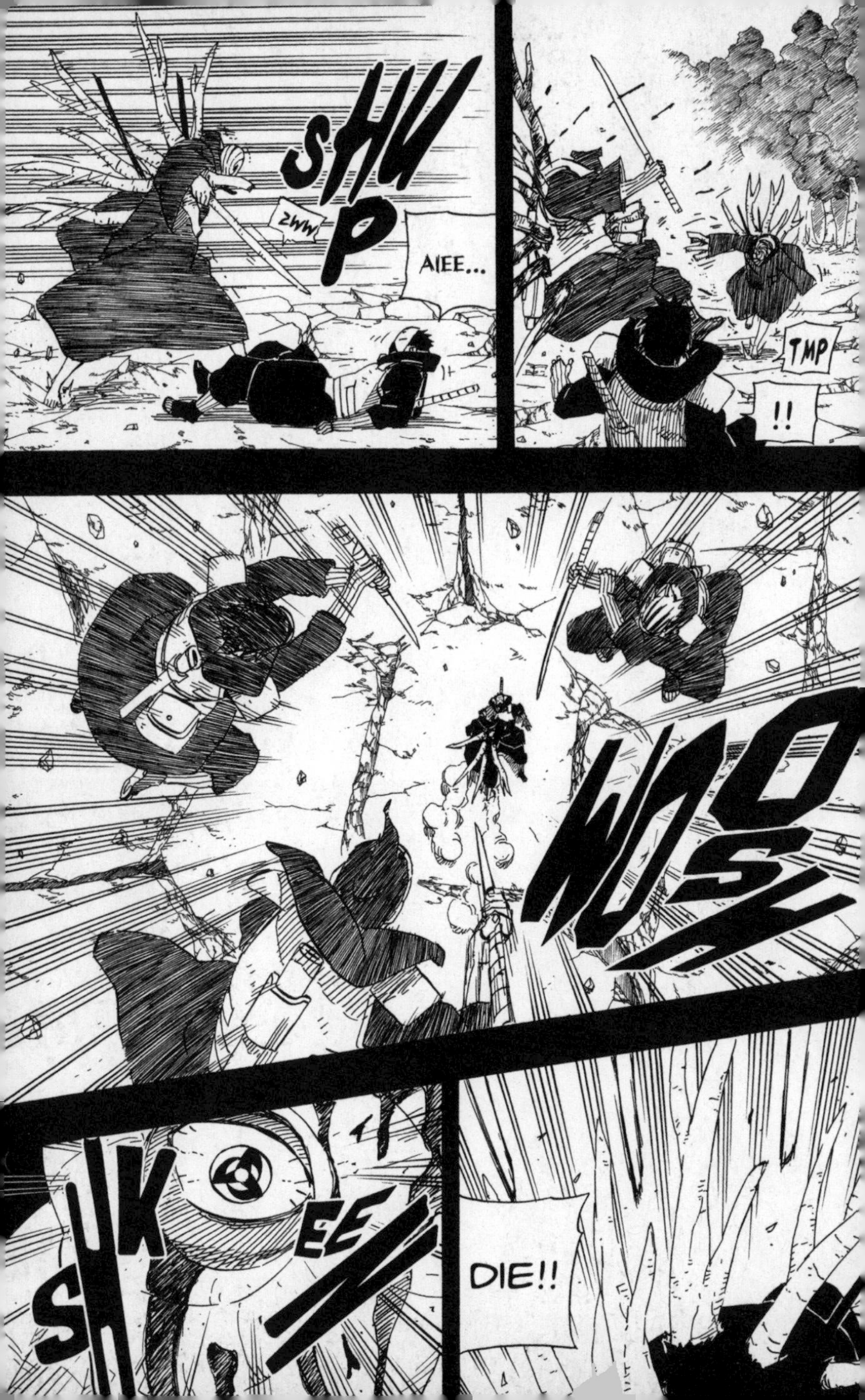
TMP
!!
SHUP
ZWW
AIEE...
WHOOSH
DIE!!
SHKEEN

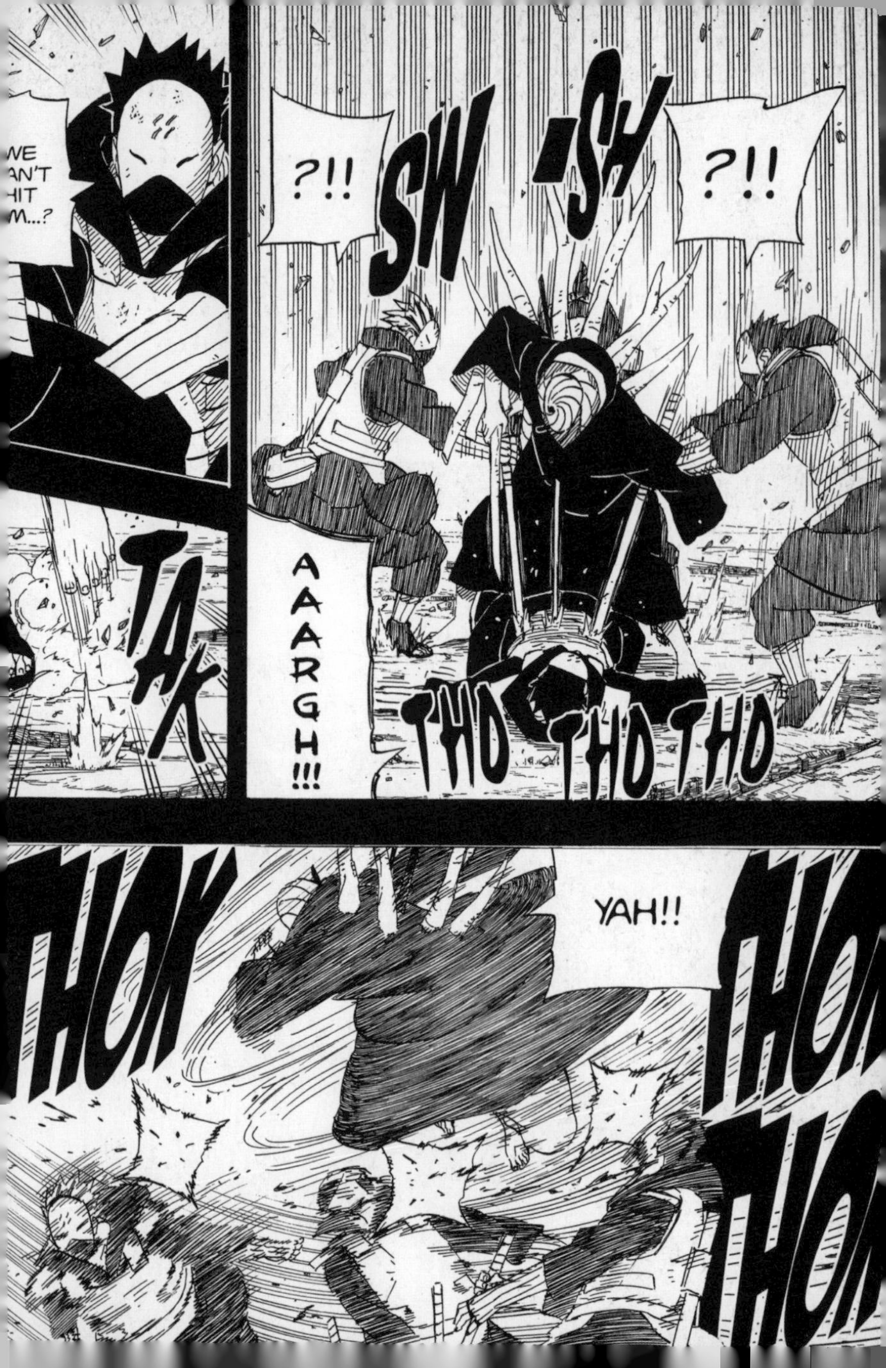

?!!
SWISH
?!!
AAARGH!!!
THO THO THO
WE
AN'T
HIT
M...?
TAK
YAH!!
THOK

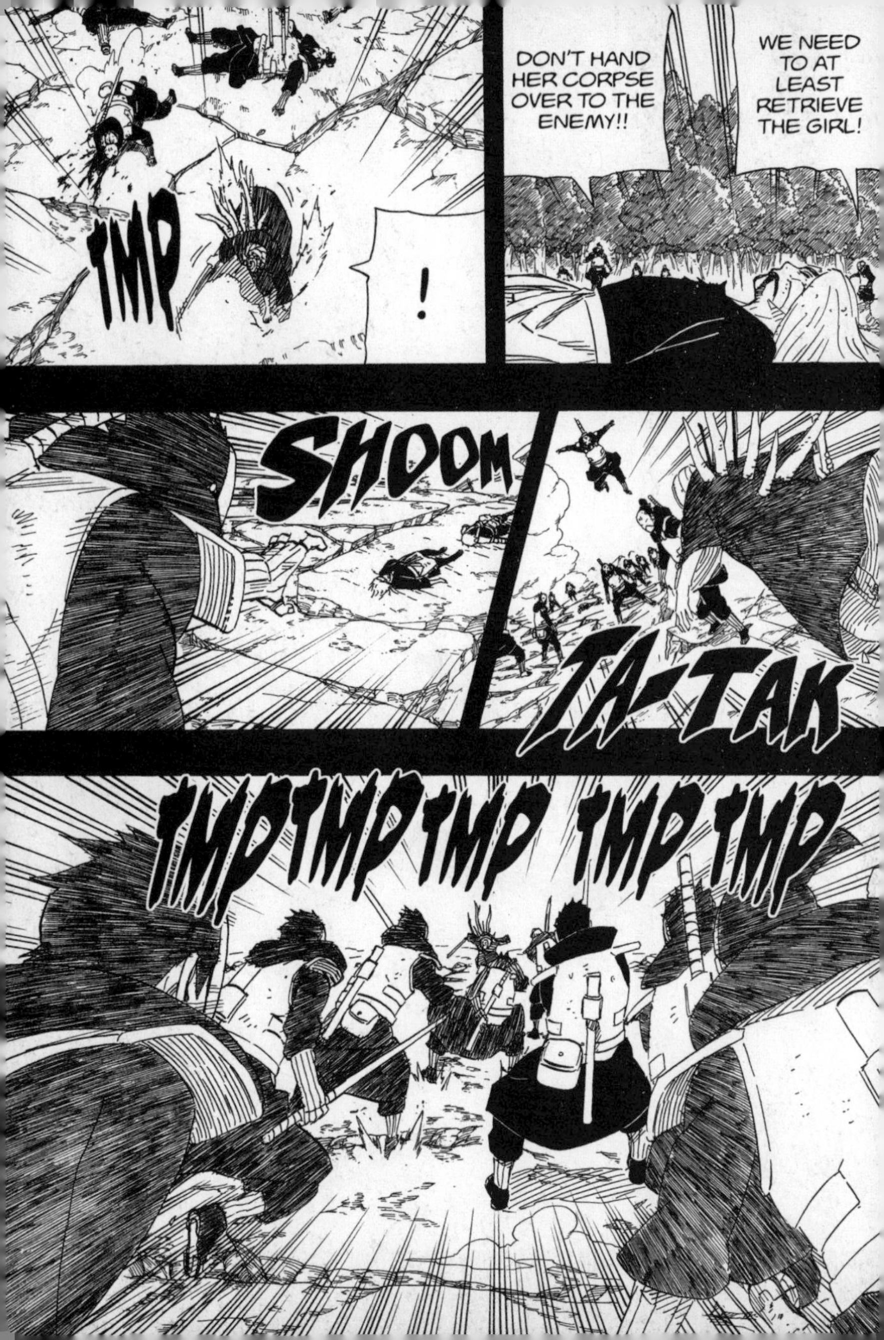
WE NEED TO AT LEAST RETRIEVE THE GIRL!
DON'T HAND HER CORPSE OVER TO THE ENEMY!!
TMP
!
TA-TAK
SHOOM
TMP TMP TMP TMP TMP

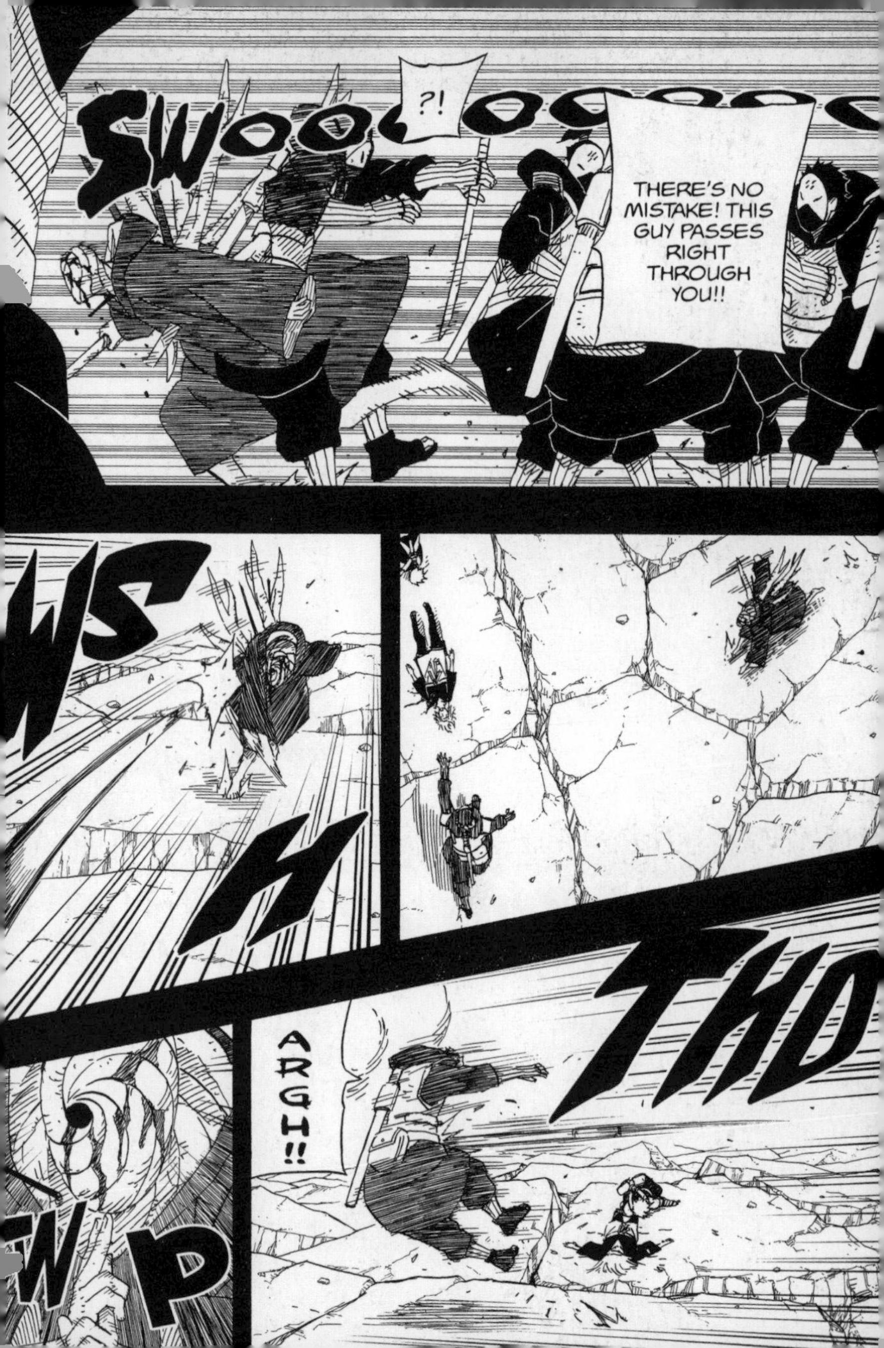
THERE'S NO MISTAKE! THIS GUY PASSES RIGHT THROUGH YOU!!
?!
ARGH!!

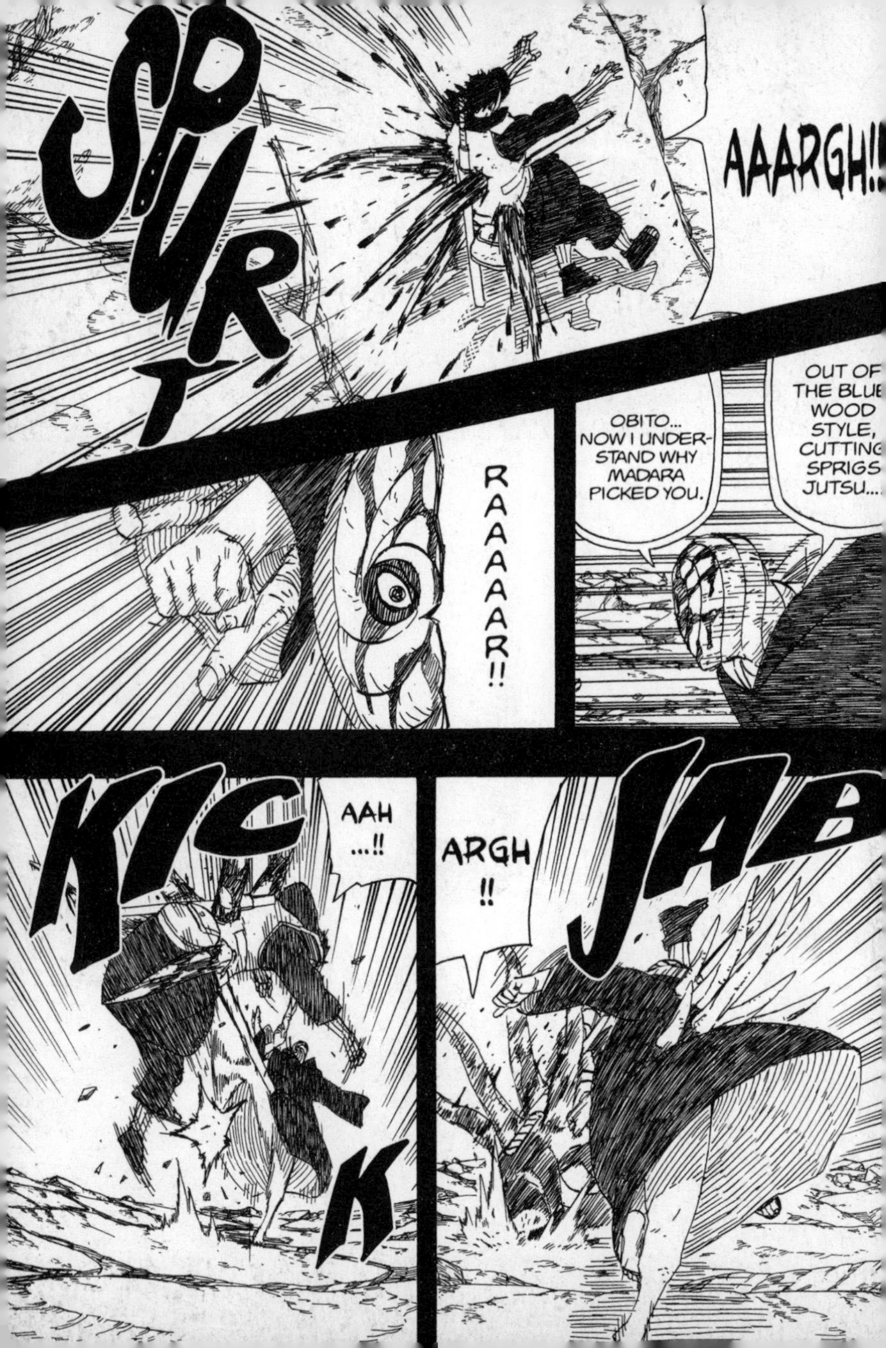
SPURT
AAARGH!!
OUT OF THE BLUE WOOD STYLE, CUTTING SPRIGS JUTSU....
OBITO... NOW I UNDERSTAND WHY MADARA PICKED YOU.
RAAAAAAR!!
JAB
ARGH!!
AAH...!!
KICK

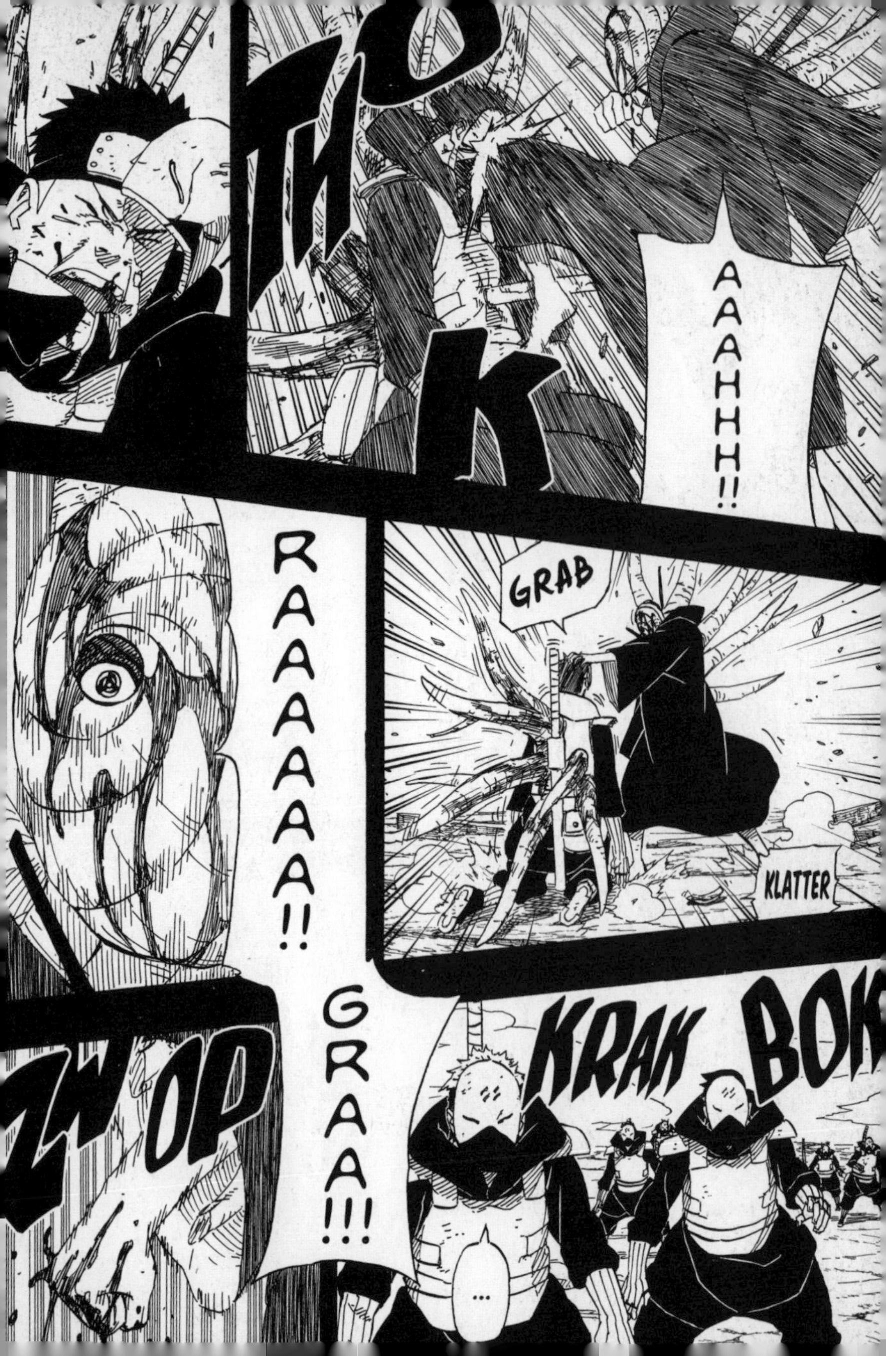
THOK
AAAAHHH!!
GRAB
KLATTER
RAAAAAAA!!
KRAK
BOK
GRAAA!!!
...
ZWOP

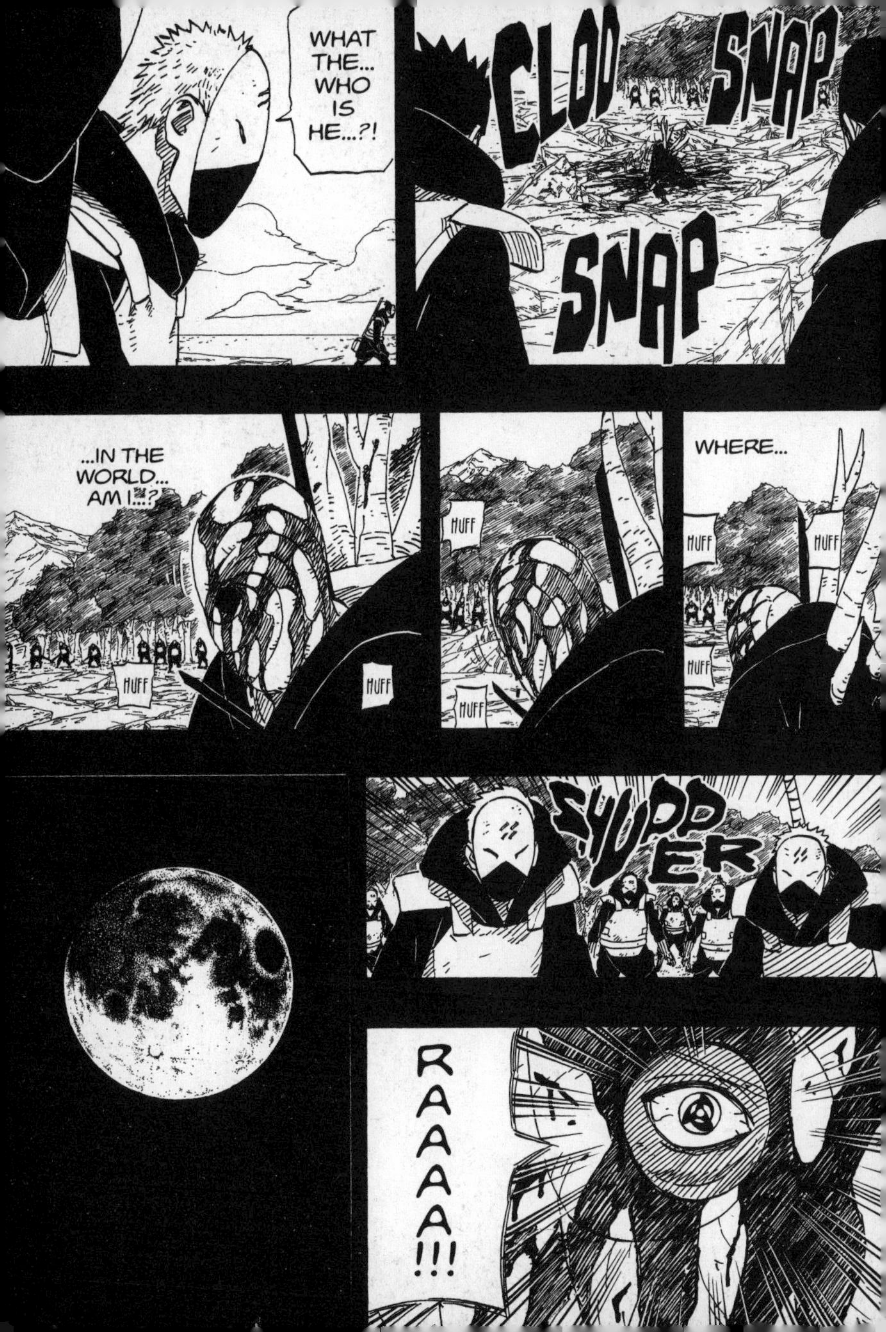
CLOD
SNAP
SNAP
WHAT THE... WHO IS HE...?!
WHERE...
HUFF
HUFF
HUFF
HUFF
HUFF
...IN THE WORLD... AM I...?
HUFF
HUFF
SHUDDER
RAAAA!!!

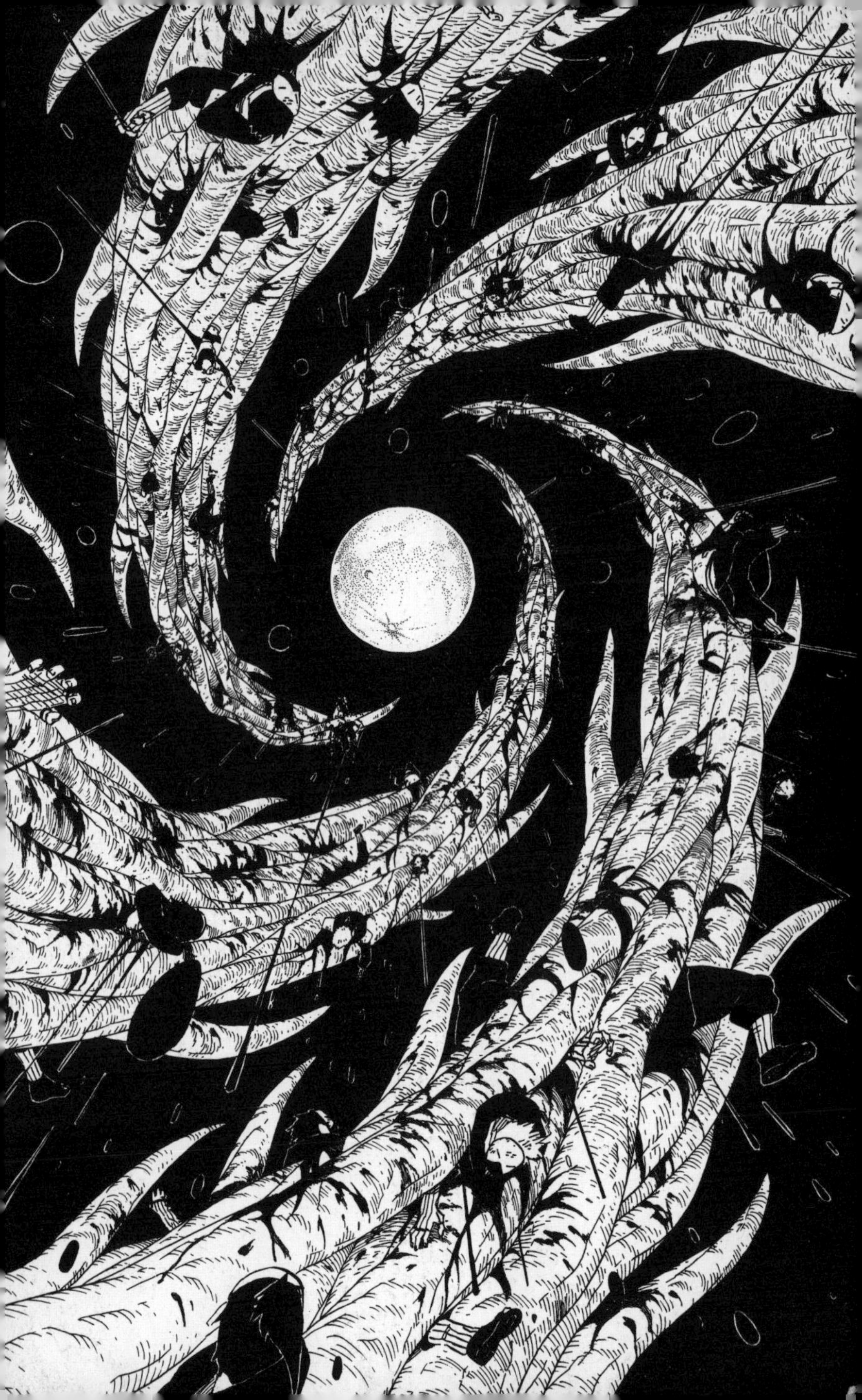

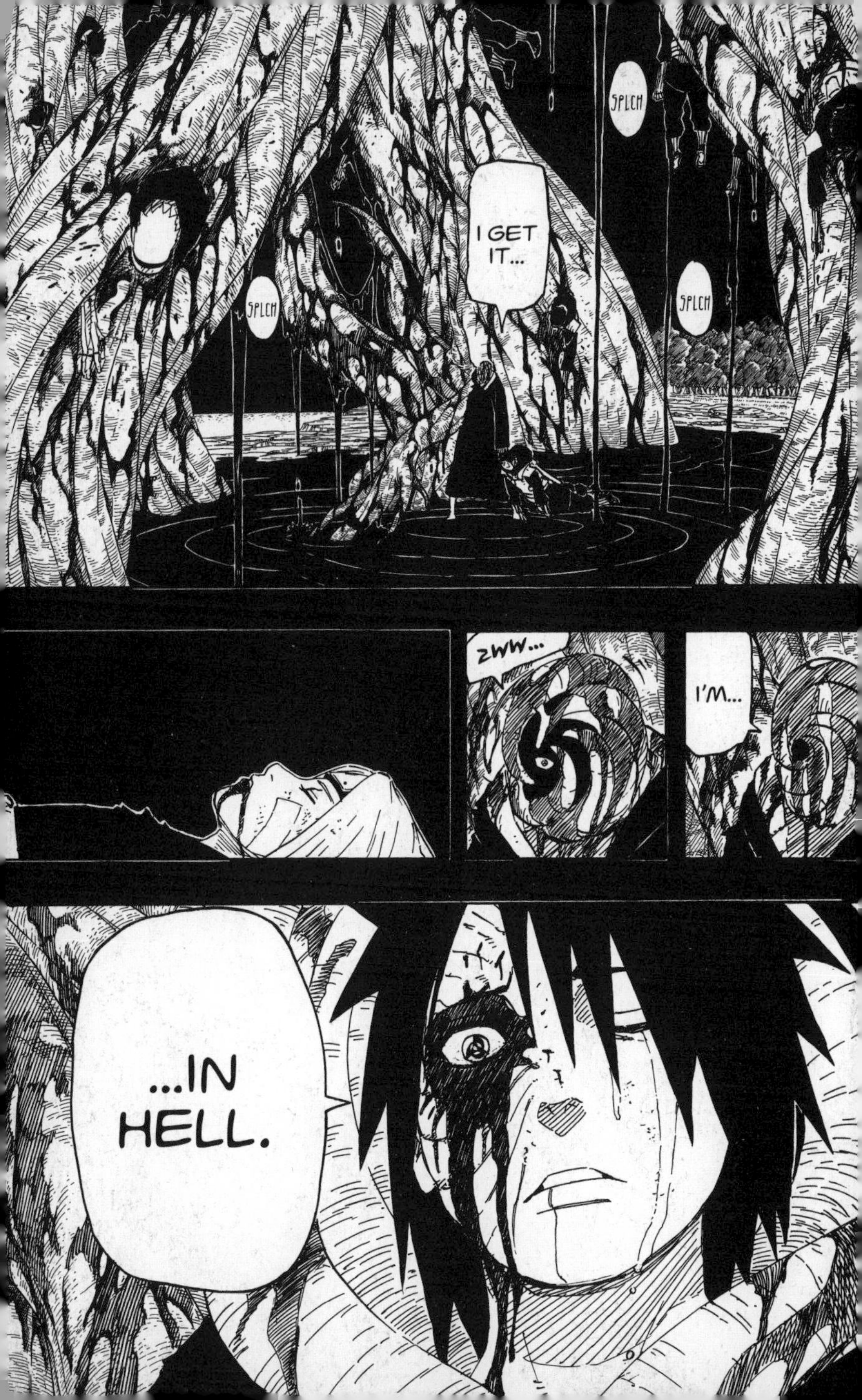
SPLCH
SPLCH
I GET IT...
SPLCH
I'M...
ZWW...
...IN HELL.

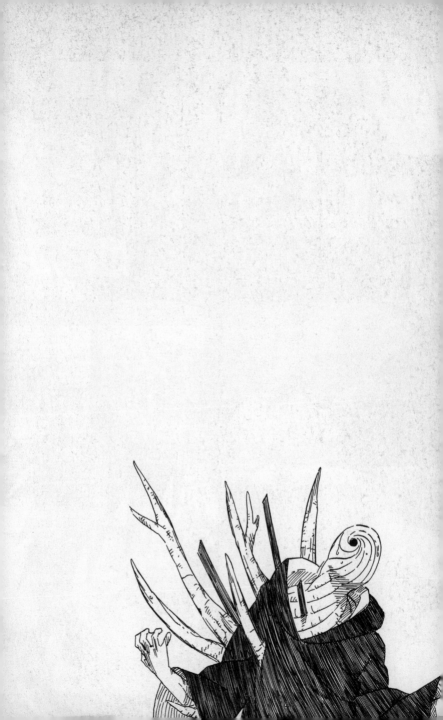

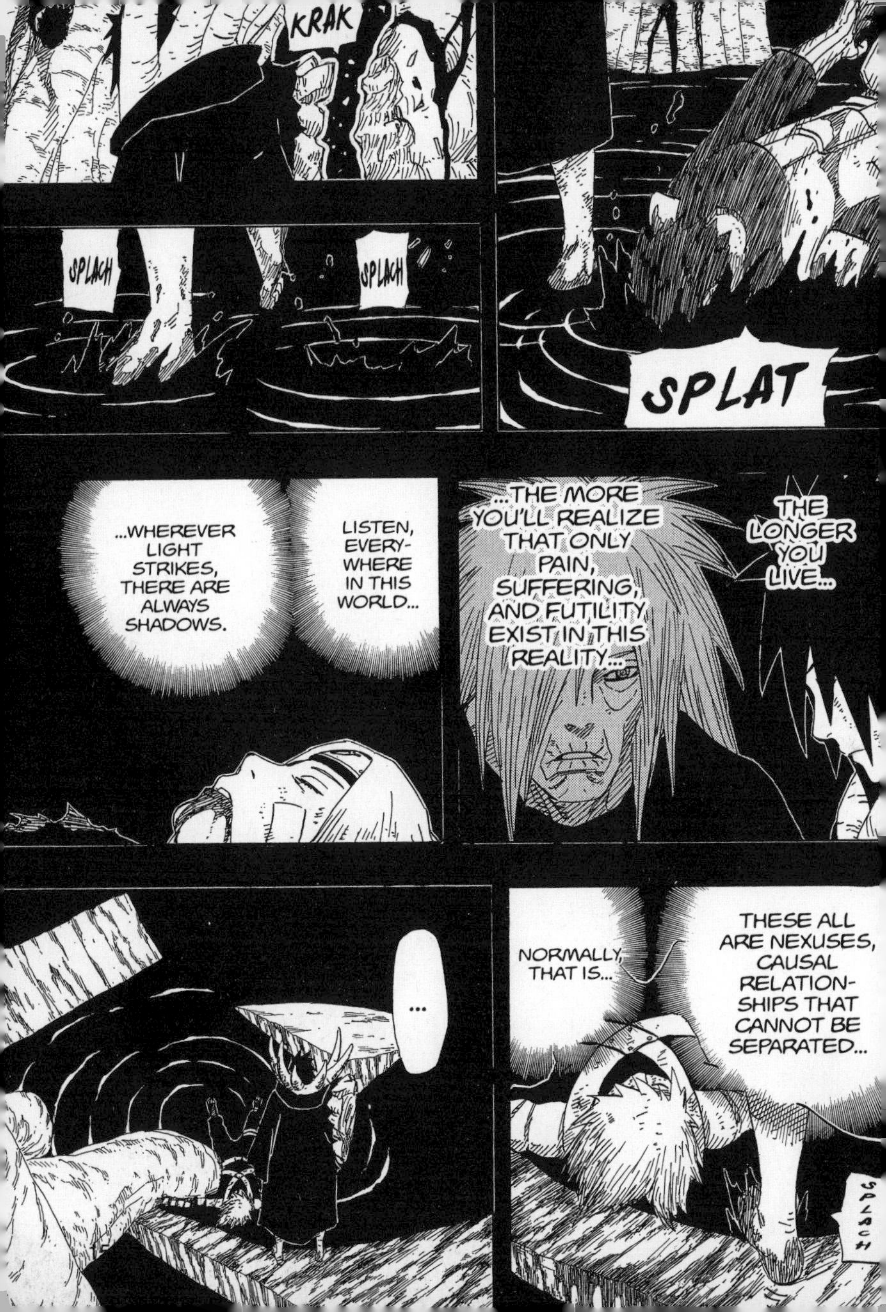
SPLAT
KRAK
SPLACH
SPLACH
THE LONGER YOU LIVE...
...THE MORE YOU'LL REALIZE THAT ONLY PAIN, SUFFERING, AND FUTILITY EXIST IN THIS REALITY...
LISTEN, EVERYWHERE IN THIS WORLD...
...WHEREVER LIGHT STRIKES, THERE ARE ALWAYS SHADOWS.
THESE ALL ARE NEXUSES, CAUSAL RELATIONSHIPS THAT CANNOT BE SEPARATED...
NORMALLY, THAT IS...
SPLACH
...

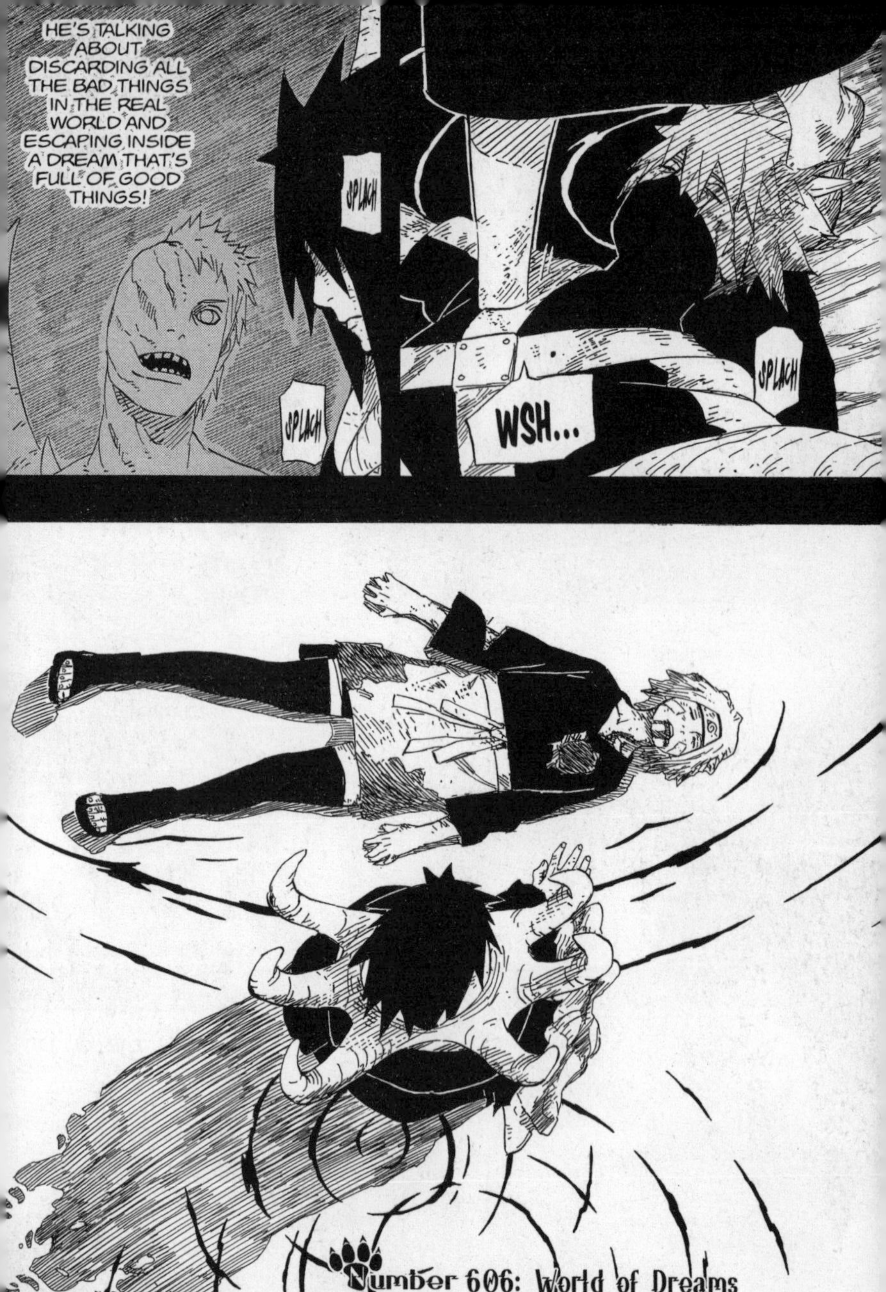
SPLACH
WSH...
SPLACH
SPLACH
HE'S TALKING ABOUT DISCARDING ALL THE BAD THINGS IN THE REAL WORLD AND ESCAPING INSIDE A DREAM THAT'S FULL OF GOOD THINGS!

Number 606: World of Dreams

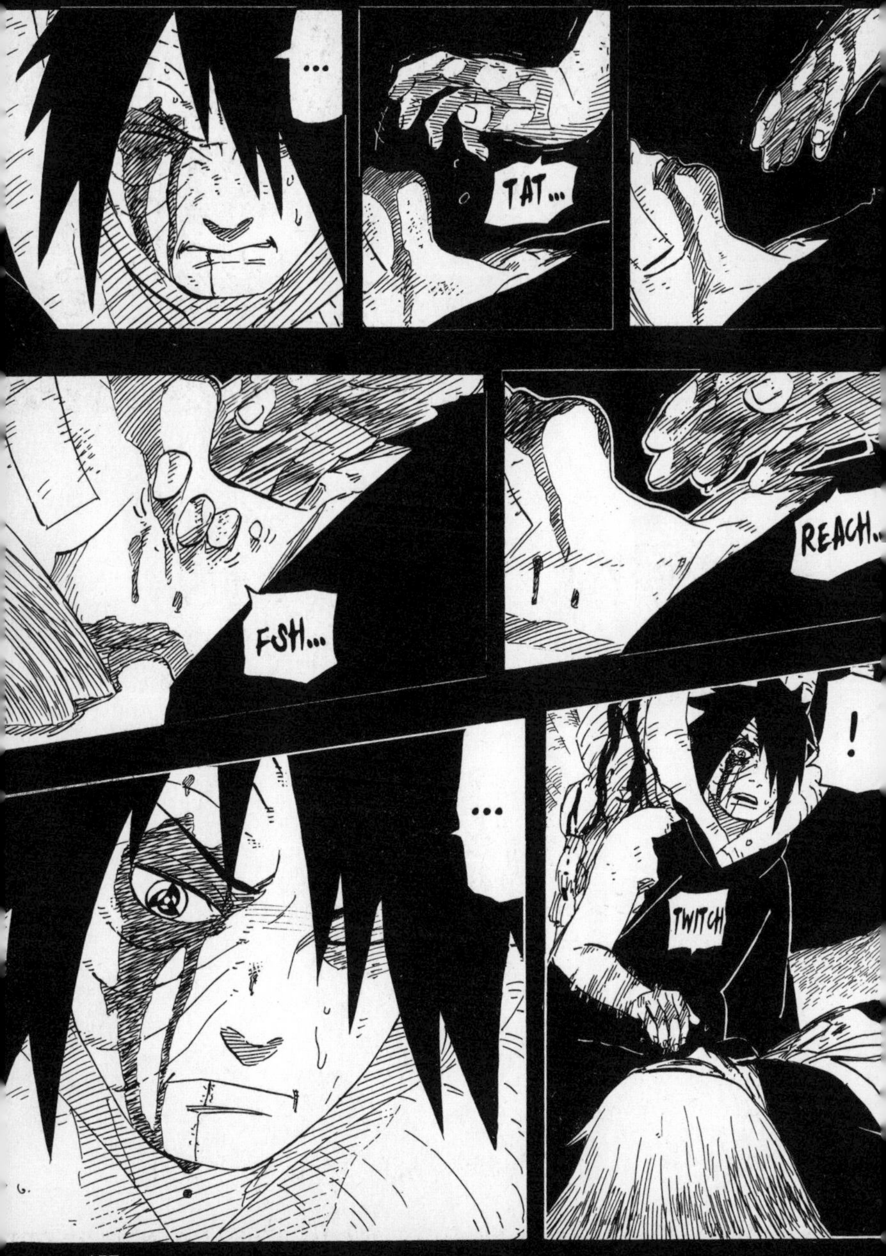
TAT...
...
REACH...
FSH...
!
TWITCH
...

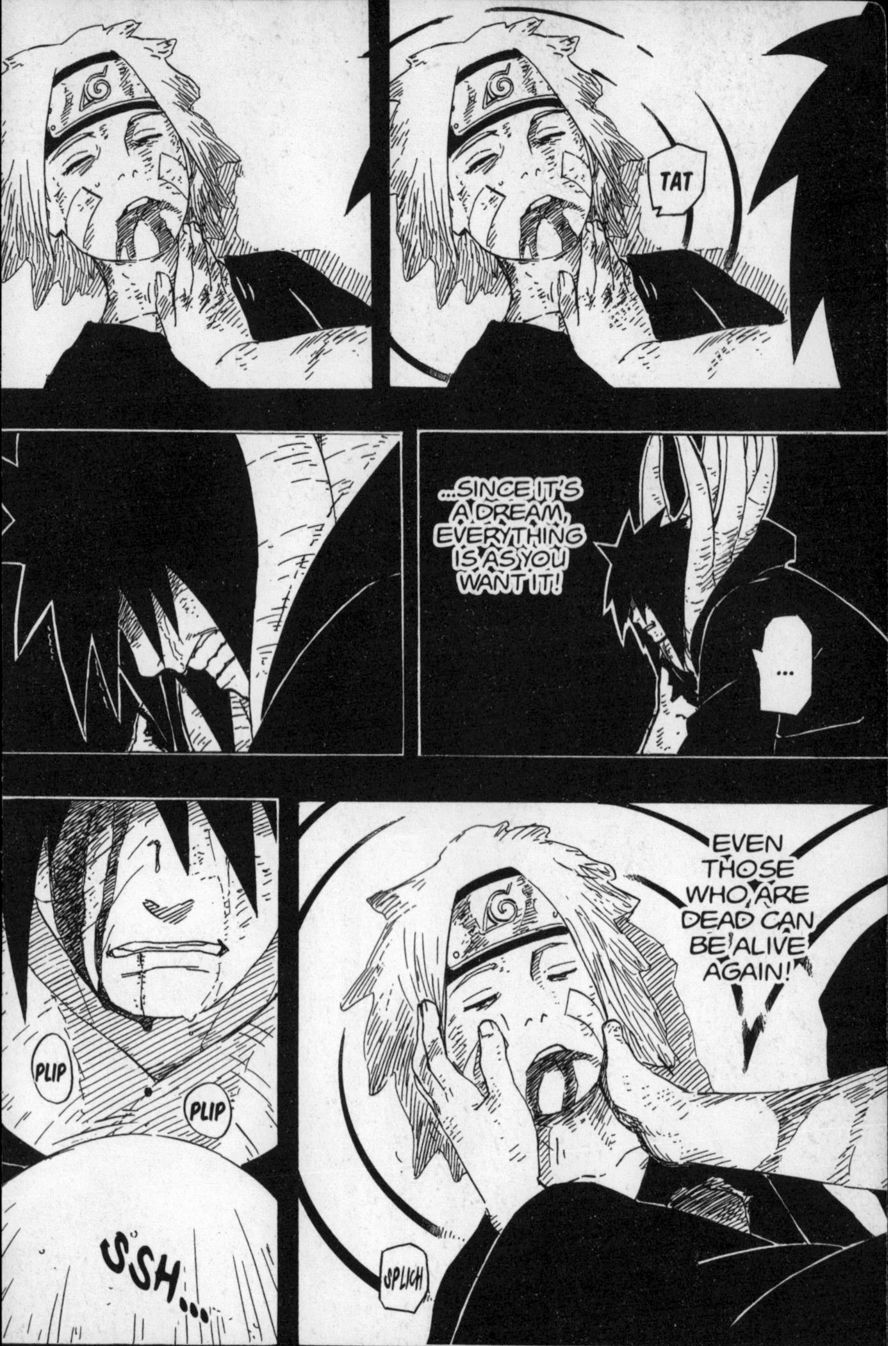
TAT
...SINCE IT'S A DREAM, EVERYTHING IS AS YOU WANT IT!
...
EVEN THOSE WHO ARE DEAD CAN BE ALIVE AGAIN!
SPLICH
PLIP
PLIP
S'SH...

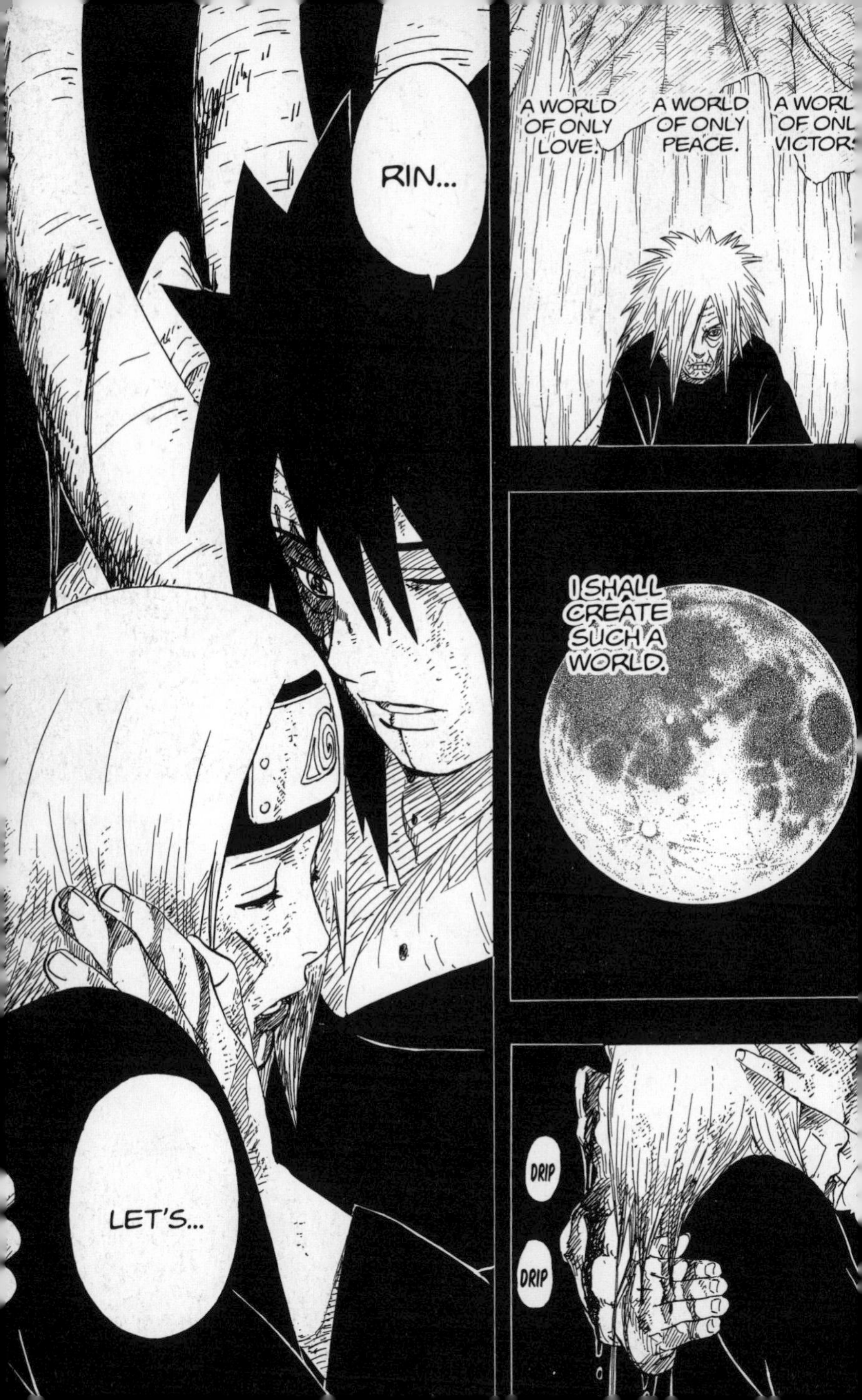
A WORL OF ONL VICTOR
A WORLD OF ONLY PEACE.
A WORLD OF ONLY LOVE.
I SHALL CREATE SUCH A WORLD.
DRIP
DRIP
RIN...
LET'S...

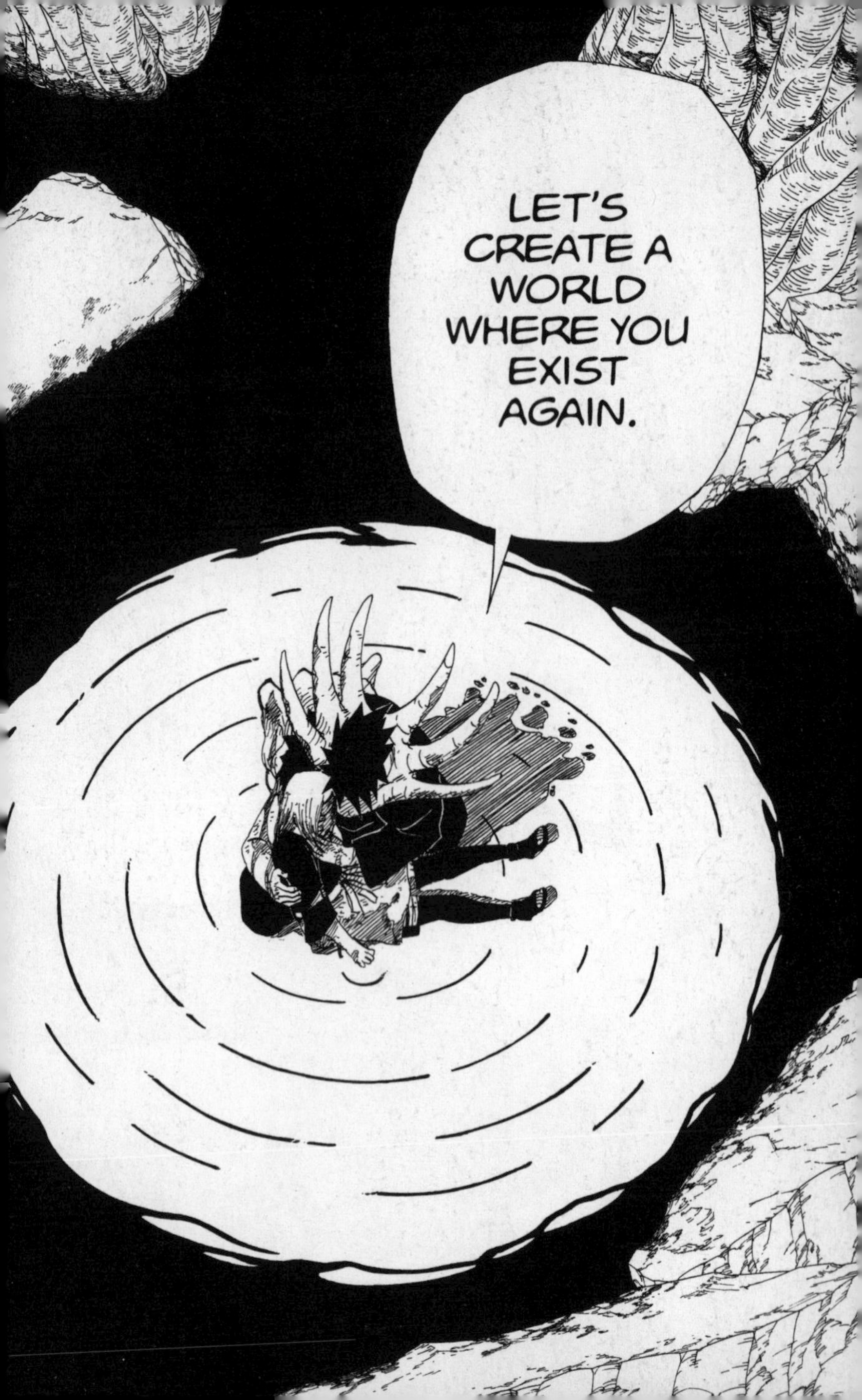
LET'S CREATE A WORLD WHERE YOU EXIST AGAIN.

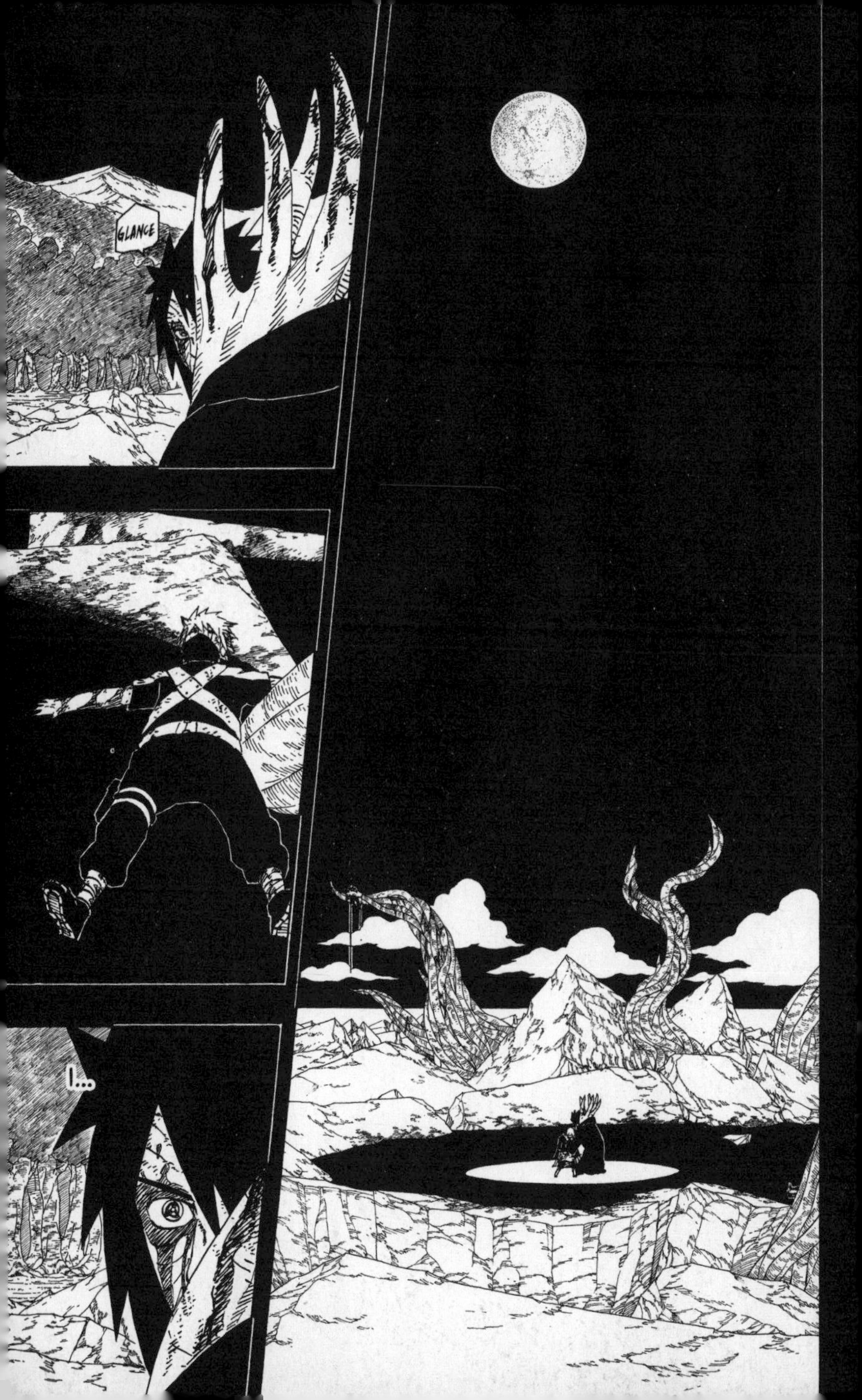
GLANCE
I...

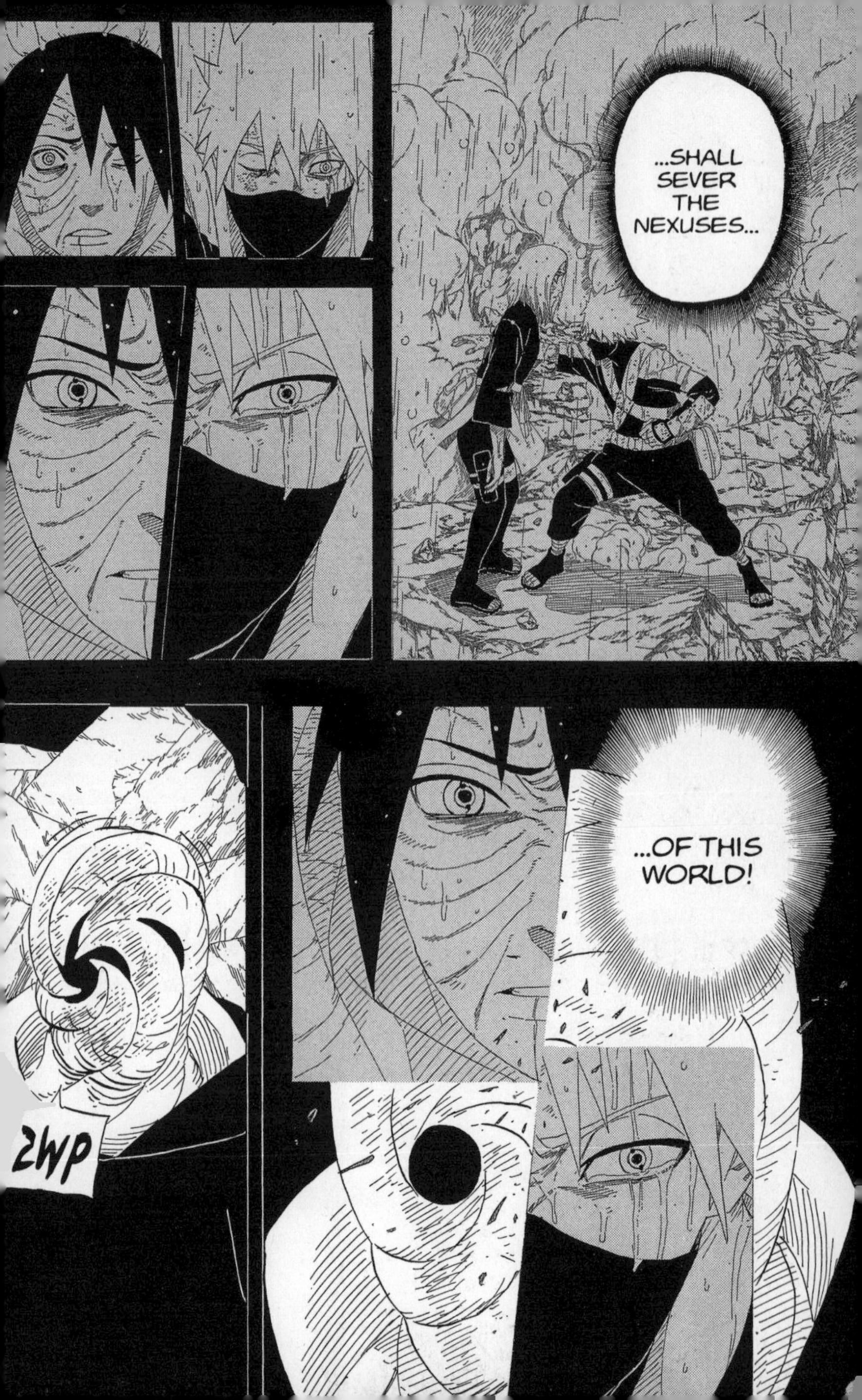
...SHALL SEVER THE NEXUSES...
...OF THIS WORLD!
ZWP

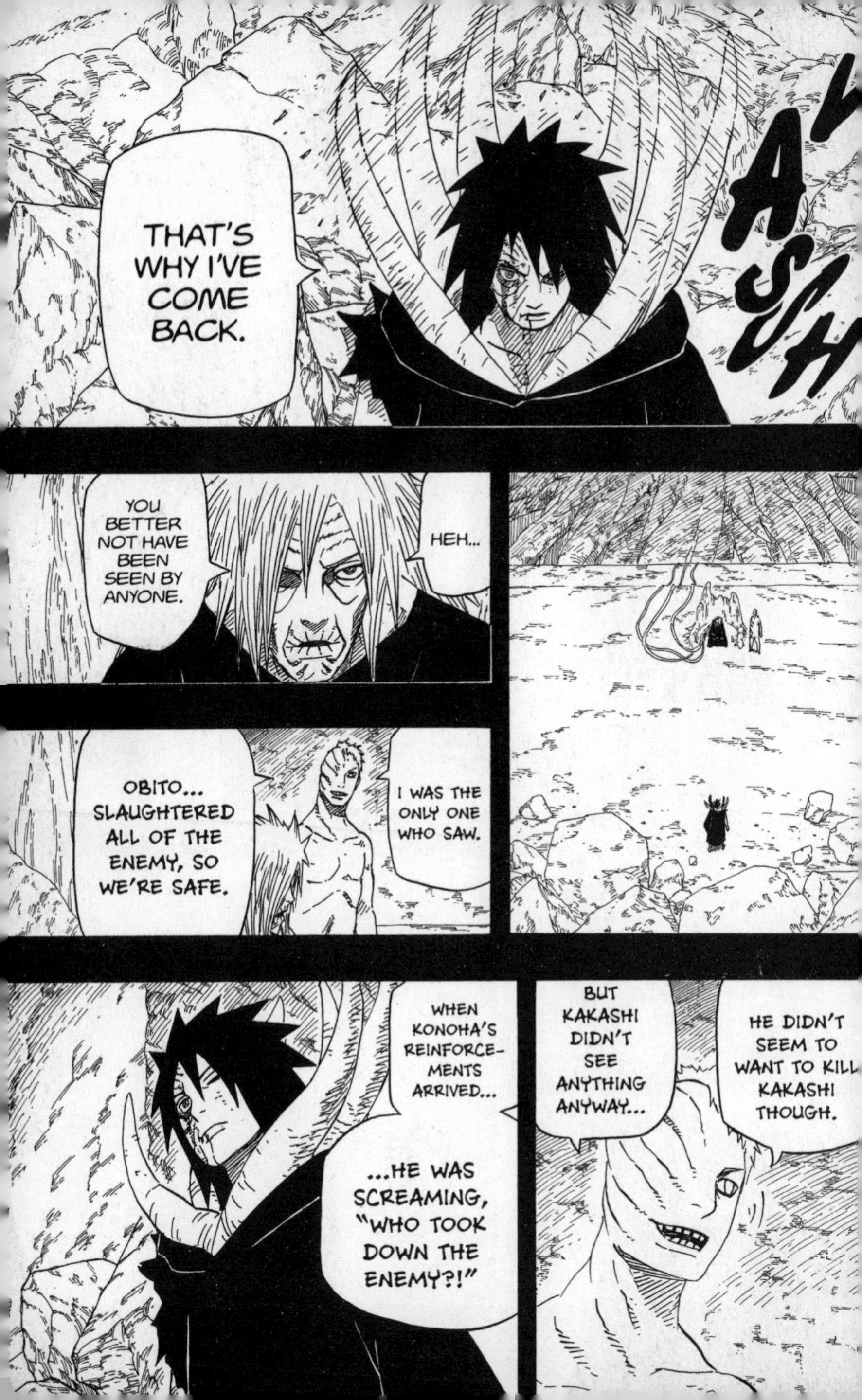
THAT'S WHY I'VE COME BACK.
HEH...
YOU BETTER NOT HAVE BEEN SEEN BY ANYONE.
I WAS THE ONLY ONE WHO SAW.
OBITO... SLAUGHTERED ALL OF THE ENEMY, SO WE'RE SAFE.
HE DIDN'T SEEM TO WANT TO KILL KAKASHI THOUGH.
BUT KAKASHI DIDN'T SEE ANYTHING ANYWAY...
WHEN KONOHA'S REINFORCE-MENTS ARRIVED...
...HE WAS SCREAMING, "WHO TOOK DOWN THE ENEMY?!"

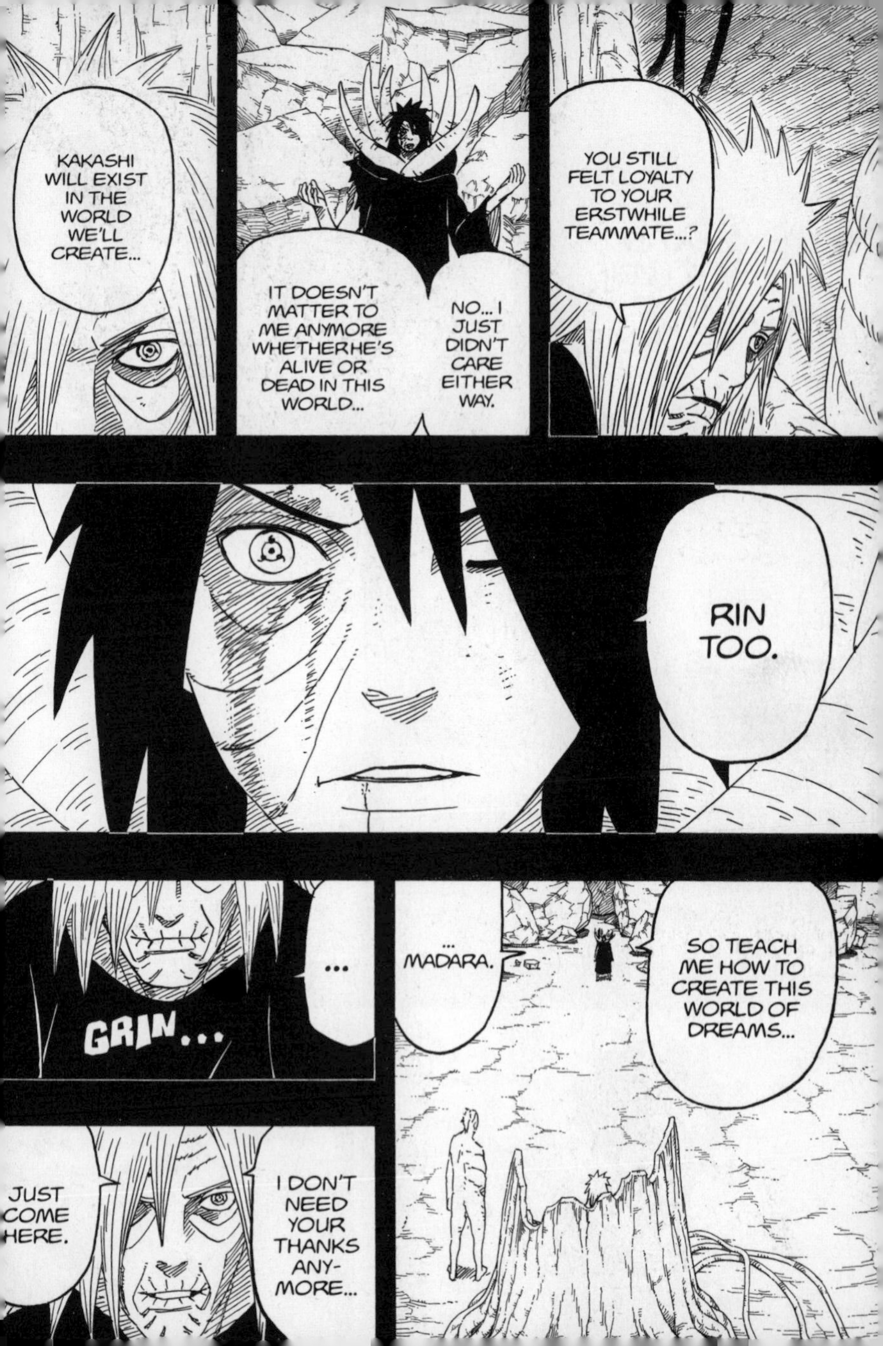
YOU STILL FELT LOYALTY TO YOUR ERSTWHILE TEAMMATE...?
NO... I JUST DIDN'T CARE EITHER WAY.
IT DOESN'T MATTER TO ME ANYMORE WHETHERHE'S ALIVE OR DEAD IN THIS WORLD...
KAKASHI WILL EXIST IN THE WORLD WE'LL CREATE...
RIN TOO.
SO TEACH ME HOW TO CREATE THIS WORLD OF DREAMS...
... MADARA.
...
GRIN...
I DON'T NEED YOUR THANKS ANYMORE...
JUST COME HERE.

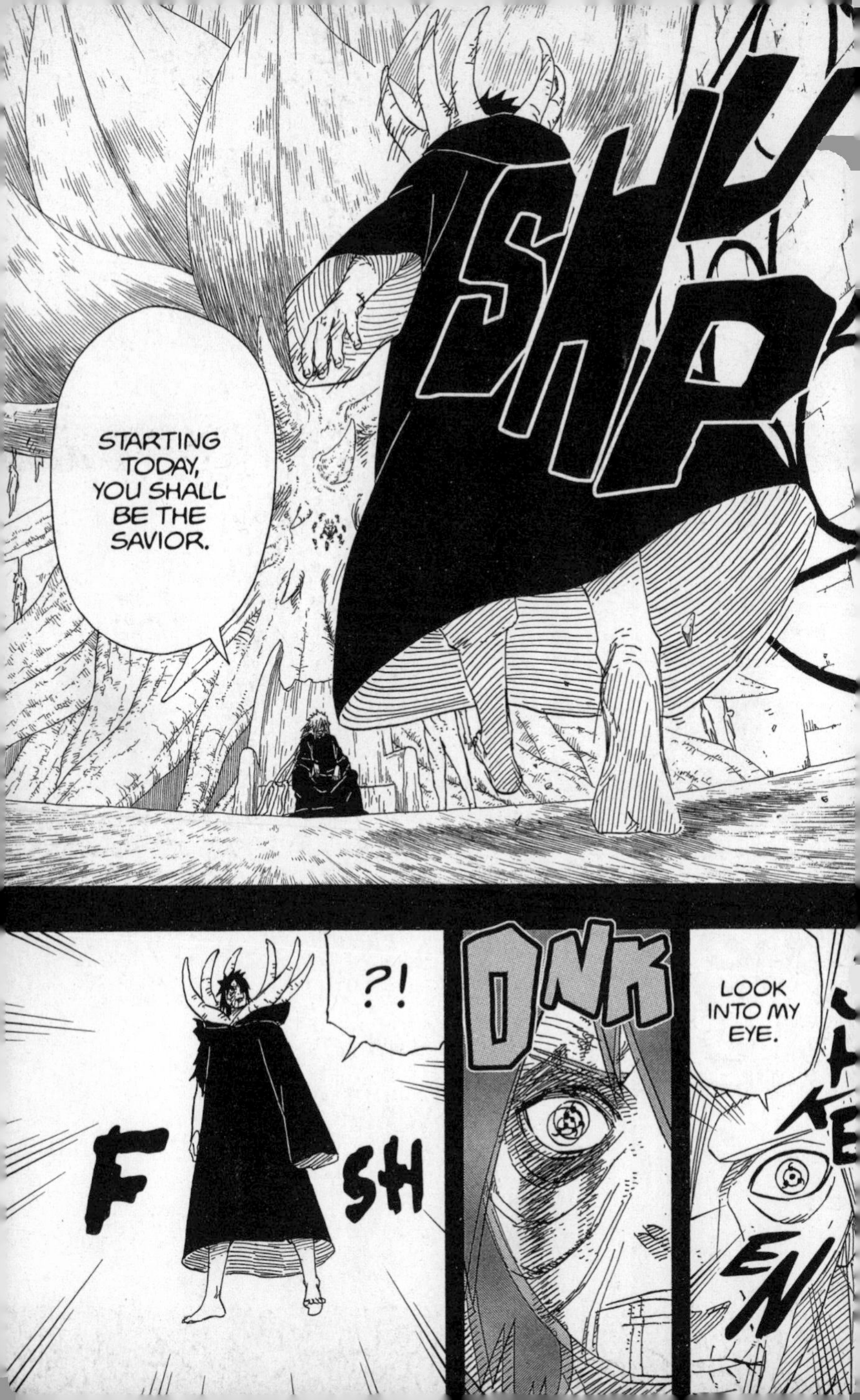
STARTING TODAY, YOU SHALL BE THE SAVIOR.
LOOK INTO MY EYE.
DNK
?!
F SH

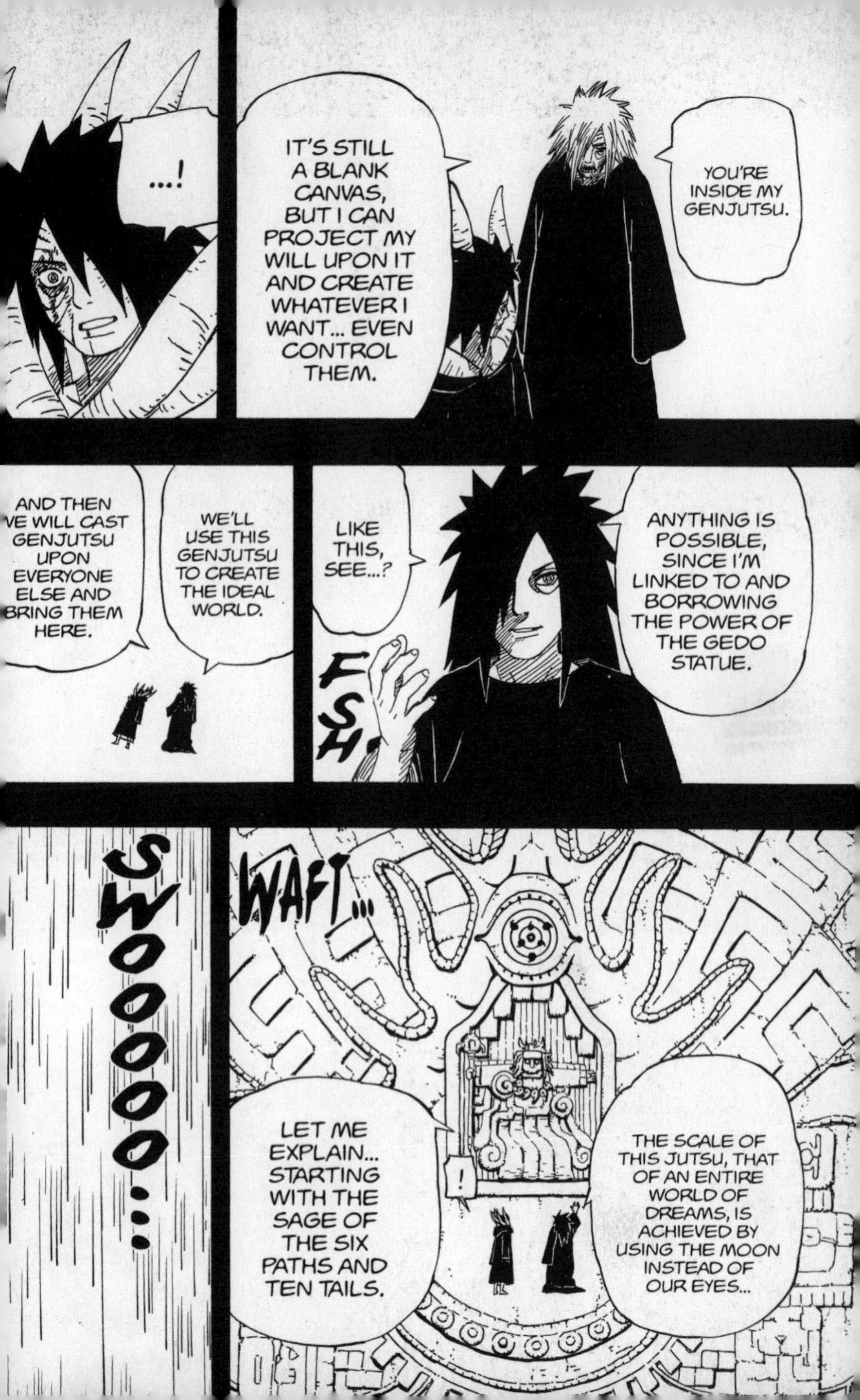
YOU'RE INSIDE MY GENJUTSU.
IT'S STILL A BLANK CANVAS, BUT I CAN PROJECT MY WILL UPON IT AND CREATE WHATEVER I WANT... EVEN CONTROL THEM.
...!
ANYTHING IS POSSIBLE, SINCE I'M LINKED TO AND BORROWING THE POWER OF THE GEDO STATUE.
LIKE THIS, SEE...?
FSH
WE'LL USE THIS GENJUTSU TO CREATE THE IDEAL WORLD.
AND THEN VE WILL CAST GENJUTSU UPON EVERYONE ELSE AND BRING THEM HERE.
WAFT...
THE SCALE OF THIS JUTSU, THAT OF AN ENTIRE WORLD OF DREAMS, IS ACHIEVED BY USING THE MOON INSTEAD OF OUR EYES...
!
LET ME EXPLAIN... STARTING WITH THE SAGE OF THE SIX PATHS AND TEN TAILS.
SWOOOOOO...

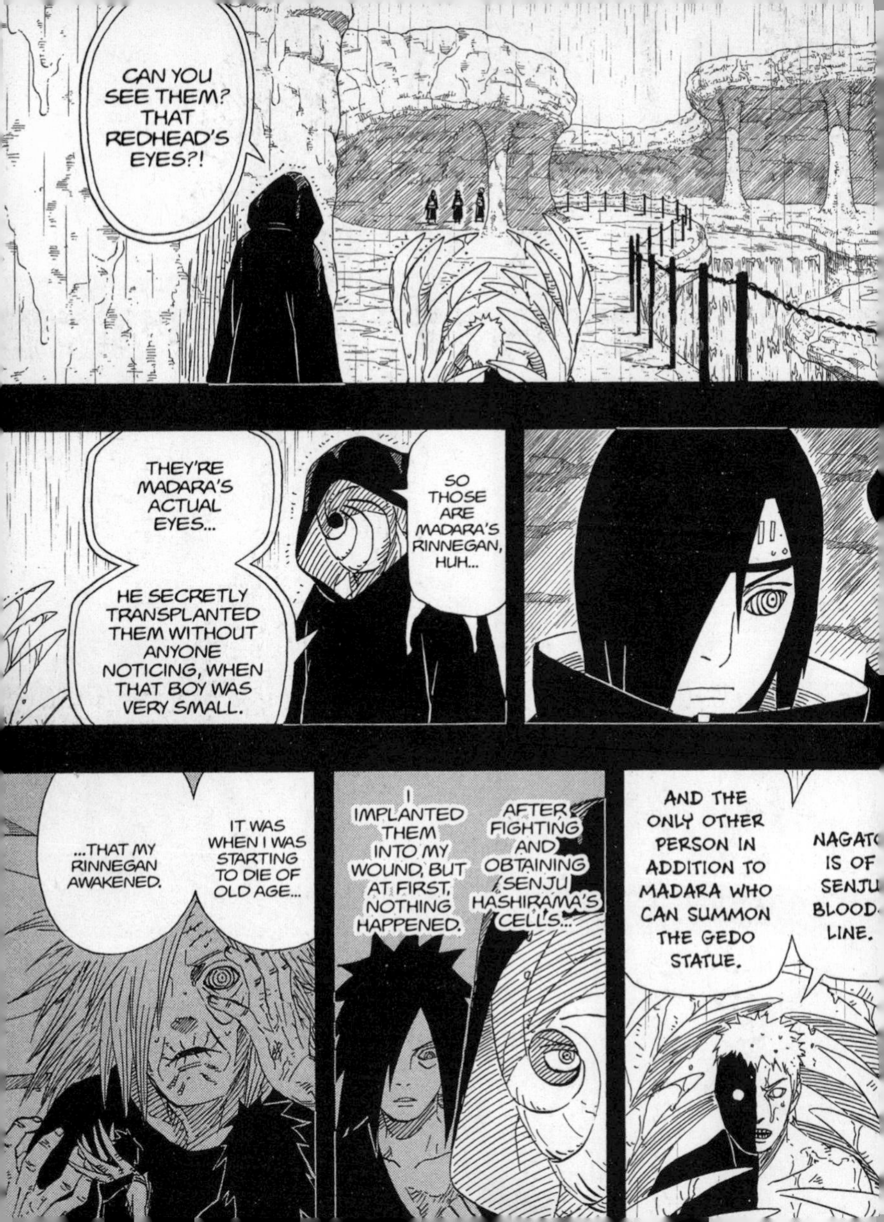
CAN YOU SEE THEM? THAT REDHEAD'S EYES?!
SO THOSE ARE MADARA'S RINNEGAN, HUH...
THEY'RE MADARA'S ACTUAL EYES...
HE SECRETLY TRANSPLANTED THEM WITHOUT ANYONE NOTICING, WHEN THAT BOY WAS VERY SMALL.
AND THE ONLY OTHER PERSON IN ADDITION TO MADARA WHO CAN SUMMON THE GEDO STATUE.
NAGATO IS OF SENJU BLOOD-LINE.
AFTER FIGHTING AND OBTAINING SENJU HASHIRAMA'S CELLS...
I IMPLANTED THEM INTO MY WOUND, BUT AT FIRST, NOTHING HAPPENED.
IT WAS WHEN I WAS STARTING TO DIE OF OLD AGE...
...THAT MY RINNEGAN AWAKENED.

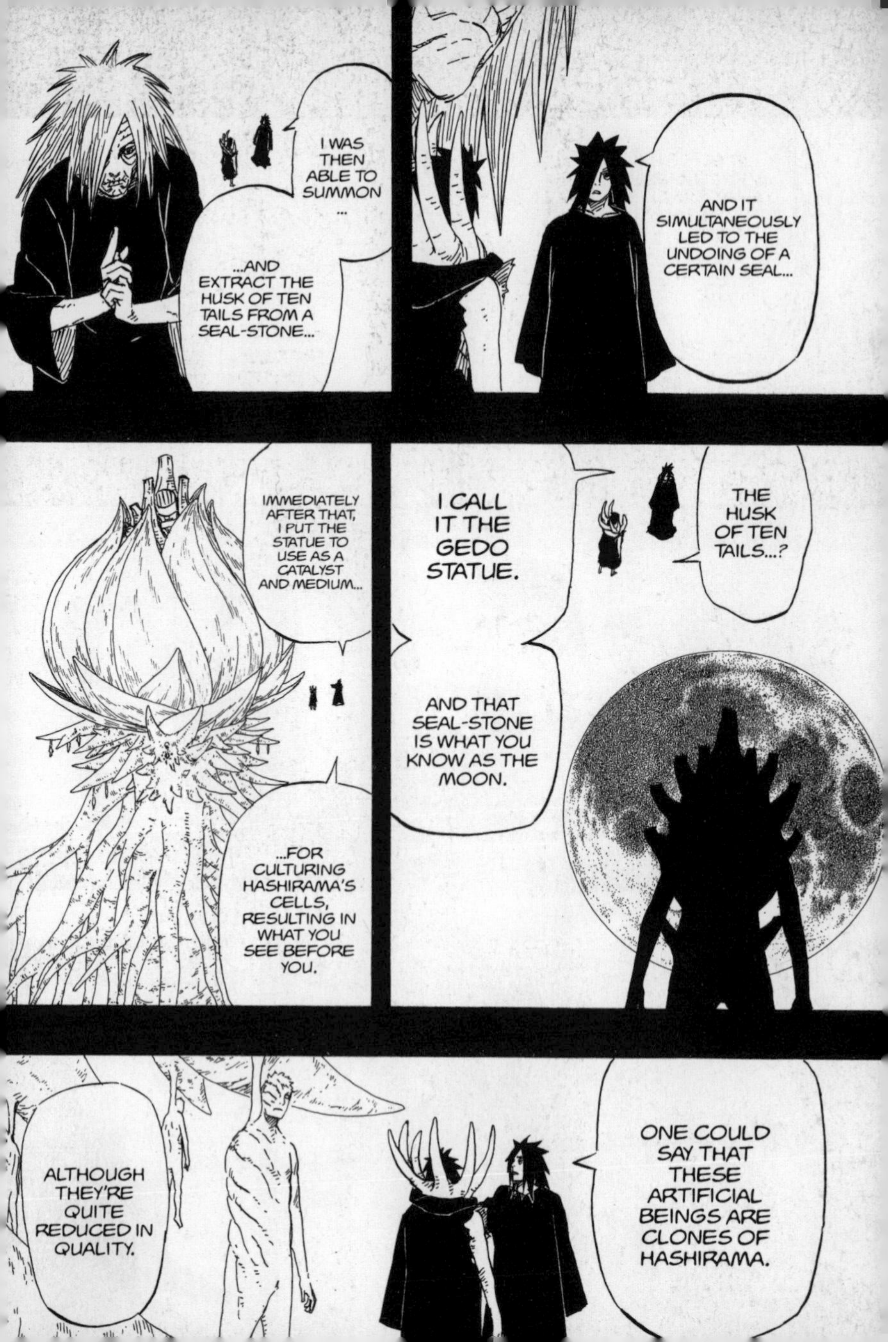
AND IT SIMULTANEOUSLY LED TO THE UNDOING OF A CERTAIN SEAL...
I WAS THEN ABLE TO SUMMON ...
...AND EXTRACT THE HUSK OF TEN TAILS FROM A SEAL-STONE...
THE HUSK OF TEN TAILS...?
I CALL IT THE GEDO STATUE.
AND THAT SEAL-STONE IS WHAT YOU KNOW AS THE MOON.
IMMEDIATELY AFTER THAT, I PUT THE STATUE TO USE AS A CATALYST AND MEDIUM...
...FOR CULTURING HASHIRAMA'S CELLS, RESULTING IN WHAT YOU SEE BEFORE YOU.
ONE COULD SAY THAT THESE ARTIFICIAL BEINGS ARE CLONES OF HASHIRAMA.
ALTHOUGH THEY'RE QUITE REDUCED IN QUALITY.

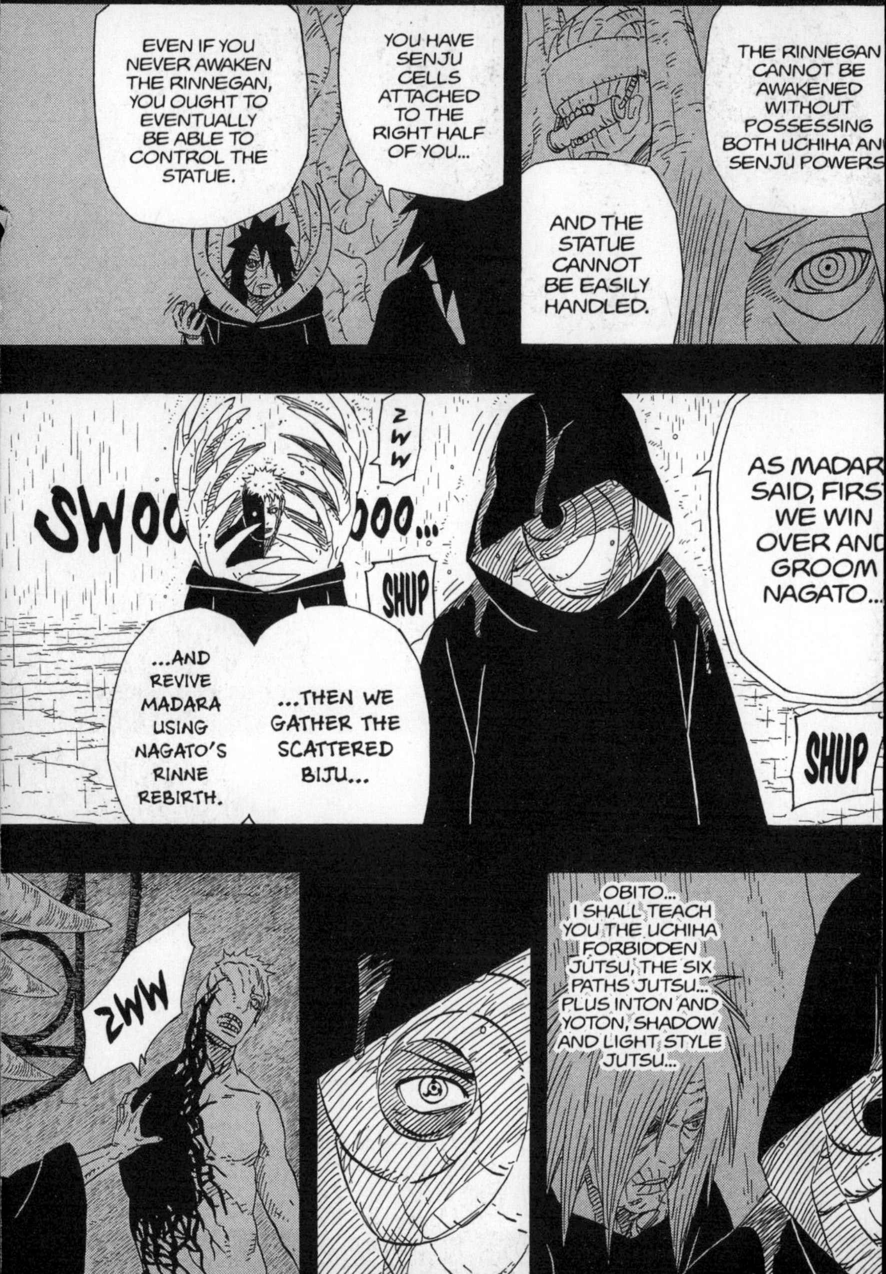
THE RINNEGAN CANNOT BE AWAKENED WITHOUT POSSESSING BOTH UCHIHA AN SENJU POWERS
AND THE STATUE CANNOT BE EASILY HANDLED.
YOU HAVE SENJU CELLS ATTACHED TO THE RIGHT HALF OF YOU...
EVEN IF YOU NEVER AWAKEN THE RINNEGAN, YOU OUGHT TO EVENTUALLY BE ABLE TO CONTROL THE STATUE.
AS MADAR SAID, FIRS WE WIN OVER AN GROOM NAGATO...
SHUP
SHUP
...THEN WE GATHER THE SCATTERED BIJU...
...AND REVIVE MADARA USING NAGATO'S RINNE REBIRTH.
ZWW
SWOO OOO...
OBITO... I SHALL TEACH YOU THE UCHIHA FORBIDDEN JUTSU, THE SIX PATHS JUTSU... PLUS INTON AND YOTON, SHADOW AND LIGHT STYLE JUTSU...
ZWW

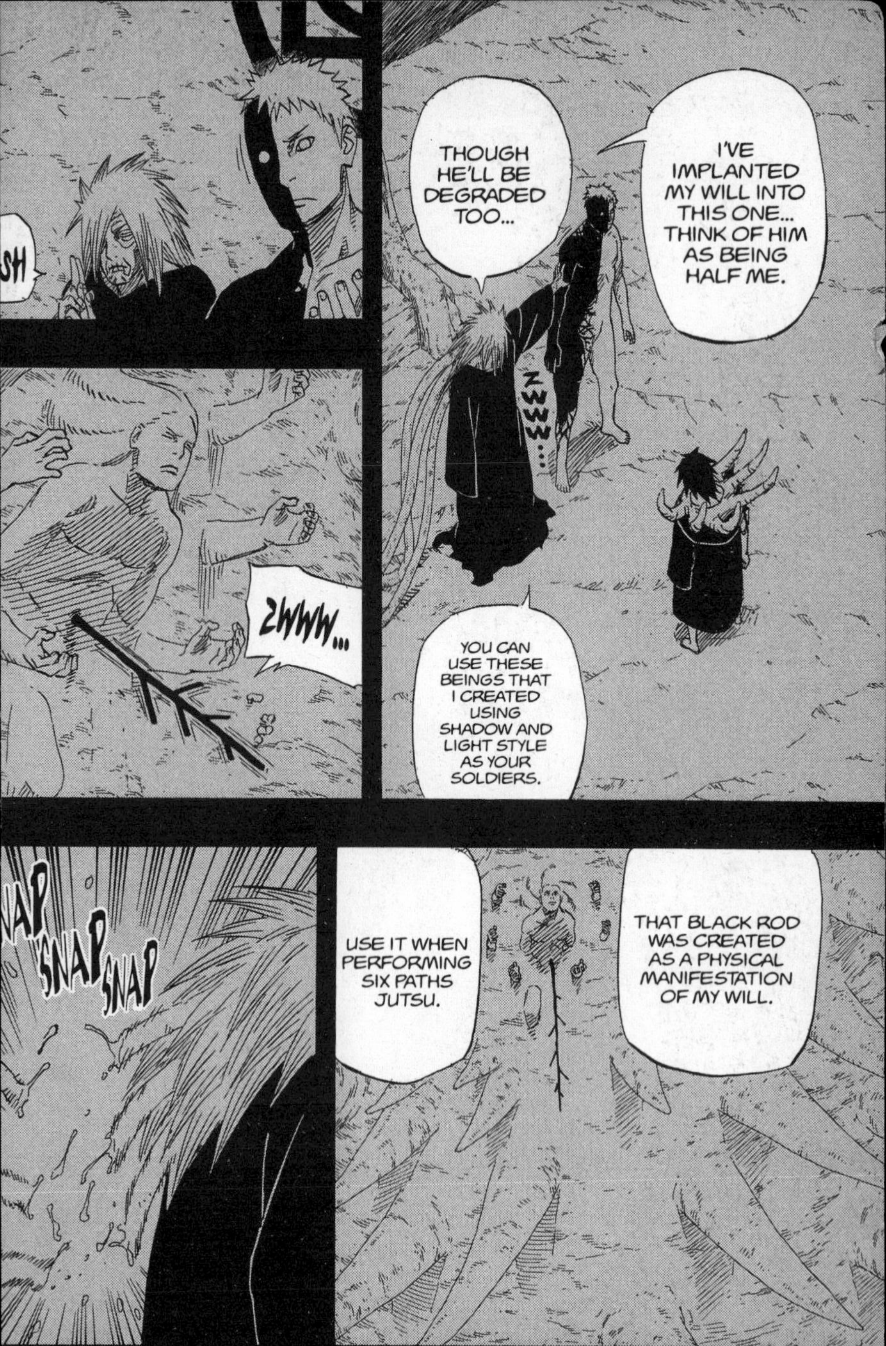
I'VE IMPLANTED MY WILL INTO THIS ONE... THINK OF HIM AS BEING HALF ME.
THOUGH HE'LL BE DEGRADED TOO...
ZWWW...
YOU CAN USE THESE BEINGS THAT I CREATED USING SHADOW AND LIGHT STYLE AS YOUR SOLDIERS.
SH
ZWWW...
THAT BLACK ROD WAS CREATED AS A PHYSICAL MANIFESTATION OF MY WILL.
USE IT WHEN PERFORMING SIX PATHS JUTSU.
NAP SNAP SNAP

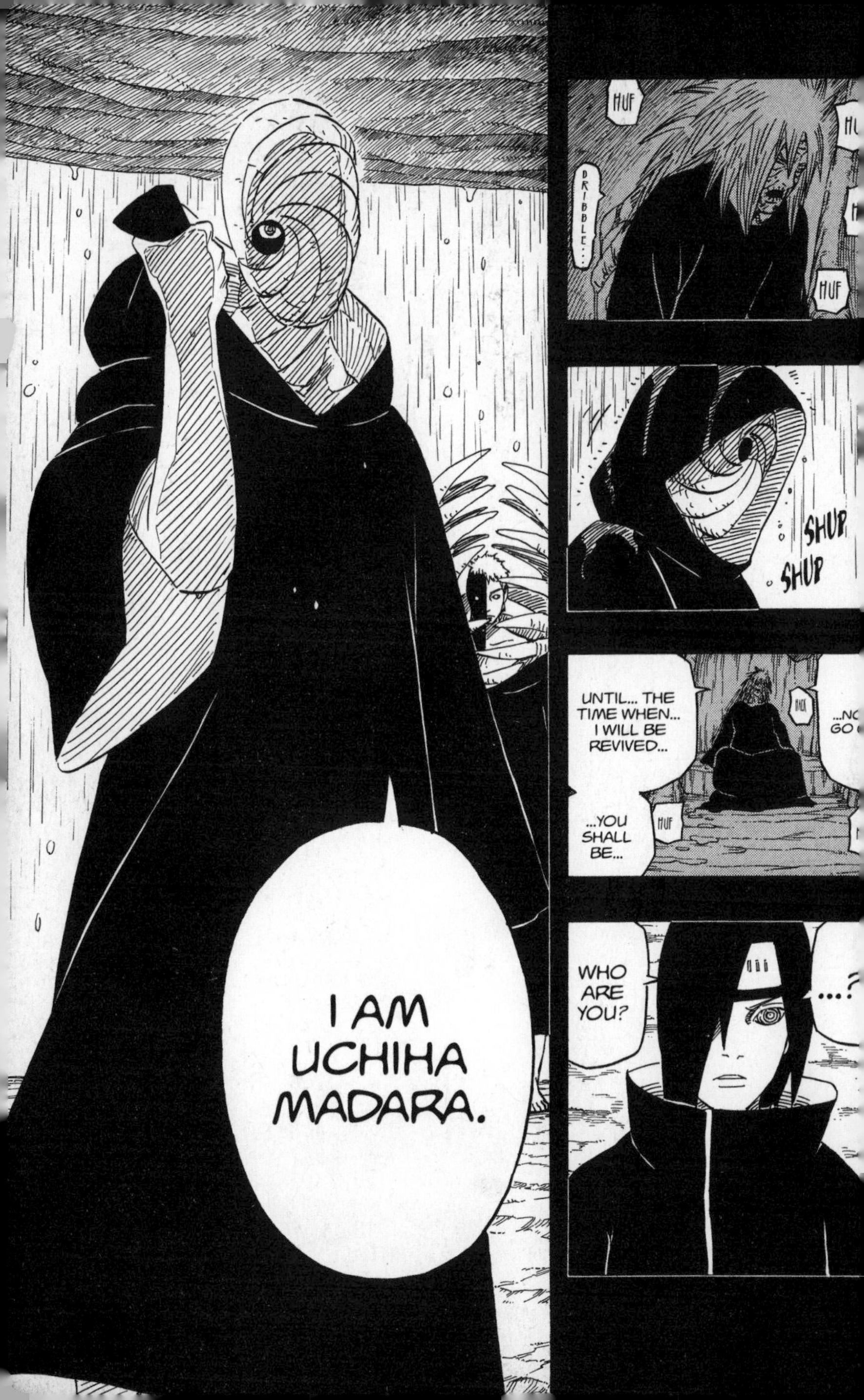
HUF
DRIBBLE...
HUF
SHUP
SHUP
HACK
UNTIL... THE TIME WHEN... I WILL BE REVIVED...
HUF
...YOU SHALL BE...
...?
WHO ARE YOU?
I AM UCHIHA MADARA.

NARUTO

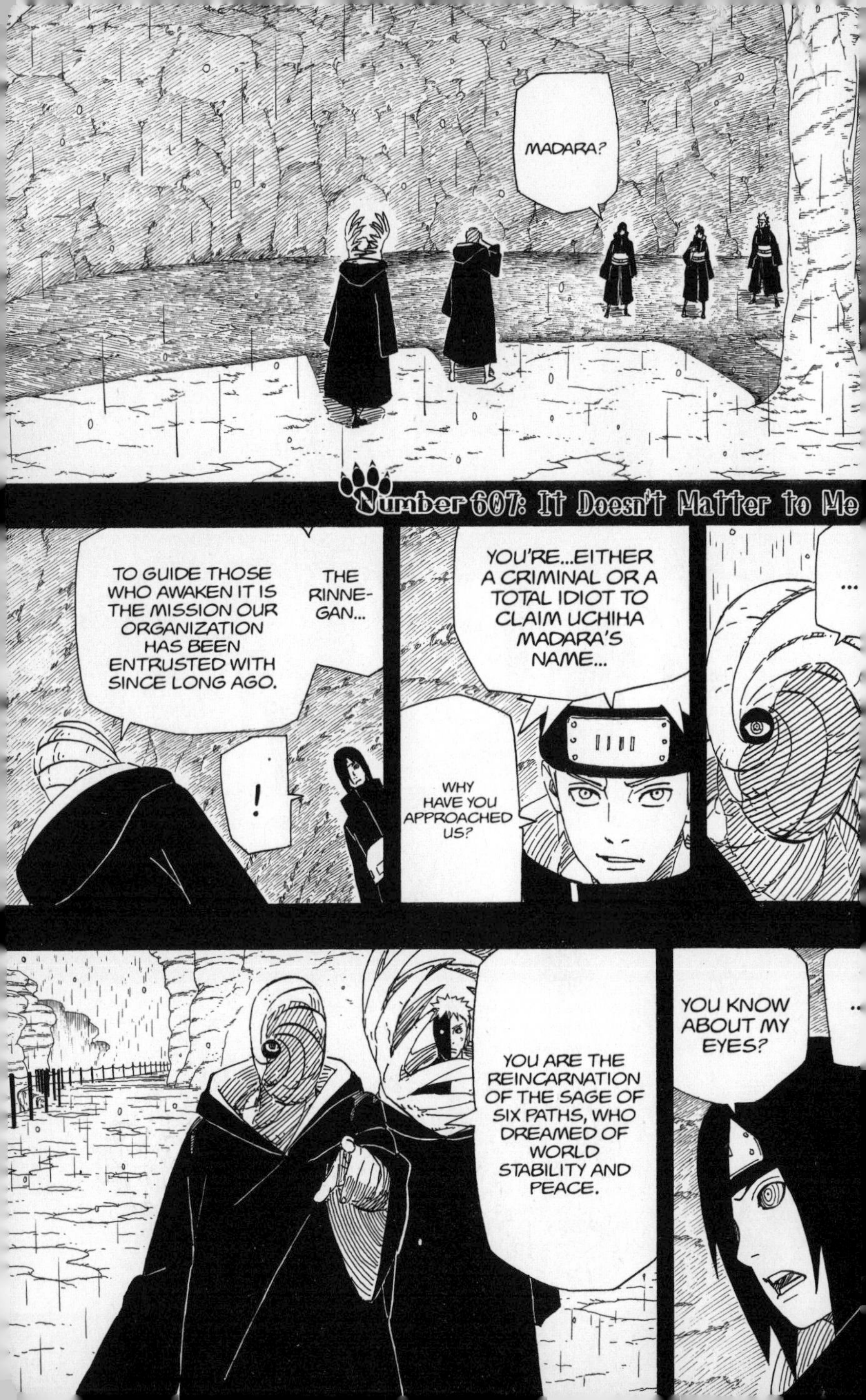
MADARA?
Number 607: It Doesn't Matter to Me
...
YOU'RE...EITHER A CRIMINAL OR A TOTAL IDIOT TO CLAIM UCHIHA MADARA'S NAME...
WHY HAVE YOU APPROACHED US?
THE RINNE-GAN...
TO GUIDE THOSE WHO AWAKEN IT IS THE MISSION OUR ORGANIZATION HAS BEEN ENTRUSTED WITH SINCE LONG AGO.
!
...
YOU KNOW ABOUT MY EYES?
YOU ARE THE REINCARNATION OF THE SAGE OF SIX PATHS, WHO DREAMED OF WORLD STABILITY AND PEACE.

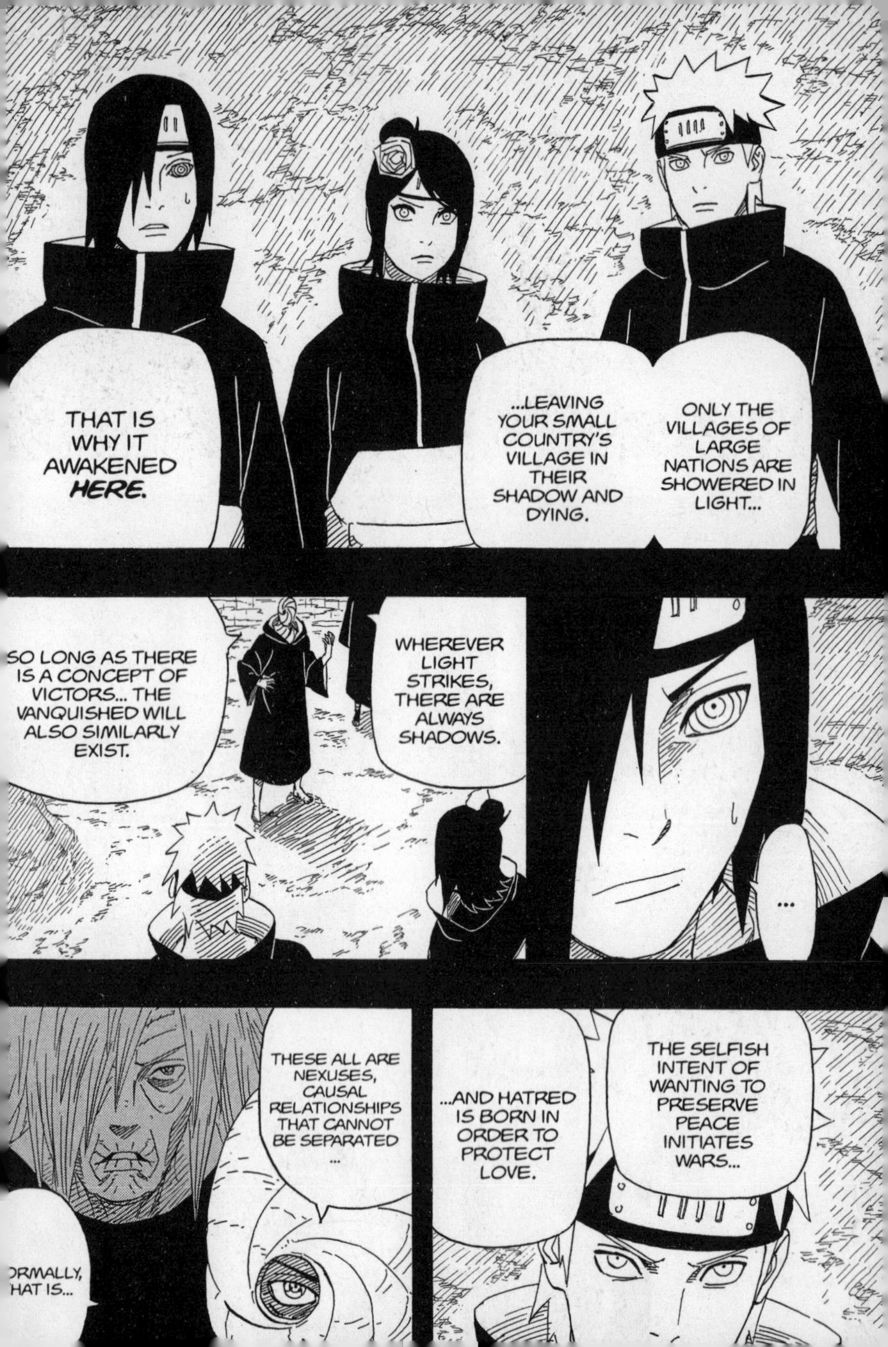
ONLY THE VILLAGES OF LARGE NATIONS ARE SHOWERED IN LIGHT...
...LEAVING YOUR SMALL COUNTRY'S VILLAGE IN THEIR SHADOW AND DYING.
THAT IS WHY IT AWAKENED *HERE.*
...
WHEREVER LIGHT STRIKES, THERE ARE ALWAYS SHADOWS.
SO LONG AS THERE IS A CONCEPT OF VICTORS... THE VANQUISHED WILL ALSO SIMILARLY EXIST.
THE SELFISH INTENT OF WANTING TO PRESERVE PEACE INITIATES WARS...
...AND HATRED IS BORN IN ORDER TO PROTECT LOVE.
THESE ALL ARE NEXUSES, CAUSAL RELATIONSHIPS THAT CANNOT BE SEPARATED...
ORMALLY, HAT IS...

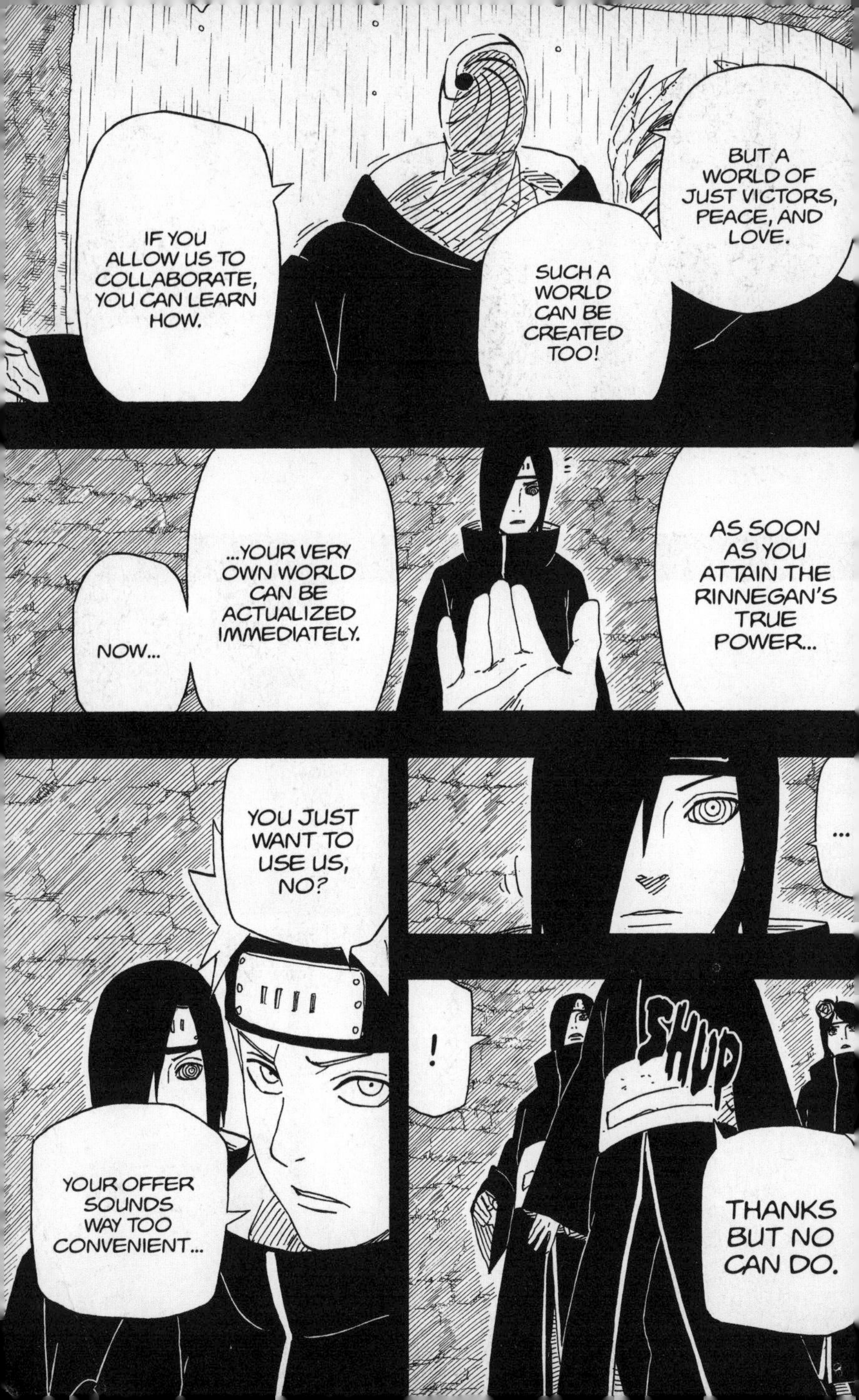
BUT A WORLD OF JUST VICTORS, PEACE, AND LOVE.
SUCH A WORLD CAN BE CREATED TOO!
IF YOU ALLOW US TO COLLABORATE, YOU CAN LEARN HOW.
AS SOON AS YOU ATTAIN THE RINNEGAN'S TRUE POWER...
...YOUR VERY OWN WORLD CAN BE ACTUALIZED IMMEDIATELY.
NOW...
...
!
SHUP
THANKS BUT NO CAN DO.
YOU JUST WANT TO USE US, NO?
YOUR OFFER SOUNDS WAY TOO CONVENIENT...

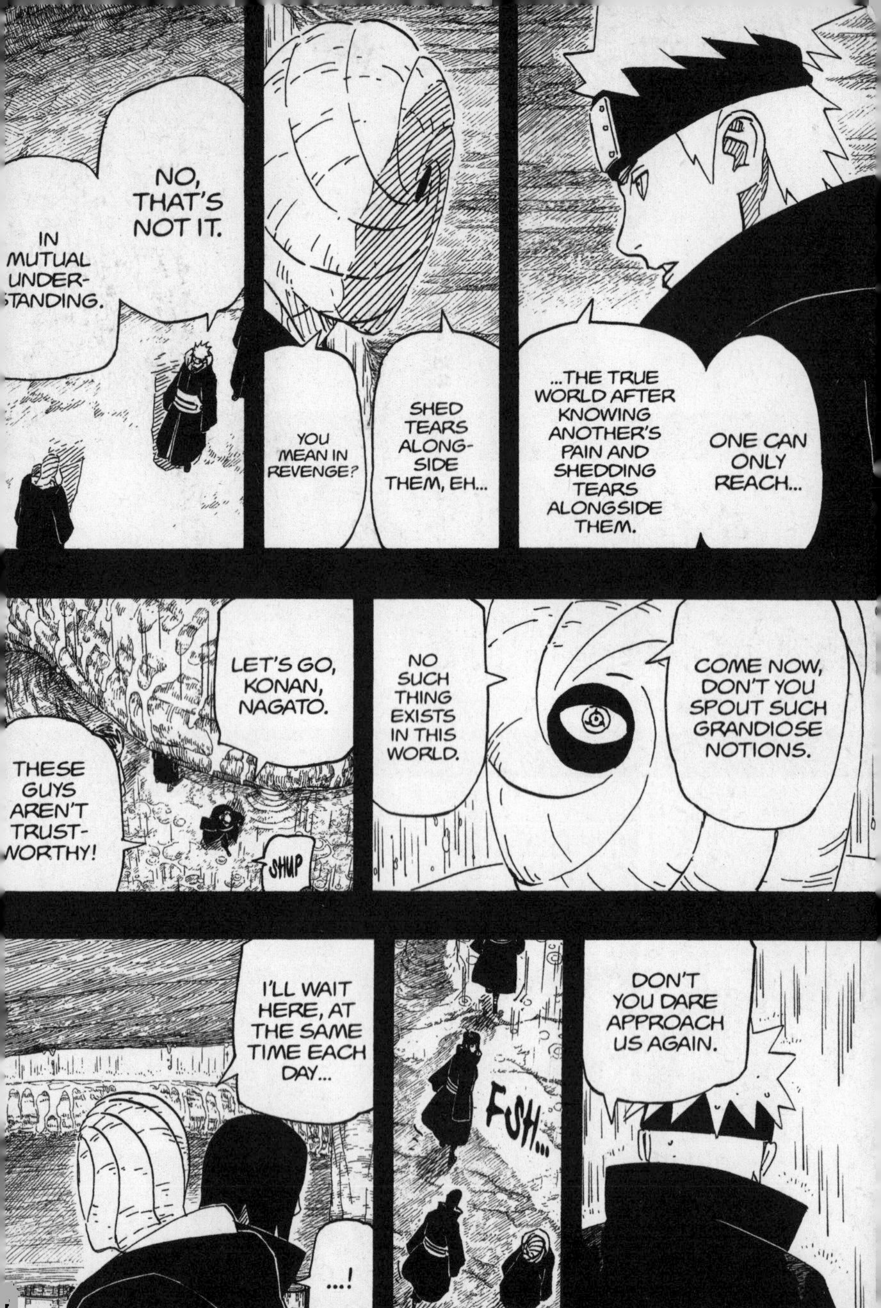
ONE CAN ONLY REACH...
...THE TRUE WORLD AFTER KNOWING ANOTHER'S PAIN AND SHEDDING TEARS ALONGSIDE THEM.
SHED TEARS ALONGSIDE THEM, EH...
YOU MEAN IN REVENGE?
NO, THAT'S NOT IT.
IN MUTUAL UNDERSTANDING.
COME NOW, DON'T YOU SPOUT SUCH GRANDIOSE NOTIONS.
NO SUCH THING EXISTS IN THIS WORLD.
LET'S GO, KONAN, NAGATO.
THESE GUYS AREN'T TRUSTWORTHY!
SHUP
DON'T YOU DARE APPROACH US AGAIN.
FSH...
I'LL WAIT HERE, AT THE SAME TIME EACH DAY...
...!

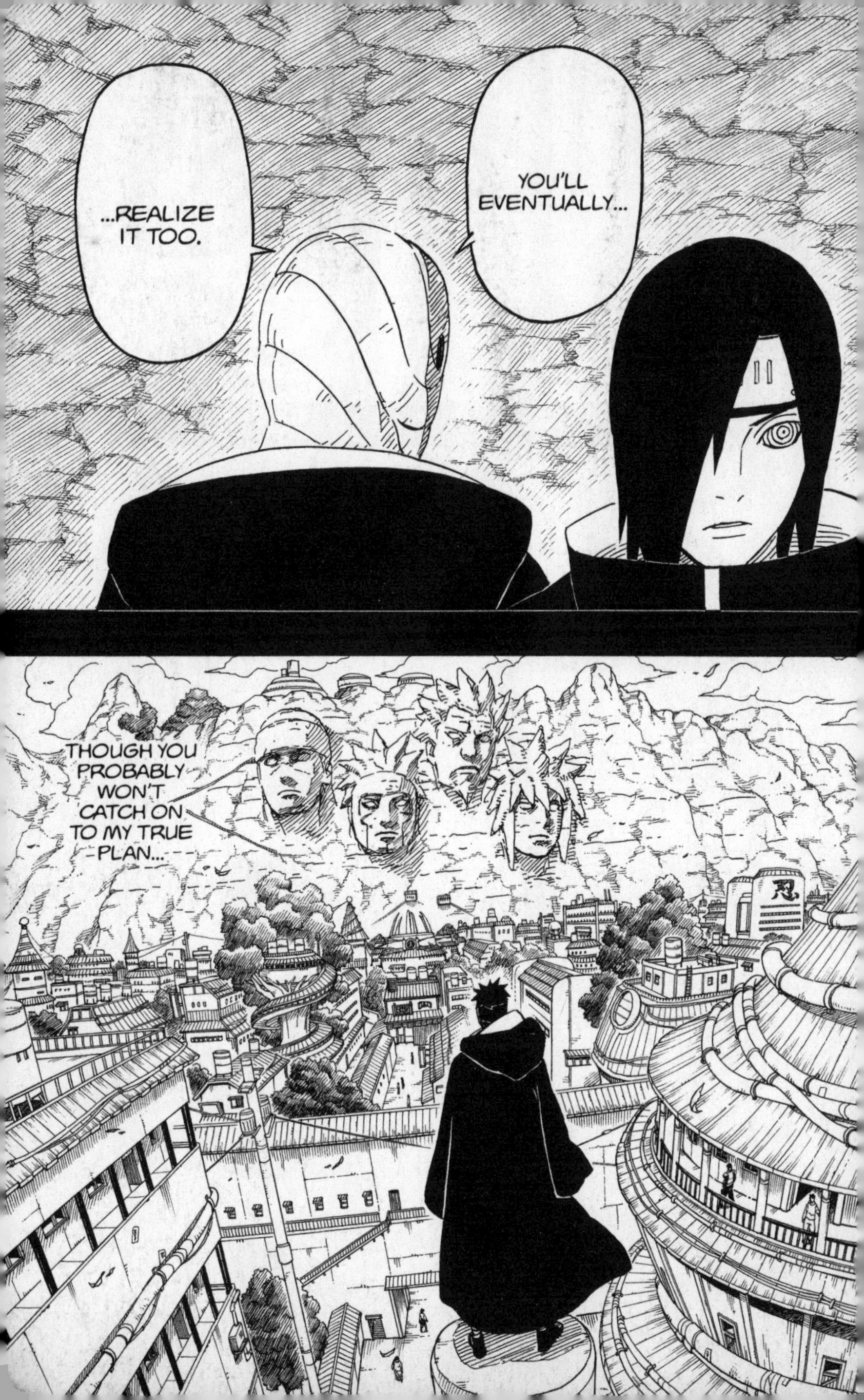
YOU'LL EVENTUALLY...
...REALIZE IT TOO.
THOUGH YOU PROBABLY WON'T CATCH ON TO MY TRUE PLAN...

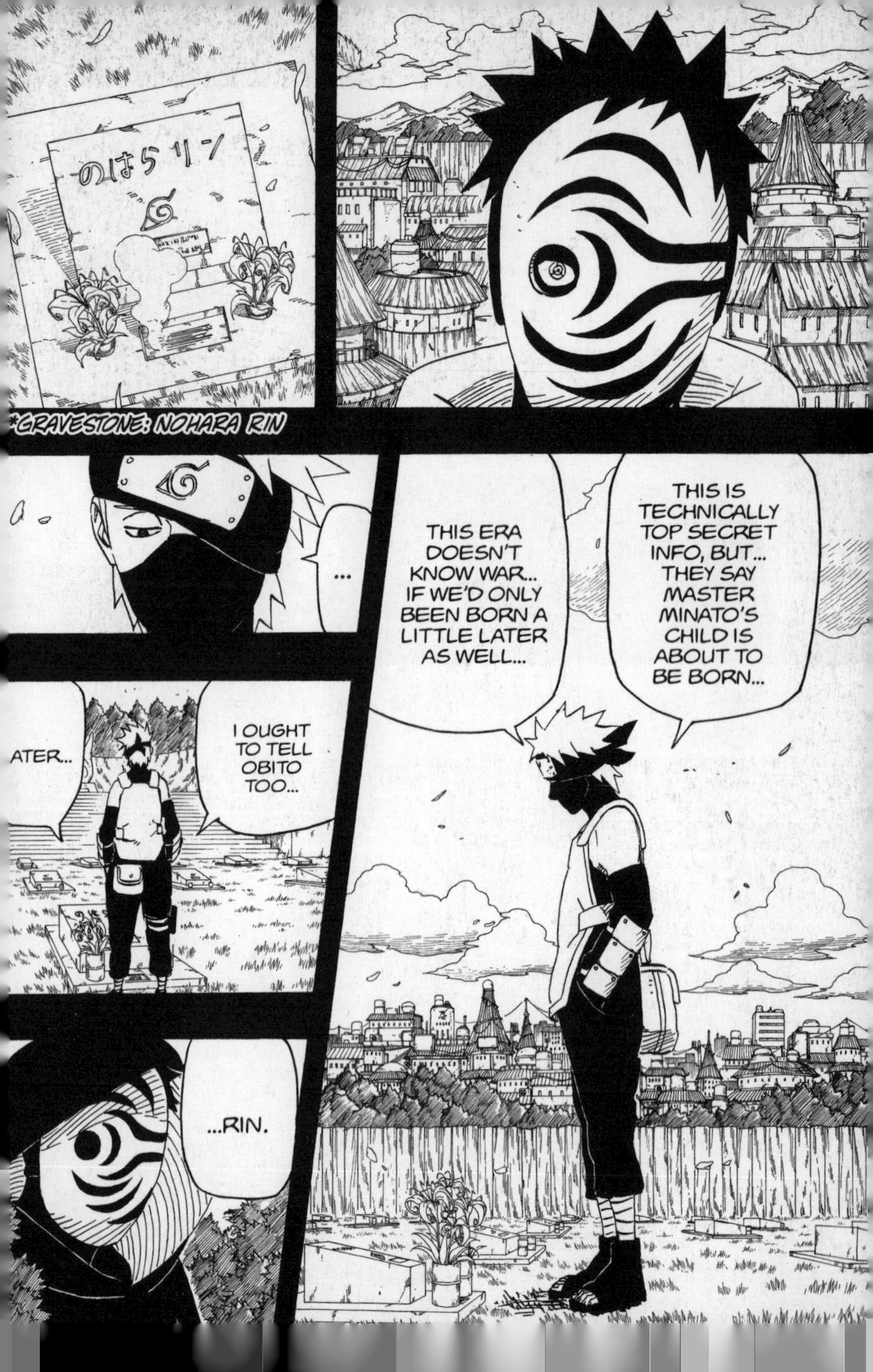
のはらリン
*GRAVESTONE: NOHARA RIN
THIS IS TECHNICALLY TOP SECRET INFO, BUT... THEY SAY MASTER MINATO'S CHILD IS ABOUT TO BE BORN...
THIS ERA DOESN'T KNOW WAR... IF WE'D ONLY BEEN BORN A LITTLE LATER AS WELL...
...
I OUGHT TO TELL OBITO TOO...
ATER...
...RIN.

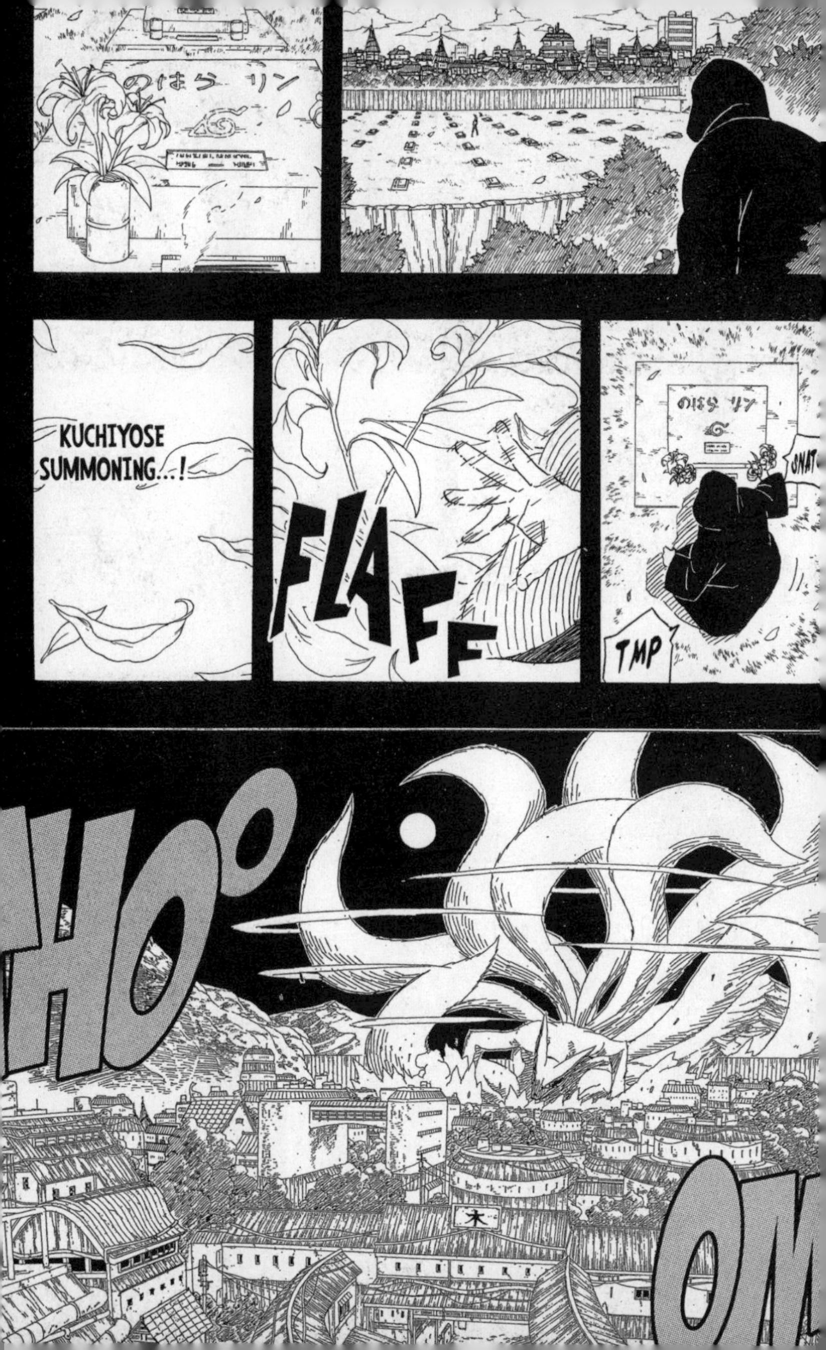
のはら リン
のはら リン
SNAT
TMP
FLAFF
KUCHIYOSE SUMMONING...!
HO
OM

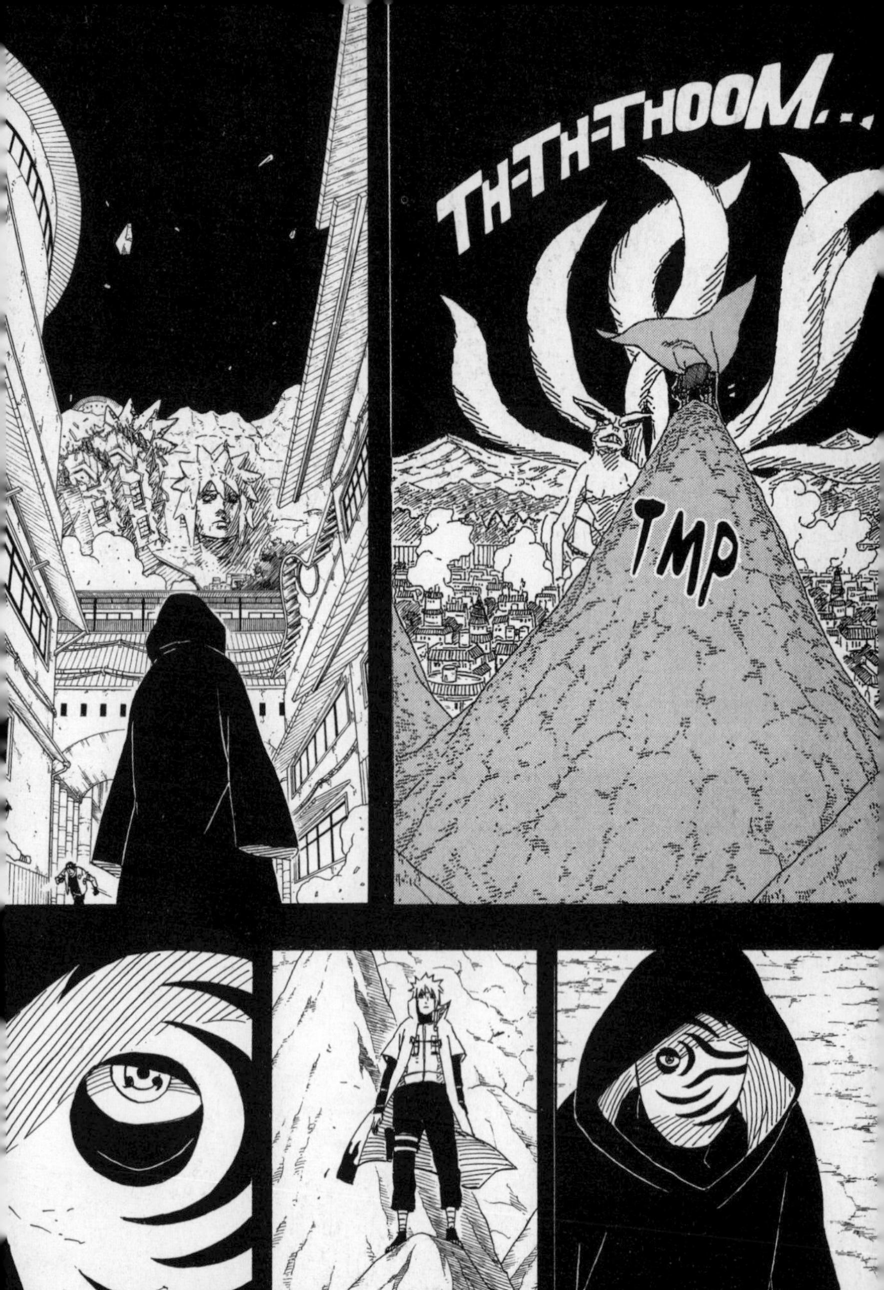
TH-TH-THOOM...
TMP

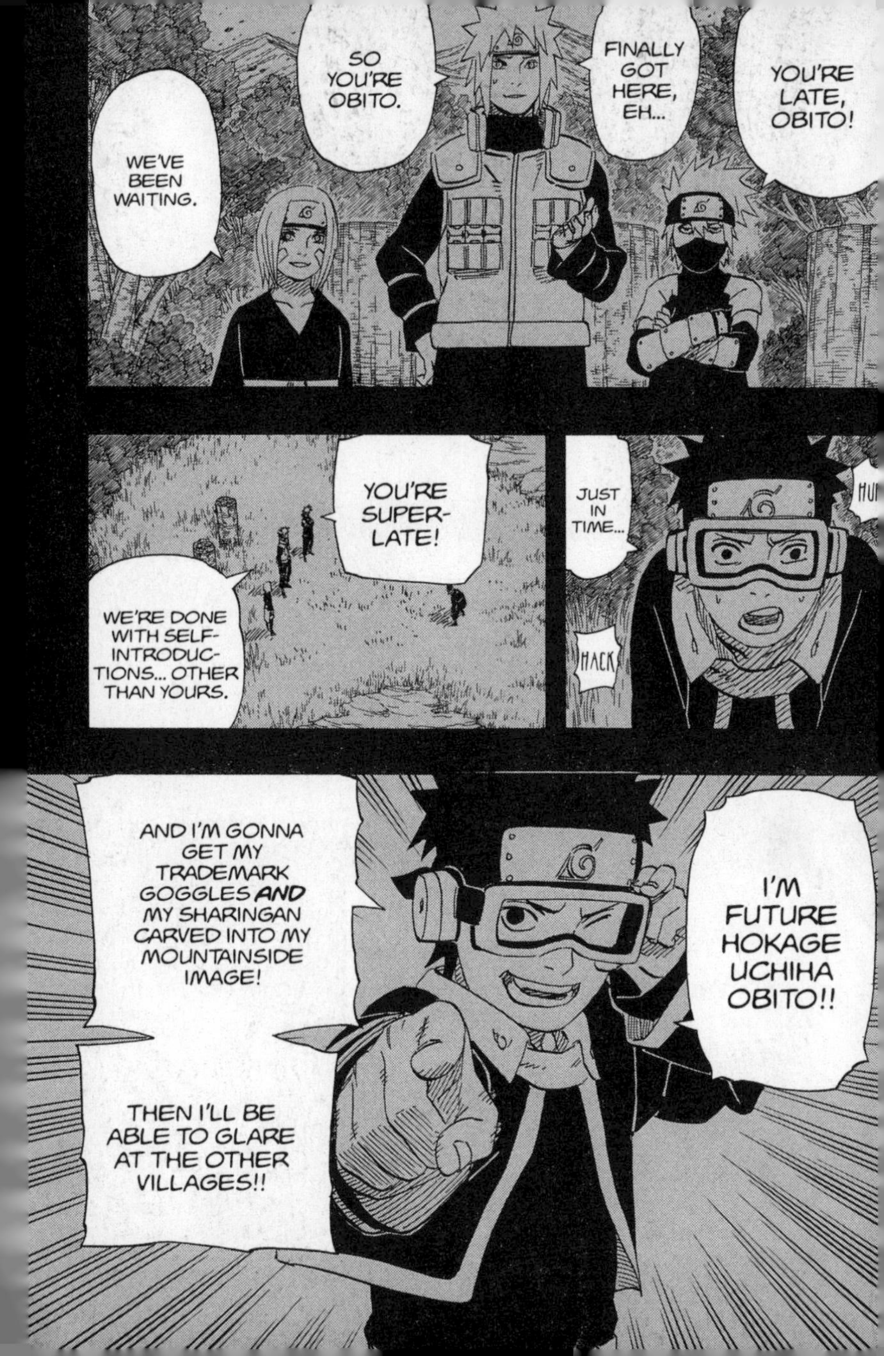

YOU'RE LATE, OBITO!
FINALLY GOT HERE, EH...
SO YOU'RE OBITO.
WE'VE BEEN WAITING.
JUST IN TIME...
HACK
YOU'RE SUPER-LATE!
WE'RE DONE WITH SELF-INTRODUCTIONS... OTHER THAN YOURS.
I'M FUTURE HOKAGE UCHIHA OBITO!!
AND I'M GONNA GET MY TRADEMARK GOGGLES **AND** MY SHARINGAN CARVED INTO MY MOUNTAINSIDE IMAGE!
THEN I'LL BE ABLE TO GLARE AT THE OTHER VILLAGES!!

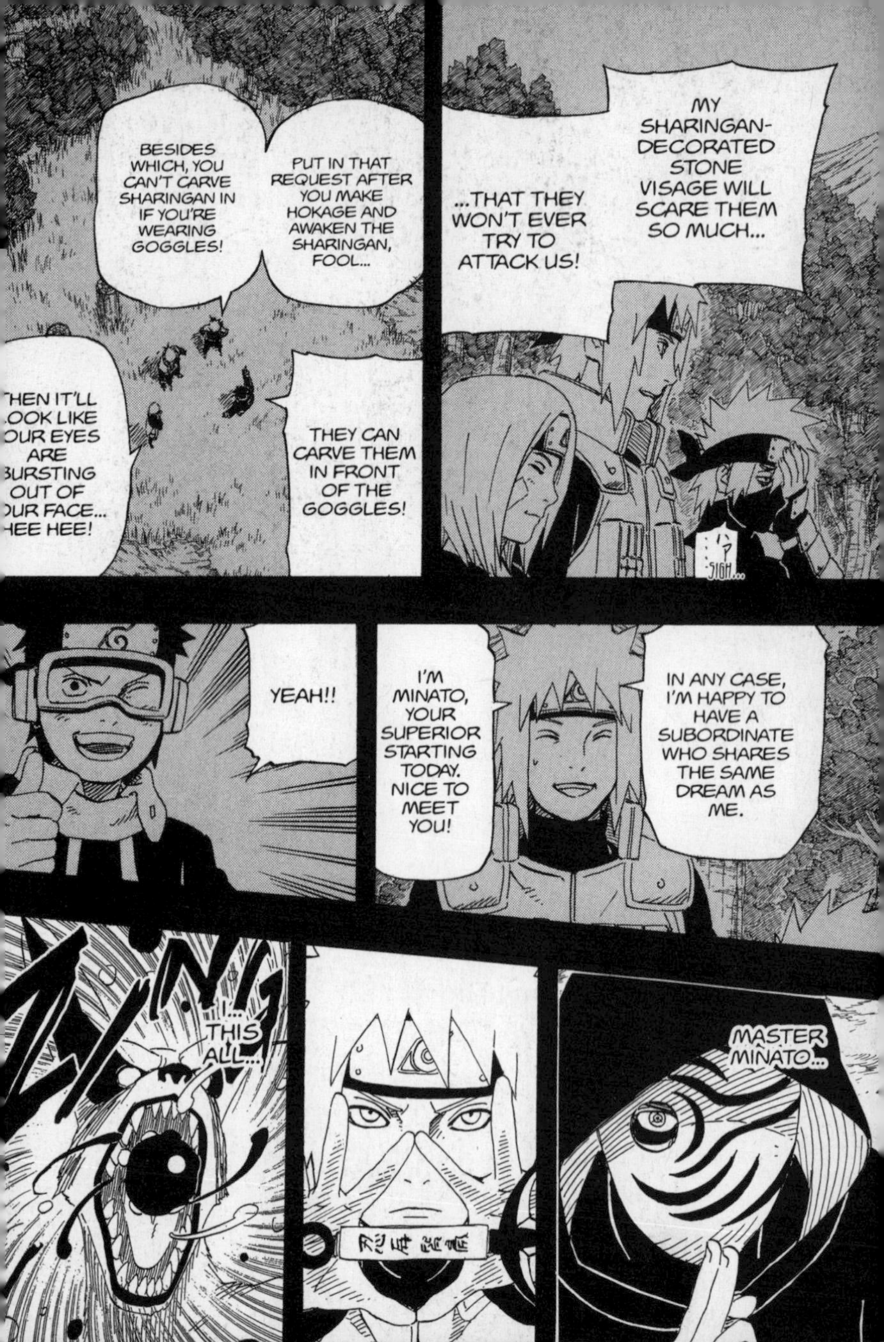
MY SHARINGAN-DECORATED STONE VISAGE WILL SCARE THEM SO MUCH...
...THAT THEY WON'T EVER TRY TO ATTACK US!
SIGH...
PUT IN THAT REQUEST AFTER YOU MAKE HOKAGE AND AWAKEN THE SHARINGAN, FOOL...
BESIDES WHICH, YOU CAN'T CARVE SHARINGAN IN IF YOU'RE WEARING GOGGLES!
THEY CAN CARVE THEM IN FRONT OF THE GOGGLES!
HEN IT'LL OOK LIKE OUR EYES ARE URSTING OUT OF OUR FACE... HEE HEE!
IN ANY CASE, I'M HAPPY TO HAVE A SUBORDINATE WHO SHARES THE SAME DREAM AS ME.
I'M MINATO, YOUR SUPERIOR STARTING TODAY. NICE TO MEET YOU!
YEAH!!
MASTER MINATO...
I... THIS ALL...

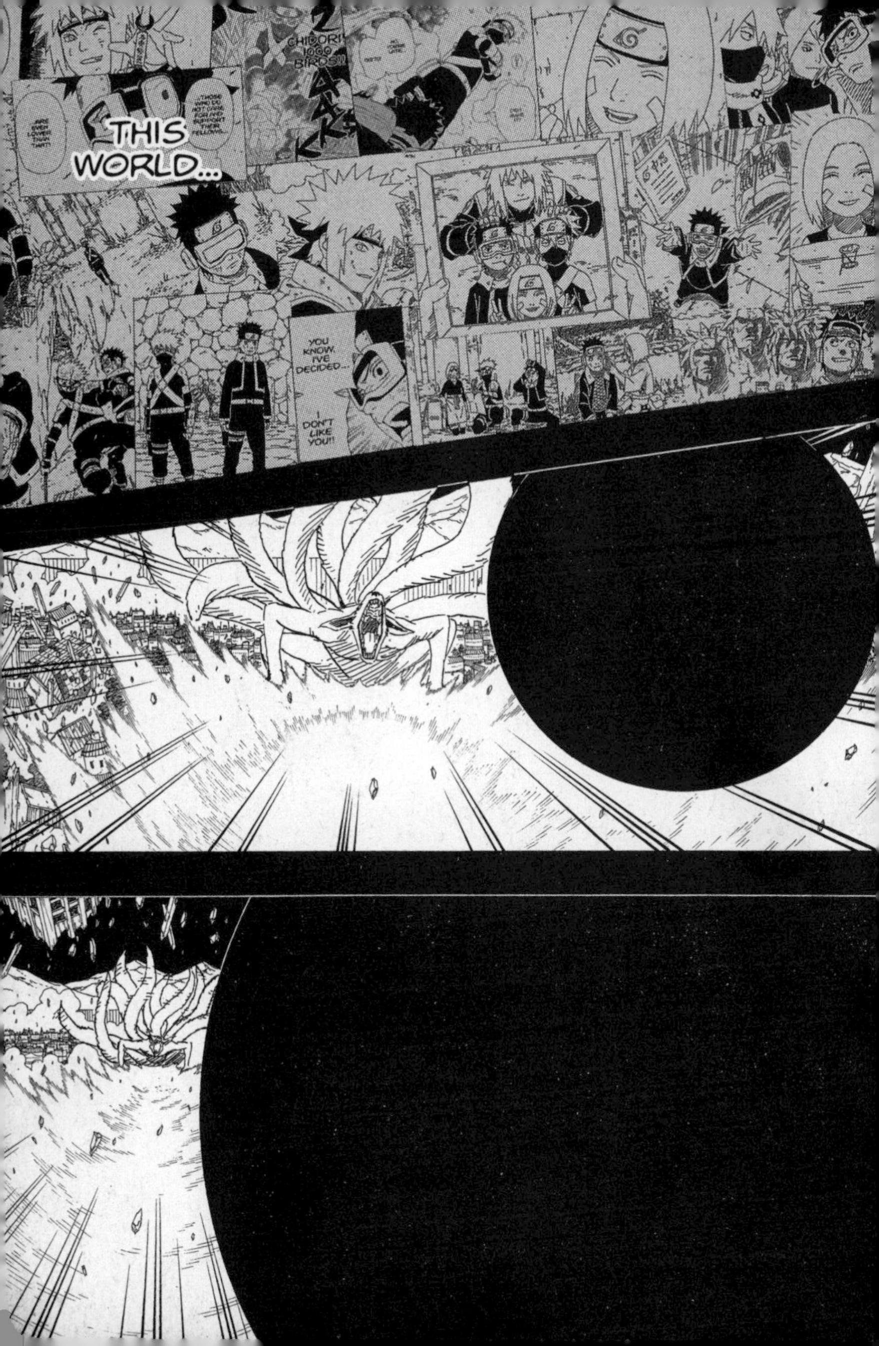
CHIDORI! 1000 BIRDS!!
THIS WORLD...
YOU KNOW, I'VE DECIDED...
I DON'T LIKE YOU!!

...DOESN'T MATTER TO ME.

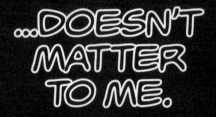

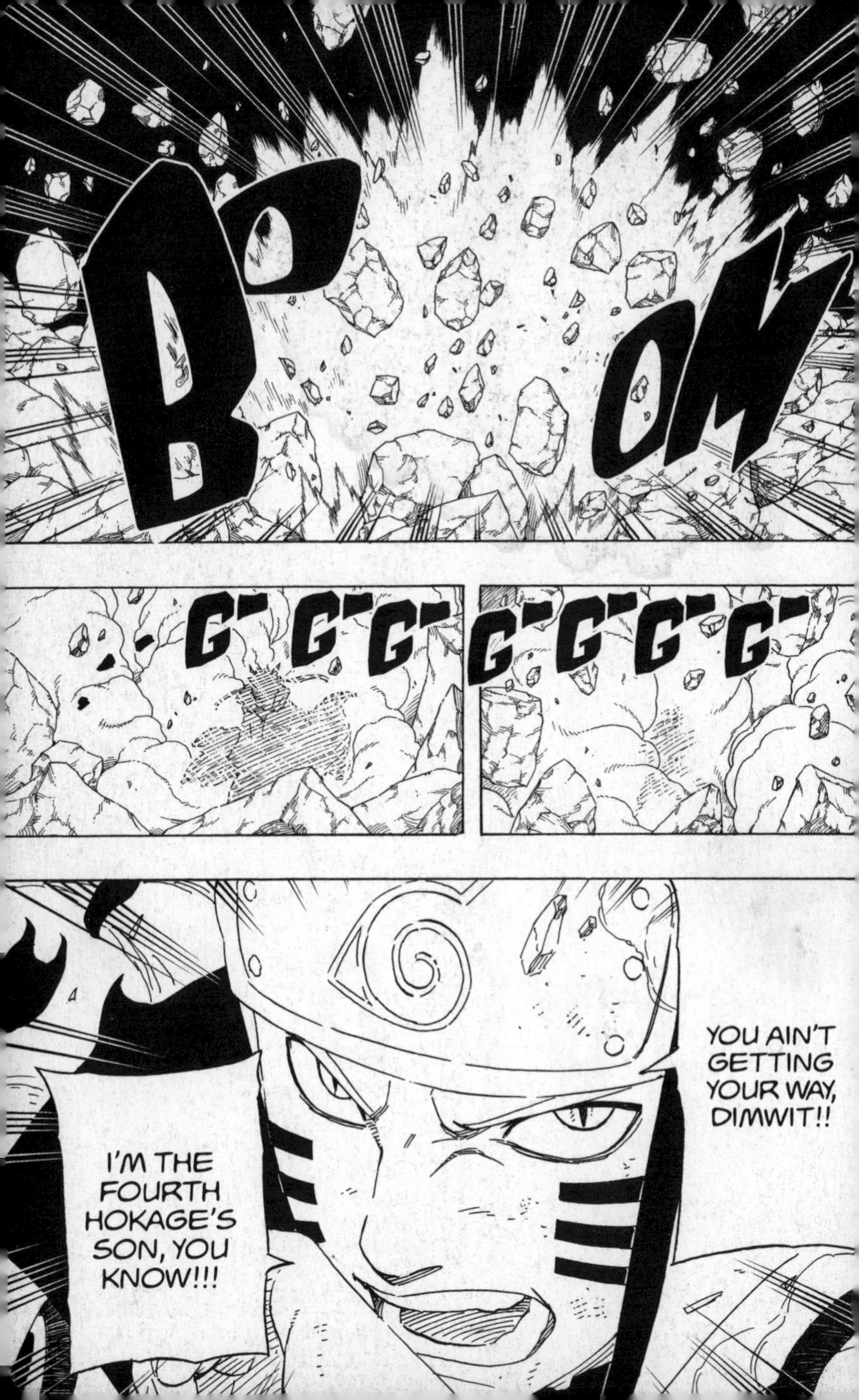
BOOM
G- G- G- G-
-G- G- G-
YOU AIN'T GETTING YOUR WAY, DIMWIT!!
I'M THE FOURTH HOKAGE'S SON, YOU KNOW!!!

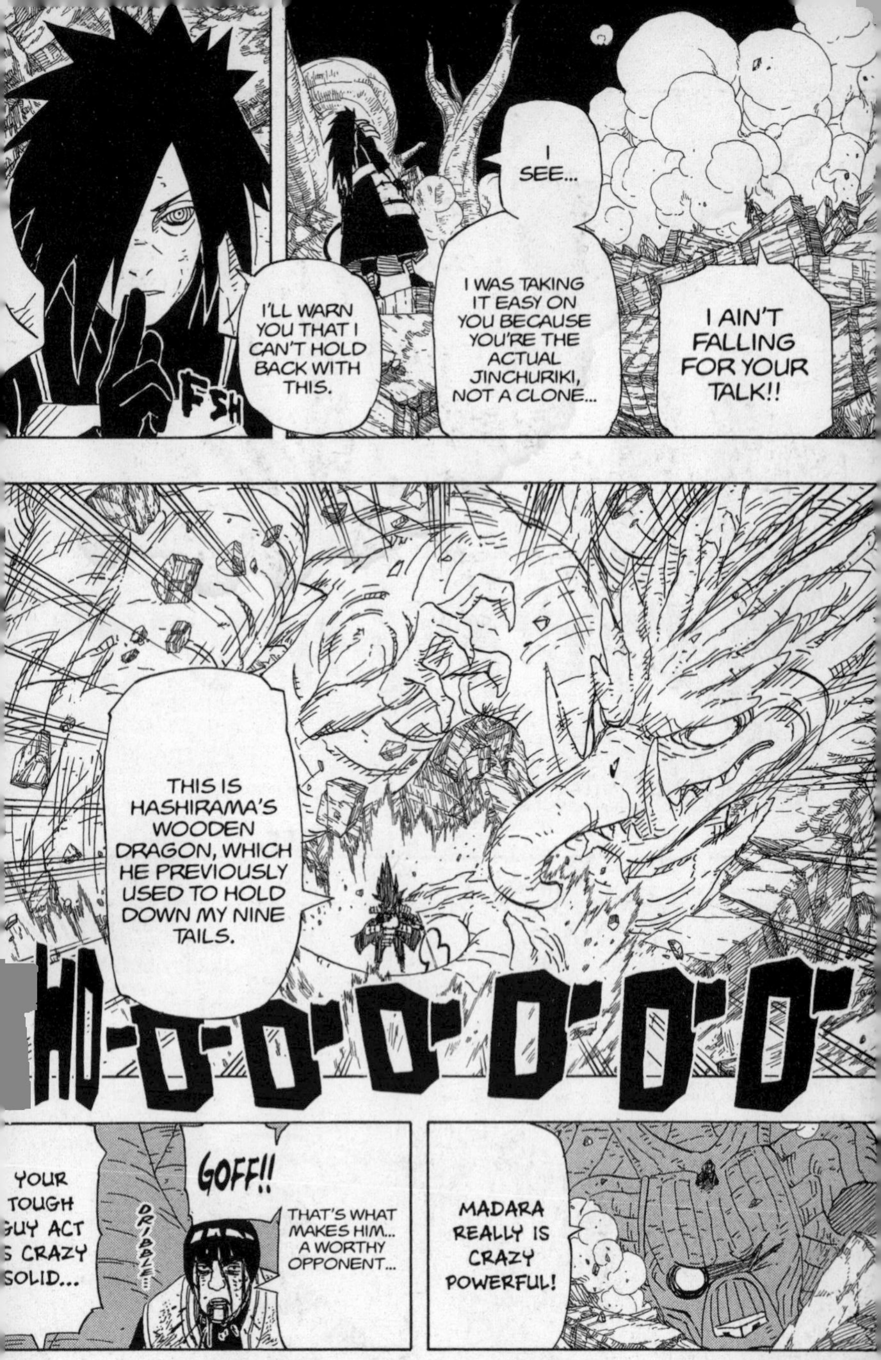
I SEE...
I WAS TAKING IT EASY ON YOU BECAUSE YOU'RE THE ACTUAL JINCHURIKI, NOT A CLONE...
I AIN'T FALLING FOR YOUR TALK!!
I'LL WARN YOU THAT I CAN'T HOLD BACK WITH THIS.
FSH
THIS IS HASHIRAMA'S WOODEN DRAGON, WHICH HE PREVIOUSLY USED TO HOLD DOWN MY NINE TAILS.
HO-O-O-O-O-O-O-O-O
MADARA REALLY IS CRAZY POWERFUL!
GOFF!!
THAT'S WHAT MAKES HIM... A WORTHY OPPONENT...
YOUR TOUGH GUY ACT S CRAZY SOLID...
DRIBBLE...

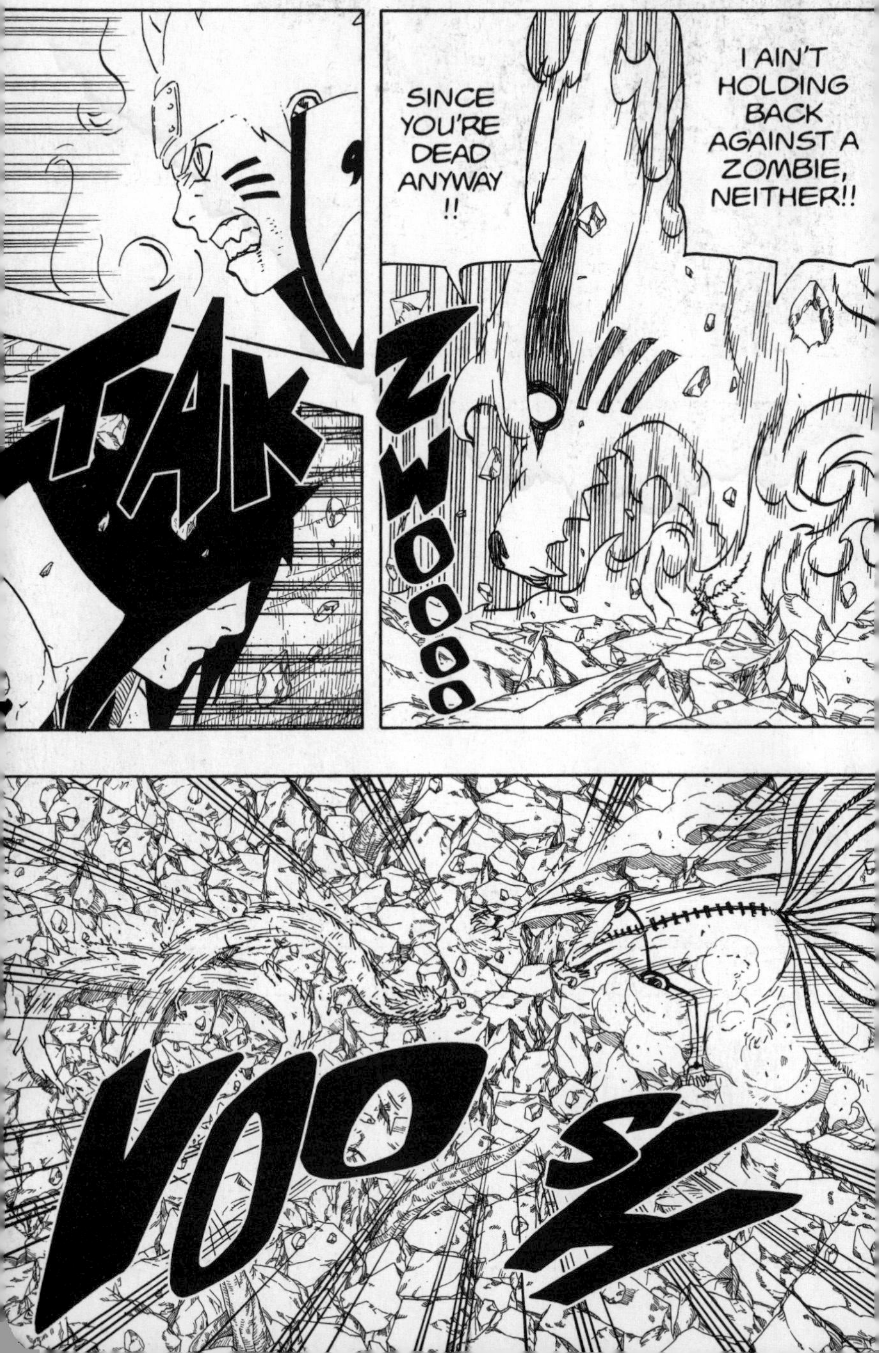
I AIN'T HOLDING BACK AGAINST A ZOMBIE, NEITHER!!
SINCE YOU'RE DEAD ANYWAY !!
ZWOOOO
TAK
VOOSH

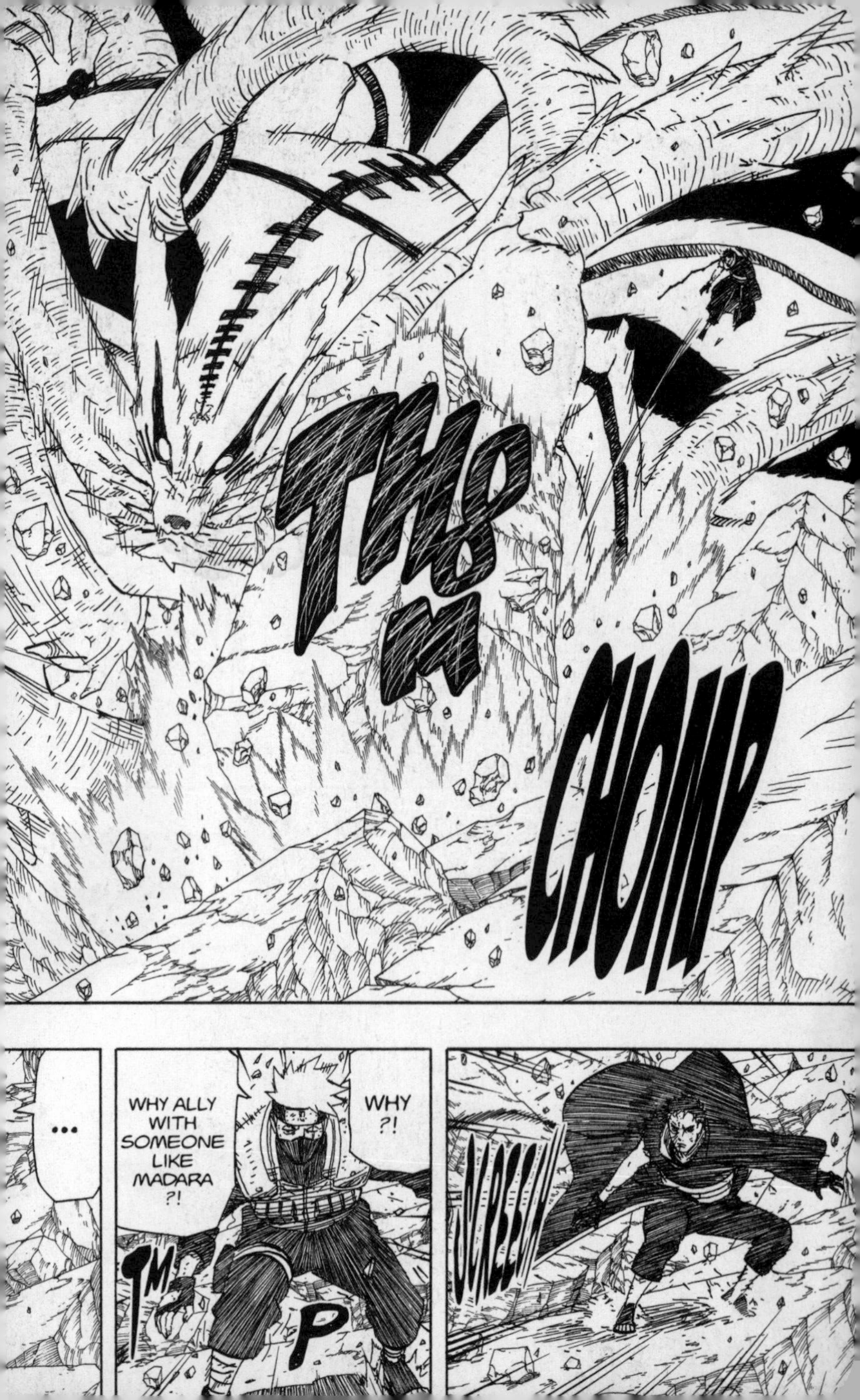
THOOM
CHOMP
WHY ?!
WHY ALLY WITH SOMEONE LIKE MADARA ?!
TMP
...

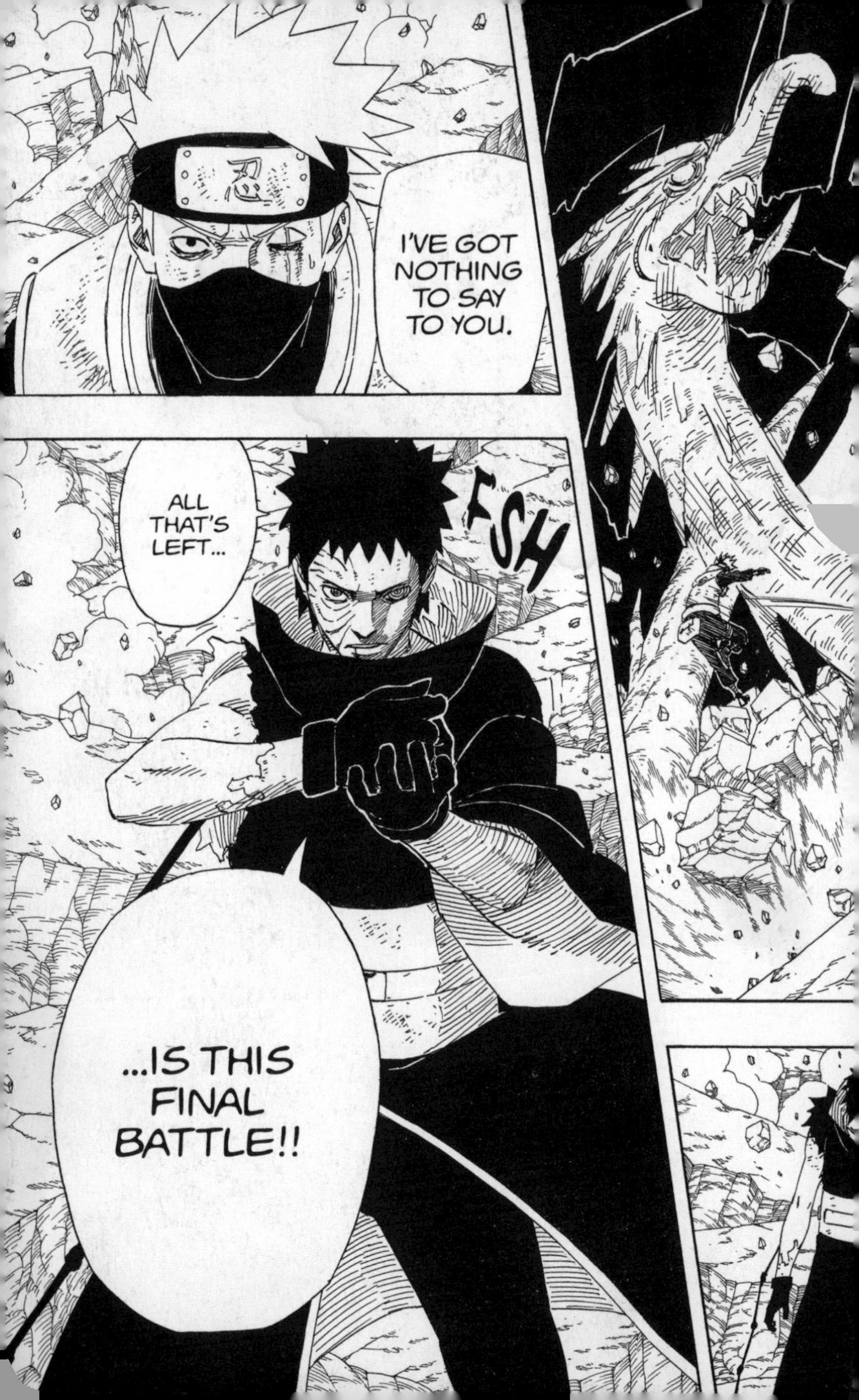
I'VE GOT NOTHING TO SAY TO YOU.
ALL THAT'S LEFT...
FSH
...IS THIS FINAL BATTLE!!

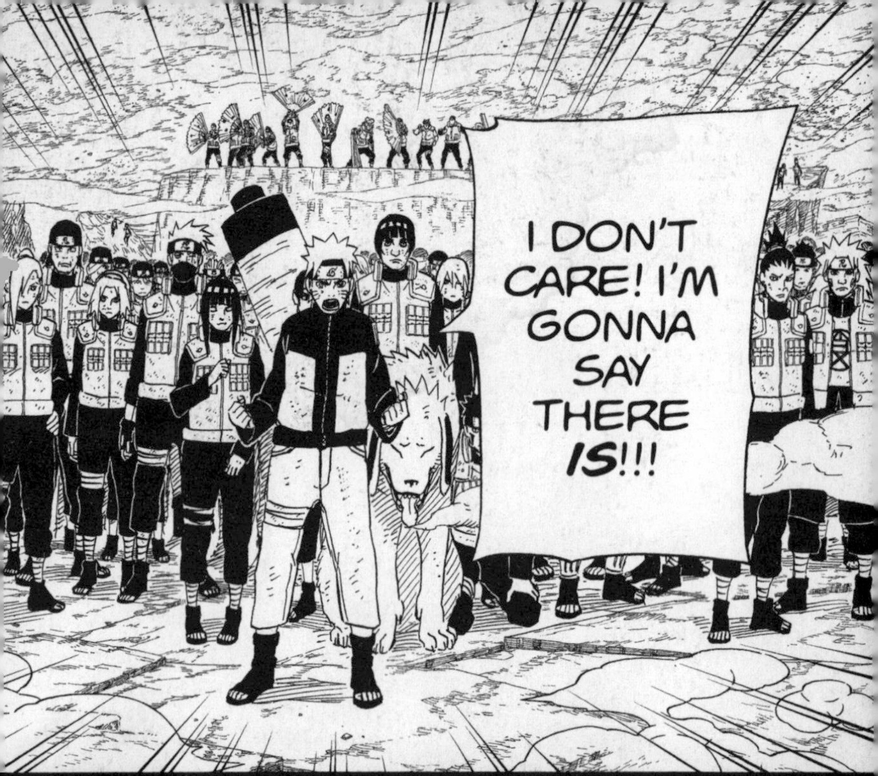
I DON'T CARE! I'M GONNA SAY THERE IS!!!

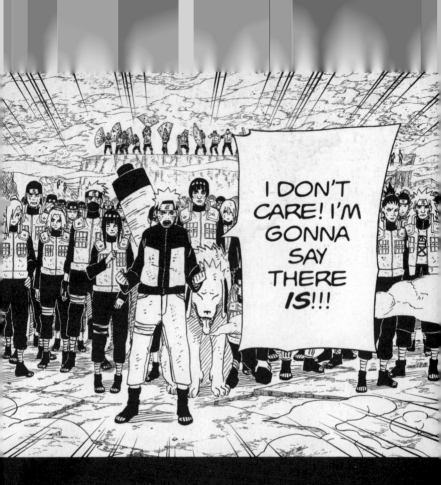

IN THE NEXT VOLUME...

TEN TAILS

The odds are against Naruto as Obito and Madara team up against him. And if things weren't bad enough, the monstrous Ten Tails is finally revived! But when all hope seems lost, Naruto will gain the support of the one thing that might give him the edge!

AVAILABLE JANUARY 2014!

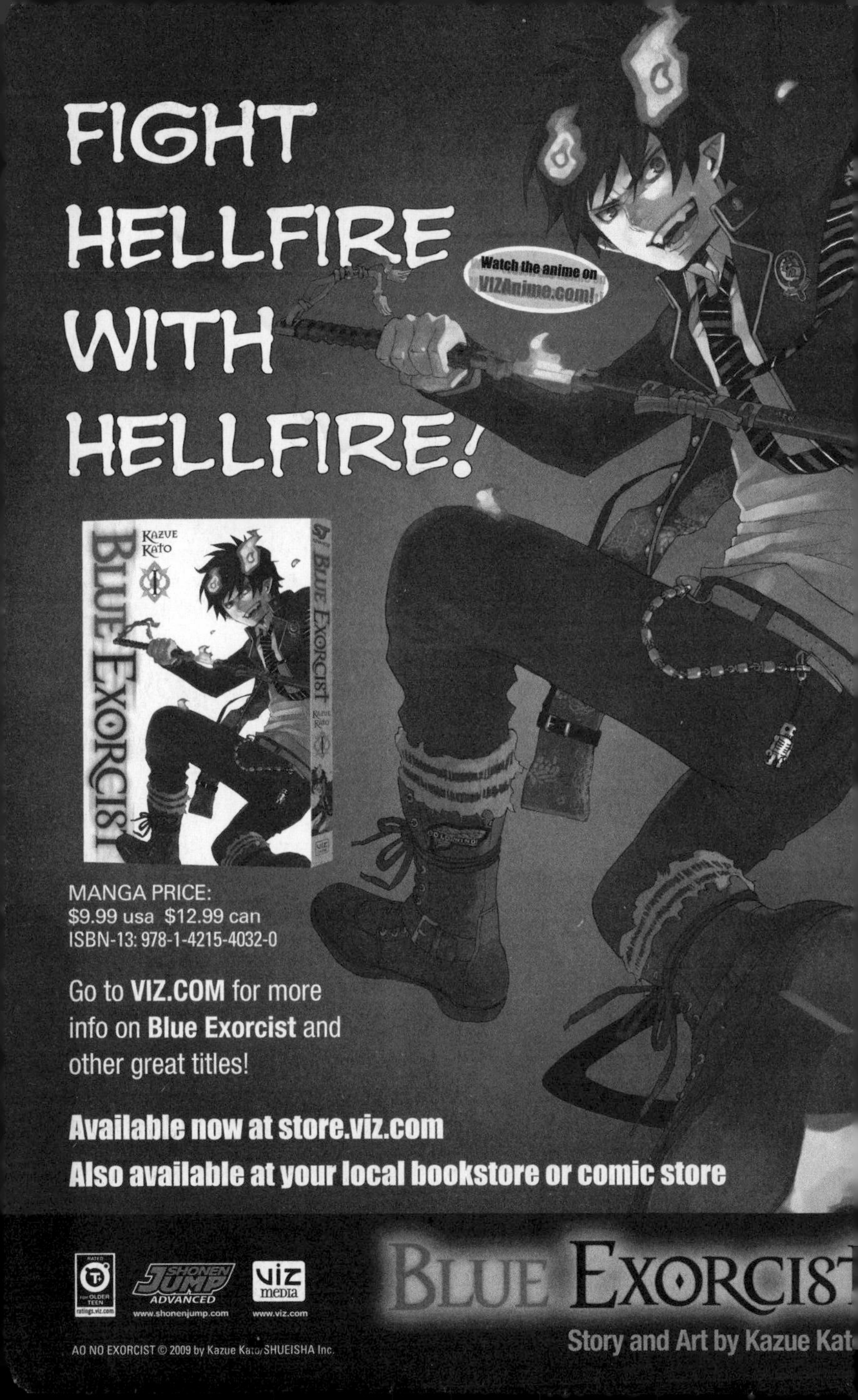
FIGHT HELLFIRE WITH HELLFIRE!
Watch the anime on VIZAnime.com!
KAZUE KATO
BLUE EXORCIST
1
MANGA PRICE:
$9.99 usa $12.99 can
ISBN-13: 978-1-4215-4032-0
Go to VIZ.COM for more info on Blue Exorcist and other great titles!
Available now at store.viz.com
Also available at your local bookstore or comic store
SHONEN JUMP ADVANCED
www.shonenjump.com
viz media
www.viz.com
BLUE EXORCIST
Story and Art by Kazue Kato
AO NO EXORCIST © 2009 by Kazue Kato/SHUEISHA Inc.

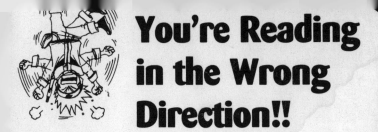

You're Reading in the Wrong Direction!!

Whoops! Guess what? You're starting at the wrong end of the comic!

...It's true! In keeping with the original Japanese format, **Naruto** is meant to be read from right to left, starting in the upper-right corner.

Unlike English, which is read from left to right, Japanese is read from right to left, meaning that action, sound effects and word-balloon order are completely reversed... something which can make readers unfamiliar with Japanese feel pretty backwards themselves. For this reason, manga or Japanese comics published in the U.S. in English have sometimes been published "flopped"—that is, printed in exact reverse order, as though seen from the other side of a mirror.

By flopping pages, U.S. publishers can avoid confusing readers, but the compromise is not without its downside. For one thing, a character in a flopped manga series who once wore in the original Japanese version a T-shirt emblazoned with "M A Y" (as in "the merry month of") now wears one which reads "Y A M"! Additionally, many manga creators in Japan are themselves unhappy with the process, as some feel the mirror-imaging of their art alters their original intentions.

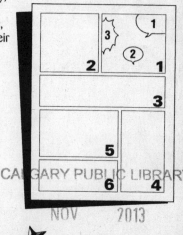

We are proud to bring you Masashi Kishimoto's **Naruto** in the original unflopped format. For now, though, turn to the other side of the book and let the ninjutsu begin...!

—Editor